D1559047

Transnational Governance

Globalization involves a profound re-ordering of our world with the proliferation everywhere of rules and transnational modes of governance. This book examines how this governance is formed, changes and stabilizes. Building on a rich and varied set of empirical cases, it explores transnational rules and regulations and the organizing, discursive and monitoring activities that frame, sustain and reproduce them. Beginning from an understanding of the powerful structuring forces that embed and form the context of transnational regulatory activities, the book scrutinizes the actors involved, how they are organized, how they interact and how they transform themselves to adapt to this new regulatory landscape. A powerful analysis of the modes and logics of transnational rule-making and rule-monitoring closes the book. This authoritative resource offers ideal reading for all academic researchers and graduate students of governance and regulation.

MARIE-LAURE DJELIC is Professor of Management at ESSEC Business School, Paris.

KERSTIN SAHLIN-ANDERSSON is Professor of Management at Uppsala University, Sweden.

Transnational Governance

Institutional Dynamics of Regulation

EDITED BY

MARIE-LAURE DJELIC
AND
KERSTIN SAHLIN-ANDERSSON

CAMBRIDGE
UNIVERSITY PRESS

CAMBRIDGE UNIVERSITY PRESS
Cambridge, New York, Melbourne, Madrid, Cape Town, Singapore, São Paulo

Cambridge University Press
The Edinburgh Building, Cambridge CB2 2RU, UK

Published in the United States of America by Cambridge University Press, New York

www.cambridge.org
Information on this title: www.cambridge.org/9780521845038

© Cambridge Univeristy Press 2006

First published 2006

Printed in the United Kingdom at the University Press, Cambridge

A catalogue record for this publication is available from the British Library

ISBN-13   978-0-521-84503-8 hardback
ISBN-10   0-521-84503-3 hardback

Contents

Figures

Tables

Contributors

MARIE-LAURE DJELIC is Professor at ESSEC Business School, Paris, France where she teaches Organization Theory, Business History and Comparative Capitalism. In 2002–2003, she held the Kerstin Hesselgren Professorship at Uppsala University, in Sweden. Her research interests range from the role of professions and social networks in the transnational diffusion of rules and practices to the historical transformation of national institutions. She is the author of *Exporting the American Model* (1998), which obtained the 2000 Max Weber Award for the Best Book in Organizational Sociology from the American Sociological Association. She has edited, together with Sigrid Quack, *Globalization and Institutions* (2003).

KERSTIN SAHLIN-ANDERSSON is Professor of Management at Uppsala University. Her current research interests center around the three following research programs: "Transnational regulations and state transformations," "Corporate social responsibility and changes in public–private relations," and "Striving for transparency in health care." Her most recent edited books are *The Expansion of Management Knowledge. Carriers, Flows and Sources* (2002, with Lars Engwall) and *Beyond Project Management: New Perspectives on the Temporary–Permanent Dilemma* (2002, with Anders Söderholm).

GÖRAN AHRNE is Professor of Sociology at Stockholm University and also a researcher at Score (Stockholm Center for Organizational Research). He has published several books on organizations and social theory. His latest book in English is *Social Organization* (1994). He has also published a chapter, "Soft regulation from an organizational perspective" together with Nils Brunsson (in a volume on soft law, edited by Ulrika Mörth, see below).

JOHN BOLI is Professor of Sociology at Emory University. A native Californian and Stanford graduate, he has published extensively on world culture and global organizations, globalization, education, citizenship, and state power and authority in the world polity. Recent books include *World Culture: Origins and Consequences* (2005, with Frank Lechner) and *Constructing World Culture: International Nongovernmental Organizations Since 1875* (1999, with George Thomas). His current research includes a project examining the impact of world culture on transnational corporations. Married with three children, he has lived for eight years in Sweden, his wife's native country.

SEBASTIAN BOTZEM studied political science in Berlin, Germany and Granada, Spain. He graduated in 2001 from the Free University of Berlin and is currently working at the Social Science Research Center Berlin (*Wissenschaftszentrum Berlin für Sozialforschung*). His research areas include transnational regulation, economic internationalization and the role of service intermediaries in globalization processes with a particular focus on the internationalization of standards in the field of accounting.

NILS BRUNSSON holds the City of Stockholm Chair in Management at the Stockholm School of Economics and he is the chairman of Stockholm Center for Organizational Research (Score). He has published some twenty books and numerous articles on issues such as decision-making, hypocrisy, organizational reforms and standardization. He is now leading a research program on rule-setting and rule-following where he is studying forms for global organizing.

GILI S. DRORI is a lecturer in Stanford University's programs on International Relations and International Policy Studies. Her research interests include the comparative study of science and technology, social progress and rationalization, globalization, governance, and higher education. She is the author of several papers and chapters on science and development, world culture, international organizations, and the role of policy regimes in worldwide governance. These interests are expressed in her recent books: *Science in the Modern World Polity: Institutionalization and Globalization* (co-authored with John W. Meyer, Francisco O. Ramirez and Evan Schofer, 2003), *Global E-litism: Digital Technology, Social Inequality, and Transnationality* (2005), and *World Society and the Expansion of Formal Organization* (co-edited with John W. Meyer and Hokyu Hwang, 2006).

ANITA ENGELS received her doctoral degree in sociology at the University of Bielefeld, Germany. She has worked on global environmental change, in the context of both industrialized and developing countries. Her fields of interest are environmental sociology, social studies of science and technology, globalization theory, and economic sociology. From 1999–2001 she was granted a postdoc fellowship at the Institute for International Studies, Stanford University, California. She now works at the Centre for Globalization and Governance at the University of Hamburg.

LARS ENGWALL has been Professor of Business Administration at Uppsala University since 1981 and has also held visiting positions in Belgium, France and the United States. His research has been directed towards structural analyses of industries and organizations as well as the creation and diffusion of management knowledge. He has published a number of books and over one hundred papers in the management area. His most recently edited books are *Management Consulting: The Emergence and Dynamics of a Knowledge Industry* (2002, with Matthias Kipping), and *The Expansion of Management Knowledge. Carriers, Flows and Sources* (2002, with Kerstin Sahlin-Andersson).

TINA HEDMO received her PhD in 2004 from Uppsala University, where she now works as a lecturer in the Department of Business Studies. The title of her dissertation is "Rule-making in the Transnational Space: The Development of European Accreditation of Management Education." Tina is presently studying the emergence of European regulation in the health care sector and the development of new modes of steering and controlling European higher education. Her research interests include re-regulation processes in these sectors in contemporary society; transnational institutionalization processes and the role and impact of non-governmental organizations in such processes.

BENGT JACOBSSON is Professor of Management at Södertörn University College, Stockholm. His research interests focus on control and decision-making in organizations, transformations in regulation and changing forms of governance. His studies focus on private as well as public organizations; business corporations as well as nation-states. He is currently heading a research program on Europeanization and Changes in the Swedish Government. Among his publications are *A World of Standards* (together with Nils Brunsson) and *Europeanization and Transnational States* (together with Per Laegreid and Ove Kai Pedersen) as well a series of books on organizing, control and decision-making in Swedish public administration.

THIBAUT KLEINER, PhD is currently working as an official in the Competition Directorate General of the European Commission. After four years as an economist in the area of merger control, he has recently taken up a new position in charge of state aid policy. He was previously researching and teaching at the London School of Economics and Political Science. He has published several articles in the field of comparative institutional analysis, strategy, organization theory and antitrust law in refereed journals and in edited books as well as a number of conference and policy papers.

MARTIN MARCUSSEN is Associate Professor at the International Center for Business and Politics, Copenhagen Business School, Denmark. He has written *Ideas and Elites: The Social Construction of Economic and Monetary Union* (2000) and *OECD og idéspillet. Game Over* (2002). He is a member of the "Centre for the Study of Democratic Network Governance" (Roskilde University Center) and he is currently working on a research project financed by the Danish Social Science Research Council on the Transnational Central Bank Community.

JASON MCNICHOL received his PhD in sociology from the University of California at Berkeley in 2002. His research interests include trends in the global governance of labor and environmental standards as well as the changing roles of firms and non-governmental organizations in regulatory oversight. He has taught at Berkeley, the University of Freiburg (Germany), and other campuses. McNichol currently serves as a program director and officer at the Social Science Research Council in New York City.

JOHN W. MEYER is Professor of Sociology, emeritus, at Stanford University. He has, over several decades, developed neoinstitutional analyses of modern organizations and national states, showing the influences of wider cultural models on the development of these "actors." Currently he works on the rise and impact of world human rights, scientific and organizational models: for instance, in Drori et al., *Science in the Modern World Polity* (2003).

GLENN MORGAN is Professor of Organizational Behavior at Warwick Business School, the University of Warwick. He is also a Research Associate of the ESRC Centre for the Study of Globalization and Regionalization based at Warwick as well as Visiting Professor at the International Centre for Business and Politics, Copenhagen Business School. He is an Editor of the journal *Organization*. Recent publications include *Changing Capitalisms? Internationalization, Institutional Change and Systems of Economic Organization* (2005; edited with Richard Whitley and Eli Moen).

ULRIKA MÖRTH is Associate Professor and Senior Lecturer, Department of Political Science at Stockholm University and Senior Researcher and Research Director at Score (Stockholm Centre for Organizational Research). She has published a book on European Cooperation on Armaments (2003) and edited a volume on soft law, *Soft Law in Governance and Regulation* (2004).

SIGRID QUACK is a senior research fellow at the Social Science Research Center Berlin (*Wissenschaftszentrum Berlin für Sozialforschung*). She holds a PhD in sociology from the Free University Berlin and has conducted research in the fields of institutional change, comparative analysis of business systems, gender and organization as well as labor markets and employment. Her current research interests focus on forms of gradual institutional change, the internationalization of professions as well as their role in transnational rule-setting.

FRANCISCO O. RAMIREZ is Professor of Education and (by courtesy) Sociology. He currently serves as the Chair of the Social Sciences, Policies, and Educational Practices Area with the Stanford School of Education. His comparative research interests include the globalization of education, the political reconstitution of gender and age, and the institutionalization of science in education and in society. He has published broadly on topics such as patterns of women's access to higher education, the role of education and science in economic development, and the interplay between education, citizenship and human rights.

LINDA WEDLIN received her PhD in 2004 from Uppsala University where she now holds a position as lecturer in the Department of Business Studies. Her research interests include institutional change and the forming and structuring of cultural and social fields, and the re-regulation of fields and of society. Her main research area is management education and knowledge, with a special focus on issues of regulation, standardization and classification in this field. She recently published *Ranking Business Schools* (2006), where she analyzes the role of rankings in forming an international field management education.

Acknowledgments

Nothing would have been possible without a cold Swedish winter! The first intuition of this book was born of the close collaboration and stimulating intellectual exchanges between the co-editors in 2002–2003, when Marie-Laure Djelic was Kerstin Hesselgren Professor at Uppsala University. Such close collaboration and regular interaction were made possible by the Swedish Research Council (*Vetenskaprådet*) – the organization that sponsors this professorship. We are both grateful for the opportunity this created for us. This project and our collaboration have proven not only fruitful and intellectually satisfying but also pleasant and at many times exhilarating.

The Swedish Research Council and the Department of Business Studies at Uppsala University also made it possible, financially, to organize a workshop in May 2003 at Uppsala, where all contributors to this volume were present. We would like to thank all participants to this workshop, including Yves Dezalay, Christoph Knill and Dirk Lehmkuhl, for what proved to be extremely rich discussions. We would also like to take this opportunity to thank Helena Buhr and her fellow Uppsala PhD students, who helped us with the practical logistics of the workshop.

From the start, we wanted to construct a tightly-knit and homogeneous volume and not merely a loose collection of chapters. This has meant a series of comments and versions, quite a few back and forth between the contributors and ourselves. We would like to express our gratitude to all contributors for their patience and understanding and for their willingness to go along with us in this direction. Parts of the introduction and some of our own contributions were presented in different workshops and seminars. Participants at the Comparative Sociology Workshop at Stanford, the Scancor Conference on Institutional Change (March 2004) and seminars at the Department of Business Studies at Uppsala University have provided us with excellent comments and criticism.

All along, we were helped by a number of colleagues and scholars who reacted to and commented on parts of the manuscript, shared their own work and engaged with us in discussions, related or apparently unrelated, that in the end proved highly helpful. We would like to thank in particular Erik Berglöf, Barbara Czarniawska, Gili Drori, Rodolphe Durand, Michael Lounsbury, Bengt Jacobsson, John Meyer, Sigrid Quack, Staffan Furusten, Woody Powell, Chiqui Ramirez, Jean-Michel Saussois, Dick Scott, Risto Tainio, Marc Ventresca, Radu Vranceanu and Udo Zander. We would also like to acknowledge the support we received from our own institutions – ESSEC Business School and Uppsala University – during the intense period when we put the book together. All contributors naturally have their own debts, both personal and institutional, and the list here would be too long.

At Cambridge University Press, we benefited from the support and professionalism of Katy Plowright and Lynn Dunlop. In the last stages of the volume, Stina Andersson has played a pivotal role. We are extremely thankful for all the energy she put in helping us format and prepare the final version of the manuscript. Leif Andersson, Alma and Milena Djelic and Philippe have been helpful in different ways – by being highly reasonable and understanding about the time this book was stealing from them!

Paris and Uppsala July 2005
Marie-Laure Djelic and Kerstin Sahlin-Andersson

Acronyms

AACSB	Association to Advance Collegiate Schools of Business
AF&PA	American Forest and Paper Association
AISG	Accountants International Study Group
AMBA	Association of MBAs
BCBS	Basel Committee on Banking Supervision
BIS	Bank for International Settlements
C&L	Certification and labeling programs
CEN	European Committee for Standardization
CENELEC	European Committee for Electrotechnical Standardization
CEO	Chief Executive Officer
CGFS	Committee on the Global Financial System of the G-10 Central Banks
CIA	Central Intelligence Agency
CISDA	Confederation of International Soft Drinks Associations
CLP	Competition Law and Policy Committee
COMESA	Common Market for Eastern and Southern Africa
CSCE	Conference on Security and Cooperation in Europe
DARPA	Defense Advanced Research Projects Agency
DOJ	US Department of Justice
EATS	Emission Allowance Trading Scheme
EBM	Evidence-based Medicine
EBRD	European Bank for Reconstruction and Development
ECA	European Competition Authorities
ECB	European Central Bank
EEC	European Economic Community
efmd	European Foundation for Management Development
EFRAG	European Financial Reporting Advisory Group
ENGO	Environmental Non-governmental Organization
EPA	Environmental Protection Agency
EQUAL	European Quality Link

EQUIS	European Quality Improvement System
ERT	European Round Table of Industrialists
ETS	Emissions Trading Scheme
ETSI	European Telecommunications Standards Institute
EU	European Union
FAO	Food and Agriculture Organization
FASB	Financial Accounting Standards Board
FDA	Food and Drug Administration
FEE	*Fédération des Experts Comptables Européens*
FIFA	*Fédération Internationale de Football Association*
FSC	Forest Stewardship Council
GATS	Global Agreement on Trade in Services
GATT	General Agreement on Tariffs and Trade
GC	Global Compact
GDP	Gross Domestic Product
GMAC	General Management Admissions Council
GNP	Gross National Product
GOV	Public Governance and Territorial Development Directorate
GRE	Graduate Record Examination
HGB	*Handelsgesetzbuch* (German commercial law code)
IAIS	International Association of Insurance Supervisors
IAS	International Accounting Standards
IASB	International Accounting Standards Board
IASC	International Accounting Standards Committee
IASCF	International Accounting Standards Committee Foundation
IATA	International Air Transport Association
ICAEW	Institute of Chartered Accountants of England and Wales
ICC	International Chamber of Commerce
ICF	International Cremation Federation
ICN	International Competition Network
ICPAC	International Competition Policy Advisory Committee
IEA	International Energy Agency
IEC	International Egg Commission
IESE	*Instituto de Estudios Superiores de la Empresa*
IFAC	International Federation of Accountants
IFRS	International Financial Reporting Standards

IGO	Intergovernmental Organization
ILO	International Labour Organization
IMD	International Institute for Management Development
IMF	International Monetary Fund
INGO	International Non-governmental Organization
INSEAD	*Institut Européen d'Administration des Affaires*
INSOC	International Network of Civil Society Organizations on Competition
INTOSAI	International Organization of Supreme Audit Institutions
IOSCO	International Organization of Securities Commissions
ISO	International Organization for Standardization
ISO/IEC	International Organization for Standardization/ International Electrotechnical Commission
LBS	London Business School
M+A	Mergers and Acquisitions
MBA	Master of Business Administration
MNC	Multinational Corporations
MP	Member of Parliament
MPS	Mont Pelerin Society
NAFTA	North American Free Trade Agreement
NGO	Non-governmental Organization
NPM	New Public Management
OAS	Organization of American States
OECD	Organization for Economic Cooperation and Development
OEEC	Organization for European Economic Cooperation
OMC	Open Method of Coordination
OS	operating systems
PAM	DARPA's Policy Analysis Market program
PEFC	Pan European Forest Certification Scheme
PUMA	Public Management Committee
SEC	US Securities and Exchange Commission
SFI	Sustainable Forestry Initiative
TABD	Transatlantic Business Dialogue
TNC	Transnational Corporations
TOEFL	Test of English as a Foreign Language
UEC	*Union Européene des Experts Comptables, Economiques et Financiers*

UKWAS	Woodland Assurance Scheme
UN	United Nations
UNCTAD	United Nations Conference on Trade and Development
UNEP	United Nations Environment Programme
UNESCO	United Nations Educational, Scientific and Cultural Organization
UPU	Universal Postal Union
US-GAAP	US-Generally Accepted Accounting Principles
WB	World Bank
WFMH	World Federation for Mental Health
WHO	World Health Organization
WTO	World Trade Organization
WWF	World Wide Fund for Nature

1 Introduction: A world of governance: The rise of transnational regulation

MARIE-LAURE DJELIC AND KERSTIN
SAHLIN-ANDERSSON

Introduction

On an experiential basis, many of us feel the impact of a "transnationalizing" world. French workers strike to prevent the de-localization of their jobs to Slovenia or China and most clothing in American stores is produced outside the United States. A German university professor is increasingly expected to belong to a transnational peer community and to adapt to career development standards greatly at odds with German academic traditions. What a European consumer gets when she buys chocolate in her local store has been defined and standardized by the European Commission. Companies around the world are going through multiple certification processes and are bound to various categories of standards – efficiency, quality, ethical or environmental ones. The list could be longer and all chapters in this volume provide further evidence of the impact of transnationalization in our daily lives.

As those examples suggest, a transnational world is not about the disappearance of rules and order. Rather, what appears striking about our times is the increasing scope and breadth of regulatory and governance activities of all kinds. The present world has been described as a "golden era of regulation" (Levi-Faur and Jordana 2005). The proliferation of regulatory activities, actors, networks or constellations leads to an explosion of rules and to the profound re-ordering of our world. Organizing and monitoring activities connect with regulation and represent other important dimensions of contemporary governance. New organizations, alliances and networks emerge everywhere. Particularly salient is the almost exponential growth of international organizations (e.g. Boli and Thomas 1999). An important task for many of these organizations is to issue rules but they may also be involved in elaborating and activating processes to monitor adoption and implementation of those rules.

1

An increasing share of this intense governance activity takes place between and across nations. Regulatory boundaries do not necessarily coincide with national boundaries. National regulatory patterns can quickly get transnationalized and transnational initiatives are having a local impact. States are active but they are themselves embedded in and constrained by regulatory actors and activities. State agencies negotiate with non-profit associations, international organizations, standard setters and corporate actors. Interactions between organizations in state and non-state sectors are complex, dense and multi-directional. The allocation of responsibilities between them is in flux and the borders between public and private spheres are increasingly fluid.

This volume focuses on governance in the transnational world and more precisely on transnational governance in the making. There is now a rich literature painting the features of a re-ordered world (e.g. Ayres and Braithwaite 1992; Cutler et al. 1999; Hall and Biersteker 2002; Slaughter 2004). There is often a sense in that literature that transnational regulations are out there and just come about – with an associated feeling of determinism and ineluctability. In contrast, we emphasize the complex, progressive and highly historical dimension of the re-ordering process that is still, very much, in the making. In fact, we propose to focus on the re-ordering process itself. In this volume, we are interested in the genesis and structuration of new modes of governance – rules and regulations and the organizing, discursive and monitoring activities that sustain, frame and reproduce them. We want to understand how they are shaped, get stabilized and change. We explore transnational governance in the making and the concomitant re-ordering of the world.

The challenge behind this book is to make sense of the complex and dynamic topography of our re-ordering world. Making sense, however, goes well beyond the description of what is visible (cf. Weber 1949) and topography means more than a surface collection of elements. We propose, in this introduction, a re-visited field perspective to capture the multiple levels and dimensions of this dynamic topography. Beyond the apparent complexity and unruly nature of contemporary transnational governance, we search for those structuring dimensions and potential regularities that frame the visible landscape and its dynamics and allow for a deeper understanding.

Revisiting some key conceptual debates and definitions

Examples now abound that point to profoundly changing rules of the game across the world in many spheres of activities – be they social, economic or political. The very definition of "rules" and "regulations," the nature of actors involved, the modes of regulatory and monitoring activities are evolving quite profoundly. In the meantime, the conceptual frameworks at our disposal for understanding processes of re-regulation are mostly inadequate. They often are mere extensions of the conceptual frameworks originally developed to understand rule-making and monitoring in a Westphalian world – where sovereign nation-states with supreme jurisdiction over demarcated territorial areas functioned in an essentially anomic international arena (Martin 2005). As such, they have a tendency to marginalize transnational regulation (Cutler 2002; Kobrin 2002). We propose that a contemporary frontier for social scientific research is to extend and reinvent our analytical tools in order to approach regulation as a complex compound of activities bridging the global and the local and taking place at the same time within, between and across national boundaries.

Transnational and not global

The label "globalization" is often used to refer to the rapid expansion of operations and interactions across and beyond national boundaries. We find this label unsatisfactory; it has become such a catchword that its meaning is highly blurred.

Transnational, we suggest in line with Hannerz (1996), is a more suitable and focused concept to make sense of the world we live in. Hannerz commented upon the two concepts as follows:

I am also somewhat uncomfortable with the rather prodigious use of the term globalization to describe just about any process or relationship that somehow crosses state boundaries. In themselves, many such processes and relationships obviously do not at all extend across the world. The term "transnational" is in a way more humble, and offers a more adequate label for phenomena which can be of quite variable scale and distribution, even when they do share the characteristic of not being contained within the state (Hannerz 1996:6).

Although the term "transnational" does not imply the disappearance of nation-states, it suggests that states are only one type of actor
amongst others (Katzenstein et al. 1998). Many connections go beyond
state-to-state interactions. As Hannerz (1996: 6) again put it "(i)n the
transnational arena, the actors may now be individuals, groups, movements, business enterprises, and in no small part it is this diversity
of organizations that we need to consider." This fits with our conviction that the exploration of a re-governing world should neither
neglect states nor treat them as the only or central mainsprings of the
re-governing process.

The label "transnational" suggests entanglement and blurred boundaries to a degree that the term "global" could not. In our contemporary
world, it becomes increasingly difficult to separate what takes place
within national boundaries and what takes place across and beyond
nations. The neat opposition between "globalization" and "nations,"
often just beneath the surface in a number of debates, does not really
make sense whether empirically or analytically. Organizations, activities and individuals constantly span multiple levels, rendering obsolete
older lines of demarcation.

Transnational governance suggests that territorial grounds and
national autonomy or sovereignty cannot be taken for granted. It also
implies, however, that governance activity is embedded in particular
geopolitical structures and hence enveloped in multiple and interacting institutional webs. Kobrin (2002: 64) saw parallels between present
governance structures and medieval states. "Although medieval 'states'
occupied geographic space, politics was not organized in terms of
unambiguous geography . . . Borders were diffuse, representing a pro-
jection of power rather than a limit of sovereignty. In the context, power
and authority could not be based on mutually exclusive geography."
With reference to Ruggie (1983), Kobrin characterized such political
structures as "patchwork."

"Patchwork" political structures mean interdependence and entanglement. Actors converge across fluid boundaries in the ways they
structure themselves, connect with others and pursue their interests.
Interdependence and entanglement reflect in part re-regulation while
driving it even further. Greater interdependence and entanglement foster the need for systematic comparisons and benchmarks and thus make
it necessary to increase coordination across countries and regions. This
in turn generates even more regulatory activity.

A re-regulated world

With the expansion of regulation has come an explosion of studies and theories (see Baldwin et al. 1998; Levi-Faur 2005). Different definitions and conceptions of regulation run through these studies. Baldwin et al. (1998: 3–4) differentiate between three conceptions: (1) regulation as authoritative rules, (2) regulation as efforts of state agencies to steer the economy, and (3) regulation as mechanisms of social control. This categorization certainly corresponds to a need for conceptual clarification in an expanding area of research (see Jordana and Levi-Faur 2004). Still, and based on our characterization of the transnational world, we find it necessary to refine further this conceptual categorization to capture the complex dynamics of contemporary re-regulation.

The categorization by Baldwin et al. (1998) points to an evolution from a narrow conception of regulation to a much broader one both in theory and practice. As we read this categorization, it tells us about four different dimensions. First, it tells us about who is regulating. Narrow conceptions suggest the centrality of the state. The broader conception points to the multiplicity of regulatory actors fighting for attention, resources and authority in multi-centered and fluid arenas. Most chapters in this volume explore the rapid de-multiplication of regulatory actors in recently regulated or re-regulated spheres – such as education, the environment, firm interactions, corporate ethics or state administration (e.g. Cutler et al. 1999; Kirton and Trebilcock 2004; Sahlin-Andersson 2004).

A second dimension bears on the regulatory mode. Rule-making has traditionally been associated, in a Westphalian world, with the coercive power of the nation-state. As such it has generally been expressed in "hard laws" and directives. A broadening conception implies a move towards legally non-binding "soft" rules such as standards and guidelines (e.g. Mörth 2004). This move follows and comes together with the explosion of regulatory actors but it also impacts upon states. The latter increasingly turn to less coercive regulatory modes as complements to more traditional coercive pressures. A third dimension is that of the nature of rules where a narrow conception assumes formal rules and a broader conception points to more informal rules. Informal rules are more flexible and thus open to interpretation and adjustment by those being regulated (cf. Kirton and Trebilcock 2004; Sahlin-Andersson 2004). Standards and guidelines are in principle voluntary and non-coercive but not always informal, as documented in this volume and elsewhere (Brunsson and Jacobsson 2000). Standardization is in fact often associated with formal reporting and co-ordinating procedures that can be heavy and constraining. A fourth dimension, finally, has to do with compliance mechanisms where the issue at stake is why those regulated do or do not comply. The evolution, there, is from the traditional association of compliance with the threat of sanctions. Even though many rule-makers do not have the type of regulatory authority traditionally associated with states, they can develop and structure regulatory sets that can be more or less coercive, for example through the connection between certain rules or standards and access to membership, resources or certifications. Compliance can also rest on socialization, acculturation or normative pressures (cf. Scott 2004).

In everyday language, a lot is being made of the contemporary trend of "de-regulation." The conceptual elaboration above, though, shows that what is at work is not so much de-regulation (in the sense of moving towards no regulation) as a profound transformation of regulatory patterns (see also Braithwaite and Drahos 2000; Levi-Faur and Jordana 2005). We witness both the decline of state-centered control and the rise of an "age of legalism" (Schmidt 2004). New regulatory modes – such as contractual arrangements, standards, rankings and monitoring frames – are taking over and are increasingly being used by states too (Hood et al. 1999). Interestingly, the proliferation and expansion of those new regulatory patterns is both shaped by market logics and has a tendency to introduce and diffuse market principles everywhere. Marketization is a force that permeates and drives transnational governance while transnational governance at the same times drives marketization further (see Djelic ch. 3).

Transnational regulation is not new but has changed and expanded, with diffusing logics going particularly from economic to social spheres (Jordana and Levi-Faur 2004). Transnational regulation is a mode of governance in the sense that it structures, guides and controls human and social activities and interactions beyond, across and within national territories. As is shown throughout this book, however, transnational regulations are embedded in and supported by other modes of governance. As a concept, therefore, governance captures better than regulation the re-ordering patterns of our contemporary world.

Governance with and without government

Governance in a world where boundaries are largely in flux is being shaped and pursued in constellations of public and private actors that include states, international organizations, professional associations, expert groups, civil society groups and business corporations. Governance includes regulation but goes well beyond. Governance is also about dense organizing, discursive and monitoring activities that embed, frame, stabilize and reproduce rules and regulations.

Theories of governance emerged in reaction to the dominant perspective that social control was mobilized by and confined in states. This was particularly striking in the political science and international relations literatures (Keohane 1982; Baldwin 1993). The catch phrase "governance without government" (Rosenau and Czempiel 1992) was precisely coined to express that reaction and as such should not be taken literally. Theories of governance do not suggest that states and governments disappear (e.g. Pierre 2000). They emphasize, rather, that the study of governance should not start from an exclusive focus on states. The role of states and governments in contemporary processes of governance should not be taken for granted (Rose and Miller 1992; Kohler-Koch 1996; Moran 2002). Rather, it should become the object of serious scholarly scrutiny (e.g. Zürn and Joerges 2005).

Governance spaces are formed as new issues arise and networks of actors mobilize to be involved, have a say or gain control (Hancher and Moran 1989). These networks are open to and inclusive of state actors but they also challenge state control (Knill and Lemkuhl 2002). Hence, research on governance needs to document the changing role of states and governments in addition to focusing on the identity of new governance actors – how they emerge, construct or transform themselves to play in the new governance game; how they interact and are interrelated.

The networks mentioned above are networks of actors – individuals and organizations – but are also discursive networks (Marcussen 2000; Kogut and Macpherson 2004). Knowledge claims and various forms of expertise shape the authority of governing actors and the legitimacy of governance activities. In other words, networks and governance processes are all institutionally embedded. Hence, research on governance needs to be sensitive to this institutional contextualization (cf. Johnston 2001; Lynn et al. 2001). Theoretical frameworks should be able to capture not only the embeddedness of particular actors or governance activities but also the entanglement resulting from multiple and multidirectional connections between actors and activities.

Exploring the rise of transnational governance: existing theoretical repertoires

There is a rich collection of theoretical repertoires that talk to the issue of transnational governance in the making. Some of those theoretical repertoires take on the issue or deal with some of its important dimensions in an explicit manner. Others are more tangentially related but our reading suggests a contribution. We organize our review of a selection of those theoretical repertoires in three clusters, each of which relates to an important dimension of transnational governance in the making. The first cluster talks to the issue of governance actors. A second cluster centres on the nature of contemporary governance processes. The third cluster focuses on embeddedness and on those cultural and institutional logics that shape and drive the re-governing process.

Governance actors

Traditionally, issues of governance and regulation have been approached in political science and in the International Relations literature from a state-centered perspective. The idea that states are the central pillars of regulation and governance within but also across national boundaries is still shaping quite a share of that literature (Martin 2005). The influence of states can be direct, through law making or other forms of regulatory activity. It can also be more indirect, through delegation at a subnational or supranational level. A number of scholars have reacted to and started to modify such state-centered perspectives, including within the International Relations community. Other contributions, talking from different disciplinary and theoretical traditions can also be mobilized for the debate around governance and its actors.

The transformation of states
A first line of reaction has been to point to the progressive "retreat of the state" in a globalizing world (Strange 1996). Many contemporary regulatory reforms have been associated with privatization and the partial dismantling of public services and welfare states (e.g. Vogel 1996).

This has sometimes been interpreted as reflecting the exportation/importation of an American mode of governance that progressively assumed quasi-universal applicability. This mode of governance diffused around the world in parallel and close interaction with the diffusion of organizing and discursive principles, particularly those associated with marketization ideas and reforms (see Djelic ch. 3).

In the process, states have in fact not withered away. Granted they may be changing, potentially quite significantly. As used by Majone (1996) and others (for a review see Moran 2002), the concept of "regulatory states" points to a significant evolution of states and the way they control and influence activities and actors. Regulatory states are not less influential or powerful than more interventionist states but they are increasingly embedded in complex constellations of actors and structures (e.g. Higgott et al. 2000; O'Brien et al. 2000). As such, their input and identity is difficult to disentangle and separate from the inputs and identities of other actors involved.

Furthermore, it becomes less and less acceptable to treat states as monoliths. State institutions are complex patchworks and this complexity becomes all the more striking now that the porosity of state institutions has increased significantly albeit differentially. In fact, boundaries may now be tighter and more rigid between sectors of state administration than between particular state agencies and other actors in the same sector or field. Going one step further, Moran (2002) argues that the concept of "regulatory state" itself may be somewhat misleading – in that it still potentially sends the signal of a central role for states in regulation and governance. Along the same line, Scott (2004) criticized a state-centered bias and introduced the idea of "post-regulatory states." The defining characteristic of "post-regulatory state" thinking is a blurring of the distinction between public and private actors, states and markets, and the introduction of a much more de-centered view of regulation that relies on mechanisms not directly associated with state authority or sanctioning power (see also Black 2002).

A related discussion is a methodological one. Many studies focus on regulatory developments in individual countries, with rare extensions into cross-national comparisons. Cross-national comparisons are enlightening because they show great variation across the globe with regard to the emergence and transformation of regulatory patterns. Still, because these studies are articulated around the nation-state as the basic unit, they tend to disregard or play down the many governing efforts that cut across and transcend national boundaries. Cross-national comparisons hence only have limited value for exploring the rise of transnational governance.

Bringing in multiple actors

Along with the idea of a retreat and transformation of states, there has been a focus on the widespread expansion of various forms of private authority (Cutler et al. 1999; Hall and Biersteker 2002). There is an interesting parallel with pre-modern (i.e. pre-nation-states) times when private authority spanning local communities was an important source of regulation and governance; the *lex mercatoria* (or merchant law) being a striking example (Berman and Kaufman 1978; Milgrom et al. 1990; Lehmkuhl 2003). The modern concept of private authority is wide and encompassing, referring to a multiplicity of governing and regulatory activities that emerge and are structured outside states. The notion of regulatory or governance networks has been a structuring intellectual common thread although the word "network" is used to mean different things.

Some contributions within the international relations literature pointed already in the 1980s to the importance of transnational social networks. Using the concept of "social networks" in its descriptive and first level sense, Kees van der Pijl and the Amsterdam school explored the sociology and political economy of transnational class formation (Van der Pijl 1984, 1998). They unearthed in the process important mechanisms of transnational governance that reproduced the class power of particular groups and associated structures of dominance – both reaching progressively a transnational scale and scope.

Haas (1989, 1992) also pointed to the importance of social networks as key mechanisms of governance crossing over state boundaries. Haas's concept of "epistemic communities" makes reference to communities of expertise and practice that are increasingly transnational while individuals in those communities retain some form of local or national influence and authority (Haas 1992). This mix can allow those groups to be powerful mechanisms at the interface between transnational and national governance activities. The understanding of "social networks" here is a more complex one. Epistemic communities are "faceless" and members generally have direct interactions only with small subsets of the community. Those communities are nevertheless powerfully connected. More than through direct and regular contacts, the "glue" is generated by common cognitive and value schemes, often associated with complex socialization processes and generally translated into "expertise", shared interests and projects (see for example Botzem and Quack ch. 13; Djelic and Kleiner ch. 14; Marcussen ch. 9).

More recent contributions talk about regulatory networks, underscoring the wide variety of public and private actors involved in rulemaking and monitoring. As Schmidt puts it, "though the hangover of the traditional focus on the state's legal commands has been felt in the study of regulation, both European and American scholars of policy networks have advanced perspectives on regulation rooted more firmly in institutional dynamics and political behaviour" (Schmidt 2004: 276). The idea of regulatory networks points to complex interconnections between a multiplicity of individual and organizational actors – interconnections that can be direct or mediated. The idea also suggests organizational, cognitive and normative frames or arenas in which those interactions take place and are structured. Finally, with a focus on regulatory networks comes a question about their legitimacy and more generally about the legitimacy of private authority. With a broadening set of rule-makers, the way of authorizing rules is likely to broaden as well. Coercive rules that rest on the monopoly of states over legal authority and physical violence or on citizens' habitual obedience come to represent only one among several forms of authorization.

In the background to many of these contributions, an important question is still the role and place of states. Whether perceived as strong or weak, states are pictured as clearly distinct from "non-state" actors. There is even a sense that the game being played around regulation and governance is a zero-sum game. If the role of non-state actors becomes more important, the expectation is that the power and influence of states will decrease in parallel. Those studies contrast state and non-state actors in the governance game. However, they do not tell us about reciprocal influence and interaction or about the transformation and reinvention that is likely to follow from regular interaction. There is no sense either of how, in the process, all those actors may in reality increase their regulatory powers – in a "win-win" kind of game.

Soft actors

The multiplicity of actors involved calls for tools that make it possible to capture complex interplays and interactions. These many actors are embedded and partly structured by other actors but they are also themselves contributing to the structuring of other actors. The concept of "soft actors" captures quite well this idea of multiple identities in flux and always somewhat blurred. With this concept Meyer (1996) emphasized a view of actors – be they organizations, states or individuals – as culturally and institutionally constrained and dependent (see also March 1981).

Hence, transnational re-regulation should not be looked at only through the prism of network connections or patterns of interaction. Activities, relationships but also actors or the development of actorhood itself are constituted and shaped by more diffuse and general cultural and institutional processes. Those cultural and institutional frames are often not directly visible but they can be studied through their effects and expressions. They can be revealed in particular if we shift our attention towards governance activities and processes.

Governance processes

Rule-making is exploding everywhere – in organizations (March et al. 2000) and in society in general, at the national but also at the transnational level (e.g. Ayres and Braithwaite 1992). A quick look at the websites of international organizations is illustrative in this respect. The OECD pays a great deal of attention to regulatory reforms. The World Trade Organization (WTO) develops regulatory schemes and the European Union is largely about regulation. Not only is regulatory pressure becoming denser and more complex in those realms where it existed before in simpler forms; it is also extending to and reaching new realms of social and human life (see Braithwaite and Drahos 2000; Kirton and Trebilcock 2004; Levi-Faur and Jordana 2005). If we take a broader view of governance, as proposed above, we can note the more general expansion not only of rule-making but also of monitoring, evaluating and auditing activities. In fact, Power (1997) characterized contemporary society as an audit society where audits explode everywhere and operations and organizations are increasingly structured in ways that make them "auditable" (see also Strathern 2000; Shore and Wright 2000).

As noted above, the rise of governance is not simply the consequence of a weakened state or of a transformed economic order. In fact, there is evidence that those latter trends may themselves be driven in part by

exploding governance on a transnational scale (see Djelic and Quack
2003; Parts II and III of this volume). Power (1997, 2003), Hood et al.
(1999) and Moran (2002) propose an alternative explanation; they
suggest that expanded monitoring and auditing activities are associated with a decline in trust. Auditing and monitoring reveal and
make transparent. Rather than building trust, though, transparency
may in fact undermine it further, leading to still more requests for
auditing and monitoring (Power 1997; 2003). This may be particularly true for processes of self-regulation that are prone to questioning.
Thus self-regulation tends to be replaced or developed into regulated
and framed if not controlled self-regulation (Ayres and Braithwaite
1992).

Hence, behind exploding governance activities there is evidence of
a distrust spiral. This distrust spiral reveals profound ambivalence in
our societies on the role of expertise, science and measurement. New
modes of governance are largely expert-based; they are often legitimized by references to science and expressed in terms of measurements
(Power 2003; Wälti et al. 2004). A general societal trust in science and
expertise is undeniably a driving force behind transnational governance
(Drori and Meyer ch. 2). In parallel, Hood et al. (1999) and Moran
(2002) point to distrust in experts, expertise and measurement as one
driver for extended governance. For example, scandals around health,
safety, environmental and other issues generate profound distrust and
a demand for even more regulation and closer monitoring. This contemporary ambivalence towards expertise and science does not only
stimulate denser governance activities. It also favors more universal
types of rules as abstract expertise tends to be highly legitimate while
practicing and individual experts often suggest distrust instead.

Governance and institutional embeddedness

Actor-centered explorations of transnational governance underscore
the highly complex interplays between interdependent regulating and
regulated actors. Studies focusing on regulatory processes point to
evolving dynamics – the activities and drives behind particular processes that create self-reinforcing pressures and loops. Institutional
theories, however, tell us that it is not enough to look at observable
flows, connections and dynamics. It is also important to understand
how those flows, connections and dynamics are themselves shaped and

permeated by culture, norms and institutions. There is now an abundant literature from which we can draw insights about the ways in which institutional embeddedness shapes exploding governance and governance, in turn, progressively transforms institutions and hence the nature of institutional embeddedness.

Towards a world society

The importance of bringing in cultural processes to understand how states in particular, but also organizations or individuals, change has most clearly been shown by Meyer et al. (1997a). World society is not only a society of powerful actors; it is a society permeated by and permeating actors with cultural values or institutional frames (Meyer et al. 1997a). These frames are shaped and diffused as global models and templates along which states (and other actors) are benchmarked and possibly transformed (Finnemore 1993; 1996a). There is no global state but the alternative to state power is not anarchy and chaos. Meyer et al. (1997a) convincingly argue that the cultural and institutional web characteristic of world society can be, at least in part, a functional equivalent to a centralized, state-like global power. The stateless but rational, organized and universalist character of world society may in fact add to rather than detract from the speed of diffusion and the global pervasiveness of standardized models and blueprints (Finnemore and Sikkink 1998).

This line of research and its elaborate theory of world society are enlightening. They bring cultural perspectives and explanations into the analysis of states, organizations and their transformation and provide evidence that actorhood is of the "soft" kind. Studies within this tradition show that states remain important regulators but that they are embedded in, shaped and fashioned by a powerful world society and its associated templates (Meyer et al. 1997a; Jacobsson ch. 10). This research has also contributed to our knowledge about key carriers of global models and blueprints (Boli and Thomas 1999, Finnemore 1996a). These studies, however, focus mostly on how global models and blueprints are diffused, potentially shaping localized discourse and/or structures and activities. We learn less on the construction, and negotiation of global models. We also lack an understanding of actual processes and mechanisms of diffusion and local reception. Finally, there is room for more work – both empirically and conceptually – on carriers. There is an extremely rich and diverse "biosphere" out there that has only recently started to be studied in and for itself (Boli and Thomas 1999; Sahlin-Andersson and Engwall 2002; Djelic and Quack 2003; Parts II and III in this volume). In particular, little attention has been paid, until now, to the double issue of power and interests. Studies combining an analysis of the activities and interests of carriers with an account of their institutional embeddedness help us capture power interplays and processes of interest formation in highly institutionalized settings with a transnational scope.

Processes of institution building

Another strand of institutional arguments draws our attention to the fact that contemporary governance does not start from scratch but sets itself in reaction and relation to earlier, mostly national, systems of rules and modes of governance (Whitley 1999; Maurice and Sorge 2000; Hall and Soskice 2001). Hence, we also need to analyze how previous governing efforts pave the way for and lead to new types of governance, how different rule-systems interact and interplay. Contemporary economic sociology builds upon the recognition that human activities, more particularly in this case economic activities, are embedded within larger institutional frames (Weber 1978; Polanyi 1944). An important share of that literature has underscored the historical significance of the national level in defining and shaping these institutional frames (e.g. D'Iribarne 1989; Fligstein 1990; Dobbin 1994; Whitley 1999; Maurice and Sorge 2000; Hall and Soskice 2001). This argument has had the merit of showing the contingence of arrangements and institutions, making it possible to introduce the idea of contextualized efficiencies. There are, however, contemporary challenges to this type of argument.

In a world where transactions and interactions increasingly take on a transnational dimension, a conceptual framework that interprets action merely as the expression of national logics becomes too restrictive. Transnational pressures – the multiplication of multinational companies, the progress of Europeanization, the intensification of transnational competition, the increasing number of international organizations and institutions, and the explosion of transnational regulation – challenge national business systems and their systemic complementarities (Djelic and Quack 2003). Recent contributions show that multidirectional interactions across national boundaries associated with the multiplication, particularly since 1945, of international organizations and institutions, contribute to the emergence and the progressive structuration of transnational social spaces and transnational ("soft") actors. An important research agenda in this stream today is the transformative impact of those transnational challenges on national business systems (e.g. Morgan et al. 2001; Morgan et al. 2005; Thelen and Streeck 2005).

Djelic and Quack (2003) suggest another angle of approach that parallels our endeavor in this volume. We should be considering how, in reverse, national institutional frames contribute to shaping and structuring transnational social spaces. The multiple ("soft") actors involved in transnational governance – corporations, state agencies, NGOs, civil society groups, professions and epistemic communities, standardizing bodies, international organizations – are themselves to various degrees associated with, embedded in or in close interaction with national regulatory traditions and institutional frames. Those actors can mobilize bits and pieces of their national legacies in the negotiation around transnational governance. Some of them may even be purely and simply fighting for the transformation of a national regulatory set into a transnational one (see Botzem and Quack ch. 13; Djelic and Kleiner ch. 14). Transnational governance in the making has a "patchwork" dimension that should not be neglected.

The travel of ideas – translation and hybridization

The world society perspective drew our attention to the homogenization of those institutional and cultural frames that structure the process of governance. Recent extensions of state-centered institutionalism wondered about, on the other hand, the reciprocal and mutually constitutive interplay of national and transnational institutional frames. A complementary question is that of the situated and micro mechanisms by which frames and ideas travel and negotiate or struggle with each other. There is a rich existing theoretical repertoire from which we can start.

Czarniawska and Sevón (1996) propose that ideas and institutions do not flow or homogenize spontaneously but that the "travel of ideas" is an active social process of translation. Ideas are picked up by actors, packaged into objects, sent to places other than those where they emerged, and translated as they are embedded into new settings (Czarniawska and Joerges 1996). Similar notions of activity are alluded to with terms such as hybridization (Djelic 1998), performative processes (Sevón 1996), editing (Sahlin-Andersson 1996) or creoliza-tion (Sahlin-Andersson and Engwall 2002). These studies take into account space and local institutional settings, embedded (or "soft") actors and time, to get a deeper understanding of how ideas, institu-tions and knowledge flow. They provide a vivid picture of the dynamic interplay between homogenization and variation.

The travel metaphor directs our attention to travel routes and carri-ers. Connections between certain actors can explain in part the routes followed and account for the speed of diffusion (Rogers 1983; Djelic 1998). In fact, some ideas or frames could become popular and pow-erful not because of their intrinsic properties but because of the ways in which they have been formulated and packaged and because of who transports and champions them (Tolbert and Zucker 1983; Czarni-awska and Joerges 1996; Røvik 2002; Westphal et al. 1997). With the structuring of transnational networks and organizations, we can expect smoother diffusion and at least partial homogenization of ideas and frames on a transnational scale (Sahlin-Andersson and Engwall 2002; Djelic 2004). While the term "travel" may give the impression that ideas flow via direct interaction, ideas can also spread as they are broadcasted from one mediating source to a wide set of possible users (March 1999: 137). For example, many international organiza-tions serve both as arenas where ideas can be told and shared and as powerful broadcasters (Sahlin-Andersson 2000).

The travel of ideas is an active process and ideas are shaped and translated differently in different settings. Carriers are active in struc-turing flows and patterns of diffusion but they are also translating the ideas they mediate, reflecting in the process their own projects and interests (Sahlin-Andersson 1996). Carriers that operate transna-tionally and global broadcasters tend in particular to generalize and theorize the ideas they champion, thus making them abstract and uni-versally applicable (see Strang and Meyer 1993).

The theoretical repertoire around the "travel of ideas" was origi-nally developed to describe what happened to management ideas as they spread. We propose that this repertoire can easily be extended to other types of ideas, in particular those shaping governance frames and practices. This makes all the more sense as there is an important direct connection between management ideas and transnational governance. We noted above that transnational governance largely builds upon soft law – standards, norms and guidelines. Many of those standards, norms or guidelines relate to organizational, administrative or management issues and quite a number in fact derive from popular management ideas (Brunsson and Jacobsson 2000, Beck and Walgenbach 2002). Ultimately, it is often not easy to distinguish between management ideas and soft regulation. As an illustration, the package of reforms known as New Public Management (NPM) started out as a "management idea" through which countries reformed their state administration (Hood 1991, 1995). After being appropriated by many countries and key international organizations, such as the OECD, the World Bank or the IMF, NPM turned into a standard (Sahlin-Andersson 2000). When ideas and practices associated with NPM became strict requirements that countries had to meet to receive IMF loans, a management idea had turned into a harder form of regulation.

Combining the repertoires to revisit the field perspective

The theoretical repertoires discussed above gave important, but partial, insights into the dynamics at play behind transnational governance. Actor-centered repertoires underscored the importance of actors, interests, initiatives and power interactions in processes of transnational regulation and governance. Studies of regulatory processes showed that regulation, once in progress, displayed its own dynamics. The contribution of institutional theories, finally, was to draw our attention towards embeddedness. Actors, interactions, regulatory and governance processes are framed and constrained by and even shaped through powerful institutional and cultural forces. Models and blueprints spread around the world and generate partial homogenization of governance forms and activities across sectors, levels and territorial boundaries. At the same time, institutional or cultural frames are not simply out there – a key question is that of their origins and emergence. Transnational blueprints and institutional frames develop historically through processes where national toolkits and actors play important roles.

Capturing multi-level institutional dynamics

The multi-level character of transnational governance is undeniably quite striking. If we want to capture this multi-level character, we suggest that it is important to overcome an analytical differentiation between macro, meso and micro processes. We need to approach evolving patterns of governance both as particular situations and configurations of actors and resources and as reflections of broader templates and forces that shape and structure our transnational world. We need, in other words, a conceptual framework that can make sense of the multi-level institutional dynamics of transnational governance.

The concept of field has been used to explore interplays across levels. Although it has become immensely popular in social sciences, this concept is rarely scrutinized in detail (but see Martin 2003; Mohr 2005). In practice, many studies tend to reduce fields to networks of actors and interactions. This, we argue, is neither enough nor satisfying. We need to find ways to combine and integrate studies of individual behaviors, interactions and processes, with studies of institutional and cultural forces, that is those forces shaping and structuring both patterns of behaviors and patterns of interactions. We find guidance and insights by plowing through the many different but complementary meanings of the field concept that have been developed and used in social sciences.

Fields as spatial and relational topographies

Variants of the field concept reveal inspiration from different disciplines. Kurt Lewin (1936, 1951) was a pioneer of the introduction of the field concept into the social sciences. His socio-psychological conceptualization built upon a combination of insights drawn from *gestalt* theory and theoretical physics. Striving to embrace the complexity of the world, he defined fields as the "totality of coexisting facts which are conceived of as mutually interdependent" (Lewin, 1951: 240). Physics inspired him to develop a topological model – a spatial view – that could depict this mutual interdependence and enable him to identify "everything that affects behaviour at a given time" (1951: 241).

From there, one line of development has been towards the modelization of topographies understood essentially as relational fields. While we certainly acknowledge the methodological contribution of complex mathematical modelization (see also Martin 2003 and Mohr 2005), we argue that it is important not to close the conceptual black box too early. Premature formalization may lead us to disregard rather than embrace complexity, all the more if this complexity is dynamic.

The introduction of the notion of organization has been another way to go. A topography populated by organizations is – to use a concept developed by Emery and Trist (1965) – a "ground in motion" and should not be reduced to a mere geographical and relational space. Warren (1967), following upon Emery and Trist (1965), coined the concept of interorganizational field and outlined the complex texture of interactions and relations in fields where organizations shape and structure individual decisions and behaviors. With a focus on community-level planning organizations in three cities, however, his field concept became closely associated with the notion of territory and geographical space. His topography remained mostly a relational one.

Bringing in the missing dimension – the notion of force

On the whole, this limited understanding of topography – in its spatial and relational dimensions – has had a tendency to prevail in social scientific uses of the concept of field. However, if we take the notion of field seriously, this limited understanding is not satisfying. We need to develop a theoretical toolbox allowing us to find how spatial and relational dimensions in field topography relate to the other key notion running through field theories in physics – the notion of force. In physics, the notion of force goes back to Newton's work on gravity and Maxwell's formalization of the electromagnetic field (Pire 2000; Martin 2003). In social sciences, this notion was creatively blended with a focus on cultural and meaning aspects – first by Kurt Lewin and Pierre Bourdieu, soon relayed by certain strands of neo-institutional theory.

Bourdieu (1977, 1984) argued that fields were held together by common beliefs in the importance of certain activities. Coherent patterns of action and meaning thus developed, even without any single actor or group of actors intentionally striving for coherence or conformity. Fields, however, are also systems of relationships and resources where dominant actors occupy central positions whilst peripheral actors continuously seek greater influence and a more central position. The struggle is in great part about and around what are and/or what will be the structuring patterns of meaning and action, the dominant frames and understandings in the field. Peripheral actors challenge dominant understandings, which they try to modify and/or displace. Central actors have a tendency to protect and defend the status quo. They may envision to bend and adapt dominant understandings somewhat, if only to anchor and stabilize them further.

When the notion of force was brought into the neo-institutional theoretical fold, it was often in association with Weberian ideas of rationalization, "iron cage" and spheres of value. Meyer and Rowan (1977)
and DiMaggio and Powell (1983), the latter explicitly using the terminology of iron cage and field, emphasized that organizations may have
a great deal in common and develop in similar ways without ever being
in direct contact with one another. Thus, the analysis of organizational
and institutional change should not focus only on interactions between
organizations but also on those cultural and normative forces that foster homogenization in a more indirect and diffuse manner. Scott and
Meyer (1983) revisited and recombined Warren's (1967, 1972) work
on interorganizational fields to talk about the duality of space and
meaning associated with the organization and development of societal
sectors.

The neo-institutionalist project has from there evolved essentially in
two directions. On the one hand, in a significant number of studies, the
focus on meaning has been lost. As Mohr (2005: 22) put it, commenting
on this evolution:

> While the project as a whole is conditioned on the assumption that it is the
> meaningfulness of space that matters, in its implementation it is the space
> itself (seen now as system of communicative structures) which is actually
> revealed through empirical analysis. Demonstrations of the homogeniza-
> tion of organizational structure are used again and again as a way to prove
> the existence and efficacy of these communicative pathways. The meanings
> embedded inside these institutional objects are left unexamined.

A partial explanation for this evolution is probably a methodological
one. Territories, interactions and relationships are (relatively) easy to
observe and measure while cultural frames and patterns of meaning are
more complex to capture. As a consequence, there is a distinct tendency
in neo-institutional literature to "create a spatial metaphor that privileges the structures of communication over the actual meanings that
flow through these structures. As a result, the communicative channels in an organizational field are not analyzed in a way that enables
these meanings to be treated as constitutive of the field itself" (Mohr
2005: 22).

While this has clearly been the dominant trend, there is nevertheless
another path – and this is to focus on meanings. Certain institutionalists have tried, in particular, to understand how cultural frames, ideas

or patterns of meaning shape and constitute new structures and new modes of action and interaction across the world (e.g. Meyer and Scott 1983; Thomas et al. 1987; Meyer et al. 1997a). The risk there, as Mohr also notes, is for spatial and relational dimensions to disappear and be evacuated. The very existence of a spatial field and the role of networks and relational patterns are in a sense wiped out by the strength and power of diffuse cultural and meaning templates. Ultimately, it seems that we still lack the conceptual tools to investigate the duality and interplay of meaning and space as constitutive of fields.

Revisiting the field perspective

In this volume, we seek to revive the institutionalist focus on the duality of space and meaning. In fact, we propose to go one step further. We understand fields as complex combinations of spatial and relational topographies with powerful structuring forces in the form of cultural frames or patterns of meaning. Hence, we see the need to integrate and combine three (and not two) dimensions as constitutive of fields – the spatial, the relational and the meaning dimensions.

We propose to look at transnational governance in the making through a revisited field perspective. The theoretical repertoires identified above help us to refine our perspective further. Fields do have spatial dimensions. However, in fields of transnational governance, spatial topographies are both complex and fluid. Spatial topographies in this context cross over traditional territorial boundaries, rendering obsolete older lines of demarcation in particular between local, national and transnational spaces. Spatial topographies in fields of transnational governance look like patchworks, or even better, kaleidoscopes. They are fragmented rather than unified; a juxtaposition of multiple sub-topographies that collide and sometimes overlap. They are also highly fluid and constantly evolving. Furthermore, those spatial dimensions are not necessarily territorial. There is, for example, a spatial dimension to negotiations structured by international organizations that is by nature extra-territorial.

Fields of transnational governance are also relational topographies. They imply, reflect and are partly constituted by and through networks. In that context the meanings of "networks" and "relational topographies" are broad and highly encompassing. First, networks do not connect only individuals, but also organizations, groups or even networks. While we should not disregard the importance of interpersonal networks, including in a transnational world, we should also wonder how those interpersonal networks articulate with other types of networks (connecting organizations, groups or networks) – the result being complex and multi-dimensional relational topographies. Moreover, relational topographies can imply varying degrees of direct contact and interaction. In fields of transnational governance, relational topographies could be combinations of tightly-knit kin or family clans with virtual networks where members may never meet or exchange and are only indirectly connected.

Fields of transnational governance are also battlefields. Building upon Bourdieu, we want to move away from the idea of benign cooperation generally associated with the concept of networks. Instead, we underscore the power and struggle dimensions of relational topographies where dominant actors occupy central positions and peripheral actors constantly struggle for greater influence and power.

Finally, fields of transnational governance are fields of forces. Those fields are crossed and structured by powerful institutional forces that altogether constitute a transnational culture or meaning system. In this volume, we identify five such forces – scientization (see Drori and Meyer, ch. 2), marketization (see Djelic, ch. 3), formal organizing (see Ahrne and Brunsson, ch. 4), moral rationalization (see Boli, ch. 5) and a reinvented democratization (see Mörth, ch. 6). When characterizing these as institutional forces, we refer to four meanings of "institutions." First, institutions are constitutive of actors, interests, relations and meanings; they push and pull activities in certain directions. This is precisely why we can conceive them as "forces" (cf. Hoffman and Ventresca 2002). Institutional forces should not be treated as external to the actors, as representing an environment to which actors are merely adapting. Second, institutional forces generally become taken for granted as the "natural" way of being and doing; they turn transparent for actors themselves (cf. Douglas 1986). Third, institutional forces are self-reinforcing. As these forces shape relations, interests and bases for activities, the actions taken carry inscribed meanings and drive activities further along the same path. Fourth, these institutional forces constitute the "rules of the game" in the transnational world, providing frameworks for judging which behavioral, organizing, discursive, and interaction patterns are appropriate.

Going one step further, we find that the institutional forces identified above foster a governance culture that heavily relies on soft rules – rules that are voluntary and to which formal legal sanctions are not

attached. Those types of rules often leave considerable space for editing the rules according to particular situations, settings and practices.
In this sense, those rules can really be said to be transnational – they
are generally elaborated so that they can be applied in different settings while leaving some degree of autonomy to localized settings and
actors. Institutional inscription is not an automatic or smooth process. It implies elaboration and negotiation of rules, diffusion, translation, appropriation and rejection, potentially stabilization and socialization. All these steps and dimensions are in themselves battlefields.
They are highly dynamic processes, full of tensions and struggles. They
involve multiple actors and interests that are both increasingly under
pressure of – if not constituted and shaped by – the same powerful transnational institutional forces and still fighting and contend-
ing with each other around and about those forces and their various
implications.

Contents of the book

This reinterpretation of the field perspective provides the backbone
around which the chapters of this volume articulate. In Part I, we
present the five institutional forces that structure fields of transnational
governance. In Part II, we move to spatial and relational topographies
and their dynamics. We document both the emergence of new types of
actors and the profound transformation of "old" actors. Finally, we
look in Part III at concrete interplays and combinations of the spatial,
relational and meaning dimensions in particular fields of transnational
governance.

Transnational institutional forces

In Part I, chapters 2 to 6 present, in close succession, five institutional
forces that structure processes and fields of transnational governance.
In chapter 2, Drori and Meyer suggest that a worldwide wave of scientization is both carried by and pushing further modern globalization.
As a result of its expanding authority, scientization encourages the
constitution of various social entities as organized, rule-making and
empowered actors that find legitimacy in references to science. Science
becomes a paradigmatic umbrella, in terms of which every aspect of
the universe can and should be interpreted and framed.

In chapter 3, Djelic follows the progressive institutional inscription of marketization. Market logics have moved, in about a century, from reflecting marginal ideas in a few liberal intellectual centres to becoming a structuring force of the transnationalizing world. Today we find that marketization permeates and structures policies, reforms, discourses and ideologies in many places in the world. This progress of marketization comes, furthermore, under a highly scientized guise, particularly reflected in the professionalization of economics.

In chapter 4, Ahrne and Brunsson show that organizing is another powerful institutional force shaping the context of transnational governance. Organizing makes it possible to create order transnationally even without a world state and a world culture. Organizing in our transnational world often takes the particular form of "meta-organizing," where organizational members are organizations. Standardization and socialization are important mechanisms that reconcile transnational ordering and the perception of autonomy that often defines member organizations.

In chapter 5, Boli presents moral rationalization as a sustaining and structuring force of transnational governance. Celebrations of virtue and virtuosity (with blame and negative feedback as correlates) become increasingly prominent in the global public realm via ritualized performance displays – world competitions, award ceremonies, rankings, accreditation processes. Virtue is the embodiment of goodness; virtuosity is the embodiment of excellence. Celebrations tend to be highly rationalized – with the assumption that virtue and virtuosity can be (scientifically) assessed, measured and compared.

Mörth, in chapter 6, draws our attention to another powerful institutional force that shapes and structures the ground for transnational governance – democracy. Rather than traditional representative democracy, the transnational world is increasingly permeated by a view of democracy that emphasizes dialogue and deliberation and the autonomy of the participating actor. The progress of deliberative democracy drives and is driven by the explosion and expansion of soft regulation.

A dynamic transnational topography

Part II and chapters 7 to 11 turn our attention towards the changing topography of governance in a transnational world. Chapters 7 to 9 document the emergence and structuration of new types of actors with increasing clout and influence in fields of transnational governance. Those three chapters look in turn at law firms, multinational firms and the transnational network of central bankers as illustrative of the new kinds of players that become involved in governance processes in a transnational world. Chapters 10 and 11 document the profound transformation of "old" actors – here states and universities – that had traditionally been more closely associated with nationally-bounded forms of governance.

Chapter 7 underscores, through the case of law firms, the important role of professions in transnational governance. Morgan shows that law firms but also legal institutions and the legal profession are actively involved in processes of transnational governance. Using competition law as exemplary illustration, Morgan considers the organizational, cultural and competence implications for law firms and the legal profession of an increasing transnationalization of governance fields.

In chapter 8, Engwall looks at multinational corporations as important actors in the topography of transnational governance. The chapter broadens the idea of corporate governance, pointing to the regular interplay between corporations and significant stakeholders in their environment such as governments, the media or civil society. A field model of corporate governance shows the double face of corporations as both strongly regulated and in active discussion and negotiation with key regulatory players.

In chapter 9, Marcussen portrays the progressive constitution of a transnational network of central banks and central bankers. The chapter points to a double development. First, Marcussen documents the historical rationalization and homogenization of the role and function of central bankers and central banks – towards independent and authoritative centers of economic and financial expertise. The chapter also shows how, progressively, a transnational network has emerged with an important impact on the production and diffusion of transnational norms and standards. The transnational network is a space for interaction and socialization – as such it is also a political arena with a significant power dimension.

In chapter 10, Jacobsson scrutinizes the rapid and profound transformation of states in the context of a shifting governance ground. Jacobsson shows how states now have to compose and negotiate with a multiplicity of other actors on a governance scene that is increasingly transnational. States, furthermore, are themselves becoming objects of regulation and increasingly subjected to different forms of pressure.

In chapter 11, Ramirez documents the profound evolution of another "old" institution – the University. Changes are in the direction of greater inclusiveness, usefulness and flexibility and are rooted in universalistic models of progress and justice. Those changes both reflect and further the significant transformation of governance and governance topographies in our transnationalizing world.

Transnational governance in the making

In Part III, we explore processes of transnational governance in the making. We look at concrete interplays and combinations of the spatial, relational and meaning dimensions in particular fields of transnational governance. In chapter 12 Jacobsson and Sahlin-Andersson report on a striking convergence of governance modes across sectors and territories. Fields and issues as diverse as the defense industry, labor markets, higher education, health care, public management and the social responsibility of corporations are increasingly governed transnationally through soft rules and in quite parallel manners. The authors explore how rule-makers create authority for themselves and the rules they produce in a context of soft governance.

In chapter 13, Botzem and Quack investigate the emergence and development, since the Second World War, of a transnational field of governance for accounting and financial reporting. This process of international standard setting is shown to be a highly political process where actors with different backgrounds enter the game with specific interests, perceptions, strategies and resources. In fact, the chapter shows how contest and conflict can become a driving force (paradoxically) of international standardization if organized within a widely accepted procedural framework.

In chapter 14, Djelic and Kleiner follow the dramatic historical development of antitrust legislation from a national (American) set of rules to a transnational system of governance. The focus is particularly on the last decade and on the various attempts to foster competition regulation everywhere, both in principle and in practice, a unique expression of that being the constitution in 2002 of the International Competition Network (ICN). The ICN is a transnational virtual meta-organization, a "community of interests" striving to push along transnationally the establishment, implementation and monitoring of standards and practices and nurturing at the transnational level a "culture" of competition.

Higher education is another domain increasingly governed transnationally. In chapter 15, Hedmo, Sahlin-Andersson and Wedlin describe and explain the progressive re-regulation of management education through the development of rankings and accreditation schemes. The interplay between various assessment and regulatory activities shapes a regulatory field where the interconnection is tight between those regulating and those being regulated. This process, they show, challenges the traditional regulatory monopoly of national states over European higher education systems. National management education systems and programs that used to be quite different before now become comparable and direct competitors on a unified market.

In chapter 16, Engels describes the creation of a market for CO_2 emissions rights. This chapter illustrates how market making is used, in our contemporary transnational world, as a rule-making frame that transcends both national environmental regulation and international environmental negotiations. This rule-making process involves many different types of actors – corporations, NGOs, industry associations, consultants and expert groups. The process, as a consequence, becomes highly unpredictable and quite risky for each particular actor. More fundamentally, there are important power and legitimacy issues with this type of governance configuration.

McNichol, finally, in chapter 17, considers a transnational NGO certification program as governance in the making. The chapter details a case study of non-governmental oversight initiatives in the wood products industry. Showing that the emergence of certification programs has been characterized by a complex logic of interaction and contestation across different constituencies and domestic regulatory arenas, the author introduces a synthetic sociological model from which to describe and explain the evolution and significance of those programs. Even if particular certification or labeling programs have limited impact, the analysis for the wood products sectors suggests that such programs may contribute to other, potentially more profound, transformations in the regulatory arena.

PART I

Institutional forces

2 Scientization: Making a world safe for organizing*

GILI S. DRORI AND JOHN W. MEYER

Introduction

In this chapter, we suggest that modern globalization, in the absence of other strong regulatory systems, has carried a worldwide wave of scientization. And authoritative scientization, in turn, created the foundation for an environment in which all sorts of social participants (from individuals to national states to corporations) can and must become organized social "actors." Turbulence in the world comes under a sort of control through scientific rationalization, relying on a natural "sovereign" in the absence of strong legal or organizational ones. As a result of its expanding authority, scientization encourages the constitution of various social entities as organized, rule-making, and empowered actors. Uncertainties are transformed from mysteries into risks that must be managed (the European version; see Beck 1992) or into opportunities for more effective action (the American version; see Peters and Waterman 1982). In this environment, we see every new science or scientist or recognized scientific finding as tending to create incentives and requirements for forceful collective rule-making and for elaborated organization, both on a global scale.

Scientization disciplines and rationalizes the chaotic uncertainties of social environments, facilitating the creation of articulate rule systems, so that social actors can organize to deal with them. And given scientization, social actors must organize to manage the newly rationalized uncertainties in order to be or appear to be sensible and responsible. They must incorporate new technologies and create organizational routines to deal with the now supposedly manageable environment, in order to be properly accountable. Also, social actors discipline and rationalize such uncertainties through collective rule-making, setting up procedural regulations and conventions even in the absence of organization. Such rule-making is governed and guided by the professional ethics of science and by the certification authority of higher education institutions; it is, therefore, conceived as value-neutral and as based on specialized expertise. Scientization thus creates a culture that demands expanded organization and rule-making.

On the other (or supply) side, scientization helps turn social participants into expanded actors who have the capacity to organize, act on a greatly expanded scale, and who are guided by professional conventions. It does this, obviously, through the greatly and globally expanded educational systems of the modern world (which establish essentially everyone as themselves actual or potential scientists; see McEneaney 2003; Ramirez, ch. 11), but also by supporting elaborated myths[1] of the empowered capacity of human agency and actorhood. These myths take the form of abstract, or theoretical, explanations of human motivation, corporate interests, or national impulses, all of which refer to the social entity as a rational and bounded entity that is ripe for decisive action.

As a result, the scientization of modern culture creates both the demand for, and the supply of, both widespread rule-making and in turn rationalized organization. We argue in this paper that scientization is a main force lying behind the extraordinary modern global wave of expansion of rationalized organizational structures. We begin by outlining the properties of this organizational revolution, and then turn to the causal role of scientization in producing it.

Expanded organizing, worldwide

It is common to note that recent decades have seen a worldwide growth in rationalized organization. Formally articulated structures, once confined to a few social locations in core countries and linked to the state and army and church or to large-scale economic activity, are now found everywhere. Associations that were once informal and community-based have been transformed into organizations and in the process have formalized their rules and regulations. Without classic bureaucracy and its forms, such groups are encircled with rules, "soft" or "hard", to define their soul and to set their boundaries. Conventional explanations have a functional character, stressing how much more complex social activities are than in the past. But this is unconvincing, in view of the spread of massive amounts of rationalized organization to countries and social locations that do not seem so complex, and that in any case have not changed in degree of complexity.

The rush for modern organizing occurs along a number of dimensions. It is important to note these, because they provide clues to the causal processes involved. The very generality of the changes across time and space and social sector make it obvious that global cultural forces, like scientization, must be considered likely candidates as causal factors.

First, extant organizations become more elaborately organized. So a modern university has a much more highly specified and differentiated structure than a university with the same functions some decades ago (March et al. 2000); similar elaboration occurs in hospitals, government agencies, business firms, schools, or not-for-profit associations. The work that these organizations perform may not really have changed so much over time, but the prescribed structure of their rules and roles certainly has.

Second, in any given social sector, there are likely to be many more organizations than in the past. A medical sector, once filled with just a few professional and service organizations tied together in informal relationships, can now have hundreds of such organizations and layers of additional organizations forming to coordinate the interaction among them (Scott et al. 2000). Over time, the medical sector has expanded considerably with the multiplication of specialized service groups, regulating and funding actors, and interest groups. Similar proliferation occurs in the sectors of mass and higher education: all sorts of specialized organizations arise out of what was once a network of more informal relationships (see Hedmo et al., ch. 15). As a result, the professional life of the academic is now filled with organizational linkages, often extending to the global level (Schofer 1999). And similarly with any given industrial sector: businesses, governments, consumers, and relevant professional groups are increasingly tied together into organizational clusters, sometimes themselves formalized through the coordination of liaison organizations.

Third, sectors of social life, once weakly organized, come to be infused with organization. This is, in a sense, true of most educational, business, or medical sectors, in which only the barest skeleton of real modern organization would have been found decades ago. In the United States, for example, mass education historically was nominally organized starting at the American "state" level, but the historians Tyack and Hansot (1982: 18) say that the average state office in 1890 had only two people – a superintendent and a secretary. Now,

of course, there are hundreds of people in these offices, and thousands
of organizations involved in the management of education. While this
increased organization occurs clearly in the more rationalized or modernized social sectors, similar structuration appears in domains where
almost nothing could have been found in a previous period. Consider
family life, for example. Some organizations now train one to play a
proper family role (e.g. parenting education or lactation consultants).
Others are apparently needed to help husbands and wives properly
argue (e.g. couples therapy or marital counseling). Still others help, on
legal, medical, or psychological bases, manage the family's treatment
of children, of its finances, or of its dissolution (e.g. divorce procedures or family courts). In these ways, layers and layers of organizations now wrap around the institution of the family and support its
maintenance.

Fourth, the expansion of social institutions that are infused with
organizational logics reveals that the nature of formalization changes
with scientization. "Formal organization" no longer means bureaucratic, in the Weberian sense of hierarchically-organized, well-defined
roles, and explicit regulations. Rather, it adds to these Weberian prereq-
uisites of explicit and predictable structures, rules, and roles, a whole
set of new standards of appropriateness. These new standards of appropriateness are built around professionalized or scientific knowledge, the
expanded human rights and capacities of participants, and expanded
principles of rationality. In this sense, current organizations mix the
formal and the informal, with clear marks of permeated boundaries
between these archetypes: corporations engage in socially responsible
initiates, while not-for-profit organizations hire professional managers
to manage their community-based affairs; and neither one of these
archetypes is bureaucratic in the traditional sense. Also, social interaction becomes less explicitly formal: team work is encouraged, social
events among all workers and with their families are routine, and
the organization often takes upon itself a friendlier mascot in addition to its logo. The informality of the formerly formal organization
often takes the form of rule-making, of softer and harder versions:
emphasis on inherent laws and on procedures allows for the organization to take a less formal and explicit form without losing control and without disengaging from its goals (see Ahrne and Brunsson
ch. 4). Many of the organizations described in this volume as transnationally entangled (from consultancy groups to treaty organizations
to transnational organizations) are explicitly, and sometime solely,

rule-makers and rule-reviewers. This trend towards the informal is carried by scientization: the notions that rules are inherent to the situation and that each social actor is a rule-generator allow for softening of regulations and of explicit roles.

Fifth, expanded organization now goes worldwide. This global extension occurs in several senses. Most obviously, organization at the global level has expanded exponentially: there are thousands of international non-governmental associations in the widest range of sectors – business, medicine, education, science amongst others (Boli and Thomas 1999). And, there are hundreds of new intergovernmental and treaty organizations, in areas from international trade and economic life to human rights and the environment (see e.g. Meyer et al. 1997b). But also, organization in great amount is to be found in all sorts of peripheral countries that had almost none of it a few decades ago (Meyer et al. 1997a). In typical developing countries, one now finds an expanded state structure with all the standard agencies; one also finds local social life organized, with parties, businesses, interest groups and civil society organizations. Much of that local public life is in fact organized around international associations – through local chapters of global educational, scientific, business, or human rights organizations. The worldwide expansion occurs, then, as structuration and growth of global organizational fields, as well as a proliferation of local-level organization.

Finally, in addition to its dramatic expansion in recent decades, modern organization also changes character. A canonical organization is, now, a social actor with empowered agency, a point made forcefully by Brunsson and Sahlin-Andersson (2000). This new social actor is not set up as a passive bureaucracy – a servomechanism reflecting the authority of an external sovereign (such as a state, a guild-like profession, or an owner). Rather, its defining characteristic is its agent-like stand. This sense of agency is a defining feature of the whole modern organizational revolution, and requires further discussion.

Organization as actor

The public organization as actor

A few decades ago, during the rise of modern thinking about formal organization, it was customary to refer to Max Weber's discussions of bureaucracy (e.g. 1964). In the post-war classics of the field, this term was routinely employed: "Patterns of Industrial Bureaucracy" (Gould-ner 1964), "Dynamics of Bureaucracy" (Blau 1963), and "Bureaucratic Structure and Personality" (Merton 1957). Now the term has receded into the background of administrative and sociological scholarship, almost entirely replaced by the term organization (see e.g. Scott 1998 for modern usages).

A major change is that the notion of control has shifted from a source external to the social entity to the entity itself. The Weberian bureaucracy and bureaucrat were obedient instruments at the hands of an external sovereign – ordinarily, the state. They operated through "imperative authority," or a chain of command descending from the center (Weber 1964: 324) and did not have autonomous agency; they were not decision-makers, but were loyal servants of the king. Their professional competencies were trained capacities to carry out orders effectively and efficiently. Of course, notions of this sort remain in some kinds of organizations and in some places: Hofstede (1980) shows that this practice remains in place in countries with strong, authorita-tive, central state sovereigns (see also Jepperson 2002), and Crozier, in "The Bureaucratic Phenomenon" (1964), makes the same point. But this conception – of formalized bureaucracy – has, by and large, been replaced by the concept of organization. The organization is certainly supposed to be accountable to various "stakeholders", but it is also an agentic and responsible decision-maker on its own. To be sure, the organization is still an embodied social entity (with addresses virtual and physical, employees, and a logo); but increasingly the organiza-tion also has a character, a will, and a responsibility. The structure of this agent-actor organization involves complex interdependencies and attempts to coordinate and control these, but nowhere is there to be found Weber's notion of "imperative control" (1964).

The organization is, in short, a multidimensionally rationalized and agentic "social actor," responsibly and autonomously controlling and coordinating complex activity in complex environments. It is a modern personage with something of a culture and soul of its own, rather than a mechanical robot. It engages in what modern analysts call decision-making. All these changes are celebrated in the recent global movement for "New Public Management" (e.g. Olson et al. 1998), which essen-tially demands the destruction of the nation-state as bureaucracy and its reconstruction as a set of highly agentic and accountable rational-ized organizations or agencies.

The professional organization as actor

The same transition has reconstructed another type of organization commonly discussed fifty years ago (Brunsson and Sahlin-Andersson 2000), namely the professional organization. "Professional," in this context, was also thought of in Weberian terms whose formulation sounds today as obsolete as "imperative control." Weber's professional was a trained and incorporated member of an authoritative status group: perhaps a traditional lawyer, doctor, priest, or professor. The ideal professional was removed from the market, and subjected to the normative constraints of a somewhat closed corporate group (Parsons 1954): the pre-modern, guild-like roots of the scheme are visible. In Parsons' words, members of such a professional class "will be concerned largely with the 'practical application' of the tradition where it can be useful to others than the members of the tradition itself" (1954: 372).

This created a problem, much discussed fifty years ago, of how such groups, both highly protected and closed, could possibly be organized. And potential conflicts between professional and bureaucratic authorities were common foci of research, though dramatic empirical evidence of conflict was low (Etzioni 1961; Corwin 1970 for discussions). A common conclusion was that in really effective professional organizations (like the hospitals of the mid twentieth century), the professionals were sovereign, and the organization was a dominated service bureaucracy.

Lately, the whole discussion of the bureaucracy–professionals tension has practically disappeared. Professional groups are still thought to wrestle for their status-group privileges and to battle over their shares of the division of labor, but fundamental crises are no longer to be found. The old bureaucracy has gone modern as an organization; and the old professional has been transformed into a skilled and well-trained organizational member. The key change is that the modern professional now cooperates and collaborates in the successful operation of the organization as actor. This does not mean submission to an alien sovereign, but rather participation in the cooperative sovereignty generated in the modern agentic organization. This marriage of the organization and professionals is routinely displayed in consultancy agencies and associations of experts (see Morgan ch. 7). By being the keepers of expert knowledge and organizing their legitimacy around such knowledge and separately from money or politics, they offer the prescriptions for organization and serve only the social good.

The private organization as public actor

The same transformation has reconstructed the old private firm. The owner (typically today a set of organizations) is now the crucial "stakeholder," and the organization itself is to be the accountable decision-maker (see Engwall ch. 8). The arbitrary authority of the old owner–manager is replaced by the professionalized authority of trained management. In addition to distancing themselves from their ownership of corporate affairs, affluent families rolled over the handling of these "private" affairs to foundations, managed by trained and certified professionals. Managerialism, with the image and logic of effective actorhood, is recognized as a dominant form worldwide, and indeed the rates of management education are rapidly escalating worldwide (Moon 2002).

Again, the issue of actorhood extends beyond the mere matter of control and authority. In the process of becoming social actors, organizations acquire a kind of soul or persona. Several activities reflect this change towards actorhood. Most blatantly, private corporations practice corporate social responsibility: they sponsor educational programs, engage in environmental activities, and support community programs to close social divides. This trend of expanding corporate social responsibility is a reflection of the new social role imagined for the private sector. With this, "doing well and doing good are not mutually exclusive" has become the new corporate and management orientation. Corporate social responsibility emerges as an affirmation of the secular religiosity of the social agent, now in the form of the for-profit corporation acquiring a sense of civil duty. Much in line with other globalization pressures on the corporate world, the global spread of corporate social responsibility rests on the universal character of morality (see Boli ch. 5). And, like other forms of organizational actorhood, it is supported by scientization and its rationalizing authority.

Actorhood and rationalization

The general expansion of organization in contemporary society has come together with a qualitative transformation from past (e.g.

bureaucratic) forms. The world according to Weber has changed into the world of modern organizational theory and ideology (Scott 1998; Hinings and Greenwood 2002).

One crucial modern dimension is the rise of the organization as an empowered, agentic, accountable and responsible actor with its own goals and plans (Hwang 2003). The modern organization is managed by professional managers, more competent at proper actorhood and decision-making than in any substantive business (Moon 2002). Its highly rationalized and transparent accounting systems tell a story of rationalized goal attainment (Jang 2000b). Modern employees are empowered participants in the organization, not passive instruments: the virtuous organization also trains its employees in further empowerment (Luo 2002). It is self-reflective and self-improving, and it constantly looks after its own quality and standards (Mendel 2001; Guler et al. 2002). With these qualities, the organization is an empowered actor, interdependent with and supported by (rather than dependent upon) other organizations.

The second dimension that distinguishes modern organization and its ideology is rationalization. On each aspect of organizational actorhood distinguished above, the modern organization has clearly defined structures, rules, and roles. But beyond these specific aspects, the modern organization links up to its internal and external environments with elaborate rationalization. For engagements with technical requirements, the organization develops safety plans, environmental schemes, and specialized arrangements for facilities and maintenance. There is also rationalized engagement with human, economic and social environments: an elaborate personnel system, structures for a systematic search for innovation and improvement, detailed scrutiny of markets and supply chains, and complex planning for future eventualities (Hwang 2003). With great precision and meticulous care, the dimensions of the organization are rationally analyzed and structured. The modern organization, in short, is not only an empowered actor. It is a personage of overwhelming articulateness and education – technically in command of itself on an extraordinary set of dimensions of social life. It can be interviewed (often having officers and units for this purpose) and trusted to give elaborate and rationalized self-reflective accounts.

Behind both these core and widespread dimensions of modern organizational evolution – actorhood and rationalization – lies modern scientization. This extraordinary cultural rationalization of the modern environment creates the transcendent claims of the organized actor to almost magical agentic responsibility. And it creates a picture of the arena of social action in which it is possible and necessary to face manageable uncertainties in a rationalized way. Science, in short, helps create both the modern empowered actor and the necessity and possibility of rational action: by nominally empowering the actor while nominally taming the environment (Drori et al. 2003: 32). Science, as an axis of modern rationalization, is a support for organizing and rule-making worldwide.

Scientization in the modern system

The extraordinary global expansion of scientific activity in the past fifty years is often noted. There is an explosion of research and teaching in every area, covering the widest range of topics; studies analyze all sorts of aspects of both physical and social worlds, from Big Bangs down to the details of neonatal life. There are quite elaborate literatures treating these developments as progress toward the human understanding of nature (Inkeles and Smith 1974; Inhaber 1977), or criticizing them as arbitrary, socially determined, and creatures of power and ideology (e.g. Mulkay 1983; Aronowitz 1988; Habermas 1993; Haraway 1996). It is not important for our purposes to assess the degree of virtue involved in scientific expansion or in its consequences. Our point here is that it is an overpowering institutional characteristic of the modern system.

Thus we emphasize the extraordinary authority of modern scientific rationalization (not its limitations or virtues). It is a striking feature of contemporary society that science speaks with highly legitimate authority on the widest range of questions. Scientific testimony can routinely dominate the proceedings of courts and legislatures, international organizations, and corporate chiefs. A few scientists inspecting the sky above Antarctica can quickly lead to a worldwide movement to change major technologies. Similarly, movements rooted in scientific research can generate major changes in the familial or educational treatment of children; and social scientific work, generating evidence of inequalities, can lead to major changes in social policy or organizational rules.

These illustrations dramatize the extraordinary global expansion of scientific activity and organization. The important points are to see how extreme the changes are and to understand how dramatically these changes may exercise authority in the modern system. This evidence illustrates the two dimensions of scientization most relevant to our analysis here. There is an exponential expansion in the numbers and empowerment of people and agencies with the certified capacity to understand and act upon authoritative scientific analyses. And there is a striking expansion in authoritative scientific analyses that offer a rationalized vision of the natural and social world and define the terms and conditions for managing it. We consider these issues of the carriers and their models as intertwined, even if analytically separate.

Expansion in formal science

There is plenty of evidence to demonstrate the expansion of scientific work worldwide (e.g. Frame et al 1977; Barnes 1985; Ben-David 1990; Drori et al. 2003). Figures 2.1 and 2.2 show the historical trends of expansion using indicators such as the numbers of science-minded organizations and agencies, national and international (Figure 2.1), or enrollment numbers in advanced education worldwide (Figure 2.2). Indeed, the higher education system is the most important channel for the transmission of the core authority of science to the societies of the world and it is the main carrier of both natural and social scientific authority (Drori and Moon 2006; Frank and Gabler 2006).

This evidence shows the exponential rate of expansion and structuration of science: from scientific agencies, to scientists, to scientific products. All these act as carriers of authoritative scientific commentary and judgment on social and natural affairs. The numbers of people and agencies with the certified capacity to assert science rises continuously and rapidly. With that rises the voice of science: these carriers, or agents, are routinely empowered to make claims in the name of science.

Penetration of scientized logics

Science grows more than in volume and scope; it also grows in the effect it has on social affairs. Scientific research agenda and findings shape the models, or scripts, with which we interpret and then construct

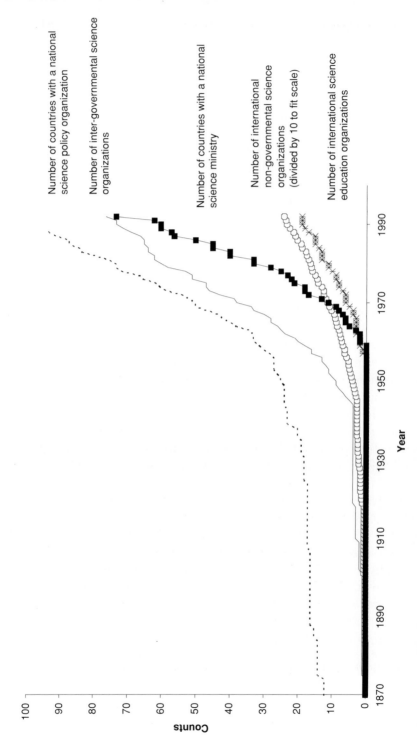

Figure 2.1 Worldwide expansion of science increasing organization and state science-related structures, 1870–1995.

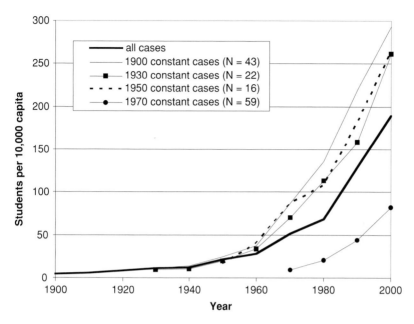

Figure 2.2 Worldwide higher education enrollment, 1900–2000, students per capita in constant case groups.

the world: the discipline of economics poses development as a social goal, medicine charts possibilities for human health, and environmental sciences warn of global warming. These fields of science define (empirically and conceptually) the terms of development (and under-development), health (and illness) and environmental sustainability (and environmental degradation). They also prescribe ways to deal with these issues and offer grounds for policy-making and change of behavior: econometric models calculate investment as one of the factors that affect prospects of national development and of corporate growth, thus encouraging investment as a standard practice; medical research asserts healthy eating habits as one of the factors that encourage longevity, thus setting diets as a growing health-related sector; and environmental scientists point to deforestation as a source of ruin, thus marking forest conservation as an action point for many international organizations and governments (see McNichol ch. 17).

The science-based identification of some issues, rather than others, as social problems immediately serves as a call for action on these issues. For example, the labeling of technological inequalities as "the global digital divide" rapidly consolidated international work to remedy the

problem and swiftly appeared as a prism for policy and action worldwide. Clearly, the diffusion of these ideas is aided by the universalistic
assumptions of science. Science is set around the delineation of natural laws, as well as social principles, both of which are derived from
observable patterns. Since these rules and principles (i.e. scientific theories) are assumed to be operating across contexts, the diffusion of the
related scripts of behavior and action tends universally to follow. Economic growth, for example, is assumed to operate similarly in Europe
as in Africa. So once liberalization of financial markets is scripted as
affecting European growth, African governments are encouraged to
establish stock markets, to relax their tariffs, and to liberalize their
energy markets (see Djelic ch. 3 and Marcussen ch. 9).

In this way, knowledge serves as a framework for action: issues that
are codified and legitimized through science set the expectations for
action and policy. Scientific theories are models, or scripts, of cosmo-
logical and ontological proportions: they reflect and assert notions of
order and of humans' role in that order. In this way, the scientization
of society is a profound process. And much like this scientization of
society, science is also being socialized, increasingly addressing social,
rather than natural or physical, matters (Drori et al. 2003). Overall,
then, scientization means the permeation of science-like logic and activities, with the underlying principles of universalism, scripts, and proac-
tion, to everyday activities. In the age of globalization, cultural rationalization of this sort, rather than state-formation at the world level,
has taken a dominant place in world affairs, in particular in regard to
transnational rule-making. Scientization is, therefore, worldwide and
a global process of rationalization.

Explaining scientization

In describing the character of the expansion of science, it is helpful to emphasize the contrasts between this expansion and some of
the traditional models of the role of science in society, which do not
adequately capture the phenomenon. There are basically two classic models that confront each other. One, associated with Robert
Merton (1938/1970, 1942/1973; see also Zuckerman 1989; Cole
1992), pictures science as succeeding because of its instrumental
functionality for the complex modernizing society: science succeeds
because it works. In reaction, critical traditions (e.g. Mazuri 1975;
Aronowitz 1988) argue that science expands, not because it works,

but because it is linked to modern structures of power and interest (including the interests of the scientific professions themselves). The first of these traditions associates scientific expansion with the instrumental problems of the complex modern system. The second tradition has a weak explanation of why science should expand at all: even if science has become the "fifth branch of government,"[2] scientists hold little direct control over sources of social power.

Nonetheless, science expands dramatically and its expansion is worldwide in character, which cannot be explained within those two traditions. The expansion of science is not concentrated in the complex core societies where it is thought most functional. While scientific research (and to a lesser extent teaching) is particularly strong in the the industrialized world policy commitments to science, such as the establishment of science ministries and national science agencies, are widespread in the third world (Finnemore 1993; Jang 2000a). Furthermore, the correlation between scientific expansion and socioeconomic development is surprisingly weak – much too weak to sustain a functionalist analysis (Schofer et al. 2000). Finally, the expansion of science is not tied to particular functional requirements of modern societies. Rather, the expansion of science is broad-ranging, far beyond any areas of special industrial or productive focus, both in particular countries and in the world as a whole (Drori and Moon 2006; Frank and Gabler 2006).

The expansion of science does not appear to be related to specific power structures. Rather, scientific activity expands on a very broad band – in research, training institutions, commercial research and development, expert communities – covering large numbers of fields, and dealing with many different issues beyond the spheres of interest of given elites. Whilst it is true that investments go into specific engineering or health issues, they also go into explorations of the universe or of biological processes, very far from particular centers of "need" or "power" in society. Furthermore, research fields in poor countries are rather similar to those in rich countries, even though power structures can vary significantly. Hence, while variations in political structure have some predictive power, they are difficult to analyze in functional terms (Drori et al. 2003).

In brief, two dimensions in the expansion of science create a challenge for traditional conceptions of the social role of science: the diffuse character of science work and the global reach of its expansion. First, science explores in one sweep grand issues like extraterrestrial intelligence or the prehistory of the human race, far beyond anything that could be considered functional or supporting of power structures. But science also addresses odd and distant questions like ice on a moon of Jupiter, as well as minute details of life, like the factors affecting which spouse takes out the garbage or the correlates of pubic hair counts per square inch. Work on questions across this broad range can be funded, published, rewarded with permanent academic positions, and gravely discussed in isomorphic communities around the world. This diffuse and wide-ranging presence shows that science is more than an instrument in modern society. Furthermore, the fact that science expands globally, across and in spite of remarkable differences in cultures, political settings, and historical legacies, and the fact that it is organized in similar ways across these social contexts, confirm its detachment from need or function.

Therefore, rather than looking at science as an instrument for efficiency or power, we propose that it is more useful to see it as a form of religion in a rationalistic modern world. It is a paradigmatic umbrella, in terms of which every aspect of the universe can be read and interpreted as set in an integrated system of "natural laws." A century or two ago, science played a somewhat similar role as the constitutive culture underlying modernity (Toulmin 1990). But the modernity it underlay then was more narrowly contained by the political structures of the modern state and army and (to a much lesser extent) the economic structures of a few industrial sectors. The science involved was often more narrowly limited to a restricted set of issues and questions. Commonly scientized topics of our time – say the physical and psychological development of children – lay out of bounds (Aries 1962). And the science of that period still reflected its origins in and conflicts with more established religions. In our own times, modernity and its scientific instruments have expanded in every direction from the macroscopic to the microscopic. They have brought every aspect of social life under scrutiny, with the looming threat or opportunity of rational organization. We return to this – our main theme – with a review and illustrations.

Reprise and illustrations

As domains of social life come under scientific scrutiny and analysis, we argue that they become increasingly susceptible to rational organization – and to agentic organization sharply distinct from traditional formal bureaucracy. Modern persons, going through education systems structured around science, have the certified capacities to bring scientific knowledge to the task of organizing technical and social activity. And given that the knowledge is itself scientifically certified and standardized, modern persons have the obligation to take it into account in managing their lives. Thus the modern organization arises, with the certified agentic capacity and responsibility to work out proper structures and routines in an ever-expanding set of domains and issues. In this way, scientization has reached into traditionally a-rationalized social spheres.

Consider, for instance, problems created by repetitive activities in the workplace. Not long ago, when a secretary was no longer able to type, little organization was required: some flowers and perhaps a gift would have sufficed to convey a response from her co-workers. The employer and corporation might offer a pension arrangement, but would be more likely simply to leave the secretary to the tender and informal care of the family system. None of the responses would convey and require a rationalized organizational structure. As the issue became scientized, with elaborated evidence and analysis, we find the creation of scientific categories – repetitive stress syndrome, carpal tunnel syndrome, and so on. This scientization of the injury produces a small-scale explosion of rationalization: organizations elaborate ergonomic programs, medical care arrangements, and the like. But many of the organizational responses occur outside the workplace itself, contributing further to the pressures towards organization: the state and insurance systems expand their disability protections; professionals arise who can allocate liabilities; training programs, both for the secretaries and for their supervisors, are put in place; specialized media and journals, some worldwide in circulation, arise; and, the organized capacity to discover and define the problem may extend to factories and offices in distant countries. Organizations that fail to deal properly with the issue come under delegitimating attacks for negligence; and a formal monitoring sector emerges to assure compliance (see Boli ch. 5).

Or consider, as a second example, the old issue of (prohibited) work on the Jewish Sabbath. Historically, rabbis and their councils, relying on their authority as religious leaders and on simple organizational arrangements, developed rules defining what was work (e.g. starting a fire in a stove) and what was not (e.g. climbing some stairs); any variation depended on each sect's religious leadership. When the modern elevator was invented, its use had to be located in terms of the traditional category of "work." Rabbis proposed various solutions to respond to this, as to other, technological changes; in this case, by and large, they frowned on elevator use because it required pushing a button (i.e. work). But a new problem was created by the invention of the modern Sabbath elevator (which works continuously during the Sabbath by opening and shutting its doors at every floor and thus does not require activation in the form of pushing a button). Since the Sabbath elevator is activated by a person's entrance into the elevator, should this act of walking into an elevator be considered a form of human intervention and, by extension, forbidden work? In our time, rabbis are less empowered to deal with such questions simply on the basis of their religious (i.e. professional in the Weberian sense) authority. Rather, their judgment comes from consultation with scientists and is anchored in a political arrangement. First, the council of rabbis called upon physicists to help them understand whether a person's entrance into the elevator is an activation of the law of gravity, and if so, whether it should be seen as representing human command or activation. This reliance on science has become routine in such judgments: rabbis now regularly consult with the scientists at the semi-academic Institute for Science and Halacha.[3] And such scholarly centers as The World Wide Halacha Center (which modernizes its name as Halachanet) are established to offer scientific answers to religious dilemmas. And, once scientific authority enters the scene, a much more rationalistic form of decision-making is put in place. Explicit organizational processes are almost by definition evoked. Some of this response is further grounded in state law and enforcement mechanisms: in July 2001 the Israeli parliament passed the "Sabbath elevator law." This law requires the new elevator as a standard in all high-rise buildings, regulates the cost-sharing procedure among the building's occupants, and offers a legal enforcement mechanism for possible violations of the law.

As a third example, we consider a story about the penetration of econometric and statistical thinking in America's military intelligence system. Interested in predicting future events, such as terrorist attacks or assassinations, DARPA's Policy Analysis Market (PAM) program was developed under retired admiral John Poindexter. The idea, based on economic thinking, was to rely on market projections compiled from surveys of ordinary people, to predict risky events. The program relied on widely-accepted econometric models of risk assessment, which have become the customary methodology in trading and betting.

The program reflected the steady post-war rise in computational power, and the use of quantitative methods for the analysis of intelligence material. The leaders called it a "refined form of polling," and derived their justifications from theoretical models in economics.

The program's ideas clearly reflect the dominance of scientific logics and of their impact on organizational formalization, in the modern system. The public debate around this program made it clear that it exemplifies an extreme case of surrender to scientized logic, specifically econometric logic. When in November 2003 the details of this PAM program were leaked to the public, a public outcry and a series of condemnations by Congressional leaders and the news media led to the cancellation of the program. What triggered the vocal public condemnation was the program's clear violation of common sense and common morality: unlike the futures market, from which the program's logic was drawn, human misery or political turmoil are not a matter for the econometrics of betting. In this sense, scientized models superseded political and moral judgments.

These cases illustrate the relatively unfettered belief in science and the progressive surrender of alternative (religious and political) logics of judgment to the logic of science. In each of these cases, the consolidation of a scientized script (of a medical condition, human–technology interface, and probability model for risk assessment) won over a social field and science became the prism for judgment, policy-making, and organizing. These cases also show how scientization constitutes both the agent-carriers (the scientific discipline, the research institute, the political unit), and the scientized script, or model, of modern social action. In these cases, scientization generated the definition of a medical condition codified into symptoms and remedies, the description of a force of nature codified into a balance with human intervention, the calculation of risk codified into econometric algorithms. Most dramatically, the democratizing tendencies of scientization influence the methodology of the PAM program. Based on scientized assumptions of statistical distribution and error terms, the opinions of lay people substituted for the judgment of the expert. Even this democratizing tendency is scientized and scripted, though: the Poindexter-led PAM program joined a growing stream of empirical work relying on "collective intelligence" (Surowiecki 2004) and the contracting firm's combinatorial product for DARPA's PAM program was called "Common Knowledge." In these, as in other forms, science has reached into various traditionally a-rational social spheres.

Conclusion – a note on globalization and global scientization

It is beyond our task, here, to put forward an extended discussion of the sources of the modern explosion of scientific research and education. We have discussed the issue at length elsewhere (Drori et al. 2003). We only make a few general remarks.

First, empirical evidence shows quite clearly when the major expansion of scientific research and training took place. With roots in the late nineteenth century (Schofer 1999), this long-term process dramatically accelerated in the 1950s, after the Second World War (Drori et al. 2003).

Second, globalization, which has marked this period, has obviously had something to do with the expansion of science. While the word "globalization" was not much used before the global economic developments of the 1980s (Guillén 2001), the phenomena that it came to represent – seen more in military, cultural and political terms – have been dramatic for over fifty years. The atomic age, rapid decolonization, the Cold War, and the stunning lessons pointing to the dangers of nationalist corporatism, fostered a spate of efforts at building world institutions. So, famously, the global intergovernmental organizational system arose and expanded; and even more strikingly the international non-governmental system grew exponentially (Boli and Thomas 1999).

Third, the effort to build a world-level political sovereignty was obviously doomed: nothing like a world state was possible. Therefore, in the age of globalization in particular, cultural rationalization of the scientized sort, rather than state formation at the world level, took the dominant place in world affairs. Science, thus, becomes a core structure in modern global rationalization.

In this context, it seems obvious – following Tocqueville's analysis of a parallel situation in American history – that social control in world society would be attempted through mechanisms of culture and socialization. Also obvious in this context is that the laws to be formulated and taught would have to be those of science (reflecting natural rather than positive law). In this sense, science provides an integrated set of principles and ideologies for a rapidly integrating world without much of a state-like political system.

In some respects, described for instance by Foucault, the modern rationalization of nature (in science) and of human life (in the discipline of the schooled person) create a field permitting the enormous exercise of technical power and control. It is easy to see the growing tentacles through which standardization and scientization penetrate each classroom, workshop, hospital room, or even family setting. And it is easy to see this as involving well-clothed power. This vision can be quite realistic, in situations in which authority to define nature and person lies in the hands of clearly-structured agents. A few people in the world, for instance, can define what is and what is not the appropriate medical treatment for millions of people, and if they operate by fairly arbitrary classificatory standards, obviously arbitrary power results.

On the other hand, it is easy to see modern rationalization in science and education as having strikingly democratizing impacts. The same science that standardizes is open to the activities of a wide and expanding range of scientists – and an even wider range of persons schooled enough in science to venture their own interpretive discourses. Nowadays, when a large piece of an Antarctic ice shelf breaks off, tens of millions of people in the world are part of the discussion of what it means and what we should or should not do about it. In the same way, the overall expansion of mass and elite education means a huge expansion in the number of active participants in the local enactment of the rationalization process. Agency is, in this sense, spread very widely – and increasingly widely – around the world.

Given the ambiguities here, we can expect a continuing conflict in social scientific analyses about the degree of centralization and concentration of power involved in the broad process of social rationalization. And the same conflict will obviously continue in discussion of the power implications of the enormous organizational expansion that results and continues to result.

There is, thus, an interesting dialectic in contemporary discussions of the scientized and organized society. We live, famously, in the society of organizations (Perrow 1979; Coleman 1982), and it is easy to drift into lines of argument about how these structures of power dominate modern society, not to mention the modern world. On the other hand, we also live in a world of rapidly expanded human rights and empowerment (Ramirez et al. 2002) and bitter criticisms of the modern system focus on precisely this point (Bellah et al. 1985; Putnam 2000).

Perhaps integration can be achieved by noting the extent to which modern organizational elaboration and concentration occur under the controls of elaborate and fairly open scientific communication systems. It is easier, under these cultural conditions, to put power together in

organizational structures, but also easier to criticize and control it from
the same cultural perspectives. Modern organizations, for instance, can
create massive inequalities, but they are legitimated under rules that
facilitate controls over these inequalities – and one can easily, with
modern data and analyses, criticize corporate exploitation in Thailand
from vantage points in London or San Francisco. In doing this, one
uses the same kinds of scientific analyses (e.g., medical, psychological,
economic) that supported the creation of the great corporate systems
in the first place.

Notes

* Work on this paper was funded by grants from the Bechtel Center at the
  Freeman Spogli Institute for International Studies at Stanford University,
  and carried out at the Institute's Center for Democracy, Development,
  and the Rule of Law. Some of the ideas presented are developed from
  Drori et al. (2003) and Meyer (2003) and reflect our collaboration with
  Francisco Ramirez, Evan Schofer, Hokyu Hwang, and other colleagues
  in Stanford University Comparative Workshop at the Institute.
1. We see "myths" as sacred and shared or uncontested truths, as is common
   usage in anthropological, and now in institutional, scholarship.
2. Referring to the structure of American political life, where government
   is formally divided among three branches (legislative, judicial and executive), and where the news media are commonly referred to as the fourth
   branch of government. In this vision, scientists are commonly called upon
   to give expert testimony to inform decision-making (Jasanoff 1990).
3. Halacha refers to the codified Jewish customs and procedural law.

3 | Marketization: From intellectual agenda to global policy-making

MARIE-LAURE DJELIC

Introduction

A distinctive feature of the contemporary period of globalization is a powerful trend towards marketization in many regions of the world. The term "marketization" refers both to market ideologies and market-oriented reforms. A market ideology reflects the belief that markets are of superior efficiency for the allocation of goods and resources. In its most extreme form, this belief is associated with the commodification of nearly all spheres of human life. Market-oriented reforms are those policies fostering the emergence and development of markets and weakening, in parallel, alternative institutional arrangements. During the last decades of the twentieth century, the dominant market-oriented reform mix has included macroeconomic stabilization, privatization, deregulation, liberalization of foreign trade and liberalization of international capital flows (Simmons et al. 2003).

Since the early 1980s, market ideology and market-oriented policies have spread fast and wide around the globe. Markets, the argument goes, are better at allocating resources and producing wealth than bureaucracies, cartels or governments. Furthermore, the global diffusion of marketization has had an impact well beyond the traditional boundaries of the economy. Marketization implies a redefinition of economic rules of the game but also a transformed perspective on states, regulation and their role. Marketization is questioning all forms of protective boundaries and barriers and having an impact, as a consequence, on social and also cultural and legal policies (Collectif Dalloz 2004; Thornton 2004).

As defined here, the marketization process points to a number of issues. There is first the issue of origins. To understand the genealogy of contemporary marketization, we have to go back to the liberal inspiration.[1] We also have to consider the alternative ideological frames historically available. We do both in the first section of this chapter. A second issue is that of ideological sustainability. For a large part of the twentieth century, the liberal inspiration has been marginalized, both in intellectual and policy making terms. Beyond the "sleeping beauty," we identify in the second section the nodes where the liberal flame was kept alive. Such an intellectual "night watch" proved essential to the liberal revival that started in the 1970s. In the third section of this chapter we describe the unique intellectual and institutional conditions of that revival.

In the fourth section we turn to the issue of global diffusion. Why and how have market-oriented reforms and ideas become so widespread during the last two decades of the twentieth century? There are essentially two ways to account for ideological and policy parallelism. The first is through "modernization" arguments. Markets emerge everywhere in a parallel and independent manner simply because they are most efficient (Friedman 2000; Lal 2000). A second way to explain convergence is through diffusionist arguments. Structures and practices tend to resemble each other due to the density of channels stimulating processes of transfer and diffusion (Powell and DiMaggio 1991; Strang and Meyer 1993; Djelic 1998; Scott 2003). We set ourselves within that second perspective and hence look at the conditions, carriers and mechanisms behind the diffusion of market ideas and policies.

Finally, the impact and consequences of the progress of marketization is another important issue. Marketization is transforming economic institutions in many countries while also reflecting upon social, political and cultural arrangements. We approach this issue in the conclusion and briefly point at the same time to the limits of the marketization trend.

Intellectual roots and alternatives

Trying to identify the precise intellectual origins of a system of thought is a thankless task. Let us start, however, from the widely shared assumption that Adam Smith's *An Inquiry into the Nature and Causes of the Wealth of Nations*, originally published in 1776, was a defining work for liberalism. This book played a key role in the emergence of the modern science of economics and was of particular influence in the stream of economics that has glorified the market (Stigler 1976; Fourcade-Gourinchas 2001).[2] The work of Adam Smith set itself in the continuity of political liberalism while strongly arguing against mercantilism and its proponents (Heckscher 1962; Schumpeter 1983: I, vii).

The liberal inspiration

Adam Smith was expanding upon the contributions of the great founders of political liberalism – John Locke in particular. For Locke, a state of nature predated the social contract. In that pre-social state, each individual was facing nature and interactions between individuals turned around that interface. They had to do with work, the products of work and property rights. Pre-political – "natural" – man was therefore a *homo economicus* (Manent 1986; Locke 1997). The social and political contract emerged only in reaction to threats and to generate collective responsibility for the respect of natural law and the protection of private property. Building upon the idea of "natural man" as economic man, Adam Smith re-affirmed both the autonomy of the economic sphere and its historical and moral precedence over other spheres of human life (Smith 1999). Adam Smith also took over the idea that the economic sphere was by nature stable, structured by "natural laws" – essentially the propensity to barter and the division of labor, competition and the invisible hand of the market.

Economic man had, according to Adam Smith, a natural propensity to "truck, barter and exchange one thing for another" (Smith 1999: I, ii, 117). The market, from this perspective, was a natural and essential dimension of social life. Each individual could obtain what he needed on the market in exchange for the things he produced. The extent and complexity of the division of labour depended upon the scale and density of the market, itself in direct correlation with demographic and infrastructural conditions (Smith 1999: I, iii). Adam Smith argued that the progressive extension and expansion of markets meant, ultimately, not only greater individual and collective well-being but also moral, social and political progress away from feudalism and tyranny and towards yeomanry and democracy (Smith 1999: I, i, 109; III).

Another "natural law," according to Adam Smith, was that markets were orderly. Order did not stem from an all-powerful regulator but from a multiplicity of transactions and their combination (Smith 1999: I, ii, 119). Through combination in the market, the greed and selfishness of individual acts turned into a morally satisfying and welfare maximizing collective order. In *The Wealth of Nations*, individuals were pictured as a-moral; the market, though, was inherently albeit mysteriously producing a progressive and moral order (Nelson 2001). The miracle of the invisible hand required, however, specific conditions and in particular that markets function freely. Smith pointed to two types of obstacles. Market players themselves could introduce disruption and "people of the same trade seldom meet together, even for merriment and diversion, but the conversation ends in a conspiracy against the public or in some contrivance to raise prices" (Smith 1999: I, x, 232). This part of Smith's argument has often been neglected but it shows deep consciousness that competitive markets were not automatically self-sustaining. Smith also strongly denounced tampering and intervention by political authorities (Smith 2000: IV, ii). That particular denunciation is an important part of the genetic link between Smith's liberalism and contemporary neoliberalism (Skinner 1999: 79).

Mercantilism and German historicism as intellectual alternatives

The idea is naturally not to reduce the history of economic thought to an opposition between liberalism, mercantilism and German historicism. Still, identities are also constituted in part through opposition and conflict. In 1776, Smith was championing political liberalism but he was also opposing and arguing against mercantilism. And later on, at an important moment for economics, during the early years of professionalization, the debate between classical liberalism and historicism proved potent (Fourcade-Gourinchas 2001). In contrast to the communist alternatives that flourished during the nineteenth century, those three intellectual traditions were compatible with capitalism and private property. They revealed, however, different conceptions of the nature and role of markets.

Mercantilism
More than a theory, mercantilism is a label that gained visibility and coherence through the violent attacks of liberal economists – and of Adam Smith in particular (Heckscher 1962; Magnusson 1994).

Mercantilists claimed that the wealth of a country was measured by its stock of precious metals. Hence a nation should control imports and exports to maximize that stock. This concretely meant an endorsement of political intervention in economic affairs. Political intervention could go in different directions. States could impose tariffs to control imports and also to protect national industries and give them time to develop. State intervention could mean aggressive political support of exports – including through military imperialism or colonialism. States could encourage the multiplication of manufactures, by providing capital or granting privileges such as exclusivity over a market or even by themselves turning entrepreneurs.

For mercantilist writers, the economy was serving a wider national project. Polity and economy were tightly intertwined and political aims had the pre-eminent role. Ultimately, foreign trade was not so different from a (peaceful) game of war and all national forces should be mobilized to wage that war. The state had a privileged understanding of national needs, national resources and their articulation. Hence, it should actively intervene, fixing priorities, combining individual efforts and controlling results. From a mercantilist perspective, reliance on private initiative was bound to favor particularistic interests to the detriment of the collective good. There was no place, in that context, for the invisible hand of a "free market". The "hand" existed but it was the highly visible one of the prince or the polity.

German historicism

The historical school of economic thought was also involved in a profound and bitter discussion with liberalism. Historicism had its roots in Germany and was highly dominant in that country during the nineteenth century. German historicists rejected the idea of natural economic laws and of universal theoretical systems (Shionoya 2001). They argued, instead, that economic "laws" were contingent upon historical, social and institutional conditions. This was a common theme but there were variations, in particular between a descriptive and a normative form of historicism.

Descriptive historicism pointed to the embeddedness of economic arrangements, underscoring the need for historically and sociologically grounded empirical economics (Iggers 1968). From that perspective, market economies had no prime of place. They should be contextualized and efficiency could not be presumed. Normative historicism went further. It connected economic trajectories with national identities – states being symbolic carriers. The consequence was militant support for the status quo that reflected the essence of a nation. This implied also a preoccupation for nation building through state-led economic policy that was reminiscent of mercantilism. Concretely, this meant that in Germany normative historicism found legitimate, towards the end of the nineteenth century, a combination of organized capitalism and strong state intervention. Such a combination, emerging together with German unification, marked as it were the culmination of the German "spirit." Progress was away from chaos, towards order; away from free or wild markets and towards organization and centralization.

In retrospect, the fate of German historicism was closely linked to two developments. First, German historicism lost the *methodenstreit* – the methodological dispute that opposed it to Austrian liberals during the 1880s (Hodgson 2001). For the Austrian Carl Menger the prime task of economic analysis was theory making and theoretical knowledge could not emerge from historical economics. Since then, this position has become uncontroversial in economics and the legitimacy of historicism was weakened in the process. A second development was the association of normative historicism with Prussian and later German nationalism. This association further contributed to marginalize historicism.

Although there is no trace of historicism in mainstream economics, it has not disappeared from the ecology of ideas. Historicism has influenced economic history (Koot 1987). It was also absorbed by early American institutionalists, such as Thorstein Veblen or Richard Ely, and is having an impact through that lineage on heterodox economics (Yonay 1998). It is probably most alive, though, in economic sociology, reflecting a Weberian heritage (Guillén et al. 2002). Contemporary economic sociologists have revived the descriptive project of the German historical school. They put markets in perspective, showing both the embeddedness of economic arrangements and the contextual efficiency of alternatives to markets (Whitley 1999; Hall and Soskice 2001; Fligstein 2001). Through the contemporary vitality of economic sociology, historicism is still indirectly present in the debate around neoliberalism.

Economic liberalism – the sleeping beauty

The first sixty to seventy years in the twentieth century were difficult for economic liberalism. The idea that economic action should take place in free markets and that state intervention should remain limited, did not convince during that period. The belief in free trade as a source of prosperity did not fare better. Almost everywhere, those years were characterized by the triumph of interventionism, and interventionism could take different forms.

Socialized property and centralized planning imposed themselves in the Soviet Union and, after 1945, in many other countries under Soviet influence. The Great Depression and its aftermaths brought Keynesianism on the policy-making scene in many capitalist countries. State intervention and regulation of markets became staple fare. The trend was only reinforced with the turn to war economies. In capitalist countries where Keynesianism was not the inspiration, the influence of Nazism or authoritarian ideologies was being felt. Here again, this meant a quasi-disappearance of market mechanisms, strong state intervention and a surge in protectionism. In parallel to this triumph of state intervention, cartelization had been progressing in most economies, championed by private actors themselves. Free markets and competition were associated with chaos and disruption, while cartelized markets held the promise of orderly and rational economic development. The consequence was a triumph of organized capitalism, at least until 1945, that extended across national borders with the multiplication of international cartels (Djelic and Kleiner ch. 14).

During those years, the prophets of free markets had not disappeared but they were a minority with scant influence on policy-making. Liberalism went "underground" and only a few scientific centers kept the flame burning. Three of those centers emerge as particularly important. The Chicago school was making its first steps, grounding the foundations for the liberal temple. The Austrian school was another important node. The small German ordo-liberal of Freiburg school finally deserves to be mentioned, if only for the "miracle" of its survival in an environment decidedly not conducive to liberalism.

Building the liberal temple – the early years at Chicago

Created in 1892, the University of Chicago was originally financed by John D. Rockefeller, the "Titan" of the American oil industry (Chernow 1998). The first head of the Economics Department at Chicago was J. Lawrence Laughlin. Laughlin was a mixture of neo-classical theorist and aggressive big business apologist – the type that seemed to "confirm the suspicion of those who regarded the University of Chicago as a tool of business interests" (Coats 1963).

The liberalism championed by Laughlin differed in important ways from Smithian or Manchester-type liberalism. His apology of the market was reconciled with the corporate and oligopolistic revolution that transformed American capitalism (Sklar 1988; Bornemann 1940). This reconciliation between markets and "bigness" has remained to this day a trademark of the so-called Chicago school of economics (Miller 1962; Nelson 2001).

The Chicago school crystallized during the 1930s around the key figure of Franck Knight (Nelson 2001). The group that emerged then would make the Chicago school famous – Jacob Viner, Henry Simons, Aaron Director, Allen Wallis, Milton Friedman, Rose Director Friedman and George Stigler (Reder 1982). Franck Knight championed free markets on moral grounds, as the best arrangements to ensure the preservation of individual freedom. Increased efficiency and utility maximization were positive collaterals, not ends in themselves (Nelson 2001).

Keeping the flame alive – the Austrian front and German mavericks

The *methodenstreit* had revealed the existence of what German historicists disparagingly called an "Austrian school". Inspired by libertarian philosophy, Austrian economists have been staunch proponents of free markets, free trade and laissez-faire (Cubeddu 1993). They have focused on the dynamics of capitalism, with the entrepreneur as core figure. Austrians are "Jeffersonians," hailing a market with multiple nodes/free individuals/entrepreneurs (Mayer 1994). The school has specificities that keep it at a distance from mainstream economics – in particular a reluctance to join the "marginal" or mathematical revolution as pioneered by Marshall, Walras and the Cambridge school (Schumpeter 1983: III, ch. v).

Carl Menger, who fought the *methodenstreit*, was an important early figure. The most famous names, though, have been Ludwig von Mises and Friedrich von Hayek. Austrian liberals were the first to argue seriously against Marxian economic thought, already in the 1880s. Von Mises' publications were a landmark in that struggle and explain in part the association of Austrian economics with staunch anti-communism (Mises 1935).

Before 1914, economists from the Austrian school enjoyed significant prestige and clout in Vienna. There were strong intellectual connections between that group and foreign colleagues, in particular Frank Knight in Chicago. However, during the interwar period, the Austrian school was increasingly marginalized. By the 1930s, with the rise of Nazism in the background, members of the Austrian school dispersed across the world. Hayeck left for the London School of Economics and in 1950 for the University of Chicago (Dostaler and Ethier 1989). Von Mises went first to Geneva and in 1940 to New York city. Most other members left Vienna to go to the United States. Migration on such a scale fostered the emergence of an "American generation of Austrian economists" (Vaughn 1994). This generation would play a significant role in the liberal revival (Yergin and Stanislaw 1998).

In Germany, liberalism was a maverick ideology until the end of the Second World War at least. In hostile conditions, a few Germans championed notions of a free market, putting their career at stake in the process. The Freiburg or ordo-liberal school was blaming collectivism, cartelization, state intervention and protectionism for the dire straits of the economy but also for the rise of Nazism. In contrast to the *Zeitgeist*, the ordo-liberal school was in favor of competition, not least as a necessary condition for political democracy (Nicholls 1984; Peacock and Willgerodt 1989).

In 1936, the ordo-liberal school published a manifesto, "Our Task". The competitive economy envisioned had neoclassical features – with multiple units, each one more or less corresponding to a private household. However, ordo-liberals did not believe in competition as a self-maintaining equilibrium – non-intervention in Germany had only brought about collusion. Markets and competitive conditions should be created and protected through legal frameworks (Peacock and Willgerodt 1989: ch. 2).

Throughout the Nazi period, the Freiburg school was a hub of intellectual resistance. At the end of the Second World War, it was neither well known nor well connected (Nicholls 1984). Things changed with the occupation of Germany and the Freiburg school became an important actor then in the transformation of German capitalism (Nicholls 1984; Berghahn 1986; Djelic 1998).

Towards a liberal revival

Throughout the first part of the twentieth century, liberalism remained a "dormant beauty," with scant influence in Europe or the United States. After the Second World War, there were important steps towards a liberal revival. The creation of the Mont Pelerin Society was a marker – opening the way to the proliferation of liberal think-tanks everywhere in the world. By the late 1970s, the liberal inspiration was back and strong on the intellectual scene. The 1980s created the political windows of opportunity that made it possible for liberalism to impose itself in policy-making circles, initially in Chile, the United States and Great Britain.

Hayeck and the Mont Pelerin Society – inventing the think-tank

In 1944, Friedrich von Hayek published *The Road to Serfdom*, where he argued that state interventionism led, inexorably, to tyranny. Nazism was being defeated; nevertheless the *Zeitgeist* was still conducive to interventionism. With a view to reviving the liberal inspiration, Hayek had the idea of bringing together like-minded individuals. The meeting took place in April 1947, at Mont Pelerin, in Switzerland. The thirty-nine participants shared a commitment to free markets and limited government albeit with varied understandings of what those meant. Milton Friedman, George Stigler, Aaron Director, Ludwig von Mises, Karl Popper and Wilhelm Röpke were all present.

At the end of the meeting, the group decided to institutionalize itself in the form of the Mont Pelerin Society (MPS). Registered as a non-profit corporation in Illinois, the society was dedicated to reviving, sustaining and spreading liberalism. Until 1967, Hayek was its president. The Mont Pelerin Society remains a virtual organization, with no headquarters, and recruits through cooptation. The society has no official publications and exists intellectually through the contributions of its members. Its website is not very informative – and in particular the list of current members cannot be accessed. In spite (or because) of this discreet touch, the MPS has been an important mechanism of the liberal revival (Mendes 2003). Membership has expanded, both in absolute numbers and in geographical reach. In 1947, 39 members came from 10 different countries; there are today around 500 members coming from 40 different countries. To this day, the MPS claims merely an advocacy role, proposing that "its sole objective is to facilitate an exchange of ideas between like-minded scholars in the hope of strengthening the principles and practice of a free society" (www.mps.org).

A measure of the intellectual clout achieved by the MPS is the number of Nobel prize winners amongst its members. Hayek received the Nobel prize in 1974. He was followed by Milton Friedman (1976), George Stigler (1982), James Buchanan (1986), Maurice Allais (1988), Ronald Coase (1991), Gary Becker (1992) and Vernon Smith (2002).

The MPS was a pioneer. It had followers and liberal think-tanks have flourished since the 1970s in the United States and elsewhere in the world (Stefancic and Delgado 1998; Mendes 2003; Krastev 2000). We only give some examples here. The Heritage Foundation (1973) and the Acton Institute (1990) brought together the liberal and Christian traditions (www.heritage.org; www.acton.org). The Ludwig von Mises Institute was created in 1982 and it has become an important seat of libertarianism (www.mises.org). The general trend has been towards an increasing presence of private and corporate interests – as evidenced for example by the Bertelsmann Foundation in Germany, the Cato Institute, and the American Enterprise Institute in the US (www.stiftung.bertelsmann.de; www.cato.org; www.aei.org).

Chicago – the new generations

In parallel with the multiplication of liberal think-tanks, the Chicago school was reaching maturity. The new generation had appropriated the philosophical insights of their teachers, in particular Frank Knight. There were two features, however, that set that generation apart. First, it jumped on the bandwagon of the "marginal" or mathematical revolution in economics and contributed to its acceleration (Reder 1982). Second, with Milton Friedman as its main spokesman, this generation re-affirmed the public and polemical role of the economist, originally explored by Laughlin.

By the early 1960s, the Chicago school in economics had acquired its unique features (Bronfenbrenner 1962). First, one finds an unconditional advocacy of the market mechanism. The Chicago economist "differs in this advocacy from many economists on his dogmatism and in assuming that the actual market functions like the ideal one" (Miller 1962: 66). Second, one finds a principled rejection of regulation and state intervention that implies acceptation of the evolutionary dynamics of market competition. This has meant, in particular, that the Chicago school has accepted "bigness." The fear of concentrated wealth, present in the work of Adam Smith, has had little weight in Chicago, much less in any case than the fear of government. Gary Becker summed it up well: "It may be preferable not to regulate economic monopolies and to suffer their bad effects, rather than to regulate them and suffer the effects of political imperfection" (Becker 1958: 109).

Third, one finds a Panglossian vision of the world. The market mechanism leads to greater efficiency, collective prosperity and individual freedom (Friedman and Friedman 1979, xv, 28: 129). Fourth, provided the state does not meddle, the market mechanism should be self-sustaining (Reder 1982). Fifth, the associated conception of human nature is that of neo-classical economics – human beings are out to maximize utility. The Chicago school has systematically explored that path by expanding the boundaries of economics, explaining theft, discrimination, marriage, fertility, child rearing (Becker 1971, 1991), legal issues (Posner 1972) or the functioning of religious institutions (Ekelund et al. 1996) through the prism of utility maximization.

Sixth and finally, the contemporary Chicago school has reconciled science and politics. The post-war generation contributed to the scientific and mathematical turn in economics while being actively involved in policy-making and political discussions. As we show below, the move to politics was initially partly accidental. Soon, though, the most vocal Chicago economists – in particular Friedman – found out that there was a "market" for their ideas and turned themselves into missionaries of market principles. Their proposals for reform:

involved either increased use of the price system, substitution of private for public production (eg. in health, education), replacement of legal compulsion by voluntary – financially induced – private cooperation or a mixture of all three (Reder 1982: 25).

Political windows of opportunity

During the 1970s, the liberal agenda moved progressively from marginality to centre stage. The process reflected in part chance and opportunities and in part the entrepreneurial flair of a few individuals who managed to identify those opportunities and ride on the wave.

In the 1970s, oil shocks created major disruptions that were reinterpreted as revealing structural fragilities. A striking puzzle was the combination of economic depression and significant inflation. "Stagflation," as the phenomenon was called, was in contradiction with Keynesian economics (Friedman 1968). The Keynesian stop-go machine appeared to be jammed. The "sleeping beauty" was out there, ready to be awaken through the search for alternative toolkits. Inspired by the liberal intellectual revival, economists and policy-makers came to blame excessive regulation and government intervention for structural rigidities. The most astounding expression of that was proposed by the British (Labour) Chancellor of the Exchequer, James Callaghan, a former trade unionist. In 1976, Callaghan pronounced Keynesianism dead and state intervention a failure.[3]

We used to think that you could spend your way out of a recession and increase employment by cutting taxes and boosting government spending. I tell you in all honesty that that option no longer exists and that in so far as it ever did exist it worked on each occasion since the war by injecting bigger doses of inflation into the economy, followed by a higher level of unemployment (quoted in Callaghan 1987).

Monetarism and supply-side economics were on their way, pointing to markets and the price mechanism as an alternative path to managing the economy.

The term "supply-side economics" was coined in the 1970s to refer to the liberal policy package that targeted stagflation. Supply-side economics were inspired by Austrian economics and libertarian philosophy and in close intellectual affinity with Chicago-style monetarism and liberalism (Leeson 1998). A starting proposition was that economic growth depends upon market efficiency and the smooth allocation of resources for production. The policy recommendation was to remove impediments to free markets and to reduce in particular state involvement. This translated into privatization, deregulation, a scaling back of welfare benefits and tax cuts. Supply-side economics also recommended free trade as a means to "healthy" competition. Monetarism, closely associated from the start with supply-side economics, had the curbing of inflation as a key objective. The argument was that free market economies were inherently stable in the absence of major fluctuations in money supply and hence in the absence of government meddling into monetary issues. Central banks, as a consequence, should be strong and independent (see Marcussen ch. 9).

The first experiment in supply-side economics took place in Chile. In 1973, a military coup backed by the CIA put an end to Salvador Allende's project of reaching socialism through reformist means. The military dictatorship turned instead to free market economics under the guidance of the "Chicago Boys." Those were Chilean economists with a PhD from the University of Chicago, who had benefited in the 1950s from a US-government program designed to counter a leftist bias in Chilean economics (Valdès 1995). The "Chicago Boys" privatized public industries and reversed the expropriation of the Allende years. They reduced trade barriers and made labor legislation more favorable to business interests. Social security was privatized and monetary policies followed Friedman's orthodoxy (Foxley 1983; Fourcade-Gourinchas and Babb 2002: 13).

Great Britain and the United States were two other early pioneers, starting even in the 1970s, ironically under Labour and Democrat governments. We have described James Callaghan's change of heart. In the United States, deregulation on a big scale started under President Carter, a southern Democrat. In 1979, President Carter put the Federal Reserve Board in the hands of the monetarist, Paul Volcker, with the mission to tame inflation. The reorientation widened in scale and scope once Margaret Thatcher and Ronald Reagan took over. Both had been strongly influenced by liberal intellectuals and think-tanks. Milton Friedman had already been a close advisor to Ronald Reagan in 1973, when Reagan was Governor of California (Leeson 1998: 45). The British Centre for Policy Studies, set up in 1974 with Margaret Thatcher as President, was the channel through which monetarism and supply-side economics found their way to Mrs Thatcher's political platform (Keegan 1984: 46–7, 81–2). In Britain, the influence of supply-side economics translated into the "systematic implementation of an agenda of deflation, privatization, deregulation and downsizing of the public sector" and into an attempt at dismantling the welfare state (Fourcade-Gourinchas and Babb 2002: 556). In the United States, deregulation was implemented on a large scale and the public and welfare sectors were pulled towards market logics. Deflation and tax cuts triumphed.

Towards global diffusion of marketization

The liberal revival had great consequences for the economic, social and political landscapes of pioneer countries like Chile, Great Britain or the United States. Its impact, however, soon became felt more broadly. The Thatcher and Reagan revolutions opened the floodgates of liberalism. They represented focal points around which logics of transnational diffusion articulated.

Diffusion and its context

The context of diffusion was characterized by five distinctive developments. First, the economic crisis of the 1970s had a nearly global impact, pointing everywhere to the limits of Keynesian recipes. Second, it increased the dependence of many countries on international financial institutions, such as the International Monetary Fund (IMF) or the World Bank (WB). Third, the fall of the Berlin Wall seemed to imply a victory of capitalism and liberalism over communism and its interventionist legacies and translated for former communist countries into dependence on international financial institutions, the United States and rich Western countries. The terrain was conducive then to an ideological U-turn in those countries – towards the "all-market" mantra and radical forms of political and/or cultural liberalism.

Fourth, the United States was rising in parallel to hegemony power – if not "Empire". Since 1945, diffusion flows have been highly skewed. Practices, ideas and institutional rules of the game have gone predominantly from the United States towards the rest of the (Western) world (Djelic 1998; Zeitlin and Herrigel 2000). This tendency has not abated; quite the contrary. Fifth, as an epistemic community (Haas 1992) but also as policy-makers, economists have gained in presence, clout and strength worldwide. The progress of this group has combined with global homogenization of the profession (Kogut and Macpherson 2003). Since there as elsewhere American hegemony was strongly felt, the Chicago style of American economics, once in progress, has spread fast and wide.

Carriers and channels of diffusion

The global diffusion of marketization has had multiple dimensions. We argue that, out of this diversity, it is possible to identify four categories of carriers or transmission channels.[4] First, we find organizational carriers broadly understood. Second, we find routines and institutionalized practices, often associated with organizational carriers. Third, we identify relational or social networks as important transmission channels. Fourth, we point to the role of normative and symbolic systems as carriers in themselves. Naturally, those are ideal types and in most empirical situations, interplay is likely.

Within the broad category of organizational carriers, we make a difference between classical organizations and network or meta- organizations (see Arhne and Brunsson ch. 4). The IMF, the WB and the European Bank for Reconstruction and Development (EBRD) are amongst those classical organizations that have played a significant part in the global spread of marketization. The IMF and the WB carry around the "Washington Consensus" – another label for what we call marketization (Stiglitz 2002). In parallel, private firms and service providers with a multinational reach are also important carriers. Anglo-Saxon firms were pioneers; today most organizations with a global ambition share at least parts of the marketization discourse and agenda.

The spread of marketization also owes a lot to organized spaces with unclear boundaries. The World Trade Organization (WTO), the Organization for Economic Development (OECD), the European Union (EU), the North American Free Trade Agreement (NAFTA), the European Round Table of Industrialists (ERT) are all variants of network and meta-organizations. They all play a part in the global move towards market logics. Their impact plays itself out in part at the level of normative frames and hence may be less perceptible, but probably more enduring in the longer term, than the coercive pressure of the IMF or of institutional investors.

Routines and practices constitute a second category of carriers. Although often associated with organized spaces, routines and practices can be influential in themselves in particular when diffusing beyond their context of origin. The setting-up of independent public agencies, for example, has ideological and structural implications that carry forward the marketization trend (Gilardi 2005). As another example, routines associated with accreditation and rankings in higher education increase competitive and market pressures in that field (see Hedmo et al. ch. 15).

Relational or social networks represent a third category of carriers. There is naturally a danger to overemphasize the importance of social networks, as is often done in micro studies of diffusion (Strang and Meyer 1993). But there is also a risk of forgetting the role that social and relational networks play in transnational and macro processes of diffusion (Djelic 2004). The transnational diffusion of marketization has historically been facilitated, we argue, by the articulation of different types of relational networks. In particular, transnational bridging networks – such as the Mont Pelerin Society – need to connect with institutionalized and powerful local networks (Djelic 2004). This ensures that ideas and practices get, first, transferred across borders and, second, lastingly appropriated including through translation locally (Czarniawska and Sevón 1996).

Normative and symbolic systems, finally, constitute a fourth category of carriers. Ideological frames or institutionalized "myths" (Meyer and Rowan 1977) are powerful because they can shape behaviors and interactions a priori. When those frames are inscribed in socialization systems, they can become invisible to embedded actors. Twenty years ago, the concept of "maximizing shareholder value" did not exist in most European countries. Today, it is a revealed truth, an unquestioned logic in many business and business school contexts across Europe. The spread of the concept and its associated normative scheme justifies in turn the implementation of routines and practices that stabilize it further. There is a self-reinforcing loop here. Ideas flow and as such they are not only carried but are also carriers. Categories and concepts such as "competition," "maximizing shareholder value," "transparency," "New Public Management," "markets," "privatization" flow across the world, carrying with them organizational, practical and behavioral implications that reinforce the marketization trend. However, diffusion also implies reception and reception calls for local appropriation, contextual decoding and "indigenization" (Scott 2003: 884). As they flow, ideas and normative categories are also "edited" (Sahlin-Andersson 1996), translated and hybridized (Czarniawska and Sevon 1996; Djelic 1998). The local decoding process – and its organizational and relational filters – should also be scrutinized.

Epistemic communities (Haas 1992) and professions are powerful combinations of our last two categories. They are anonymous social networks bound together through shared normative and symbolic systems. Epistemic communities and professions have been instrumental for the global spread of marketization and as such deserve to be singled out here.

Mechanisms and logics of diffusion

Those carriers and transmission channels function according to different types of logics. We identify three categories of logics that resonate loosely with the categorization of diffusion channels. Here again, in most situations of diffusion, interplay is likely. This categorization is an alternative to the classical typology of diffusion mechanisms (coercive, mimetic, normative) proposed by DiMaggio and Powell (1983).

We point first to political logics. By that we mean logics reflecting power asymmetries and dependence. Political logics can translate into coercive pressures but also into voluntary imitation of what appears more "efficient," more "modern," more "rational" or more "scientific" (see Boli ch. 5; Drori and Meyer ch. 2). The influence of financial institutions such as the IMF or the WB provides a good illustration of political logics. Those institutions work through mechanisms of "conditionality", conditioning credit lines upon the implementation of policies and reforms. During the last two decades, dependent countries have been coerced in this manner towards the adoption of neoliberal reform packages (Stiglitz 2002). The influence of the European Union on candidate or potentially candidate countries is another good illustration. Integration is strictly conditioned upon a package of structural adjustments and reforms, many of which stimulate the progress of marketization in those countries. For potential candidates, with no definite time horizon, pressure may be more indirect and self-inflicted through voluntary imitation.

A second category of diffusion logics are those associated with processes of social interaction. By social interaction, we mean various forms of direct interface and exchanges that often take place within and across social networks. Social interaction logics played a part in the constitution and spread of neoliberal think-tanks and also in the appropriation of the neoliberal agenda by British and American governments for example. When we consider the transnational diffusion of ideas, we argue that social interactions should be at the same time wide and deep (Djelic 2004). Global epistemic communities or advocacy networks are an interesting illustration of that. They combine transnational peer interaction with national or local strategies of influence towards key institutional and organizational nodes (Marcussen ch. 9; McNichol ch. 17; Djelic and Kleiner ch. 14).

Finally, structuration and socialization processes point to a third category of diffusion logics. Here, by structuration, we refer to a process by which the rules of the game are set and constituted to reflect a particular ideology and associated practices. Those framing schemes themselves can diffuse. They may then have an impact on practices, behaviors, interactions and shared beliefs through percolation and progressive socialization. Structuration logics can combine with political and/or social integration logics. Structuration pressures will be all the more powerful if framing schemes become deeply institutionalized and possibly invisible for socialized actors. The progressive accession of the Chicago school to a dominant position in the economics profession is a good example. Early steps in that direction revealed political and social interaction logics. Today, the influence is largely explained by the structuration power that tradition has achieved. The Chicago school agenda to a great extent shapes the rules of the game in the economics profession – in training institutions, publication outlets and academic networks.

Conclusions: The global mantra of marketization and its limits

Since the early 1980s, the spread of marketization has meant, in reality, deep transformations with economic, social and political dimensions. Market-oriented macro-economic policies – privatization, deregulation and liberalization – have spread rapidly (Ikenberry 1990; Eising 2002; Henisz et al. 2004). Kogut and Macpherson (2004) document such rapid diffusion in the case of privatization. Pioneer experiments were those of Chile under General Pinochet and Great Britain under Mrs Thatcher. The real explosion, though, happened in the late 1980s and in the 1990s, in spite of mixed evidence by then on the merits of the British program (Vickers and Yarrow 1988). Trade liberalization also progressed during that period while the global spread of monetarism meant the diffusion of the ideology of central bank independence and associated institutional transformations (see Marcussen ch. 9). Marketization has also translated into financial liberalization with a global structuration of the financial field (Van Zandt 1991; Ventresca et al. 2003) and the increasing isomorphism of financial institutions, organizations, practices and discourses across the world (Simmons 2001; Kleiner 2003a). The same happened with the idea of competition. The fight for competitive markets has become a nearly global one, in principles and structures if not always in practice (Djelic and Kleiner ch. 14).

Marketization has also implied a transformed approach to the role of states and to regulation. There are essentially four trends here. First, states increasingly delegate some of their rule-making and rule-monitoring power to independent regulatory agencies (Gilardi 2005). Second, regulatory philosophy is increasingly moving towards structured self-regulation. Regulatory areas are "privatized," turned into "markets" where many different actors interact and negotiate to reach a point of equilibrium expected to be efficient (see Hedmo et al. ch. 15; Engels ch. 16; McNichol ch. 17). In parallel, "control" is replaced by "audit" (Power 1997). The difference is subtle but significant: political fiat is displaced by "independent technical or scientific expertise" (see Drori and Meyer ch. 2) and monitoring authority is in part privatized. Third, states and administrations across the world are going through the "new public management" revolution (Hood 1995; Christensen and Laegreid 2001). This essentially amounts to a "managerialization" of state bureaucracies – with greater transparency, a preoccupation with efficiency and "customer" orientation, the generalization of competition and market mechanisms within and across administrative units. Fourth, the idea that the state could – and should – disengage from certain social and welfare activities has gained ground. Private pension schemes have emerged as a consequence (Weyland 2003) and the health and education sectors are having to deal with competition and market pressures (see Ramirez ch. 11).

The progress of marketization can also be measured through its impact on firms and forms of governance. During the 1990s, "outsourcing" and a focus on "core competencies" became all the rage. Both trends reflect the belief that markets allocate resources and orient strategic development more efficiently than managers or bureaucracies. Everywhere the 1990s have been marked by the expansion of stock markets and by increasing numbers of listed firms. This has in effect put financial markets at the core of many industries – with an influence on strategic and governance choices (Tainio et al. 2003).

This progress of marketization has been associated and in close reinforcing interaction with the increasing presence, power and expansion of cultural liberalism (Meyer and Jepperson 2000). Cultural liberalism places the individual at the centre, with a surprising and worldwide expansion of standardized ideas about individual rights, powers and competences (see e.g. Drori and Meyer ch. 2). This progress of the "individual" goes well beyond the human person. Animals themselves are increasingly treated as "individuals." In our liberal marketized societies, corporations also are "individuals" in that sense and, by extension, state agencies too.

Although the global progress of marketization is undeniable, there are limits to its reach. Limits stem from political and ideological resistance as the strength of the anti-globalization movement illustrates. Limits stem also from local translation, editing and hybridization that mitigate the progress of marketization (Czarniawska and Sévon 1996; Sahlin-Andersson 1996; Djelic 1998). While market logics have advanced in all Western European countries, national welfare schemes, for example, have not been dismantled to the extent one would expect (Deacon 2005). Limits are also visible in processes of "decoupling": the marketization revolution does not always go down from discourse to implementation. One naturally has to add a geographic if not cultural dimension to that mapping of limits. Certain regions, like sub-Saharan Africa, are on the margins of the marketization revolution. Other parts of the world, coinciding more or less with George W. Bush's definition of "rogue states," resist and reject, politically and culturally, the progress of marketization. Finally, building upon the story we have told here, one could speculate about another limit to the progress of marketization. Crisis and dissatisfaction with economic performance could combine with and stimulate the (re)emergence of "sleeping beauties" – sets of ideas and associated policies that could have been dormant for a long while without fully disappearing. History tells us that this type of ideological long wave is not impossible.

Notes

1. Throughout this chapter, "liberal" will be understood in the European sense of the term.
2. This influence is undeniable even though the historiography points to incompatibilities between parts of Smith's work and the most extreme forms of neo-liberal argument (Viner 1960).
3. This part of Callaghan's speech was drafted by Peter Jay, his son-in-law, who was strongly influenced then by the work of Milton Friedman (Keegan 1984: 91).
4. Our categorization is compatible with that of Scott (2003) although slightly different. Scott identifies four broad classes of "carriers" or "vehicles": symbolic systems, relational systems, routines, artifacts (Scott 2003: 882).

4 | *Organizing the world*

GÖRAN AHRNE AND NILS BRUNSSON

Introduction: Explaining global order

In the modern world it is conspicuously easy to communicate and inter-act with people all over the globe. Communication and interaction are facilitated by common systems of distinction and by our ability to pre-dict the behavior of our counterparts. An air ticket can be used all over the globe because there is agreement on the meaning of the series of codes printed on it, and because there are common classification systems used to describe organizations such as airlines and individuals such as pilots; furthermore we expect airlines and pilots to act in a sim-ilar manner wherever we encounter them. Because it is easy to predict the behavior of people and organizations, it is possible to interact with them with little knowledge about their personal traits or histories. To many modern observers, this high degree of order is remarkable, and has played a significant role in fostering the popularity of the concept of globalization.

For most of the twentieth century, scholars have referred to the nation-state as a primary source of order, although within restricted territories, through first a common organization, the state; and sec-ond a common culture, the nation. Modern states constitute one of our clearest examples of complete, strong and complex organizations (Ahrne 1998) and cultures are often assumed to follow state borders (Hofstede 1980). With this background, the absence of a world state and a coherent world culture makes global order all the more intrigu-ing. Still, conceptually there is some continuity: concepts related to organization and culture have been used by scholars interested in glob-alization, although these concepts are often presented in different forms than when explaining national orders.

Focusing on the cultural dimension, some argue that there is more of a common global culture than generally assumed. Ideas are spread all over the globe, usually from a Western centre (Thomas et al. 1987;

Robertson 1992; Boli and Thomas 1999). There are some common conceptions about how natural and social worlds function, and there is a repertoire of identities and norms for behavior that are shared the world over, at least by elites.

Alternately, we could use organization as an explanatory factor. Because there is no world state, we cannot expect global organization to be a copy of the type of organization that we observe in the nation-state. Instead, some scholars have argued, there are more partial and split organizational orders in the form of multinational companies, with activities spanning the globe (Teichova et al. 1986). Others have pointed to looser arrangements of organizational forms. Thus individuals or organizations are described as cooperating in "networks" (Castells 1996; Håkansson and Johanson 1998). Such networks are organized to some extent, although they do not constitute formal organizations.

Other concepts combine cultural and organizational aspects; the concept of international "regimes" has been used to describe the Bretton Woods Agreement and GATT, for example. Regimes include organizational aspects such as written rules and established decision-making procedures for cooperation as well as such cultural aspects as common conceptions and norms (Krasner 1983; Katzenstein et al. 1998).

"Institution" is another common concept. Institutions can be defined as "socially constructed, routine-reproduced, programs or rule-systems . . . accompanied by taken-for-granted accounts" (Jepperson 1991: 149). Common institutions, almost by definition, facilitate communication and interaction; they contain both cultural and organizational elements. Scott (1995) distinguished between three pillars of institutions: cognitive, normative and regulative. The cognitive pillar concerns people's conceptions of "the nature of reality and the frames through which meaning is made," the normative pillar concerns ideas of right or wrong and includes both values and norms, whereas rule setting, monitoring and sanctions are examples of the regulative pillar. The first two pillars refer to what we define as cultural aspects and the third pillar to what we define as aspects of organization.

Because cultural and organizational processes are different mechanisms for creating order, many of their causes and effects remain obscure if we collapse them into a single concept. We believe that it is useful to distinguish more clearly between organization and culture than is implied by the use of concepts such as regime or institution. This distinction seems particularly important when we are interested not only in the "demand side" of order (how organizations and individuals are affected by elements of organization or culture), but also in the "supply side" (how these elements are produced). It will also reveal more clearly the extent and nature of the interrelationship between organizational and cultural processes. Finally, we believe that a confusion of cultural and organizational aspects can lead to underestimating the fundamental importance of organization in creating global order.

In this chapter we compare culture and organization as sources of order and discuss how they contribute to global order. We also analyze two particularly important forms of global organization: standards and meta-organizations.

Culture and organization as different systems of order

Culture concerns values and meanings that are shared within a group or collective of people. Several aspects have been distinguished in writings about culture, one of which concerns the way the world is constructed. Culture can give explanations of both natural and social processes. Moreover culture supplies distinctions. Cultures contain a set of possible identities and generate certain status orders. Culture provides notions of what is good and bad and sets norms. It gives a sense of what is worth striving for. Culture as a realized signifying system is embedded in activities that are not directly considered to be cultural (Williams 1981). A common culture is a powerful facilitator of communication and interaction.

In the traditional sense, cultures emerge from common experiences and memories. Three components of such shared experiences can be distinguished: a sense of continuity among the experiences of succeeding generations, shared memories of events which have been turning points of a collective history, and a sense of common destiny (Smith 1990: 179–80). Culture understood as a whole way of life is a concept with a background in anthropological field studies, and several writers on culture have recently warned against implementing too extensive a use of the concept. Culture is not everywhere, is their argument, and it is necessary to try to understand where culture "begins and ends" (Hannerz 1996: 43; cf. Archer 1988). Williams (1981: 207) emphasized the importance of distinguishing the economic system, the political system, and also a kinship system from the general signifying system of a culture. It is also important to distinguish culture from organization.

Like culture, organizations are systems that facilitate communication and interaction, but they are actively created by people, often for these very purposes. Organizations have certain features that facilitate communication and interaction. They have members and they have an authoritative centre – a management[1] – with a high and special status. Management has the right to issue commands and rules prescribing the actions of organization members. Like a culture, organizations are systems that enhance cooperation and restrain competition: in organizations, authority is monopolized. Authority is restricted by formal constitutions, rules about rule-making and commanding, and by informal limitations in the zone of indifference of its members (Barnard 1968); the centre does not have an unlimited right of control.

Rules constitute a particularly important element of organizations (Weber 1964; March et al. 2000). In formal organizations, only management has the right to issue binding rules (directives), and rules constitute a crucial instrument for control and coordination. Rules facilitate behavioral predictability and they can also be designed in a way that directly supports coordination. Moreover, compliance with rules and commands is enhanced by management's right to information about members' actions and its right to issue sanctions. The ability of organizations to concentrate resources facilitates information gathering and the issuing of sanctions.

Also, organizations are powerful instruments of distinction. They construct identities and classifications. Most basically, they give people identities as members and non-members, and they have an accounting system that classifies certain resources as belonging to the organization. Members are given more detailed identities with the help of categories such as departments and positions and a status in the form of a hierarchical order.

Organizations are attempts at stabilizing interaction and classifications and they are generally described as stable, inert and inflexible. But compared with cultures, they are flexible having the potential for more rapid change. New commands and rules concerning actions and classifications are issued routinely, organizational members are exchanged and new systems of information and sanctions emerge.

Whereas culture can be defined as that which is not decided, an essential aspect of organization is decision-making – the conscious choice of acting in one way rather than another (Luhmann 2000). Organizations are actively created as the result of decisions by specific persons, including sometimes by an individual. Decisions play a crucial role in organizations (March and Simon 1958). Organizations have goals and alternatives whereas cultures do not. Organizational rules are similar to social norms in that they are scripts for behavior, but rules are decided by people and have authors, whereas norms grow out of a social setting and have no authors. Furthermore, whereas identities and status may be culturally determined, they can also be decided by organizations.

Decisions have important effects: they dramatize control and discretion by portraying decision-makers as being causes of subsequent actions and as making choices of their own free will. And since being a cause of one's own free will is the way of becoming responsible (Aristotle 1984, Book III, Ch. 1), decision-makers assume a high degree of responsibility. Organizations constitute the most powerful earthly system for concentrating responsibility. The management of an organization is responsible for what that organization does, in both a legal and moral sense. Management even tends to be responsible for organizational actions over which it has no control. Other members have correspondingly less responsibility: to be a subordinate in an organization implies a substantial reduction of responsibility. It is difficult to attribute responsibility for cultural phenomena to one person or group, but it is easy to find heroes and scapegoats in the organizational world.

Moreover, decisions dramatize uncertainty (Luhmann 2000). Decisions are attempts at creating certainty and determining what the future will look like. They also create uncertainty by demonstrating that the future is chosen and could be otherwise. So, whereas culture can be defined as that which is not contested, organizations and their decisions are wide open for criticism and opposition.

In contrast to culture, decisions and organizations are projects with a significant potential for failure. Although organizations are, for good or bad, able to achieve great things, many of their attempts at control and choice fail to generate what is desired or predicted. This type of failure is an important theme in the empirical literature on organizations, whereas the literature aimed at helping managers in their work has produced endless dreams about and instruments for avoiding such failure. Whereas the study of culture is a study of what has succeeded or the study of results, the study of organization tends to be a study of attempts – the study of both failures and successes.

Culture and organization: Interaction

Although culture and organization are different systems of order, in practice they interact. The very phenomenon of organization and its widespread popularity, can be understood as the result of certain cultural phenomena, such as globally shared conceptions of actorhood. And most organizations benefit from at least a minimum of cultural elements that are common to their members. Members tend to share certain values or ways of understanding the world. In organizations there is no need to make decisions about things that are already culturally regulated unless management wants to break with such notions. So organizations have a cultural foundation. Organizations go beyond culture by creating more distinctions and scripts for behavior than can be offered by common cultural elements. Moreover, organizations often break with culturally shared conceptions such as reciprocity or traditional notions of justice and fairness.

Organizations may breed specific "organizational cultures," i.e., habits, customs and norms common to the members. (Alvesson and Berg 1992; Martin 2002). For some time such organizational cultures may enhance interaction and facilitate production, but sooner or later they will be perceived as obstacles and be challenged, since they will be difficult to decide away. Organization can be seen as a layer of conscious decision-making and thinking about how to do things that lies between a more general culture and locally emerging organizational cultures. Organizational decision-making partly builds on and partly fights both forms of culture.

A situation in which culture and organization completely coincide is a situation in which the organization becomes more or less invisible and everything is perceived as cultural. The idea of the nation-state can be seen as a model for such a perfect overlap. The laws of a state have been regarded as codifications and expressions of existing norms and customs (Dahlkvist and Strandberg 1999). What is outside the nation-state is both another culture and another state.

However, this model has scarcely been realized; the cultural homogeneity in actual states has never been complete (Anderson 1983).

Culture, organization and global order

Both culture and organization are important concepts for understanding global order, but not in their all-encompassing forms: there is no one world culture nor is there one world organization. Instead global order can be understood as the result of scattered cultural and organizational elements and their interplay.

In its original sense, a common culture is a unique and consistent combination of numerous cultural elements concerning conceptions, values, morals, the nature of the world, and a whole way of life. A culture is mediated and more or less unconsciously learned by people who interact over long periods, and it presupposes both continuity and a common territory. Under this definition, a world culture is difficult to imagine (Smith 1990).

However, the concept of culture can also be used in a narrower sense. For instance, one can think of professional cultures that exist and are reproduced within certain groups of professionals like doctors or lawyers. In this sense, cultures may become "conventions of global interaction" as occurs, for instance, among traders in investment banks (Knorr Cetina and Bruegger 2002). Or one can think in terms of particular cultural elements such as "cultural frames" or "cultural institutions" (Drori et al. 2003) that spread over the globe. Such cultural elements include common conceptions and elaborate theories about identities, for instance theories about the individual (Meyer 1986). There are also common conceptions about how the social and natural worlds operate, particularly in modern science (Drori et al. 2003; Drori and Meyer ch. 2), and some common *virtues* or norms spreading around the world (Boli ch. 5). Common identities, conceptions and norms among people in different parts of the world clearly facilitate communication and interaction. Rather than constituting whole life worlds, such cultural elements pertain only to certain limited aspects of social life. On the other hand, they may be combined with other cultural elements and become integrated into wider national or ethnic cultures. In these ways cultural elements may contribute to a global order.

In a similar way, formal organizations such as states or firms contain all organizational elements, such as members and resources, an authoritative centre issuing commands and rules, and systems of information and sanction. But more important for understanding global order is the fact that single organizational elements, like single cultural elements, can exist on their own. A conspicuous feature of the contemporary world is that elements of organization are dispersed over the social landscape without being integrated in formal organizations.

Sometimes we find membership without any other organizational element. For instance, Greenpeace has so-called "support members", who are not subsumed under any organizational hierarchy and who have no rights or duties as to information or sanctions. Many individuals and organizations offer rules for others in the form of standards. Examples of standardizers include organizations such as Amnesty International; the World Wide Fund for Nature (WWF); the International Organization for Standardization (ISO). Others, such as Human Rights Watch or the Financial Times, collect information about how entities such as states or business schools follow various standards and disperse this information in their rankings (cf. Hedmo et al. ch. 15; Jacobsson and Sahlin-Andersson ch. 12). Certification institutes combine information with a specific form of sanction by issuing certificates announcing that others have met their specific standards.

Elements of organization are crucial for establishing global order. For one thing, advanced means for communication and interaction, such as international mail, air travel and telecommunications, are often described as technical aspects of globalization (Scholte 2000), but they all require extensive organizing; without organization, they would have been mere technical possibilities rather than realities.

In the remainder of this chapter we present two forms of organization: standardization and meta-organizations. Standardization in its pure form means the production of rules without the support of any other organizational element. Meta-organizations are, in principle, complete organizations containing all organizational elements, but they have organizations rather than individuals as their members. We believe that those two forms are the most important examples of global organization. And because they represent extremes, they are good illustrations of the organizational concept. They are alternatives and complements to a cultural order: they are the results of decision-making and can provide order even with a lack of common culture. They are also supported, though, by some cultural aspects.

Standardization

Standardization constitutes a particular form of rule-setting. By rules we mean explicit, almost always written, statements that prescribe how certain actors must behave in certain situations. Rules are powerful instruments for creating distinctions and predictability. All classifications require rules. And if we have knowledge that people follow certain rules, their actions become highly predictable. Classification and predictability are closely related; rules are valid for some categories of people in some types of situations (March and Olsen 1989). Thus in order to predict behavior, we must know the type of person involved in what type of situation.

Traditionally, rules have been viewed as closely connected to formal organization (Weber 1964). However, in the modern world, an increasing number of rules exist outside formal organizations (Brunsson 1999; Brunsson and Jacobsson 2000). There are many individuals and organizations that provide rules for others even though those rules are not combined with the hierarchical authority of formal organization. In this sense, those rules are non-binding or voluntary. Rule setters have assigned such rules different names, including recommendations, guidelines, advice, etiquette, best practices, or standards. We subsume all these terms under the concept of "standard." Standards are the most important organizational element that can be found outside organizations. Almost any area of life has standardizers and standards.

There are standards directed at firms and commercial life without which much of the existing international trade and global commercial activities would be impossible. There are, for example, standards for what things should be called; standards for the technical design of commercial products and their parts; standards for the eco-labeling of products that affect their competitiveness (cf. McNichol ch. 17); standards for production processes, such as "quality standards" or "environment standards"; and standards for accounting and for contracting (cf. Botzem and Quack ch. 13).

States are the victims of a growing number of standards and standardizers, including standards for how they should treat their citizens (issued by Amnesty and others), or standards issued by economists and the OECD for how states should run their economies, organize their administrations, protect the environment (cf. Jacobsson ch. 10).

Firms are the targets for standards from management experts for how to manage and organize. The personal lives of people are targets for other standardizers who know how we should write and speak, how we should manage our marriages, plan our careers, bring up our children, develop our personalities.

A large and increasing number of these standards are directed at people and organizations regardless of their nationality. Although not binding for anyone, a great many standards have a strong impact and are followed and respected by many individuals and organizations throughout the globe. The present degree of global order would not have been achieved without standards.

Standards, culture and organization

Unlike cultures but like complete organizations, standards are clearly man-made. Standards have a definite source: it is possible to find the organization which, or individual who has authored a standard. Standards are the result of decisions and thereby easily invoke the idea that they could be different or not exist at all. But whereas organizations often evoke protests and complaints, this is rarely the case for standards because of their non-binding nature. Standardizers have a limited responsibility compared with organizational managers issuing directives because they make only "half a decision": standardizers can only recommend a standard; it is up to others to decide if they will follow it. In this way, the follower must accept most of the responsibility for acting in accordance with a standard and for its results. It makes little sense to complain or protest about standards one does not like; instead the common and commonly expected reaction is just to refrain from adopting such standards.

Managers of organizations are limited in number, restricted in their rule-setting by constitutions and expected to create rules that are consistent and form a coherent system; these are all factors which decelerate rule production. In contrast, the capacity of standardizers is practically endless: the number of potential standardizers is almost infinite and they have the right to set as many standards as they please. Standards can be produced even more quickly, easily and cheaply than organizational rules and their production requires no elaborate organizational procedures such as democratic decision-making (cf. Mörth ch. 6). So standards abound. The advertising of standards tends to involve some cost and to be a slower process, but modern mass media are great helpers here.

Although there is an ample supply of standards, there is little guarantee of demand. In contrast to managers, standardizers do not have immediate access to other organizational elements to support their rules. So generally we would expect more failed standards than failed directives; all forms of organization are prone to failure but standardization even more so. And the way to succeed is somewhat different from the situation within organizations.

Organizational managers can refer to their hierarchical position and point out who has authored the rules in order to convince members to follow them. In contrast, standardizers do not have such obvious authority and must claim authority in other ways (Tamm Hallström 2004; Jacobsson and Sahlin-Andersson ch. 12). Moreover, standardizers are unlikely to convince others of their standards by pointing only to themselves; they have to refer to the quality of the standards as well. Some standardizers, such as WWF or Amnesty, try to convince others that they should follow their standards because the standards lead to good consequences for those other than the standard followers. Other standardizers place greater emphasis on the followers' interests, providing advice intended to increase the probability that the followers can reach their goals. Such standards – the standards of management gurus or eco-labels, for instance – can be sold for a price. Also, one can convince people to follow some standards merely by referring to the fact that a lack of adherence will make interaction and communication impossible; in this case, the exact contents of the standards are of less importance.

The following of norms and directives is preceded by identity. For example, in most cultures women and men tend to follow somewhat different norms. And organizational members follow organizational directives because they are defined as members of a given organization, and because they have a certain position in that organization. In the case of standards, however, identity sometimes follows rule compliance rather than the other way round. One may create a certain identity by choosing to follow certain standards. For example, the only way to present oneself seriously as an environmentalist is to follow the standards of an environmental organization. And for the past decade it has been difficult to convince others that one's company is of a high quality without following some quality standard. The ability of standards to determine identity and status is a further argument used by standardizers to encourage adoption; by following the standard, followers are able to demonstrate that they are certain kinds of people or organizations or that they are superior to others.

Whereas both culture and organization are systems of little competition, standardizers and standards are regularly exposed to competition. The ease with which standards can be produced is one reason for competition. In addition, standard setting itself may evoke further standard setting – one way to avoid adopting or to challenge an existing standard is to produce another standard. Thus the very act of setting a standard may evoke active competition. A fundamental cause of competition is that people are free to choose to follow a given standard. This freedom and the resulting competition constitute obstacles for standardizers who want to influence others or sell their standards for a price. On the other hand, as is the case for markets, freedom of choice and competition, or the possibility of competition, constitute the major legitimizing grounds for standardization.

Standards are important instruments for interaction and communication when there are few other forms of organization and little common culture. But elements of a common culture or organization also help standards become more effective, as long as these elements are consistent with them. For instance, in the modern world, many actors, situations and problems are increasingly believed to be essentially the same or to belong to the same category regardless of the local setting (Strang and Meyer 1993). This commonality of actors, situations and problems leads to the idea and argument that they should naturally be treated in a similar way and be susceptible to the same general rules. For example, people all over the globe are increasingly assumed to be individuals with similar needs, rights, duties and problems (Meyer 1986), making it natural to think that they should follow the same standards. When more and more entities are defined as "organizations", the number of potential followers of the standards offered to organizations increases proportionally (Brunsson and Sahlin-Andersson 2000).

Moreover, modern science produces general knowledge about these broad categories, and what is or claims to be scientific knowledge has great authority in modern society. There is, therefore, an opportunity for a standardizer to create authority by relating to this scientific authority, arguing that its standards are based on the latest scientific findings or on the eternal truths of science (cf. Drori and Meyer ch. 2).

Hence, many standardizers are active not only in setting standards but also in propagating identities and conceptions that support their rules. For instance, Amnesty tries to reinforce ideas about the individual and individual rights. WWF tries to make people share its values concerning nature. Sometimes standardizers are even able to turn their standards into norms, making large groups of people internalize them. Other standardizers try to build their standards on existing conceptions and norms, offering standards that contain more elaborations and specifications of what many people already believe is basically right. For example, quality standards were found to be sold to customers by convincing them of the idea that they managed an "organization" (rather than a school, for instance), and quality standards are essentially an elaboration of common conceptions of what it means to be an organization (Henning 2000).

Likewise, many standardizers try to combine their rules with more elements of organization. They may try to recruit members and enrol presumptive rule-followers in rule-setting processes in order to secure their commitment. For instance, environment organizations may engage industry in standard setting for industrial processes and products (Boström 2003; cf. also Engels ch. 16; McNichol ch. 17). Standardizers such as Amnesty install information systems by which compliance to their standards is monitored. Others try to introduce a form of sanctions by establishing formal certification procedures, as in eco-labeling, which clearly distinguish those who successfully follow the standards from those who refrain from or do not succeed in doing so. Others, like ISO and CEN, try to establish monopolies for their standards. Or standardizers refer to "third parties", i.e. agents who have power or authority over others and can coerce or convince these others to follow a certain standard. Such parties may be public opinion, consumers, large corporations with great power over their sub-contractors, or states with legislative power.

Meta-organizations

Although standards help to achieve order, by themselves they represent just one organizational element. One can also try to achieve order by using as many organizational elements as possible. Such attempts often end up in a meta-organization – an organization with organizations rather than individuals as its members. Some well-known examples of meta-organizations are the UN, the EU, the WTO, IATA (International Air Transport Association) and FIFA (Fédération Internationale de Football Association). Meta-organizations are important tools for achieving global order. They usually carry names such as federations, communities, unions, leagues or associations, but these names should not be confused with analytical concepts for organizational form, such as state, firm or association (Polanyi 1968).

In contrast to state federations or business combines, which also have organizations as members, meta-organizations have the association rather than the state or the firm as their form. Member organizations can leave the meta-organization at will while this is not the case for subsidiaries in combines or federal states.

The members of meta-organizations may be states, firms or associations. Typically, meta-organizations recruit members on the basis of similarity (cf. Marcussen 2004). The members of the EU are European states, IATA has airline companies as its members and FIFA organizes national football associations.

There are theories about federations and business combines, but meta-organizations have received little if any theoretical treatment. Most meta-organizations are relatively unknown, usually less well known than their members. Who has heard of large meta-organizations such as World Federation for Mental Health (WFMH), International Egg Commission (IEC), Confederation of International Soft Drinks Associations (CISDA), or International Cremation Federation (ICF)?

The number of standards that have been issued throughout the world is overwhelming, and it would be extremely difficult to calculate their number. The number of meta-organizations is more limited and according to our estimates in the year 2003, at least 10,200 international meta-organizations existed.[2] About 10 percent of these have states as their only members.

The existence of meta-organizations is not a new phenomenon; nor is it exclusively international. There are many national meta-organizations that have existed since the nineteenth century. For instance, labor unions and trade associations have often been organized into meta-organizations. However, almost 90 percent of the international meta-organizations that existed in 2003 were founded after

1950, and 25 percent of all existing international meta-organizations have been established within the past 12 years.

Fields with the greatest number of international meta-organizations include development, research, education, and industry. UNESCO, with 196 member states, is the organization with the greatest global coverage. Another meta-organization which spans most of the globe is the Universal Postal Union (UPU), with members from 190 countries. The International Organization of Supreme Audit Institutions (INTO-SAI) has members from 185 states. Many sport federations have also global coverage.

One explanation for the large and rapidly increasing number of meta-organizations is the comparative ease of establishing them – at least compared with organizations with individuals as members. Few resources are needed (van Waarden 1992) and the resources can usually be acquired from member organizations – entities that tend to have substantially more resources than individuals. Also, most of the potential members are well-known organizations and are often limited in number, thus easy to identify and recruit. Often finding five to ten members is enough to launch a meta-organization; there are many meta-organizations with some tens of members, some with a membership in the hundreds, and few with more than a thousand members. Among the 72 international meta-organizations founded in 2002, only 8 had more than 100 members, the highest number being 351. And once recruited, members tend to stay: turnover is typically low.

Meta-organizations are attempts at establishing order among members; they are formed in order to facilitate interaction and communication among organizations belonging to a certain, typically narrow, field. Some meta-organizations are formed to restrict competition among members or, in the case of cartels, to abolish most competition. Some meta-organizations combine restriction to and enhancement of competition by defining which organizations are allowed to compete and which are not. Then competition is sometimes obstructed or protected in relation to organizations that are not members, while competition among members is both encouraged and enhanced with common directives and standards. Such is the case in sports, and in the EU's establishment of a common market. Compared with stronger organizing attempts, such as the merging of interacting organizations into one organization with individuals as its members, a meta-organization can more easily be designed to ensure competition among members because members still exist as separate organizations.

Many meta-organizations try to create order not only among their members but also outside their own boundaries. They attempt to influence the distinctions of others, for example in a way that improves the status of their members in society at large. By belonging to a certain meta-organization, a member can demonstrate that it is a certain type of organization, for instance a particularly serious and concerned one. Also, many meta-organizations want to influence decisions in other organizations – the legislation of states, for instance – in a manner which they believe will further the interests of their members (Jutterström 2004). To affect outside order, a meta-organization must sustain and support similarity among its members and be able to speak with one voice.

Standards and meta-organizations

Compared with standards, meta-organizations involve more organizational elements. One example is concentration of responsibility. The existence of an authoritative centre and its right to set binding rules make meta-organizations more responsible than standardizers. Meta-organizations and their rules attract more criticism and protests than do standardizers and standards. Meta-organizations such as WTO or World Economic Forum evoke not only protests, but also more organizational efforts, particularly in the form of counter-organizations. For instance, the World Social Forum was founded as a response to the World Economic Forum meetings.

The potential spread of standards is wider than is the spread of rules in meta-organizations: rules in meta-organizations are exclusive to members, whereas standards are available to everyone. Furthermore, as in all organizations, the number of rules is more restricted than is the case with standards.

On the other hand, rules in meta-organizations have a greater potential for being followed than standards. Thus, the setting of standards is a more uncertain method for those who want others to follow their rules, but the number of potential rule-followers is greater. However, meta-organizations have an ability to increase their scope of influence and spread their rules that is unavailable to standardizers and individual-based organizations: they can create their own members and thereby increase the number of rule-followers. Many meta-organizations are active in establishing member organizations in efforts to increase their coverage. This is common practice among, for

instance, trade unions and trade associations, and among sports federations (Liljeros 1996).

Organizations and meta-organizations

Meta-organizations function somewhat differently from organizations with individuals as members (Ahrne and Brunsson 2005). Like
individual-based organizations, meta-organizations have, in principle,
access to the whole set of organizational elements that we have identified. In practice, however, the strict use of all these elements by a
meta-organization would constitute a threat to the unique identity and
sovereignty of each of its members. Members themselves are organizations that need a certain autonomy and right to make their own
decisions; otherwise their *raison d'être* in the eyes of their own members, customers, or others would be eroded.

The identity and status of a meta-organization are contingent upon
the identity and status of its members. Members are typically better known and seemingly more important than the meta-organization
itself; in fact many meta-organizations present themselves by listing
their members. An EU in which France and the UK were exchanged
for Turkey and Romania would be a significantly different organization. Likewise, the absence of rich, important or high-status organizations can decrease the interest of all other organizations in joining or
remaining within a meta-organization. Hence, the meta-organization
is highly dependent on single members.

Because of the need to maintain a high degree of member sovereignty
and the tendency to be dependent upon single members, central authority in meta-organizations is comparatively weak. It is stronger than for
mere standardizers, but it tends to be weaker than in individual-based
organizations. This feature of meta-organizations particularly applies
to coordination and decision-making. In principle, all members should
be equals, and this principle does not allow much of a hierarchy. Even
a division of labor among members is difficult to achieve, particularly
when the purpose is to maintain and develop similarity rather than
difference among members.

Furthermore, meta-organizations have a limited ability to concentrate their resources, as most available resources are typically
controlled by members. Negative sanctions often require a stronger
central authority than that possessed by meta-organizations, and
the extreme sanction, exclusion, is rarely realistic. Positive sanctions

require less authority but more resources, and given the resource limitations of most meta-organizations, positive sanctions of any importance are difficult to mobilize. Moreover, a meta-organization will not necessarily have the resources or the legitimacy to obtain information about exactly what is happening inside its member organizations. Large members in meta-organizations are able to ignore rules, as for instance in the OECD (Noaksson and Jacobsson 2003) and in the EU. The rules that are easiest to enforce are often the ones required for membership.

We have argued above that organization is prone to failure. Although failure of a standard is more common in the implementation than in the decision phase, meta-organizations often fail even to make decisions. Such failures often have to do with significant differences amongst members of meta-organizations.

Member organizations in a meta-organization share certain similarities but there are also differences in such attributes as number of members and amount of resources; those differences can be quite radical (cf van Waarden 1992). For instance, both Japan and Malta are members of the United Nations; they are similar in some respects, the most important of which is their statehood, but they are enormously different in size and resources. Such great differences easily create diverse interests and conflicts that are not easily solved. Differences among members often lead to a contesting of their equality, especially by larger and richer members which argue that they should have more votes than smaller members.

Uncertainty around appropriate voting rules makes many meta-organizations strongly prefer consensus, even if it reduces the organization's scope of action. If all members do not agree on a decision, there is no decision. This right of a member to veto decisions is sometimes formalized. Consensus decision-making also helps meta-organizations retain members and allows members to preserve their autonomy and identity as organizations (Braithwaite and Drahos 2000: 487).

Strategies and strengths

Although meta-organizations exhibit weaknesses compared with individual-based organizations, they are significant organizational entities, and they often find ways to solve at least some of their problems. For example, a common solution to the problem of making unanimous decisions is to issue voluntary standards rather than binding directives (Ahrne and Brunsson 2004b). These standards have many names: recommendations, policies, conventions, declarations, white books, and green books, among others (Ahrne et al. 2000; Brännström 2004). Although the standards are voluntary, one should not underestimate their possible effects; there is often little immediate compliance with the standards but, over time, a majority of members comply.

Meta-organizations have difficulty creating common conceptions and norms because they create interaction among organizations rather than people: the people who interact are representatives of member organizations. They are members of the members and not of the meta-organization. In order to counteract this condition, meta-organizations often try to involve many people within their member organizations by creating arenas and arranging meetings. One telling example is the so-called "open method of coordination" that has been practiced in the EU (Jacobsson 2004; Mörth ch. 6). Such activities indicate a belief that it is easier to turn standards into norms than to turn them into directives.

The central authority and external positioning of meta-organizations are often strengthened by their ability to establish and maintain a monopoly, an ability that derives from the small number of potential members. If all relevant members have been recruited in one meta-organization, it is difficult, if not impossible, to form a competing organization because this will require convincing members of the original meta-organization to desert it. And because fellowship with other member organizations is a primary motive for joining a meta-organization, it is difficult to start a process of desertion. So there is often only one meta-organization for a certain purpose and for a certain kind of organization.

The significance of many meta-organizations also derives from the fact that they are embedded in a broader cultural and organizational context that sanctions their creation and authoritative role. For instance, the EU has actively promoted the creation of European trade organizations and these in turn have promoted the creation of national trade organizations (Jutterström 2004). Such a context strengthens the meta-organization both externally and internally.

Conclusion

We have attempted to contribute to an understanding of the high degree of global order characteristic of our contemporary world. We have argued that culture and organization are important sources of world order, but that they come in dispersed forms – in the form of cultural and organizational elements. In particular we have emphasized the importance of organizational elements in creating global order.

There is a risk that the importance of organization is underestimated in analyses of global order, for several reasons. First, because organization is often taken to mean only complete formal, individual-based organizations, other forms of organizing outside and between formal organizations are easily overlooked. Second, even important formal organizations such as those that issue standards as well as the majority of meta-organizations are relatively unknown and their identities are weak. Standardizers and their standards may seem unimportant because they rely on voluntary rules; and meta-organizations suffer from "thin" identities because they must not be seen to threaten the autonomy and identity of their member organizations. Third, most organization theorists have explicitly or implicitly concentrated on organizations with individuals rather than organizations for members (for an explicit treatment, see March and Simon 1958), leaving the important form of meta-organization underanalyzed. Fourth, in contrast to culture, all forms of organizing are attempts rather than results. Attempts often fail and results are often contested and criticized. Yet we argue that the impact of organization is much stronger than all these factors would suggest.

The spread of some cultural elements is a precondition for the creation of the forms of organizing that we have discussed. Organizing, however, goes beyond culture. And organizational elements have the potential to be more rapidly changed and spread than cultural elements. Even if there are many organizational failures, the number of organizational attempts is so overwhelming that there is room for many successes as well. And sometimes failure in the short run does not preclude success in the long run; for instance, many standards in meta-organizations, such as the EU, have turned over time into binding directives or even something close to norms; or compliance has increased even though rules have remained as standards (Aldestam 2004; Österdahl 2004).

Through standardization and meta-organizations, much global order has been established, increasing the chances for communication and interaction. But what kind of order is this? Standards typically lack territorial restriction, but they are specialized and functional, and often incoherent. Meta-organizations provide greater coherence, but generally only in a narrow and specialized field. Both meta-organizations and standards are compartments of order among similar actors throughout the world. But they are seldom connected to compartments that exist for other functional specializations. The result is a somewhat disordered picture of numerous and narrow compartments, such as air-transportation, banking or different sports stretching across the globe, each covering some small portion of issues or interests but ignoring others and leaving many issues and questions untouched. Also, most standards and all meta-organizations primarily provide an order among organizations rather than among individuals.

This picture is in stark contrast to an order of nation-states: states are individual based organizations, bound to a territory rather than to a function, and can deal with a wide range of diverse issues within that territory. The traditional order of nation-states presents a checkered order among individuals, whereas the emerging global order, facilitated by standards and meta-organizations, is a kind of striped order among organizations. There seems to be little reason why the stripes would convert to squares: it is hard to think about fields of standardization or meta-organizations as proto-states, i.e., as embryos to a world-state.

Notes

1. The words "management" and "managers" are used throughout this chapter to indicate the top of the hierarchy of any organization, be it a firm, state or association.
2. By "international" we mean that the organization has members from at least three countries and is also financed by members in at least three countries. The figure 10,200 is based upon organizations listed in the *Yearbook of International Organizations 2003/2004*. The Yearbook contains no list of meta-organizations, but for most organizations, it presents information about types of members. We counted that at least 90 percent of international organizations have other organizations as members.

5 The rationalization of virtue and virtuosity in world society*

JOHN BOLI

All human beings are born free and equal in dignity and rights. They are endowed with reason and conscience and should act towards one another in a spirit of brotherhood. (Article 1, Universal Declaration of Human Rights)

We will conduct our business openly, with honesty, integrity and trust. We will respect human rights in all our activities. We will obey the law and operate in accordance with the highest ethical standards; we will expect the same from our partners, contractors and suppliers. (Unocal Corporation Statement of Principles, 2004)

This year's laureate in Chemistry is being rewarded for his pioneering investigation of fundamental chemical reactions, using ultra-short laser flashes, on the time scale on which the reactions actually occur. (Royal Swedish Academy of Sciences, awarding the 1999 Nobel Prize in Chemistry to Ahmed H. Zewail)

Created in 1957, the World Federation of International Music Competitions is dedicated to establishing a global network of internationally recognized organisations that through public competition discover the most promising young talents in the great tradition of classical music. (World Federation of International Music Competitions 2004.)

Introduction

It should hardly be necessary to insist on the breadth and complexity of the latest phase of globalization. Economic, political, cultural, and technical dimensions of globalization have received a great deal of attention (e.g. Robertson 1992; Appadurai 1996; Held et al. 1999; Micklethwait and Wooldridge 2000; Scholte 2000; Stiglitz 2002), but the moral dimension remains relatively unexplored. The moral dimension is rough terrain; hard data is scarce and causal processes are nebulous in what is still seen as an amorphous arena of religious faith, a-rational convictions, and philosophical presuppositions. In this chapter I explore speculatively the formalization of two aspects of the moral order (Wuthnow 1987) that is deeply embedded in world culture: virtue and virtuosity. I offer an unavoidably subjective reading of world culture's moral foundations and rationalized structures, relying on example and anecdote rather than systematic data. My hope is that this initial exploration of the global moral order, limited though it is, can prompt others to bring the moral dimension more directly into global analysis.

Outward manifestations of the global moral order are certainly familiar. Complaints about globalization resound throughout the global public realm, bemoaning the plight of sweatshop workers, political prisoners, marginalized indigenous peoples, tropical rain forests, and much more. Transnational social movements mobilize massively to identify the sins of corporate capitalism, oppressive states, and global governance organizations like the IMF and WTO (Keck and Sikkink 1998; Smith and Johnston 2002). Underlying these complaints and movements are moral principles and values, that is, conceptions of virtue that are presumed to be globally valid. Ambitious projects to establish a universal "global ethic" (Küng 1998) have emerged, especially among ecumenical religious groups, while codes of ethics and systems for monitoring companies in the name of corporate social responsibility are expanding rapidly (see Jacobsson and Sahlin-Andersson ch. 12). Ethics codes and monitoring systems translate the global moral order into rationalized mechanisms that seek to promote virtue in the operations of daily life.

Identifying, advocating, and implementing virtue are enterprises rooted in the normative dimension of the global moral order. Similar rationalization is underway with respect to the cognitive dimension, or virtuosity. Virtue is the embodiment of goodness; virtuosity is the embodiment of excellence. Virtuosity reflects the instrumental dimension of moral assessment in which superiority of performance or capacity is demonstrated. The global rationalization of virtuosity is evident in world records and world championships, professional and academic credentialing, prizes for scientific research and literary production, and much more.

To explore these normative and cognitive aspects of global moral construction – virtue and virtuosity – I begin with an analysis of the global moral order. I discuss the degree of moral capacity associated with different social entities and analyze globally constructed conceptions of virtuous behavior. I then consider the sacred core of the world moral order and the abstract principles and instrumental technologies related to them. Against this background, the next section develops the concepts of virtuosity and virtue and their relationship to the two principal purposes of human endeavor, progress and justice. In the remainder of the chapter I flesh out this abstract analysis with empirical examples of the celebration and certification of virtuosity and virtue in world society. I consider variability in the degree of rationalization and in the types of social units involved. This analysis leads to a set of patterns and topics for research that could be explored with comprehensive empirical data.

Methodological note

While my analysis of the moral order is inevitably subjective, it is grounded in two bodies of raw data. The first is the many formal documents generated by states, IGOs, NGOs, and companies that present principles, values, actions, and institutions defining the good and the excellent (cf. the epigraphs that open this chapter). The second is the general information and discourse of the global public realm. This surely means that I select too many American, European, or Western constructs to the neglect of other increasingly globalized cultural complexes.[1] I should also note that I do not treat here the often heated global debate about the moral order and its presumed universality. Much of what I discuss below is vigorously contested, and opposition to global moral absolutes is well known. To keep this paper within bounds, though, I must leave exploration of these complexities aside.

Exemplars of good and evil and the moral construction of actors

One way to approach the global moral order is by considering exemplars of good and evil, that is, the saints and devils of world society. In the twentieth century, obvious global saints include Mohandas Gandhi, Albert Schweitzer, Mother Teresa, Nelson Mandela, Martin Luther King and the Dalai Lama. Besides these individuals, some groups, particularly non-governmental organizations, might qualify as paragons of virtue: Amnesty International, *Médecins Sans Frontières*, Red Cross/Red Crescent, the World Wildlife Fund. Individual devils include Idi Amin, Nicolae Ceausescu, Adolf Hitler, cult leader Jim

Jones, drug lord Pablo Escobar, perhaps Osama Bin Laden (though glorified in some parts of the world). Groups or quasi-groups possessed by the devil are more numerous than their saintly counterparts: the Ku Klux Klan, Aum Shinrikyo, the Unification Church, skinheads and white supremacists, anarchists, perhaps al-Qaeda (again with qualification). Dreadful exemplars of evil also include certain states or regimes, such as the Nazis, South Africa during apartheid, Burma, Chile under Pinochet, Rwanda and Zimbabwe. In severe cases, such states have become pariahs in world society. On the other hand, examples of virtuous states or regimes are not easily adduced, though one could perhaps make the case for Sweden (1960s to early 1980s) or Allende's Chile.

In pondering such exemplars, it appears that most virtuous actors are individual people. Individuals are constructed as capable of knowing good and evil and choosing between them. Moral demands apply mainly to individuals and moral failure damages individuals most. International law increasingly employs this perspective, making individuals rather than states the subjects of law to an ever greater extent (Bassiouni 2003). The individual focus of world-cultural morality is especially evident in codes of ethics constructed by international organizations (for example, for architecture, accounting, geneticists, physicians, social researchers). Virtually all such codes have individuals as their subjects; even business ethics codes follow suit in that corporate compliance is to be implemented by individuals.

Collectivities, by and large, are seen as amoral actors. Niebuhr (1960) made this the linchpin of his analysis: individuals are capable of virtuous action but collective actors are not. In particular, powerful actors, states and corporations, are deemed amoral. According to prevailing world-cultural doctrine, their concern for self-interest (*raison d'état*, profit) makes them respect rules of propriety only expediently. In international regime theory, for example, states agree to collective regulation only when it lowers transaction costs, reduces the negative impact of competition, and makes the behavior of competitors more predictable (Krasner 1983; Young 1989). The same argument is supposed to account for collective regulation among corporations: they agree to technical standards, pricing structures, or codes of ethics only insofar as such agreements serve their individual interests.

The dominant explanation for the amorality of states and corporations is the pressure of systemic competition. States that try to abide by moral principles will be destroyed by ruthless rivals; corporations cannot afford morality because unprincipled competitors will under-cut them. Rational actors are always prepared to cheat (Collins 1982); propriety can be ensured only if it is imposed by a central authority. At the global level, however, no such authority is operative. States can impose principled behavior on corporations under their jurisdiction but the world polity is peculiarly anarchical.

The key idea that emerges here is that morality depends on the capacity to choose. If the actor has no choice, moral judgments must be suspended. We may blame the state or capitalist system for much evil but we cannot hold individual states or companies responsible.

Another sort of amoral actor is the ethnic group (and, *mutatis mutandis*, the "nation"), which is typically seen as a creature of self-interest. An ethnic group may cooperate with other groups but it does so strategically. If threatened, it may resort to violence. Like states and corporations, ethnic groups lack an integrated self. Hence, because they have no collective soul they cannot behave morally.

Not all collectivities are constructed as amoral, however. One class of organizations stands out for its apparent moral capacity: the voluntary association. Charity and relief organizations, human rights groups, environmental bodies, even sports clubs and hobby groups are seen as doing good or promoting virtue. Above I mentioned several international associations that seem to be especially virtuous. Few such bodies are seen as unremittingly evil, though white supremacist and terrorist groups stand out as important exceptions.

Voluntary associations have three properties worth noting. First, the theory of action they embody holds that they are, in essence, the free and rational expression of individual human members. They are not collectivities in an emergent-property sense; their meaning and value are associated not with a reified whole but with their individual parts. Their "conscience" is thus the individual consciences of their members.

Second, the non-compulsory character of voluntary associations is crucial to their moral capacity. Voluntary associations assemble individuals to achieve desired ends through uncoerced action. Crucial to this mode of operation is their freedom from the constraints of competition. Operating "between states and markets" (Wuthnow 1991), voluntary associations pursue collective goods that are self-enhancing: the more successful they are, the more "everyone" benefits. Cooperation and coalition-building are their hallmarks. Even associations acting as self-promoting interest groups tend toward inclusion and cooperation.

They are not pushed to amorality by the concern for national security or the bottom line.

Third, the most virtuous voluntary associations are those that reject self-interest in favor of altruism. Virtue becomes evident, in the global moral order, through the sacrifice of self-interest in the name of the greater good. Thus, voluntary associations are no ordinary collective actors. They are the collective counterpart to the moral individual. They pursue self-interest much less than ascriptive or coercive organizations because they are committed to serving the other, sometimes at great cost to the self. In doing so, they are imbued with moral authority.

In sum, of the primary actors of world culture, only individuals are fundamentally morally capable. States, corporations, primordial and interest groups are seen as amoral, but a special form of organization, the voluntary association, is also capable of virtue. This neat categorization is too simple, of course. States are not always seen as amoral; they often seek to present themselves as morally responsible actors and some states are at times deemed virtuous because of their "progressive" social policies. Corporations, too, often project self-images of moral commitment, perhaps to fend off complaints about moral transgressions but also because their directors may take the precepts of corporate social responsibility seriously (e.g., Max Havelaar, the Body Shop, Patagonia; see Boli et al. 2004). More often, though, states and corporations dwell in the shadows of immorality or amorality.

Having sketched the construction of goodness and evil in contemporary world culture, I take up next the content of the moral order itself.

The global moral order[2]

Virtue

At the heart of the global moral order is the sacred. The sacred stands outside of society, transcendent, immutable, eternal. The sacred gives meaning and value to human action; it compels reverence, respect and fear. It is the font of morality, the framework for distinguishing the laudable from the forbidden. Affirmation of the sacred is *ipso facto* virtuous; transgression is evil.

Acts of transgression are especially helpful in understanding the moral order. Murder, rape, assault, battery, kidnapping – these are severe transgressions (felonies), for the individual is truly sacred (Goffman 1956, following Durkheim 1961; Dumont 1986). Categories or groups of individuals are also deemed sacred; international law makes a formal crime of genocide, that is, the wholesale destruction of a nation or "people." Transgressions against the environment – pollution, habitat destruction, and the like – indicate the sacrality of nature. Wherever we find claims of transgression, we find a sacred element as the subject of concern.

We can also ponder the transgressions of pariah states to identify the sacred. In Khmer Rouge Cambodia, transgressions included political imprisonment, torture, and murder; in South Africa, explicit inequality; in Burma, repression and self-imposed isolation, cutting off the people from progress and development. Again we find people, often as categories of individuals (Cambodian peasants and intellectuals, South African blacks, etc.), as those being transgressed.

Turn the matter around. What sacred did Mother Teresa uphold? In her selflessness she aided the poor and the marginalized, affirming the dignity and worth of all humans as fundamentally equal. Her example suggests that principles such as equality and universality are inherent in the sacrality of the individual. It also suggests that mechanisms protecting and promoting sacred individuals – e.g., impartial justice, education, religious teaching – are crucial to the doing of virtue.

These and other ways of pondering the sacred moral core lead to several key observations:

(1) The global sacred order resembles the structure of moral capacity: individuals are the primary sacred entities while states and corporations are attributed little sacrality. Voluntary associations are also non-sacred but identity-supplying collectivities (nations, primordial groups, the family) are clearly sacralized. So too is the one grand collectivity that includes all individuals, humanity as a whole.

(2) Many of the principles that underlie virtuous behavior derive from the sacred individual and primordial group. Righteousness is demonstrated by opposing oppression (Amnesty International), fighting inequality (Gandhi, Mandela), preserving life (*Médecins Sans Frontières*), protecting persecuted groups (Martin Luther King, Dalai Lama), and so on.

(3) Contrary to what one might expect, virtue does not inhere in the rationalized technologies of world culture (cf. Meyer et al. 1987; Meyer 1994; Boli and Thomas 1999). In themselves, neither scientific advance, nor technical progress, nor bureaucratic management are blessed enterprises. Rather, these are the realms of virtuosos – Nobel Prize winners, high-tech innovators, and the like – whose shine is far more instrumental than moral.

(4) Again, perhaps surprisingly, global virtue does not especially inhere in the affirmation of traditional sacreds. Pope John Paul II's virtue derived from his championing of the downtrodden, not from his devotion to God. The world moral order is primarily secular. Religion's spiritual precepts must be translated into this-worldly action to garner significant moral accolades.

(5) Nature is attributed a good deal of sacrality, worthy of protection (e.g., animal rights) in itself (cf. Frank et al. 1995). For ecological extremists, nature's sacrality trumps all; humanity is nothing but a parasite.

(6) Refusal to acknowledge the universal validity of the global moral order is itself a serious transgression. Self-interested action and national self-determination are legitimate but they must not subvert the sacred order.

Figure 5.1 offers a tentative sketch of the substance of the global moral order. At the core are sacred entities: individuals, certain types of collectivities, nature, and humanity as a whole. Around the core are principles derived from the sacred entities: dignity, equality, rights, protection, identity, and so on. This is the central sacred mass, transgressions against which offend moral sensibilities and mobilize efforts to restore sacrality. Around them clusters a diverse array of instrumental mechanisms that are presumed to promote the two dominant purposes of human action, rationalized progress ("development", in a broad sense) and justice (equality of opportunity, equality before the law, access to basic resources, and so on; see Nisbet 1980, Meyer et al. 1987, Meyer et al. 1997a).

While instrumental mechanisms of science, exchange, technique, professionalization, education, and the like, have little inherent moral value, they gain luster to the extent that they enhance and empower the sacred core entities. They also tend to become sacralized in their own right through the familiar Weberian process by which instrumental rationality displaces substantive rationality.

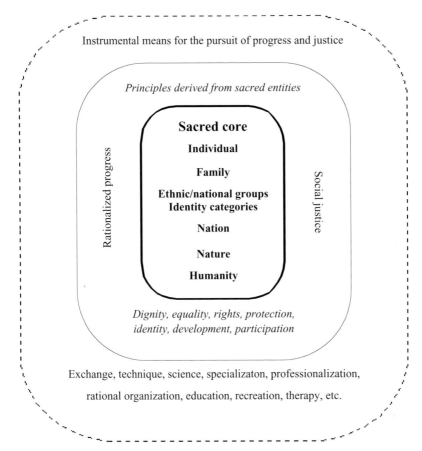

Figure 5.1 The sacred of the global moral order.

Virtuosity

In considering virtuosity I shift gears by beginning with a broad-ranging data source, the two volumes of Gale Research (2000) listing honors, awards, and prizes awarded throughout the world (see the illustrative lists in Table 5.1). Most awards and prizes recognize exceptional performance, especially in technical or rationalized domains. Enormous numbers of awards are given for research (in everything from acoustics to zoology), industrial activity (accounting to wood products), and applied technology (aeronautical engineering to welding). Also common are humanities and literary awards as well as music, visual,

Table 5.1. *Global/international award examples*

Holistic virtuosity	Competitive virtuosity
Advertising	Agrarian cinema and video
Architects	Bidding (bridge)
Astronautics	Bocce
Broadcasting	Calligraphy
Casting (film, theater)	Children's theater or stories
Conceptual furniture	Choirs
Crystal growth	Creative writing
Hydrology	Design
Imitation Hemingway	Engineering
Machinists (chief mechanics)	Harps
Natural history	Horseshoe pitching
Oncology nursing	Information processing
Photography	Islamic heritage
Plastics research	Jewish deaf
Property assessment	Marketing
Protection of monuments	Mensa members
Public relations	Music composition
Secretaries	New instruments and bows
Standards users	Ploughing
Structural engineering	Road safety
Surface finishing	Study of the world refugee problem
Thermographers	Video works
Violin makers	Wildlife photography
Women in film	Wind ensembles
	Young statisticians from developing countries

Holistic Virtue
Badminton (service to federation)
Dag Hammarskjöld award
Defense of religious liberty
Dialogue between cultures
Global paragons
International humanitarian law
PEN/Newman's Own (press freedom)
Prevention of blindness
Service
World citizen humanitarian

Note. Source: Gale Research (2000).

and performing arts prizes. My rough estimate is that over 90 percent of the awards in these volumes recognize virtuosity, that is, specialized excellence or superior performance.

Virtue, in the form of selfless service to others, is evident in awards for community service, volunteering, public service, human rights, and humanitarianism (the lower portion of Table 5.1). Often bestowed by voluntary associations, these awards are relatively rare; the subject index suggests that all virtue-oriented categories combined account for fewer awards than chemistry, engineering, or literature alone. Many virtuosity awards contain language about service to the "greater good" (e.g., contributions to "French culture" or "Greek culture") and many recognize contributions to abstract branches of knowledge or the professions, but explicit mention of moral virtue is absent for the vast majority.

While the Gale Research volumes are hardly comprehensive – they omit practically all awards given by schools, churches, individual companies, local governments, and so on – they indicate widespread certification of virtuosity. This certification reflects the dynamic dimension of the global moral order: virtuosity is the achievement of human progress in all its multifarious forms. In the case of world records and in many contests and competitions (the right-hand column of Table 5.1), human progress is concretely demonstrated through measurement procedures. Athletes jump higher and swim faster; supercomputers perform more gigaflops; engineers produce materials with unprecedented tensile strength.

Virtue, by contrast, is not progressive; it is good. Virtue is embodied by those who commit themselves to the other grand purpose of human action, social justice. Moral progress may be an elusive ideal, but virtuous action is recognized both locally and globally in the good deeds of the virtuous. The contrast seems clear: virtuosity is doing well, while virtue is doing good.

Yet virtuosity and virtue are more closely intertwined than at first appears. Here it is worth recalling Weber's (1958) Protestant ethic thesis: for Protestants generally, and for Calvinists especially, the pursuit of virtuosity (disciplined, productive work) became a sign or signal of virtue.[3] Virtuosity was not virtuous in itself, but virtue was linked to ascetic self-discipline – a strict form of rationalized virtue – that helped generate and legitimate the pursuit of rationalized progress as a central human purpose. Though transformed by secularization and the compartmentalization of religion, this ethic remains relevant to the global moral order: progress signifies virtue to the extent that it helps realize the good. Progress is thus morally justified by its purported usefulness in protecting and empowering individuals, families, primordial groups, and other sacralized entities as they strive for self-actualization. In this light, virtuosity is also positively morally charged. Virtuosity shows that progress has enabled ever more remarkable human achievements that signify the enhancement of sacred entities. Thus, both virtuosity (via progress) and virtue (via justice) carry the global moral order.

Moral displays and demands: Celebration, certification, criticism

Virtuosity and virtue become prominent in the global public realm via ritualized performance displays: world competitions in sports, beauty, writing, and musical performance; award ceremonies sponsored by associations, industries, and governments; proclamations recognizing sterling performance or exemplary service. These expressive celebrations of virtuosity and virtue dramatize commitment to the global moral order "for all the world to see," transforming the virtuous or virtuosos into Durkheimian totems representing the sacred entities of the moral order. Most often, the celebrated entity is the individual; less commonly organizations, usually national associations, international NGOs, or companies. Significantly, collective entities – the family, ethnic and identity groups, even the nation – rarely receive recognition.

Expressive celebrations are one side of the coin; the other is the search for sinners. Champions of the moral order, especially global civil society organizations, insist on conformity to the moral order on the part of powerful global actors (states, transnational corporations, and IGOs). They remind world citizens (Boli 1999) of their obligation to protect and promote the sacred core and they diligently work to identify those who fail to do so. Their criticism often takes the form of shaming and moral exhortation, but they also go further by generating mechanisms for the certification of virtue, paralleling the certification of virtuosity mentioned above (cf. Jacobsson and Sahlin-Andersson ch. 12).

In a world of impersonal, distant relationships and organizations (Simmel in Levine 1985), the certification of virtuosity and virtue helps alleviate the classic problem inherent in contractual relations: a purely contractual society is doomed because no mechanism can be devised to ensure the honoring of contracts (Durkheim in Bellah 1993: 86–113; see also Collins 1982). Trust is imperative, and Durkheim found that trust must be grounded in a precontractual commitment to good faith via the *conscience collective*. Disinterested certification of competence (virtuosity) or goodness (virtue) is supposed to provide the trust that is indispensable to contractual relations (in markets, games, scientific research, etc.) and, therefore, to progress and justice.

Certification processes – the rationalization of virtue and virtuosity – are a double-edged sword: angels are anointed (certification glorifies the qualified or the superior) and sinners are criticized (shame is heaped on moral violators). Both anointing and criticism are undergoing rationalization at a rapid but uneven pace. An example at the low end of rationalization is criticism in the form of a demonstrator carrying a placard proclaiming, "WTO = Worst Trade Organization." The demonstrator points the finger at a purported sinner but the placard is a bit vague about the details. At the other extreme, to be anointed as an environmental angel via the ISO-14001 certification process, a company must undergo a thorough assessment by an independent auditor. The global trend is toward rationalized forms of certification but not in every domain, as I show below.

Types and examples of variable rationalization

Table 5.2 catalogs rationalized virtuosity and virtue in world society in terms of a crude dichotomy of low versus high rationalization. Celebration and certification appear for both virtuosity and virtue; the table adds criticism on the virtue side. Criticism about lack of virtuosity (incompetence) is rare in global discourse. Violations of the moral order are sins that arouse the *conscience collective* but incompetence carries no such moral charge.

Beginning with the left-hand column of Table 5.2, celebrations of low-rationalization virtuosity are legion. They include holistic awards determined by the subjective judgments of committees, panels of experts, and the like, for example engineering awards, film festival winners, research and Nobel prizes. Also common are competitions crowning global champions in such domains as musical performance, games, sports, and essay writing. Global business INGOs offer

Table 5.2. *Rationalized virtuosity and virtue in world society: Types and examples of low and high rationalization*

Low rationalization

	Virtuosity		Virtue	
Celebration	*Certification*	*Celebration*	*Certification*	*Criticism*
Holistic awards, Global 500 companies	Honorific memberships	Holistic awards, UN World Heritage sites	Conduct code monitoring	Speeches, Statements, Demonstrations

High rationalization

	Virtuosity		Virtue	
Celebration	*Certification*	*Celebration*	*Certification*	*Criticism*
None	World records (Guinness records), Credit ratings, Technical standards, ISO 9000, Product tests, FDA approval, Professional licensing, Educational testing, Educational degrees, Drug tests, IEA	None	Sainthood, Audits, ISO 14000, SA 8000, DJ Sustain. Indexes, Internet trust orgs	Expert reports, analyses, Statistical indices

similar holistic awards by naming a "company of the year" and global honor rolls of successful companies (especially *Fortune's* Global 500) are widely known.

The cell for high-rationalization celebrations of virtuosity is empty. For both virtuosity and virtue, rationalization almost always entails certification processes that focus more on documentation and measurement than celebration per se. For example, the Olympic athlete who wins the women's heptathlon is celebrated for her victory by the unrehearsed cheers and flashing cameras of adulatory spectators, a decidedly unrationalized (yet ritualistic) ceremony that nonetheless depends on certification of her virtuosity through exacting measurement methods. Highly rationalized celebrations of virtuosity – elaborate rituals requiring long training, specialized knowledge, and a complex sequence of exact movements – are exceedingly rare. Even the recipients of Nobel prizes need know little more than table etiquette and how to speak into a microphone to execute their roles properly at the celebratory banquet given in their honor.

In the virtuosity certification column, honorific memberships bestowed by prestigious professional societies are the main type of low-level rationalization. Both global and national bodies are relevant since many national academies (of, for example, science, literature, the arts) bestow internationally recognized honors. Especially noteworthy among more highly rationalized forms of virtuosity certification are systems designed to solve Durkheim's problem of precontractual trust, including credit ratings for businesses (Moody, Standard and Poor), technical and quality standards produced by ISO/IEC. Similar trust-building occurs through product testing by public and independent private organizations. Much of this certification is handled by national-level organizations, such as Underwriters Laboratories and the US Food and Drug Administration; a less rationalized but still systematic type being consumer surveys. Yet national testing sometimes has global reach (FDA drug certification, for example), as do some forms of national licensing and educational certification (for example, the Educational Testing Service's GRE and TOEFL tests).

The last two examples of high-rationalization virtuosity certification in Table 5.2 represent uncommon types. Drug testing, which often relies on global standards and procedures, is unusual for its dual function: it both certifies virtue ("clean" athletes are in conformity with the moral order) and qualifies individuals for the certification of competence.

The final example, the comparative testing project by the International Association for the Evaluation of Educational Achievement, involves rationalized virtuosity certification that ranks entire countries. Many such statistical rankings are commonplace (patent productivity, GDP/capita, infant mortality rates) but the IEA effort is unusual in that it is specifically designed to produce such rankings.

The right-hand columns of Table 5.2 catalog types and examples related to virtue. Holistic awards based on subjective judgments (low rationalization) are again common, celebrating those who help the poor, fight corruption, promote international peace, or protect nature. Best known, perhaps, are the Right Livelihood awards (the "alternative Nobel prizes"). Another example is UNESCO's World Heritage list of some 750 cultural or natural treasures that are of value to humanity and therefore are to be protected in perpetuity.

Processes devoted to the certification of virtue appear to be concentrated in the world of business. Most common by far is the formal auditing of company accounting, another highly rationalized (though imperfect) solution to Durkheim's problem (cf. Botzem and Quack ch. 13). But virtue certification is less concerned with trust than with corporate social responsibility. Companies are expected to adopt the "triple bottom line", adding ecological and social considerations to their concern for profits (cf. Jacobsson and Sahlin-Andersson ch. 12). A low-rationalization form is conduct code monitoring by INGOs and independent firms; more highly rationalized forms include ISO 14000 environmental standards and the Social Accountability 8000 (SA 8000) certification process (see also McNichol ch. 17). Other examples of highly rationalized virtue certification include online systems to assess and certify the trustworthiness of would-be sellers and buyers (e.g. feedback systems on ebay), the absence of child pornography on "adult-entertainment" web sites (certified by Adult Sites Against Child Pornography, an industry association), and the Thawte Web Server Certificate (certifying individual identity). An interesting example mixing both virtue and virtuosity is the family of Dow Jones Sustainability Indexes, which track the financial performance of companies committed to environmental and social sustainability.

In the far right-hand column of Table 5.2, criticism, the absence of virtue is at issue. Low-rationalization criticism by self-appointed guardians of the global moral order comes in many forms, from speeches to street demonstrations to press releases. Backing up these

Table 5.3. *Rationalized virtuosity and virtue in world society:*
Entities and assessors/auditors

Principal entities assessed				
Virtuosity		**Virtue**		
Celebration	*Certification*	*Celebration*	*Certification*	*Criticism*
Individuals	Individuals	Individuals	Companies	Companies
(Companies)	Companies	(INGOs)		States
(Countries)	Products	(Companies)		IGOs
	(Countries)	(Countries)		(Countries)
Assessors/auditors				
Virtuosity		**Virtue**		
Celebration	*Certification*	*Celebration*	*Certification*	*Criticism*
INGOs	INGOs	INGOs	INGOs	INGOs
(National orgs)	States	National orgs		
	Companies			
	(National orgs)			

Note. Entities in parentheses account for a small proportion of the respective activity.

actions (i.e. high-rationalization criticism) are scientific studies and reports, statistical analyses, systematic data gathering regarding human rights violations (Human Rights Watch) and government corruption (Transparency International), and so on. Global critics have learned that hard data, comparative rankings, and other forms of expert-generated knowledge carry greater weight than mere invocation of the global moral order, however eloquent and impassioned it may be.

Units and assessors/auditors

Table 5.3 catalogs the entities involved in assessing virtuosity and virtue. The upper half shows entities that are assessed while the lower half identifies entities that do the assessing. Working through the table from the upper left cell, note first that celebrations of virtuosity praise individuals far more than other entities. Teams receive accolades as well but often these too are individualized, with one or two players taking most of the bows. Much less widespread are celebrations of companies and countries. Individuals are also prominent in the certification of virtuosity, as the subjects of professional licensing, educational degrees, and honorary memberships, but perhaps equally prominent are companies and products.

The upper right cells of Table 5.3, cataloging the entities assessed for virtue, largely resemble the corresponding cells for virtuosity. Celebrations of individual virtue far outstrip those for other entities, in line with the global moral order's characterization of individuals as the only authentic moral actors. Most celebrated are those who risk their lives or sacrifice their own comfort to help the poor or the oppressed. INGO virtue is also celebrated, though much less frequently, for selfless commitment to promoting the moral order, especially in the face of great danger (e.g., *Médecins Sans Frontières*, winner of the Nobel Peace Prize in 1999). Rarer still is the celebration of company virtue, which occurs mainly in the form of "ten best" or "100 best" lists with respect to the environment, working conditions, and the like. Countries may be celebrated holistically as global exemplars (e.g., Sweden for its welfare provisions) or for virtuous action in specific dimensions (e.g., the Nordic countries for low infant mortality rates). Thus, country rankings have relevance for both virtuosity and virtue.

Certification of virtue involves mainly companies, in the variety of forms discussed above: accounting audits, ISO 14000 environmental standards, Internet trust systems, and so on. This is hardly a mystery. As the far right-hand column indicates, companies are criticized as the great sinners of world society, along with particular states and a few IGOs (above all the IMF and WTO). Companies are taken to task as polluters, exploiters, or cultural imperialists (Starr 2000; Klein 2002; Notes from Nowhere 2003). The IGOs are lambasted for favoring global capitalism and sinful companies at the expense of workers, local cultures, and the environment. Critics demand that companies, IGOs, and major states use their enormous power and resources responsibly, i.e., in accordance with the moral order. Note, though, that neither INGOs nor individuals feel the sting of criticism to any substantial degree, with the exception of the occasional tyrant.

The lower half of Table 5.3 catalogs the implementers (assessors and auditors) of the global moral order. Most evident, across the board, are INGOs. INGOs in highly rationalized sectors (for example, technology, science, professions and sports) account for a large portion of virtuosity celebrations and certifications. Humanitarian, human rights, political activist, and similar INGOs do, on the other hand, much of the celebrating and certifying of virtue. INGOs dominate most of all in the criticism column. They are the "conscience of the world" (Willetts 1996), the moral crusaders harping constantly on the sins of the powerful (Falk 1999; Bello and Mittal 2001).[4] The ubiquity of INGOs as assessors and auditors bears out the Boli and Thomas (1997) argument that INGOs are especially central in world-cultural development. More than any other type of global actor, they define virtuosity, sponsor celebrations, bemoan global sins, and certify competence and righteousness across a wide range of domains.

National associations (domestic NGOs) are also important assessors and auditors. They sponsor many international awards and prizes, mainly for virtuosity, and they do much professional certification (along with states). Companies have a more modest role, engaging mainly in financial certification through auditing processes, but private firms also conduct ISO 9000 (virtuosity) assessments and ISO 14000 (virtue) certification. IGOs, meanwhile, are conspicuous by their absence. Sometimes they join the chorus of moral criticism through condemnatory resolutions (e.g., by the UN, the OAS, or the EU). Otherwise their contribution is limited primarily to the statistics they gather, which are used by INGO gadflies to identify and decry inequality (UN *Statistical Yearbook*), environmental damage (UNEP reports), violations of worker rights (ILO studies), etc.

Patterns and topics for research

Tables 5.2 and 5.3 point toward a number of patterns that I will develop further in this penultimate section as topics for systematic research. The first pattern undergirds this entire essay as a broad empirical generalization: the post-war period has witnessed rapidly expanding moral mobilization, that is, exponential increases in the recognition and rationalization of virtue and virtuosity. Why this is so is a difficult question that I address in the conclusion.

A related issue is the increasing automaticity of the rationalization of virtue and virtuosity. For example, a specialized scientific INGO founded in 2005 would be likely to institute a global award much sooner than a similar INGO founded in 1980. Similarly, a newly discovered dimension of inequality (say, lower average incomes for left-handed people) would more rapidly lead to criticism of corporations (for anti-sinistral discrimination) in 2005 than in 1975. Moral sensibilities are increasing; activation of the global moral order is more routine.

A third topic is the relative frequency with which different social entities are celebrated. If the individual is indeed the primary sacred entity and the key source of social value, systematic data should show that celebrations focus mainly on individuals (note the prevalence of the individual in the cells of Table 5.3). Celebrations of secondary sacred entities such as the nation (countries) and various types of groups should be less frequent but nonetheless more common than celebrations of companies and states since the latter entities are conceived as instrumental organizations of no moral capacity. Voluntary associations will also be celebrated rather rarely because they are seen not as entities in their own right but as collections of individuals, who should properly be the focus of celebrations.

The assumption that celebration serves primarily to reaffirm the moral order has an important implication for the rationalization of virtue and virtuosity. Celebrants may not celebrate just as they please; they must respect the boundaries and mystery of sacred entities. Because rationalization is necessarily intrusive (disenchanting), involving analysis, control, and measurement, celebrants should be hesitant to rationalize celebratory rituals. This is why the cells in Table 5.2 for highly rationalized celebrations of virtue and virtuosity are empty: high rationalization is legitimate for certification but not for celebration.

For certification the opposite conclusion applies. Trust and confidence are deemed essential for the successful pursuit of progress and justice, yet trust and confidence are jeopardized by the conception of individuals, organizations, and states as self-interested actors. The rising individualism of world culture (Boli 2005) only exacerbates this problem. Hence the impetus to develop effective mechanisms that can overcome the inherent untrustworthiness of rational actors, be it companies (which lack inherent moral capacity) or individuals who are prey to the temptations of deceit and swindle. Systematic data therefore should reveal that the certification of virtue and virtuosity normally involves a high level of rationalization.

Another topic for research depends on the distinction between two major forms of global authority: the legal-rational form wielded by states and IGOs, which is backed by states' coercive capacity, and the rational-voluntaristic form epitomized by INGOs (Boli 1999), which relies on the sovereignty and capacity for reasoned discourse of empowered individuals acting through non-coercive self-governing structures (cf. Jacobsson and Sahlin-Andersson ch. 12; Mörth ch. 6). Rational-voluntaristic authority assumes trustworthiness, sincerity, and commitment to collective welfare on the part of individuals. By contrast, legal-rational authority uses the implicit threat of force to constrain the self-interested behavior of individuals (and other entities). It therefore seems plausible that greater rationalization occurs in domains directly controlled or regulated by states or IGOs, while domains subject primarily to INGO governance display less rationalization.

My final topic applies to the criticism and condemnation that arise when violations of the moral order occur. One might expect moral criticism to vary with the severity of the violation: those who kill, injure, or enslave individuals or groups will be most strongly criticized or condemned. While severity is undoubtedly important, it may be overridden by another factor, the (perceived) power of the purported violators. For example, the primary targets of the anti-globalization movement are transnational corporations and major IGOs (Boli et al. 2004). Their sins are economic exploitation, cultural imperialism, environmental damage, and the like. But these moral violations are less horrifying than such gross transgressions as mass rape, murder, or the wholesale destruction of villages – sins routinely committed by both rebel and government forces in civil wars. The puzzle here is that these armed factions receive far less global criticism than the IMF, Shell Oil, the WTO, or Freeport McMoRan. The solution may lie in the fact that armed factions in peripheral countries are seen as less threatening to the global moral order because they have neither global ambitions nor global capacity. Criticism intensity thus may vary more directly with the power and reach of the violators than with the severity of the violations.

Conclusion

To close this speculative endeavor I return to the issue of the rapid and global rationalization of virtue and virtuosity in recent decades. How are we to account for this trend? One facile answer verges on tautology: in an era of rapid globalization, activation of the global moral order increases in tandem with other dimensions of globalization. If "everything is going global," the moral dimension goes global as well.

This argument is not quite as simplistic as it appears. In the previous phase of rapid globalization, from the 1860s to the First World War, global mobilization around virtue and virtuosity also increased rapidly. This period ushered in the Nobel prizes, the modern Olympic Games, rules of war, anti-slavery and temperance movements, women's rights movements, and so on.

As explanation this generalization can be strengthened with ideas derived from Wuthnow's (1989) analysis of major cultural/ideological movements of the modern era (Protestantism, the Enlightenment, socialism). Like resource mobilization theorists (Tarrow 1994; McAdam et al. 2001), Wuthnow stresses the importance of expansive economic and social conditions for the growth of cultural movements. In periods of strong globalization, I suggest, movements that anchor themselves in the moral order are especially likely to flourish. By aligning themselves with the sacred and championing principles of excellence (progress) and goodness (justice), such movements gain a wider hearing, attract more enthusiasts, and generate more resources than movements that are inconsistent with or ignore the moral order.

A similar argument emerges with respect to Weber's signature issue: the sweeping rationalization of social life in general over the past several centuries. If knowledge (science), production, markets, leisure activities, occupations, organizations, polities, and so much more are undergoing thoroughgoing rationalization, should we not expect the moral dimension to follow suit? This question may put the cart before the horse. Until at least the eighteenth century, in the West the most highly rationalized organization was the Roman Catholic Church and the most highly rationalized form of knowledge was Christian theology. Weber saw these leading forms of rationalization as crucial foundations for the broader rationalization of the West (cf. Collins 1980). There is thus much to be said for the view that the systematic moralizing of the Church paved the way for the more secular version that originated primarily in the West but globalized in the nineteenth century.

Another factor, more relevant to virtue than virtuosity, is the decentralized nature of contemporary world society. Legal-rational authority is fragmented at the global level; coercive mechanisms to rein in self-interested actors are weak. Aware of this global governance void, individuals and organizations feel compelled to take action against moral violators on the basis of their commitment to the global moral order. If

an effective world state should emerge, such moral mobilization probably would decrease.

My final issue has not appeared above but is surely on the minds of
many readers: Does the rationalization of virtue and virtuosity actually make moral violations less likely, or enhance perceptions of trust
among contracting parties? Obviously, short-term effects are often
weak. Yet there is good reason to believe that moral mobilization and
instrumental certification matter a great deal in the long run. For example, over the past two centuries moral mobilization has helped end
slavery, improve the status of women, reduce harmful automobile emissions, and legitimate same-sex relations. Certification has made medical
care safer, reduced earthquake damage, increased product reliability,
and facilitated labor mobility. Such trends are uneven but nonetheless
striking. Even more striking are the effects on world-cultural models of
actors: states, companies, and individuals are under ever greater pressure to be responsible, effective, globally aware citizens of the world.
Actors frequently fail to satisfy the demands of the moral order but
they are increasingly likely to be called to account for doing so.

The effectiveness of moral mobilization is indicated not by the
absence of violations but by the finger-pointing that violations provoke.
The effectiveness of certification is indicated not by its routine role in
occupational sorting but by the hue and cry that arises when credential fraud is revealed. Perhaps more than anything else, the hypocrisy
that is so evident among the powerful – their expressed commitment to
egalitarian progress that is belied by exploitative or destructive behavior – is a sure sign that the rationalization of virtue and virtuosity is
a major force in world-cultural development. Hypocrisy indicates the
vigorous presence of the moral order and its guardians. Its absence is
possible only when the moral order has been entirely shunted aside
(Ellul 1978).

Notes

* I thank participants in the Uppsala workshop, and the editors, for their
comments and suggestions. Thanks also to colleagues and students at
Emory and to participants in a conference at the University of Arizona
where I first presented some of the ideas developed here.
1. The biases may be less troublesome than they appear in that non-Western
cultural arenas are increasingly enmeshed in world culture and quibble
little about most aspects of the moral order discussed below. For example,

Islamic discussions of human rights challenge a narrow range of articles in the Universal Declaration of Human Rights (mostly having to do with women and the family) but accept most of its content and underlying foundation (Little et al. 1988; Mahdudi 1980).

2. In this section I build primarily on Durkheim's (1961) sociology of religion and Ellul's (1973, 1977) analysis of secular sacralization, along with the work of Berger (1967), Douglas (1966), Dumont (1986), Geertz (1980), and Goffman (1956).

3. This insightful idea was suggested to me by the editors.

4. Of course, companies and IGOs, stinging from the barbs of INGO moralism, disagree, considering INGOs irresponsible, unaccountable, and unrealistic; see Bond (2000).

6 Soft regulation and global democracy

ULRIKA MÖRTH

Introduction

This chapter focuses on global processes of re-regulation and democratization. First, the argument in the chapter is that soft regulation is becoming increasingly important in regional and global governance and that the use of soft regulation opens up for a broad spectrum of actors in regional and global regulation processes. Indeed, state actors must share legislative power and authority with international organizations on the one hand, and with multinational companies and representatives of civil society, on the other (Boli and Thomas 1999; Hall and Biersteker 2002; Knill and Lehmkuhl 2002). Democratic discussions co-evolve with this global re-regulation. Democracy is pursued and professed, but also challenged by expanding schemes of soft regulations.

My interest in these intertwined regulative and democratic developments is normative. In what ways does soft regulation challenge our traditional understanding of representative and liberal democracy, based on a clear division between the public and private sphere? Can private actors be held accountable for the decisions they take? Perhaps we should instead see private actors' participation in the decision-making process as part of a more deliberative understanding of democracy? It might be argued that a re-defined democracy is developing with globalization and re-regulation. The importance of soft regulation in regional and global governance raises fundamental questions about which democratic principles and standards we should emphasize – accountability or deliberation. It also brings to the fore the consequential issue of whether democracy beyond the nation-state is possible. Can international organizations, like the EU, be democratic, or is democracy only possible within nation-states? The empirical basis for this chapter stems from the most advanced "experiment" of democracy beyond the nation-state, namely the European Union.

The idea of soft regulation that is proposed here is quite close and parallel to the concept of soft law. A generally accepted definition of soft law is that it consists of "rules of conduct which, in principle, have no legally binding force but which nevertheless may have practical effects" (Snyder 1993: 198). The difference between soft and hard law is that hard law entails the possibility of legal sanctions whereas this is non-existent in the case of soft law. Thus, soft law lies somewhere between general policy statements and legislation (Cini 2001; Mörth 2004). Soft regulation is like soft law – a form of authoritative rule-making and a legitimized act of power. One could of course argue that there is a fundamental difference between soft law and soft regulation in the sense that law is associated with the legal system whereas regulation has more to do with social interactions. I argue, however, that soft regulation is a function of authoritative rule-making and that it therefore challenges the traditional dichotomy between law and non-law. In addition, soft regulation also challenges the distinction between private and public actors. Paradoxically, we seldom talk about law and authority when we observe how private actors exercise power. Instead, less politically sensitive concepts are used, that are not linked to legal and political systems (cf. Knill and Lehmkuhl 2002).

Using the term "law" to talk about soft regulation allows us to point to the fact that soft regulation is closely associated with changes in authority patterns and democracy. In turn, this makes it necessary to raise the issue of democratic legitimacy: how can regulations that are increasingly shaped by actors other than the state be democratically legitimate? Thus, for the purposes in this chapter – to analyze soft regulation with a focus on democratic implications – soft regulation and soft law are used as coterminous terms.

Two systems of authority

Authority, defined as legitimate power, can be based on government or governance. These two authority systems are ideal types and are often in practice interlinked and dependent on each other (see Table 6.1). It is, however, important to make a distinction analytically between them. This is so because the two authority systems are based on very different ideas of regulation; both with respect to who the legitimate regulators are and what kinds of regulatory patterns should be used. Furthermore, the two systems – government and governance – reflect

Table 6.1. *Two systems of authority*

	Government	Governance
Modes of regulation	Hard law	Soft law
Regulators	Public actors	Public and private actors
Democratic model	Representative and state-centric	Deliberative and societally-based
Democratic reform	Hierarchy and parliamentarization	Open structures and network-building

two different democratic models associated with distinct values and principles. This means that the two authority systems give different perspectives on global and regional regulation and on the question of democracy beyond the nation-state. In order to analyze the democratic implications of soft regulation in regional and global politics, it is essential to discuss how soft regulation can be accommodated into these two democratic models.

Government and democracy

The authority system of government is based on rules that are coercive – hard law – and elaborated by elected politicians, especially parliaments. These parliamentary bodies can be national, regional (the European parliament) or potentially global. Thus, traditional authority is characterized by the domination of hierarchy and monopoly for rule-setters, the latter being in most cases state actors. The democratic legitimacy for this system of authority is that associated with representative and liberal democracy – a democratic model that emphasizes the importance of a hierarchical chain of power and accountability. The democratic procedure is aggregative, which means that individual votes are aggregated in national elections (majoritarian democracy). People's opinions are expressed in general parliamentary elections and democratic reforms tend to be focused on hierarchy and parliamentarization (Olsen 2003). Within this particular democratic frame, the distinction between the public and private spheres is quite significant and essential. The public, often coterminous with the state, is the authoritative rule-maker and legislator. The private sector, profit and not-for-profit organizations, can take part in the public rule-making processes according to two interest meditating systems – pluralism or corporatism (Schmitter and Lehmbruch 1979). The former system is often characterized in terms of voluntarism and competitive non-hierarchical order whereas the latter is characterized by a compulsory, non-competitive and hierarchical order.

A legitimate question is how far this model of democracy can possibly apply beyond the nation-state? If we consider this model and tradition, democracy beyond the nation-state is dependent on the possibility of creating a representative democratic model or government on the regional or global level. There are basically two lines of argument within the government school of democracy on whether democracy is possible beyond the nation-state. Robert Dahl represents those who argue that international organizations cannot be democratic (Dahl 1999). In his understanding of democracy, democracy above all has to do with popular control over the personnel and decisions of the state. This important democratic standard is, according to Dahl, impossible to create at the international and global level (Dahl 1999). In this line of thinking, which clearly has its origin in the democratic theory debates of the nineteenth and twentieth centuries, the connection between the demos, citizenship, electoral mechanisms, the nature of consent, and the boundaries of the nation-state is taken for granted (Held 1995). Another matter is if international organizations are effective and good at solving problems (Dahl 1999). The perceived choice and dilemma between effective problem-solving and a democratic process is a classic theme in democratic theory. The dilemma between output legitimacy and input legitimacy is often discussed in terms of a zero-sum game: one has to choose between having acceptance through system effectiveness or acceptance through democratic procedures (Zürn 2000).

According to the second line of argument, here represented by David Held, there is no longer any congruence between the majority culture and the overall political culture within the nation-state. According to Held's theory on cosmopolitan democracy, democracy is extended to the international and global level. In short, Held's proposals include a global legal system, a global parliament "to which all global bodies would be accountable . . ." (Dryzek 1999: 31–2). Held's vision of a cosmopolitan democracy is clearly an extension of liberal and representative democracy. He envisions a democratic model at the global level similar to the democratic institutions that structure the nation-state. In contrast to Dahl, he believes that democracy can be global but that this requires a global parliamentary system.

Thus, both Dahl and Held have a clear government perspective on democracy. They differ, however, in their view on whether liberal and representative democracy is possible beyond the nation-state or not. Whereas Dahl says that this is not possible, Held argues that it is possible to create global parliaments, global political parties and other important institutions that would allow representative democracy to function at a more than national level, whether regional or global.

A conclusion at this stage is that soft regulation in regional and global politics is indeed a problem if we also want these regulations to be decided upon in a democratic way, with "democratic" referring here to a model of "representative democracy." The reasons for the difficulty are that the traditional liberal and representative democratic model emphasizes the importance of a clear chain of command and control which is difficult to achieve in global politics and in processes of regulations in which private actors participate.

Governance and democracy

The authority system of governance is based on rules that are legally non-binding. Governance rests upon multiple authorities that are not necessarily public. Rules are decided by both public and private actors. This means that the traditional distinction between private and public spheres, so fundamental in the liberal thinking of representative democracy, can be questioned. Furthermore, the public sphere is not necessarily state-based but can consist of private actors; non-profit organizations and profit organizations. The global public domain cannot be analyzed in terms of states and interstate relations but as a domain in which states are embedded in a broader "institutionalized arena concerned with the production of global public goods" (Ruggie 2004: 500). Thus, various private actors take part in authoritative regulatory processes (Cutler et al. 1999; Hall and Biersteker 2002). The regulatory processes in systems of governance result in soft law or soft regulation. The latter can be of several types but their main and common feature is that they cannot be associated with legal sanctions. In practice, however, the border between hard law and soft regulation can sometimes be difficult to uphold (see the following section on the European Union, in particular the open method of coordination (OMC)).

The democratic model behind the authority system of governance is deliberative and societally based. People's opinions are formed in ongoing public dialogues and discussions. Indeed, one important rationale for questioning liberal and representative democracy is that political issues change. "We are less concerned with growing enough food or producing enough houses, than with the effect of modern agribusiness and the consequence of urbanization" (Barnett 1996: 171). Drawing from Beck's argument of the risk society, Barnett claims that the party politics of representative democracy were constructed to deal with non-reflexive issues and not with the new modernity of a reflexive risk society. "Humans have left the cycle of fate and entered a world whose parameters are now man-made" (Barnett 1996: 172; Dryzek 1999). The idea that individuals and societies are increasingly able to reflect upon and chart their own course into the future, rather than adapt to fate or the flow of events, is encapsulated in recent work by theorists such as Ulrich Beck, Anthony Giddens and Scott Lash on the concept of reflexive modernization. In a society in which complex issues must be balanced against each other – economic concerns (for instance growth, wealth), social concerns (for instance inclusion or exclusion), ecological sustainability and political democratic concerns (for instance accountability, participation) – "it is less obvious who are the experts and how to adjudicate the necessary trade-offs involved" (Olsen 2003: 6). Thus, the fact that issues change and require more participation from ordinary people challenges the traditional democratic system of hierarchy and parliamentarization.

Furthermore, democratic reforms in systems of governance are focused on open structures and network building (Olsen 2003; cf. also Ahrne and Brunsson ch. 4; Drori and Meyer ch. 2). This means that regional and global regulation is not necessarily viewed as weak because of its lack of legal sanctions. Instead social sanctions and processes of socialization are viewed as powerful compliance mechanisms. This type of power instrument is evident in OECD and other international organizations that pursue ideational power rather than power based on the possibility of enacting legal sanctions in cases of noncompliance (cf. Djelic and Kleiner ch. 14; Marcussen ch. 9). During recent years the European Union has also begun to use soft regulation rather than its traditional hard law legislation (see below; see also Jacobsson ch. 10; Jacobsson and Sahlin-Andersson ch. 12).

There are basically two variants of deliberative democratic theory pointing to possibilities of creating democracy beyond the nation-state: one radical interpretation and one more traditional interpretation. The radical interpretation of deliberative democracy entails a fundamental critique of the democratic model based upon hierarchy and parliamentarization, whereas the traditional interpretation focuses on how deliberation can be achieved within the liberal and representative democratic system. The core ideas of deliberation in both variants are that democracy should be more direct, reflexive and dialogic (Barnett 1996). According to Frank Cunningham, deliberative democracy presumes an open discussion among equal citizens. (Cunningham 2002) Deliberative democracy also implies that legitimate decisions and rationality can only be achieved through deliberation and that this deliberation takes place according to certain procedural rules (Premfors and Roth 2004).

John Dryzek proposes a rather traditional interpretation of deliberative democracy. Dryzek argues that Held's state-centric and liberal democratic model at the global level will only reproduce the limits that exist at the national level. Instead Dryzek argues that democracy at the global level must revolve around discourses because of the lack of institutional hardware (formal rules). In other texts Dryzek discusses deliberative and discourse-oriented democracy as a complement to the traditional liberal and representative democracy and its institutions (Dryzek 2000). Thus, in Dryzek's texts the state is regarded both to be part of the problem for establishing societal democracy and a part of the democratic solution! Dryzek makes the distinction between liberal constitutionalist deliberative democracy and discursive democracy that seems to capture the important distinction between a light version of deliberation, that is within the liberal representative system, and a more profound break with that system (Dryzek 2000).

A radical and more consistent theory of deliberative democracy beyond the nation-state is presented by Paul Hirst. Although Hirst does not use the term deliberation I would nevertheless categorize his thinking on democracy in that tradition of democratic thinking because of his critique of the state-centric and hierarchical democratic system. Indeed, Hirst's critique of liberal and representative democracy is harsh. The institutions that democracy has become identified with – "national parliaments, political parties, and the majority choices of the citizens of a homogenous political community – seem less than effective means of organizing the new politics" (Hirst 1997: 30). According to Hirst, liberal democratic politics are stagnant. His democratic vision is to re-organize democracy from the state to voluntary and democratically self-governing associations (Hirst 1994).

In contrast to the corporatist tradition, Hirst argues that associative democracy does not encompass the traditional conception of the "modern state as a compulsory organization that claims a monopoly over the right to determine the forms of governance within a definite territory" (Hirst 1997: 115). Hirst is also critical of the traditional distinction between the public and private spheres, so fundamental in the formal, liberal and representative understanding of democracy. "The public sphere is based on representative government and the rule of law . . . The private sphere is that of individual action, contract, and market exchange, protected by and yet independent of the state" (Hirst 1997: 116). Hirst argues that "in fact both state and civil society are made up of large complex organizations, and the boundary between the two is not at all clear" (Hirst 1997: 117).

Thus, both Dryzek and Hirst emphasize the importance of societally-based deliberation. They differ, however, in their view on whether this deliberation must take place within a liberal representative democratic system or whether a deliberative democratic system must break with our traditional system of representative democracy.

Hirst's idea of a democracy based on society, rather than the state, fits well into the discussion in recent years on the emergence of a global civil society. Indeed, the global civil society does not fit into the traditional authority system of government and its emphasis on the state-centred democratic model within the nation-state. The global civil society refers to "a vast sprawling non-governmental constellation of many institutionalized structures, associations and networks within which individual and group actors are interrelated and functionally interdependent" (Keane 2003: 11). These groups do not accept that decisions taken within the World Trade Organization and other inter-governmental organizations are made democratically legitimate within the democratic systems at the national level. Instead, a more direct democratic process of legitimization is required at the global level. The crucial and contested question is, as the discussion of the different democratic schools shows, whether this global democratic system is possible or even desirable. What is clear is that those who argue for a more radical break with the state-centered democratic model have a more difficult position than those who defend the current system, or who only want to reform the current system.

To sum up, the relationship between soft regulation and global and regional politics is less of a problem under a governance authority system than in the framework of a model of government as described above. In the model of governance the focus is more on deliberation than on a clear chain of command and control. The democratic problem within this model is that soft regulations are rarely a function of a truly deliberative and societally-based process and instead are often decided upon by a technocratic elite or else are reflecting strong power imbalances.

We will now move on to the empirical analysis and see what the European Union owes to both authority systems – that of government and that of governance. We also consider what that might mean for soft regulation and democracy.

The European Union

The European Union (EU) is to a large extent based on the authority system of government. The democratic legitimacy of European decision-making is based on national representative democracy (national parliaments) and on the emerging European representative democratic system (the European parliament). In the academic and political jargon the power base of the EU is often described in terms of intergovernmentalism and supranationalism. The former term means that the EU is about states and interstate relations whereas supranationalism means that various supranational actors (often public) are important to understand the dynamics behind the European integration processes.

The so-called democratic deficit in the EU is often interpreted as the lack of democratic accountability. There is, however, no consensus on how to reduce this deficit. For those who argue that the EU's power base should be more one of intergovernmentalism, the democratic problem is often viewed as a problem within the nation-states. The adherents to a more supranational EU see a greater degree of representative democracy at a European level as the solution to the democratic problem of the EU. Both of those solutions are in any case very much focused on democratic reforms in terms of hierarchy and parliamentarization. The EU's democratic problem is met by reforms that strengthen the hierarchical chain of command and control and either give more powers to national parliaments or to the European parliament. The reforms are focused on the EU's formal legislative process – the community method – where the European Commission presents legislative acts. The Council of Ministers (the governments of member states) and the European Parliament then pass and endorse these acts, in their role as the EU's legislative powers.

During recent years, new ways of characterizing the EU have emerged that do not consider it as based either on intergovernmentalism or supranationalism. The EU can instead be described as a system of multi-level governance in which actors (private and public) and levels (national and regional) are strongly interdependent. The regulatory mode within this system is not necessarily formal legislation but rather soft regulation. One case in point is the open method of coordination (OMC). In the European Council's meeting in Lisbon in 2000 it was decided that the OMC should be used to make Europe the most competitive and dynamic knowledge-based economy in the world. This economic goal is intended to be accomplished by co-ordination between the member governments' economic and employment policies rather than by traditional hard legislation. The power mechanism in the OMC and in other forms of soft regulation is not the threat of legal sanctions but instead peer pressure, peer review, benchmarking and the system of name and shame (see Boli ch. 5; Jacobsson and Sahlin-Andersson ch. 12).

The OMC has a democratic potential based on deliberation and participation by societal actors. Indeed, the OMC seems to mobilize the participation of a wide range of various actors such as social partners in the labor market and other civil society actors (Jacobsson 2004). This was explicitly mentioned by the European Council (de la Porte and Nanz 2004); the reform to introduce the OMC formally was legitimized as a move towards deliberative democracy and not as a reform designed to work towards a more satisfying representative democracy. Another matter is of course whether this reform will be successful or not from a democratic point of view.

The OMC and other forms of soft regulation are also linked to the formal legalization process within the EU – what is otherwise called the community method. Indeed, in practice the two systems of authority – government and governance – are often difficult to separate from each other. The OMC and other forms of soft regulation can therefore be interpreted both as part of the traditional chain of command and control and as outside the government model. Indeed, some critics of soft regulation argue that it has a weak democratic base in the traditional democratic model whereas others argue that soft regulations are covered by the decision-making processes of representative democracy (Frykman and Mörth 2004).

The OMC is not an isolated phenomenon in the European Union. In addition to its use in economic policy and employment policy, the method is used for regulating environmental policies and sustainable development. In time, health issues, educational policy, immigration policy and even tax issues will to a large extent be regulated by soft regulation rather than by hard law (see also Jacobsson ch. 10). In the summer of 2004, the EU government announced that the goals within the stability and growth pact would be achieved through coordination and political peer pressure rather than by coercive legal rules.

One interesting feature in these processes of soft regulations is that they are seldom presented and legitimized as law. This is not only evident in the EU but also in other international organizations. I would argue that many soft regulations are law in disguise (Mörth 2004). The UN Global Compact initiative and agreement is one case in point. The agreement was not presented as soft law or regulation, by the actors involved (Sahlin-Andersson 2004). The idea behind the initiative was instead to distance it from law and from legal regulatory frameworks. As in other cases of soft law there are no legal sanctions attached to the Global Compact. Instead of outlining clear sanctions for those not complying with the principles, the initiatives are based on the assumption that there are independent observers who watch and scrutinize the actions taken and who can point to those who are to blame (see Boli ch. 5; Jacobsson and Sahlin-Andersson ch. 12). A lack of reference to soft law is also clear in other international organizations, for instance, within the OECD (Marcussen 2004).

Many organizations avoid the term law. The very word "law" seems to be avoided because it has the unwanted connotation of coercion, hierarchy and supranational decision-making – the authority system of government. It can, however, be argued that there is a tension in and a gap between the way the rules are legitimized and presented on the one hand and the meaning of the rules on the other hand. International organizations must present themselves as flexible and modern and thus avoid any reference to coercion and command and control if they want to make agreements with private actors. Modern organizations are less prone to use hierarchical authority, and so become advisory rather than directing. Even organizations like the European Union with the potential and the ability to use hard law seem to follow this modern trend of soft regulation. Thus, soft law is an attractive form of regulation and governance because it is considered to be modern (Ahrne and Brunsson 2004b) and in line with modern ways of organizing (Ahrne and Brunsson ch. 4; Drori and Meyer ch. 2).

It can also be politically convenient to describe and present rules as non-law to avoid a discussion of the democratic implications of the fact that important decisions are made outside the traditional and formal government system. Indeed, law can be regarded as the very essence of public authority. If, however, making law is also part of other forms of authority structures with a weak link to the traditional democratic institutions (parliaments), the very idea of the linkage between government-law and democracy can be questioned. The crucial question is of course whether soft law is linked to governance or government. Analytically the answer is easy (see above) but in practice it can be difficult to separate the two systems and rules. Indeed, soft law can be a precursor to binding legal instruments, which means that it is not always linked to governance, but it is often also closely linked to the traditional steering mode of government.

There are different ways of transforming soft law into hard law. One way is legal: the European Court of Justice or another legal institution interprets the voluntary rules as legally binding. There are also less obvious and less formal ways to transform soft law into hard law. The perception of rules is an essential mechanism in deciding whether soft law will be transformed into hard law (Aldestam 2004). If the actors – the rule followers – believe that the rules are legally binding they will act accordingly. Other indirect ways of transforming soft law into hard law are conditionality clauses. EU directives often prescribe certain standards to be followed in order to implement the directives. The World Bank and the International Monetary Fund undergo a process whereby the soft rules gradually evolve into harder law. The incorporation of soft rules into the conditionality clauses of loan agreements, arrangements and programs by states in economic distress is one of the mechanisms by which soft law is transformed into hard law (Spiliopoulou Åkermark 2004; cf. also Djelic ch. 3).

One obvious way of transforming soft law into hard law is by political decisions. At the European Council in Laeken in December 2001 it was decided to convene a Convention composed of the main parties involved in the debate on the future of the EU prior to the next inter-governmental conference (Presidency Conclusions 2001). In the final constitutional treaty of the European Union (August 2004), one finds several references to soft law. The regulation of economic policy and employment policy will be conducted through co-ordination (Article 15). In the overall paragraph on the Union's legal acts the possibility of recommendations and opinions is mentioned. In Part III of the treaty the possibility of using soft law (especially guidelines and indicators) is mentioned in connection to various policy areas such as social policy, employment policy and health policy. What is missing in the constitutional treaty, however, is an explanation of the democratic legitimacy of soft law when it is weakly linked, or not linked at all, to traditional law-making. Indeed, this lack of constitutionalization of soft law as an essential mode of regulation and the lack of consideration for its democratic implications is surprising given that the OMC and other forms of complex relationships between soft law and hard law seem to increase in importance over time.

How can we then explain the lack of more general and principled considerations about soft law in the draft treaty? There are no easy answers to this question. It is clear, however, that every constitution, national or European, often includes an element of flexibility. It could be counter-productive, then, to include a more specific declaration of how the OMC and other deviations and developments from the community method (the hard law-making process in the EU) should be used. This is especially true for the EU, which can be regarded as a moving target that must reach decisions on political issues that seem to be more controversial and diverse than at any previous point in EU history. There is, therefore, a functional explanation for the lack of general regulation in soft law in the treaty. A normative explanation is that soft law is not considered to be a problem because it does not challenge the community method and the traditional chain of command and control. Clearly, the treaty follows the logic of government and there are few elements in the draft that one could identify as belonging

Table 6.2. *Two systems of authority and the European Union*

	Government	Governance
Modes of regulation	Hard law: the community method	Soft law: the open method of coordination
Regulators	Public actors: the Council of Ministers and the European parliament	Public and private actors: the European Commission, civil servants from national agencies/ministers and interests organisations (profit and non-profit)
Democratic model	Representative and state-centric	Deliberative and societally-based
Democratic reforms	Hierarchy and parliamentarization: Treaty establishing a constitution for Europe	Open structures and network-building: very few reforms (the Lisbon European Council 2000)

to a governance-like system. It could also be the case that soft law is not mentioned other than in terms of references to the OMC and to guidelines for various policy areas, because the authors of the draft treaty wanted to avoid the very term "law." The connotation of the word is profound because it is strongly linked to the power of the legislator – the very essence of every democratic system. By using terms other than "law" one can avoid a debate about power and accountability in a system in which actors other than the national parliaments enact law.

To sum up, Table 6.2 encapsulates how the EU is based on the two authority systems of government and governance. In the government system the community method dominates. The legislation is decided by the Council of Ministers and the European parliament. The reforms in the constitutional treaty focus on how to strengthen the chain of command and control. In the governance system the use of the OMC and other forms of soft law dominates. These regulations are the function of deliberative processes between public and private actors. Democratic reforms are practically non-existent. Instead, the EU transforms gradually and informally in the day-to-day integration process towards a more network-based system with a very weak traditional democratic base. My conclusion is that the representative model of democracy is not sufficient to make soft regulatory processes, for instance the OMC, democratically legitimate. Although traditional legislative actors have a formal role to play within these soft regulatory processes, the regulations are formed in a governance system. What is lacking in the EU are reforms that would give the governance system democratic legitimacy. These reforms should not be targeted towards more hierarchy and parliamentarization but rather towards open structures and networks according to deliberative democratic principles and values.

Conclusions

Soft regulation is analytically connected to the authority system of governance that in its turn is closely linked to a deliberative and societal-based democratic model. The dominant democratic model in the Western world has, however, historically been based upon the authority system of government and liberal and representative democracy. Democratic problems are often perceived as the lack of hierarchy and parliamentarization. Indeed, in the recent draft of a constitutional treaty for Europe, the reforms are mainly that of strengthening the national parliaments and the European parliament. Regulatory processes that result in soft regulation are thus more or less outside the formal constitutionalization process. We could therefore end up with a wider gap between two parallel systems in the EU: government and governance. The former system is democratically legitimate, although not without its problems, but the latter system will have a much weaker democratic base if any. The risk is of course that soft regulation will be in the hands of civil servants, private actors and other actors that have a weak democratic base in the system of government. At the same time those actors who have a strong base in that system – the politicians – are held responsible for the decisions. The paradox is thus that those who have the power cannot be held accountable and those who are accountable have no power. Indeed, it can be argued that what is sometimes brought forward as one solution to the EU's democratic deficit – to involve more societal actors in the soft regulatory processes – can instead be seen as the very problem for reaching enhanced democratic qualities in the EU (cf. Eriksen and Fossum 2002). Deliberation takes place but only among experts and seldom with ordinary citizens. We are dealing with deliberation in which new types of knowledge are created and formed among experts with a scientific rather than political base for the development of arguments (see Drori and Meyer ch. 2). These deliberations are not necessarily democratic. They are often held behind closed doors and do not include ordinary citizens.

In this chapter I have conducted a normative analysis of the democratic implications of developments around soft regulation. In my work on soft regulation and democracy, I have realized that the word normative is interpreted in very different ways. Some researchers even want to avoid being normative altogether. In my understanding the term 'normative' has very little to do with your own opinions and what you think would be the best way to solve problems. Instead, it has to do with raising the important questions – the different choices and options – on democracy and other normative issues. The demand for making private actors democratically accountable because they are important actors in decision-making processes may seem a rather neutral and objective statement, but it can also help to reproduce our traditional understanding of democracy (cf. Wälti et al. 2004). Indeed, the traditional solution to the perceived democratic problem would be to strengthen the political control over private actors or to see to it that power is in the hands of public actors. Reforms should thus focus on hierarchy and parliamentarization. I believe, however, that it is important to base our analysis of soft regulation and democracy on a broad and deep understanding that there may be different ways of achieving and organizing democracy. In line with Ruggie, I believe that we need new 'perceptual equipment' in order to understand and analyze the shift from modern authority relations to post-modern structures of authority that are less focused on the divisions between private and public spheres (Ruggie 1993). This shift does not only challenge our traditional understanding of authority but also the very idea that democracy can only be state-based and primarily a prerogative for parliaments.

A recurrent critique of deliberative democracy is that it lacks realism. Who are those that are eligible to take part in the deliberations – those who are affected by the decision, those who are experts in a particular field or every single citizen? How should the deliberations be practically organized – by referendums, town meetings or by the Internet? There are in my view two most promising and interesting aspects of deliberative democracy, especially of the more radical interpretation of deliberative democracy. The first is the very idea of idealized deliberations and rational arguments among people (Goodin 2003) which leads to the view that democracy should be more direct, reflexive and dialogic. People are expected to be able and willing to take part in important local, national, regional and global decision-making.

Secondly, the conceptual and normative debate about deliberative democracy has shown that democracy is not necessarily a choice between aggregation of preferences in an instrumental and problem-solving fashion, on the one hand, and democracy based upon an ethnic and cultural homogenous society, on the other. The latter understanding of democracy makes the existence of a people – demos – the prerequisite to democracy. Deliberative democracy, however, separates between ethnic values and culture, on the one hand, and political rights, on the other. In this way democracy does not require a culturally defined demos and can therefore be created well beyond the nation-state. Democracy in the European Union is rights-based rather than based on common ethnic and cultural values (Eriksen and Fossum 2000). Democracy is understood as something more than just general elections and party politics.

PART II

A dynamic transnational topography

7 Transnational actors, transnational institutions, transnational spaces: The role of law firms in the internationalization of competition regulation

GLENN MORGAN

Introduction

The emergence of systems of transnational regulation and governance in the last decade has been a considerable challenge to authors studying patterns of business and management from an institutionalist perspective. One view, expounded most clearly in Whitley, is that "as long as the nation state remains the primary unit of political competition, legitimacy and definer and upholder of private property rights, in addition to being the predominant influence on labor market institutions, many characteristics of business systems will continue to vary significantly across national boundaries" (Whitley 2005a: 224). Inevitably such arguments are countered by contrary claims showing how, in specific areas, forms of transnational governance are emerging, what Djelic and Quack refer to as "the progressive transnationalization of a few actors, strategies and logics" (Djelic and Quack 2003: 11).

In this chapter, I examine this issue through distinguishing three elements – transnational social spaces, transnational actors and transnational institutions. As transnational phenomena, each of these elements emerges out of the dynamics of globalization and the weakening of nation-states as frameworks for economic coordination. However, each of them emerges out of different processes and this affects how their interdependence evolves. By distinguishing these elements, it becomes possible to understand the broader phenomenon of the emergence of a transnational sphere as complex and contingent.

I explore these ideas through examining transnationalization in relation to competition law. As Djelic and Kleiner (ch. 14) show, the emergence of transnational governance of competition law is very recent.

Similarly, until relatively recently, law firms in most countries were local, dealing with home based markets and clients. During the 1990s, however, increasing numbers of large law firms began to internationalize in part to serve multinational clients whose interests, for example, in the field of competition issues and antitrust policies, crossed over national jurisdictions. This phase was characterized by what Evenett et al. describe as the "merits and practicalities of reconciling national antitrust law and enforcement with an increasingly global marketplace" (Evenett et al. 2000: 1).

The chapter proceeds in the following steps. In the first section, I argue that it is necessary to distinguish three interacting aspects of this process – transnational social spaces, transnational actors and transnational institutions. In the second section, I use this framework to explain more clearly the nature of international law firms and how they relate to the emerging transnational sphere of competition law. In the third section, I consider a particular example of transnational competition law in action: the clash between the US and the EU competition authorities over the proposed GE-Honeywell merger and the role of law firms in this process. In the concluding section, I use this example to develop further the basic argument that the way in which transnational spheres of regulation and action are constructed varies according to the different logics and speed in which transnational social spaces, actors and institutions develop across different sectors and countries.

Elements in the emergence of the transnational sphere

There are three elements in my concept of a transnational sphere. These elements are transnational social spaces, transnational actors and transnational institutions. Firstly, it is important to reflect on the terminology of "transnationalism" itself. What does it mean and why use it in comparison to terms such as "global" or "international?" Hannerz argues that "the term 'transnational' . . . makes the point that many of the linkages in question are not 'international' in the strict sense of involving nations – actually, states – as corporate actors. In the transnational arena, the actors may now be individuals, groups, movements, business enterprises, and, in no small part, it is this diversity of organization which we need to consider" (Hannerz 1996: 6;

see also Morgan 2001a). So whilst "international" is usually taken to refer to relations between states and "global" to refer to a distinct level of territorialization (i.e. across the whole world), "transnational" can encompass a variety of different types of actors and different sorts of connections across varying numbers of national boundaries.

In identifying empirically and theoretically a transnational sphere of analysis (Khagram and Levitt 2004), it is necessary to distinguish between transnational social spaces, transnational actors and transnational institutions. From an empirical point of view, an increasing share of our life takes places in transnational social spaces (see Morgan 2001a for the different ways in which this occurs). Large firms, for example, are increasingly transnational social spaces. As such, they facilitate flows of individuals, ideas, capital, technology, products and services, knowledge etc. across national contexts – but within organizational boundaries.

The concept of a transnational actor is more complex. We describe firms as "actors" in the sense that whatever their internal divisions and conflicts, they also display a pattern of coordinated collective action based on internal processes of control, monitoring and discipline. The firm as a transnational social space, therefore, needs to be distinguished from the firm as a transnational actor. Are firms national or transnational actors? One strong argument has been that firms might internationalize their activities but remain predominantly national in their modes of action, control and coordination (Hu 1992; Hirst and Thompson 2000; Doremus et al. 1998).

The clearest argument to the contrary is presented in the path-breaking work of Bartlett and Ghoshal (1989). For Bartlett and Ghoshal, the transnational is a distinctive type of firm. They state that transnationals "decide task by task and even decision by decision where issues should be managed. Some decisions will tend to be made on a global basis, often at the corporate centre . . . ; others will be the appropriate responsibility of local management." (Bartlett and Ghoshal 1989: 209). For them, the firm is a "differentiated and inter-dependent network . . . integrated with a flexible coordinating mechanism" (ibid: 210). Essential to this is the idea of cross-national learning. What emerges as the transnational is a new actor where the dominance of a single national origin and set of practices and processes is no longer the defining feature of the firm. Some authors have been sceptical about

Bartlett and Ghoshal's notion of the "transnational firm." They have argued that becoming a transnational social space in the way described actually undermines the possibility of becoming a transnational social actor, as the loosening of hierarchical authority and the development of heterarchy and network relationships bring to the surface differences between national institutional settings and create conflicts and games within the firm (see e.g. Kristensen and Zeitlin 2005; Morgan 2005; Whitley 2005b). As a result, the firm finds it difficult to take coherent action or to develop a strong shared identity.

The discourse of "transnational capabilities," however, suggests that the firm has the power to coordinate effectively its members across different national spaces, to enable them to learn from differences across contexts, to implant this learning within its procedures to produce new improved practices and to reproduce these capabilities over the long term as individuals move in and out of the organization. This is not simply a question of a management commitment to learning across national boundaries expressed in activities such as shared management development, global knowledge management systems and information databases, international project teams etc., though all these may contribute to the development of the firm as a transnational actor. It also implies that the routines, practices and actions of the firm are transnational, not national. Whitley (2005b) argues that the fundamental barrier to this lies in the way in which national institutional contexts remain the dominant career reference point and source of reward and reputation, knowledge and learning for most individuals. Whitley's expectation is that in most cases, the employees of multinational corporations (MNCs) will be oriented to "national" labor markets (both internal and external) and this will constrain interest and commitment to the development of transnational capabilities. Of course, firms may well recognize this and try to counteract it through expatriate assignments, appraisal systems designed to reward international cooperation, etc. but the degree to which such mechanisms are successful and create a "transnational" management group or the firm as a transnational actor is difficult to determine.

Finally, we can consider the idea of "transnational" institutions. In the context of the issues explored in this chapter, transnational institutions are constructed as ways to reduce uncertainties and risk for actors involved in economic transactions across national borders (Morgan 2001b). They are "transnational" in Hannerz's term because they cannot be reduced to agreements between national states (commonly labeled "international" institutions) but are, on the contrary, distinctive emergent properties from the actions of public and private actors across diverse national contexts and across diverse spatial levels. More problematically, however, transnational institutions may take two forms. On the one hand, they can effectively consist of the imposition of one single national model (e.g. Americanization as discussed in Djelic 1998; Zeitlin and Herrigel 2000) on a number of contexts via the creation of a single transnational rule-making authority. On the other hand, they can emerge from multicentered and multileveled types of processes in which "national interests" are one set of constituents but not the only one and not necessarily the most effective one. In the former case, it is clear that the dominant actors are likely to be "national" and the struggle to make the transnational institution a distinctive level of reality is likely to be continually frustrated by actors whose primary interest is in getting the institution to follow their own preferred pattern built out of national institutional contexts. In the latter case, where no one set of national actors is able to exert predominance, the emergent process of compromise and negotiation is likely to interact with and stimulate the development of transnational social actors, i.e. social actors for whom making the transnational institution work in a coherent and effective way becomes the main objective even in the face of resistance by powerful "national" level actors. Neoinstitutionalism suggests that as actors and institutions coevolve, they create path dependency and lock-in and thus a form of stability is developed. As an emergent set of rules of action, cognitive frameworks, normative commitments become common, then institutions are reinforced and develop their own trajectory and their own significance for actors.

Broadly speaking, firms have been becoming transnational social spaces quite rapidly over the last two decades, though the extent of this varies across sectors and countries. Transnational institutions have been building more slowly and, as one would expect, this process is subject to more complex forms of determination than is the creation of transnational social space inside the firm. In particular, transnational institution building like other forms of institution building is subject to political and social pressures and reflects the relative strengths of particular nation-states. The overall uncertainties of transnational institution building are high, the timescale uncertain, the response of key actors and social movements unpredictable. Part of the reason for this is that transnational actors are difficult to create as identities are socially embedded in distinctive national and regional settings. Actors are often better characterized as "national in orientation" but "transnational in effects." This means that they engage with transnational institutions in a way which undermines the "transnationalism" and instead encourages reversion to patterns of national and international power politics. As a result, the change process is likely to be episodic (rather than incremental), discontinuous (rather than continuous) and reversible (rather than uni-directional). When there is a lack of powerful actors supportive of institutions, institutions themselves will remain relatively weak, fragile and subject to frequent and rapid change. It is the mutual constitution of actors and institutions that creates stability and certainty. If transnational institutions are to become significant, they need to become arenas which shape and are shaped by transnational actors.

Competition law as an emergent transnational sphere

The growth of multinationals over the last decade has been characterized primarily by cross-border mergers and acquisitions. As Djelic and Kleiner show in chapter 14, this means that many national regulators have to consider any mergers and acquisitions proposal for its impact on competition. As national regulators have different procedures and processes, even with similarity of broad principles, this multiplies regulatory costs and leads firms (and regulators) to seek ways to reduce these problems. Developing a common transnational framework for competition regulation is a proposed resolution to this problem. As Djelic and Kleiner argue there are many interested participants in the outcome of competition law. However, few of them are as continuously and closely interested or expert in its development as lawyers. How do they act in relation to the development of this transnational sphere?

Since the early 1990s, there have been an increasing number of law firms with a presence in multiple national jurisdictions. The Global 100 law firms list produced by *The American Lawyer* on an annual basis and measuring firms in terms of turnover consists entirely of US and UK firms. In the 2003 list, UK law firms occupy four of the top ten places in the Global 100, the rest are from the US.

Table 7.1. *The global top ten law firms 2002 ranked by gross revenue*

Rank	Name	Location	Gross revenue 2001–2 in $
1	Clifford Chance	UK	1,409m
2	Skadden Arps	US	1,225m
3	Freshfields	UK	1,060m
4	Baker & McKenzie	US	1,000m
5	Linklaters	UK	917m
6	Allen & Overy	UK	834m
7	Jones, Day, Reavis & Pogue	US*	790m
8	Latham & Watkins	US*	769m
9	Sidley Austin Brown & Wood	US*	715m
10	Shearman & Sterling	US	619m

* indicates the firm is a national firm, i.e. multiple offices in the US but very limited involvement overseas.

US firms dominate the list of the Global 100 primarily because of the huge internal market for corporate legal services in the US. However, these US firms are often less international than the UK firms, preferring to focus on high value activities around financial markets in the US. Frequently this means that their offices outside the US are limited to London plus a small number of other cities in Europe and Asia such as Brussels, Paris, Frankfurt and Tokyo. Of the top ten, US law firms (measured by profitability per partner), Skadden, Arps is the most international with offices in eleven countries (see Table 7.2). The top US firm in this list, Wachtell, Lipton, Rosen & Katz only has a New York office. The second in the list, Cravath, Swaine & Moore, only has offices in New York and London.

Overall, the mean is of 5.2 overseas offices and 4.6 countries in which the top 10 US law firms are present. The top 10 UK firms, on the other hand, have an average of 19.7 offices overseas in an average of 14.2 countries.

Compared with, for example, other professional services areas (accountancy, advertising and consultancy), law firms are limited in the extent to which they constitute themselves as transnational social spaces. If we took a simple measure of transnational social space in terms of presence in different countries, the top 100 firms by turnover would vary from 1 (just in the home base) through to 33 (Baker McKenzie). The big four accountancy practices would generally boast

Table 7.2. *Number of offices overseas of top ten US law firms (ranked by profit per equity partner)*

Rank	Name	Number of overseas countries in which firm is present
1	Wachtell, Lipton, Rosen & Katz	0
2	Cravath, Swaine & Moore	1
3	Simpson Thacher & Bartlett	3
4	Kirkland & Ellis	2
5	Milbank, Tweed, Hadley & McCoy	5
6	Davis, Polk & Wardell	6
7	Paul, Weiss, Rifkind, Wharton & Garrison	4
8	Sullivan & Cromwell	7
9	Skadden, Arps, Slate, Meagher & Flom	11
10	Cleary, Gottlieb, Steen & Hamilton	7

Note. Table derived from *Financial Times*, 22 March 2004 and websites of firms (January 2005).

Table 7.3. *Top UK law firms (ranked by Chambers Global on reputation)*

Rank	Name	Number of overseas countries in which firm is present
1	Clifford Chance	21
2	Freshfields	18
3	Allen & Overy	19
4	Linklaters	20
5	Lovells	18
6	Herbert Smith	8
7	DWS	10
8	Norton Rose	15
9	Ashurst Morris Crisp	9
10	Slaughter and May	5

offices in all recognized nation-states in the world, a figure currently hovering around the 150 mark.

The US law firm model is of particularly limited transnationalization with a very small number of overseas offices and limited reliance on overseas earnings or activities. The overwhelming impression of these

Table 7.4. *Lawyers outside home jurisdiction (from The Lawyer,*
14 January 2005)

Firm (all UK based unless otherwise stated)	Lawyers outside home base %	Profit per equity partner 2004 (£k) Average profit per equity partner = £504k
Baker & McKenzie (US)	83	364
Freshfields	66	678
Coudert Brothers	64	257
Clifford Chance	62	579
White & Case (US)	59	618
Lovells	57	590
Norton Rose	57	405
Linklaters	55	646
Allen & Overy	53	628
Simmons	52	275

law firms is that they are national rather than transnational. They act
as US firms with international interests, rather than constituting either
a transnational social space or a transnational actor. The situation is
rather different with regard to the UK firms, as Table 7.4 and Table 7.5
show. In two of the firms, overseas business was worth nearly
60 percent of total turnover and in the others between 40 percent and
50 percent. Overseas business is important to the UK firms and does
not detract from their overall earnings.

Earnings from German business and the presence of German partners appears particularly crucial for the UK firms as revealed in
Table 7.5.

These figures reflect the fact that UK law firms have increasingly
gone in for mergers with existing law firms, particularly in the European context. Given that mergers amongst partnerships can only occur
on the basis of agreement, a significant condition in these deals has
been the retention of local partners in positions of dominance. UK
international law firms are shifting significantly towards being transnational social spaces, characterized by strong and diverse national institutional interests encompassed within a fragile and complex international governance structure. They are more transnational social
spaces than the US firms but this leads to potentially more conflict

Table 7.5. *Turnover and number of partners in UK global firms comparing UK and German proportions (adapted from Morgan and Quack 2005a)*

	Freshfield	Clifford Chance	Linklaters	Lovells	Allen & Overy
Turnover 2002					
London/UK (£ mill.)	330	398	378	240	362
Germany (£ mill.)	180	109	102	70	34.6
Global (£ mill.)	800	978	720	390	647
UK as % of global	41.3%	40.7%	52.5%	61.5%	56.0%
Germany as % of global	22.5%	11.1%	14.2%	17.9%	5.3%
UK and Germany as % of global	63.8%	51.8%	66.7%	79.4%	61.3%
Partners 2004					
London/UK	179	232	205	162	191
Germany	166	112	95	80	30
Global	522	640	498	342	425
UK as % of global	34.3%	36.3%	41.2%	47.4%	44.9%
Germany as % of global	31.8%	17.5%	19.1%	23.4%	7.1%
UK and Germany as % of global	66.1%	53.8%	60.3%	70.8%	52.0%

between partners than the creation of a common identity (Morgan and Quack 2005b).

Transnational institution building: The case of competition law

The transnational sphere penetrates increasingly deeply into the strategic and operational decisions of firms, which increases the requirement for legal advice that can evaluate the consequences of action in multiple national and international jurisdictions. This is particularly clear in the sphere of competition law. In the case of the GE bid for Honeywell, for example, the firm's lawyers had to file notifications in not just the US and EU of its intent to merge but in twenty-five other jurisdictions as well. Competition regulation reflects the basic concern within capitalist economies of ensuring that firms are not allowed to dominate markets. Different societies have understood these relationships in distinctive ways (see Gerber 1998; Djelic and Quack 2005) but as the issue has become more international, greater complexities emerge over the rules and jurisdictions. Thus a merger between two firms from a single country may have a different impact on market dominance issues in other countries from the impact in the home base. Therefore, competition authorities in all the countries affected may have to consider the proposals and can in theory challenge and bring a stop to the whole process. Within the EU, mergers above a certain size are referred not to the national authorities but to the EU Competition Commission in an attempt to avoid duplication of effort and increase flexibility and responsiveness to pan-European mergers. Across the US, Europe and Japan, more informal methods of communication have been pursued in order to reduce uncertainties.

These issues are reflected in the emerging literature in this area (Gerber 1998; Braithwaite and Drahos 2000: Ch.10; Devuyst 2001; Djelic 2002; From 2002; van Waarden and Drahos 2002; Djelic and Quack 2005; Djelic and Kleiner ch. 14) that emphasizes the gradual emergence of a set of transnational institutions as ways of avoiding the potential confusion of multiple regulators. The argument can be broadly summarized as follows:

- The European level of competition regulation is emerging as a *sui generis* sphere of transnational governance.
- This is part of a broader convergence of competition regulation standards occurring throughout the world and predominantly influenced by the US antitrust model.
- This convergence is characterized less by the imposition of shared legal standards by governments and more by an emerging transnational community of actors who are developing shared practices and understandings around the sphere of competition regulation through continued interaction and dialogue in a range of institutional and network contexts – an example of the emergence of 'soft law' (cf. Mörth ch. 6; Jacobsson and Sahlin-Andersson ch. 12; see also Djelic and Kleiner ch. 14; Marcussen ch. 9).
- This convergence is having consequential effects on national contexts and on firm level strategies and structures. It therefore reflects a gradual but important transfer of both power and influence towards transnational forms of governance and away from the national level.

What characterizes competition regulation is the gradual emergence of transnational institutions in terms of "a competition policy and competition institutions that function along quite similar principles" which "owe a lot, indeed, historically to American models" (Djelic 2002: 234).

It is interesting to examine the GE-Honeywell case in the light of these considerations. The GE-Honeywell bid was huge in terms of size. It was between two US companies and approved by the antitrust arm of the US Department of Justice; yet the EU rejected the bid on grounds that it would adversely affect competition in the EU. The result was a bout of recriminations and conflict that revealed underlying issues about the development of the transnational sphere. GE had looked at buying Honeywell in 1999 but had considered its stock price too high. During 2000, however, its price plunged. In October 2000, a merger deal was in the process of being struck with United Technologies when Welch (the CE of GE who was within months of a pre-announced retirement) at the last minute offered a higher price for Honeywell. In strategy terms, the logic of the deal was clear if complex in detail and difficult and uncertain in terms of implementation. Wall Street audiences were initially skeptical. In spite of its record of acquisition and successful integration, GE had never tackled anything as big as Honeywell and achieving the synergies and complementarities would require massive management focus on restructuring and downsizing some areas. Moreover, Honeywell could drag down GE's overall performance because of its relatively slack market positioning. Welch on the other hand described the deal as "a home run," "exciting as hell."

As with most international mergers, lawyers played a significant role at a number of levels. Corporate counsel on the funding of the merger was more or less entirely Wall Street dominated. The main lawyer involved for GE was John Marzulli from the Mergers and Acquisitions group at Shearman & Sterling, one of the top mergers and acquisitions law firms in New York as measured by value of deals. Representing Honeywell was Peter Atkins from the Mergers and Acquisitions (M+A) group in Skadden, Arps (seventh in the league of US M+A advisers in 2003 measured by value). Both Marzulli and Atkins are star lawyers (or "rainmakers" in popular terminology) in their respective firms and practice areas. M+A lawyers in the top firms are amongst the elite of the elite, moving in the same circles as top bankers. Large law firms like Shearmans are complex places in terms of hierarchies of status and competition between partners. In organizational terms, the firms are divided up into distinct practice areas and the fees paid to the firm reflect both the prestige of the practice group and the lawyers within it. Generally it is the lawyers within the M+A or corporate finance practice group who generate the highest fees and are the most valuable for the company. They stand closest to the centers of capital and the advice which they give is, in theory, highly customized, suited to the specific circumstances of the case. Their advice is partly technical (i.e. what the law allows etc.) but it also has a strong social aspect. It accesses for the client networks of information, reputation and legitimacy. In general, in professional services firms, the more standardized the problem, the lower the fees. Standardization makes competition easier and more transparent. It allows firms to substitute junior employees for partners and thus enables partners to spread their time across more clients (Morgan and Quack 2005b).

Whilst corporate finance and M+A activities are at the top in terms of prestige, status and reward, other practice areas have different positions and networks. Antitrust practice groups, for example, are likely to find themselves called on by the M+A lawyers to help with specific areas of a broader deal. In the US, antitrust lawyers are likely to have strong linkages into the government (the Justice Department, in particular), the courts and universities. Their prestige and status is more linked to political and governmental connections. They are less likely than their M+A colleagues to be connected to top business leaders and bankers. These differences are overlaid with issues of geographical location where law firms are spread across a number of offices. The Wall Street connection is strongest for those based in offices in New York. For antitrust lawyers in the US, Washington DC is clearly a central location though it implies distance from the corporate centre in New York. Members of antitrust practice groups in London, Brussels and Frankfurt, for example, may deal with the local consequences of Wall Street dominated deals, implying a further distance from the centre of corporate power.

Certainly this seems to have been the case with the GE bid. Welch's main concern was how the deal could be financed and how Wall Street would see the merger. Regulatory issues were not at the top of the agenda. Welch's decision to jump in at the eleventh hour meant that any regulator's expectations about pre-notification, private dialogue on potential trouble spots could not be met. Given all their previous experience, Welch and his advisers well knew the way in which the US Department of Justice would deal with the case. They could have expected that the deal would be scrutinized and that they would have to agree to certain divestitures. But it seems that the European dimension was not even raised in the initial stages. The following appeared in the Wall Street Journal 15 June 2001 (as the deal was sinking):

GE failed to anticipate the kinds of questions it would be asked in Europe. At his October news conference, Mr. Welch even dismissed specific questions about the 58-year-old Mr. Monti, whom he later conceded he had underestimated . . . GE conceded yesterday that the Honeywell deal came together too quickly for it to consult its European merger lawyers, Chris Bright of Shearman & Sterling and Simon Baxter of Clifford Chance.[1] But the company's top lawyer says both later signed off on the proposed transaction. Moreover, Honeywell, which had just been through a harrowing negotiation with the same EU lawyers in an earlier merger with AlliedSignal also told GE it anticipated no particular troubles.

The failure to involve European lawyers reflected the way Shearman and Sterling and most other large US firms work. Wall Street is the primary focus; after that Washington DC and the response of the Department of Justice; only after that might issues of other jurisdictions arise. In other words, they acted like a national firm, pushing their own agenda through their transnational social space in the expectation that this would not be resisted. Shearman & Sterling were not a transnational actor. They failed to coordinate and cooperate across national borders and this contributed to GE's problems.

This can also be seen by turning the perspective round to the institutions themselves. There are two levels to this analysis – the EU level itself as an effort at transnational institution building and the more global level of developing common standards and expectations across the US, Europe and wider. With regard to the EU, procedures and processes for antitrust decisions were emerging slowly. Whilst regulations had been put in place in the 1990s and decisions were coming through the system, this was still an early phase in institutionalization where the influence of certain individuals, most obviously in the late 1990s the EU Commissioner for Competition, Mario Monti, could be felt. In contrast, of course, the US had a long tradition of antitrust activity and whilst it is obviously true that this was affected by the broader political environment, there was a stability that was lacking in the European context.

In the EU at this time, the official line was that mega-mergers created economies of scale that eventually destroyed smaller competitors. The long-term consequence of this loss of competition would be detrimental. This position was an emergent process coming out of the Commission; not simply the imposition of any EU member. It reflected what Caparoso and Stone Sweet (2002) refer to as "the institutional logics of European integration," an emergent reality for actors that is distinctive and separate from the national sphere.

In comparison "influenced heavily by conservative economic and legal thinkers mainly at the University of Chicago, the US began to focus on the effect a merger would have on prices, innovation and product development rather than the fate of companies left to compete with the new entity. In short, the new approach placed less emphasis on market analysis and more on economic analysis" (Wall Street Journal, 3 July 2001). This has become known as the difference between the substantial lessening of competition (SLC) test[2] which US competition regulators are now using and the "dominance" test (where it is the fact of dominance per se, i.e. having a high market share) which is the preferred European model (see Venit and Kolasky 2000).

Within a month or so of the merger announcement, a few commentators were beginning to suggest that the EU side of regulatory approval might be more difficult than Welch had expected.[3] *Forbes* magazine predicted on 27 November 2000 that "there may be antitrust problems and, from a most surprising source, the European community . . . Monti's main focus is something called portfolio theory which refers to the range of products created by combining two behemoths. That's precisely the issue at the heart of GE/Honeywell. 'GE is buying a high-tech company with 90% overlap with the things we [already] do . . .' Welch crowed in announcing the pact. Where Welch sees profit, Monti sees 'collective dominance'." (*Forbes*, 27 November 2000). Forbes also predicted that competitors in Europe would soon start lobbying the EU to turn the deal down on the grounds of "dominance." Meanwhile, GE postponed formal notification of the deal to the EU until early February "in order to address concerns informally before the antitrust review clock starts ticking" with Jack Welch visiting Mario Monti in January "to discuss moves that could facilitate approval of the acquisition" (*WSJ*, 30 January 2001).

By this time, the US Justice Department investigation was already well under way. Although the press referred to the likelihood of a "tough review" (*WSJ*, 14 December 2000), the same article also stated that "an initial evaluation by a Defense Department task force hasn't identified major competitive issues that might derail the huge acquisition." By early May, the Department of Justice (DOJ) had agreed to the merger subject to GE selling Honeywell's helicopter engine unit and allowing new competition in the maintenance and overhaul of Honeywell aircraft engines and auxiliary power units,. In this respect, Shearman & Sterling's lawyers had used their skills, qualifications and networks as might have been expected. The antitrust practice group leader, operating out of the firm's New York office, was at this time Kenneth Prince who had appeared regularly before the DOJ and the Federal Trade Commission since 1975. In Washington DC, the partner in the antitrust practice group was Steven Sunshine, a former Deputy Assistant Attorney General in charge of merger enforcement at the DOJ antitrust division (1993–5) where he supervised the review of all merger transactions and directed the government's challenges to the transactions where necessary. Another partner in the practice group, based in New York, was Wayne Dale Collins who had also served as a Deputy Assistant Attorney General in the DOJ antitrust division in the first Reagan administration.

In Europe, on the other hand, the lawyers were facing a more complex environment with fewer resources. The main Shearman & Sterling partner in Europe, Chris Bright, who ran GE's defense, had only joined the firm in 2001 after the opening shots in the deal had been made. He came from Clifford Chance where he was head of the European competition practice for two years having moved from Linklaters in 1999. His experience whilst at Linklaters included secondment to the UK Department of Trade and Industry as an advisor in the competition policy division. Bright was being helped by Simon Baxter, a relatively junior partner (since 1998) in the Clifford Chance office in Brussels who specialized in competition law. At this point, Shearman & Sterling did not have a Brussels office and therefore depended on others to act for them on the spot – in this case, Bright's former colleague at Clifford Chance, Simon Baxter.[4]

The opening of the formal antitrust enquiry in the EU revealed that many more issues and objections were being raised than in the US, particularly around the possibility that GE might be able to use its power in so many different areas relevant to aircraft manufacture and financing as to keep out competitors. In late February, in spite of personal representations by Welch to Monti, the European regulators informed GE that the merger would be subject to a detailed Phase II investigation and therefore could not hope to get clearance until July at the earliest. In response, GE offered a number of minor remedies including what were termed "behavioral commitments" to limit their activities in bundling and dominating the market. GE refused to go any further on the grounds that further divestitures would undermine the logic of the business case for the merger and thus on 3 July 2001, the EU delivered its verdict that the merger was "incompatible with the common market." As GE refused to make further concessions, the merger was dropped.

The case demonstrated a fundamental problem for multinational companies in the multiplication of jurisdictional regimes. How were they to know whether a merger proposal would get through in both the US and the EU? The problem was two-fold. Firstly, at least as far as US commentators were concerned, it was unclear what the EU model was (Venit and Kolasky 2000). In terms of EU process, decisions on competition were taken by the Commission on the advice of the Commissioner. In the US, if the DOJ could not reach agreement with the parties to a merger, it would take its case to the courts where it would have to prove its case. US commentators argued that this was much fairer and took decisions out of the political arena in a way which was not the case in the EU. The EU also welcomed opinions of competitors on the deal in a way which was not favored in the US.

The second major aspect of the problem was the contrast between the US and the EU in terms of the underlying principles. The distinction between the SLC model and the market dominance model has already been discussed. What is of more significance, however, is the underlying framework within which this distinction was constructed. In terms of personnel, US commentators were scathing about the limited economic backgrounds of European investigators. Increasingly, US regulators and lawyers have come to share a standard methodology of economic analysis developed through the Chicago School of economics and now comprising an integrated field of knowledge around issues of law and economics (cf. Djelic ch. 3). The qualifications of the Shearman partner, Collins, a JD and a PhD in mathematical economics reflects this integration. Such a combination, which would be very difficult to find amongst UK and other European lawyers, is not unusual in major US firms. This integration of law and economics around a liberal, monetarist economic and political agenda became known in the 1980s as the Washington consensus and has since been highly influential as a framework for reshaping societies either through internal reform or, more broadly in the world, through the influence of the World Bank and the IMF (Dezalay and Garth 2002a, 2002b; cf. also Djelic ch. 3; Marcussen ch. 9). As Dezalay and Garth (2002a and b) reveal, this is a powerful combination of academic knowledge, expert power and dominant political and economic interests in the US. It brings together different professions, such as lawyers, accountants and management consultancies, into a matrix of power that influences whole societies through US diplomacy and the activities of US dominated world institutions (cf. Botzem and Quack ch. 13; Djelic ch. 3; Djelic and Kleiner ch. 14; Marcussen ch. 9). The deep institutionalization of the Washington consensus in firms and politics generates deep unease in Europe where it is not clear that there is a distinctive alternative.[5] In this sense, the GE-Honeywell merger brought to the surface the impact of these processes not just on "developing countries" but on the EU where officials were battered by US lawyers and officials with accusations of incompetence for a failure to understand the new economics of law and competition.

In a typical reaction, for example, Shearman & Sterling gave a clear indication that they perceived the European approach as essentially "amateurish" and politicized:

The biggest single issue that remains is a lack of confidence in the Brussels systems and how this may be addressed. There remains wide discomfort (far more than attaches to any other system) with the approach taken by the Commission to merger investigations . . . The Commission has less refined analytical tools and less certain policy goals when compared with the US agencies . . . The Commission has significantly fewer resources available for each investigation and is less able to resolve issues identified in the allotted time. (Shearman & Sterling Client Publication, "What's new in antitrust" January 2002.)

Shearman & Sterling go on to link these inadequacies with firstly the ability of the EU Commissioner to escape the rigorous public exposure of arguments which comes in the US from the necessity for the antitrust section of the DOJ to go to court, and secondly the "political" nature of decision-making on the operation of competition law.

The decision on the GE-Honeywell case therefore raised substantial questions about the EU transnational institution building process in the sphere of competition and antitrust policy. What principles should underlie it and how should it relate to the US model? Two important moves took place in response to these conflicts as political authorities saw the difficulties created by the possibility of further clashes. First, the EU established a review of its merger policy and sought comments from interested parties. 120 bodies responded and 25 percent of them were law firms or associations of lawyers. Eight UK based and seven US based law firms responded to the review; the other law respondents were firms from France, Germany, the Netherlands and Scandinavia as well as professional associations from Europe and the US. In late 2002, the EU came back with draft proposals. As well as new suggestions on the process and the criteria for deals to be referred to the EU rather than being dealt with at national level, the Commission agreed to create a post of Chief Competition Economist in the Directorate General for Competition (as a way of partially assuaging US concerns about the lack of technical economic expertise). However, it also appeared to retain the dominance test (rather than switching to the SLC test) whilst allowing for an efficiency defence to ameliorate over-interventionism on the basis of the dominance test. Secondly, the EU and the US competition authorities established the International Competition Network as a means of converging standards through negotiation and networking (see Djelic and Kleiner ch. 14). In this sense, there are ongoing activities aimed at creating a transnational framework for competition law that can provide multinationals with a reasonable level of predictability and certainty. As global merger activity has declined since 2001, the emerging consensus has not yet been severely tested.

Transnational institution building, actors and social spaces: Conclusions

The events described reinforce the importance of distinguishing between transnational social spaces, transnational actors and transnational institutions. Transnational social spaces are increasing in importance as multinationals grow and develop. This is generating a broad range of problems for national and transnational institutions. The influential participants in the formation of transnational governance are only partially transnational themselves. Many key actors are nationally based and seek to influence the transnational institutions on the basis of their national interest (cf. also Botzem and Quack ch. 13; Engels ch. 16; McNichol ch. 17). This leads to increased conflict around transnational institutions and particularly around the degree to which they become reflective of a particular dominant national context.

From a theoretical point of view, this approach suggests the need to go beyond the simple dichotomy between transnational and national. The national and the transnational clearly coexist but what is interesting is how they interact and coevolve. Whilst our social spaces are becoming more transnational, our capacities to resolve the problems emerging from this do not seem to be keeping pace. Many powerful actors still follow their national patterns and this leads them to interact with emergent transnational institutions in ways that exacerbate difference and conflict.

The example of competition law reveals the significance of US law firms with limited capacities for transnational action. Individual actors within the firms tended to retain strong ties to their local labor market and their local professional knowledge base. These organizations basically work as "national firms with international operations." They are first and foremost American, with practices, processes and powers rooted in the dominant US conception of how competition law should work. By contrast, the EU is a social space with a variety of different traditions in competition law. Over the last two decades, these traditions have been placed into a setting where the necessity of resolving their differences has become essential. The outcome of these processes is the emergence of a transnational (EU) based view of competition law, distinct from national traditions and embedded in practices, processes and networks spanning different European contexts. At the same time, however, the EU is also faced with strong external pressure to take on a particularly powerful (American based) model of competition law. The result is a complex process of uncertain institution building in which national actors are highly significant and "transnational actors" limited in their powers and role.

This framework provides the possibility of moving towards an understanding of a diverse range of areas of transnational institution building in the economic sphere. An interesting comparison would certainly be with the dominance of the Big Four accounting firms and the gradual establishment of two dominant standards for financial reporting (cf. Botzem and Quack ch. 13). It is relatively clear in this case that the firms themselves were both beneficiaries and proponents of standardization, thus facilitating their presence across the world. What is less clear is how far the model of standardization was based on emergent transnational processes or on the imposed dominance of US practices. It is also not clear how far these firms have developed transnational capabilities and can therefore be considered transnational actors, or whether on the other hand they are basically federations of national partnerships (Morgan and Quack 2005a; 2005b).

In conclusion, an empirical and theoretically informed account of the emergence of transnational institutions needs to be sufficiently complex to capture the uncertainties and problems of these developments. By distinguishing between transnational social spaces, transnational social actors and transnational social institutions, it is possible to unpack and understand the various rates of change and conflict around particular transnational institutions. Without considering these various elements, we may overestimate the extent of change and the degree of emergence of a transnational sphere.

Notes

1. In fact, Bright and Baxter were not "merger" lawyers but members of the antitrust competition practice groups of their respective firms – an important nuance of status difference that the WSJ ignored.
2. Today, a "substantial lessening of competition usually is taken to mean a reduction in consumer welfare (or more precisely an increase or facilitation in the exercise of market power to the detriment of consumer welfare)" (Shearman & Sterling's Comments on the Merger Review Green Paper, 29 March 2002, p. 17).
3. It is worth noting that these events were taking place around the time of US presidential elections. Commentators have noted that strong US political pressure seemed to play "a decisive role in garnering European approval of major transactions between American companies" (*Defense Daily International*, 3 November 2000). The hiatus created by even normal elections (never mind chad-affected ones such as the Gore–Bush

election of 2000) could affect the US government's ability to press the interests of its companies.

4. In July 2001, Shearman & Sterling opened a Brussels office.

5. Interestingly one of the most articulate statements of a European alternative comes from an American, Rifkin (2004). See also Garton Ash (2004).

8 | Global enterprises in fields of governance*

LARS ENGWALL

Introduction

Although global enterprises existed before the Second World War, they grew considerably in importance during the second half of the twentieth century. Labeled multinationals in the 1960s (Vernon 1977), more recently called global or transnational corporations (Bartlett and Ghoshal 1989), they have been a focus for intensive research in international business (see Forsgren and Björkman 1997; Birkinshaw and Hood 1998; Magretta 1999; Calori et al. 2000; Dunning 2000; Johnson and Turner 2000). They have been growing organically, but also, to a large extent, through mergers and acquisitions. The events at the beginning of the twenty-first century in the pharmaceutical and telecommunications industries provide significant examples of this development. Many of these global companies are now so large that their turnover is higher than the GNP of nation-states. These circumstances appear to provide them with considerable power in relation to governments. However, this does not mean that states are unimportant, nor are they relics of times gone by (cf. Jacobsson ch. 10). Even fierce proponents of the new system of world affairs like Friedman (2000) admit their significance.

Against this background, issues of corporate governance have become more and more in focus. However, so far discussions and analyses have mainly focused on the relationships between owners and management, leaving other actors in the governance field out of the analysis. This chapter suggests that such an approach has serious limitations and that wider perspectives should be used. In addition to this broadening of perspectives, it will also be argued that corporations increasingly have a tendency to use boundary-spanning units and different types of intermediaries in their interactions with counterparts exercising regulative forces. Finally, the chapter presents a field model of corporate governance.

Governance as a reciprocal interaction with counterparts

The traditional approach to corporate governance has been, as mentioned above, a focus on the relationship between principals (owners) and agents (managers). As the former have delegated operations to the latter, they run the risk that managers may not be acting entirely in their interests. Therefore, in economic analysis, the issue of corporate governance is seen as an issue of owners monitoring managers. Some early contributions were made by Alchian and Demsetz (1972), Jensen and Meckling (1976) and Fama (1980). They were followed by a number of important studies in the 1990s (Fligstein 1990; Roe 1994; Blair 1995; Monks and Minow 1995; Keasey et al. 1997) and in the present decade (Barca and Becht, 2001; Carlsson, 2001).

Although the literature mentioned here deals with an important problem in corporations, there are reasons to consider it as taking a too narrow approach to corporate governance. First, it is evident that the relationship between owners and managers is not unidirectional. Instead, it is reciprocal. Even if owners try to influence managers, the latter also have a great influence on owners through different means, such as road shows, media encounters, strategic actions, etc.

Second, the concentration on owners in the analysis of corporate governance means that a number of other significant counterparts and stakeholders of the corporation are left out of the analysis. In this chapter we point to the importance of three such counterparts: governments, the media and civil society.

Governments

The political science literature makes a basic distinction between politics and markets (Lindblom 1977). It addresses the question regarding the division of labor between elected politicians and economic actors in markets. This question goes back to classical political debates on the role of the state. In recent decades this question has again become particularly visible due to strong tendencies to diffuse market principles (Djelic ch. 3) and open up markets (Yergin and Stanislaw 1998). Deregulation has thus occurred in various markets and has had significant effects, particularly in financial markets (Khoury 1990; Engwall 1994, 1997). This does not mean, however that politics are no longer important for corporate governance. Governments are still significant actors, as they always have been. Thus, although today we see more market solutions (Strange 1996), governments nevertheless still provide the rules of the game, which, in turn, institutionally oriented economic historians have found to be an important prerequisite for prosperity (North 1990). Of course, the rules and the tendencies for intervention have changed in the process of marketization (Braithwaite and Drahos 2000; Kipping 2002; see also Djelic ch. 3; Marcussen ch. 9). However, this development has not implied the abandonment of regulation (deregulation) but rather changes in the rules of the game (reregulation).

In their relations to corporations, governments set the rules for corporate action through executive actions (first branch of government), legislation (second branch of government) and judicial actions (third branch of government) (Siebert et al. 1956). As legal frameworks have undergone continuous change as a result of internationalization, the balance of power between the different levels of government has shifted. In discussions related to the European Union, it has been common to speak about Europe as a multi-level governance system, where national, regional and European levels are interrelated (see Mörth ch. 6; Jacobsson ch. 10). Regulation by governments has become more differentiated. The levels are definitely not disconnected – European competition policies have, for instance, been copied by national governments – but the expansion in different layers of rule-making significantly changes the environments for businesses (see Djelic and Kleiner ch. 14). However, as pointed out above, the relationship between corporations and governments is reciprocal. It is not only that governments influence corporations; corporations also influence governments.

The media

In addition to the above-mentioned three classical branches of government – the executive, the legislative and the judicial – the political science literature has long mentioned the press as a fourth branch (Siebert et al. 1956). Due to the expansion of broadcasting and other means of communication there are today reasons to extend the definition of this fourth branch of government to the media in a wide sense.

In the last decades, the role of the media in corporate governance has changed dramatically through a strong expansion of business coverage in media. A recent study by Grafström (2002) of the Swedish development during the last twenty-five years provides evidence regarding this change. In the mid-1970s radio and television did not treat business news as a separate category, while today they devote substantial time to this type of news. The period has also seen the expansion of a business press, starting with the foundation of the business daily, *Dagens industri* in 1976, which has become a great success. It increased its circulation in the 1990s by 56 percent, at the same time as the total circulation figures for the Swedish daily press declined by 13 percent (Grafström 2002: 30–1). Simultaneously a shift has occurred in the economic news from macro-economic and labour-related issues to reports on individual companies. Similar developments have been observed in many other countries. Internationally the successful expansion of the London-based *Financial Times* is particularly worth mentioning. Rockoff (1999) labels this broadsheet as "a truly international newspaper [and] one of the world's most respected business titles" (p. 197).

Of course it can be argued that media companies do not always live up to their role as a fourth branch of government, as they uncritically report information provided by corporations, building images of corporate heroes and reinforcing speculative tendencies. One illustrative example of the latter is provided by a study by Hadenius and Söderhjelm (1994), which showed that the business press, and also to a certain extent the general national press, was rather uncritical in the period leading to the Swedish banking crisis. However, there is also evidence that different kinds of media play a very significant role in the removal of corporate leaders, something that has been illustrated, for instance, by the fall of the former corporate hero, Percy Barnevik in 2002 (Carlsson and Nachemson-Ekwall 2003). They have also become increasingly significant as scrutinizers of the social responsibility of corporations. All in all, these examples thus again emphasize the reciprocal character of the relationship between managers and their counterparts, in this case the media.

Civil society

Although individuals in democratic societies have opportunities to influence the political leadership – which in turn is instrumental for corporate governance – and the fourth branch of government may defend their interests, there is considerable evidence that many do not find this influence satisfactory. As a result we have seen a number of initiatives among citizens at all levels – local, national and international – to take action outside the ordinary political system. In other words, segments within civil society become frustrated over their low degree of influence and therefore gather in different kinds of social movements. Some observers, like Useem (1984) and Strange (1996), see these as a response to the retreat by governments in a period of market liberalization.

The governance through grass roots action takes many forms in terms of organization. Although protest movements are basically spontaneous and non-hierarchical, there is a tendency over time to find more structured forms. Well-known examples of such organizations are Amnesty and Greenpeace, with their long records of scrutinizing civil rights and environment issues. However, there also exist a large number of other organizations all over the globe representing segments of civil society, including the Earth Island Institute, the Institute for Global Communications, JustAct, OneWorld, Oxfam, the Rainforest Action Network, and Womankind Worldwide to mention only a few (Warkentin 2001).

The activities of those organizations representing civil society have indeed influenced corporate behavior (see for example McNichol ch. 17). One significant such change is an increasing emphasis on the social responsibility of business entities, i.e. how companies are serving society as a whole and not only owners. This tendency is not uncontroversial, however. Milton Friedman, among others, already in the 1960s (see Friedman, 1962: Chapter 8) argued that such broader considerations are inappropriate and illegitimate in relation to owners. On the other hand, it cannot be ruled out that such concerns may benefit both short-term and long-term profit. Once again we can note that the relationship between managers and their counterparts is reciprocal.

The four counterparts in action

Actors and actor groups

A closer look at the four counterparts identified here reveals that they are far from being homogenous. Instead, each counterpart category brings together several different types of actors and actor groups, some being national, others spanning national borders (see Table 8.1).

Table 8.1. *Further specification of the actor groups within the four counterparts*

Counterpart	National	Cross-border
Owners	a. *Institutional investors* such as national insurance companies, investment trusts, investment companies, and domestic governments b. *National private investors*	a. *Institutional investors* such as international insurance companies, investment trusts, investment companies, and foreign governments b. *International private investors*
Governments	*National ministries and government agencies* such as the inspection of finance and agencies for competition and consumer protection	a. *International UN agencies* such as FAO, UNESCO, UNCTAD, OECD, the World Bank b. *EU Directorates and Agencies*
Media	a. *National broadcast media* b. *National print media*	a. *International broadcast media* b. *International print media*
Civil Society	a. *National human rights organizations* b. *National environmental organizations* c. *Other national organizations* such as Public Citizen in the US	a. *International human rights organizations* such as Amnesty and Human Rights Watch b. *International environmental organizations* such as Greenpeace c. *Other international organizations*

Among *owners*, an important distinction to make is that between institutional and private owners, the former becoming more and more significant through the development of insurance companies and investment trusts. Owing to their huge capital bases they have the capacity to put strong pressures on corporations. However, it is not uncommon for these institutional owners to vote with their feet rather than with their voice, nor do they necessarily take an active part in the governance of the corporations in which they own stocks (Hellman 2000; Davis and Steil 2001). In this way the traditional governance mechanism has, in some corporations, become less strong. This is particularly the case for foreign owners, who take a portfolio management approach with a focus on short-term performance. Nevertheless, corporate directors have tended to place increasing attention on international financial markets through road shows to various financial centers (cf. Tainio et al. 2003). A significant feature behind this interest has been the introduction of different types of options programs linked to the development of share prices (Carpenter and Yermach 1999).

With respect to *governments*, national ministries and government agencies constitute important domestic counterparts. Among them, units such as the inspection of finance and agencies for competition and consumer protection play significant roles both in determining the political rules of the game and then ensuring that these rules are observed. Among actors in the government area should also be counted individual ministers and politicians, who from time to time give their views on corporate behavior. In the last few years this has particularly been the case with respect to executive compensation.[1]

Across borders it is relevant to point out different UN agencies such as FAO, UNESCO and UNCTAD, and others like OECD and the World Bank. Similarly, on the European scene the different European Union directorates and agencies have become highly relevant for corporate governance. Often mentioned in recent years have been the antitrust measures taken by the Commission putting an end to merger plans. Two examples are the intended merger between General Electric and Honeywell in 2000 and the intended takeover of the French Legrand by Schneider (Carlsson and Nachemson-Ekwall 2003: 111). The European Commission rejected both with reference to antitrust arguments (see Djelic and Kleiner, ch. 14, for more on the diffusion of antitrust regulation).

In times of globalization and growth of multinationals the question of jurisdiction of governance has become particularly relevant. There are risks in the choice by multinationals to locate different kinds of operations according to the advantages of various regulations. This in turn may become an element in the competition between areas for employment, which eventually may lead to an adoption of the least common dominator.

Among the *media* it is relevant to make a distinction not only between national and cross-border media, but also between broadcast and print media. The former is growing in importance, although newspapers still have a strong position, particularly in some countries, like Sweden. However, the growth of broadcast media has no doubt been significant for corporate governance. The reporting process for radio and TV is more rapid, and requires CEOs to perform live. The earlier opportunities to check article manuscripts and to suggest changes are no longer available, which in turn has led to a strong need to improve the ability to handle reporters. Although the last decades have seen considerable internationalization, these confrontations are often most intense and aggressive in the company's domestic country.

Among organizations representing *civil society* there are two issues in particular that have attracted the attention of concerned citizens: human rights and the environment. With respect to the first issue, Amnesty, with activities in many countries, is probably the best-known movement emanating from civil society (Clark 2001; Power 2001; Gibney 2003). Greenpeace has a similar strong status on the second issue (Bohlen 2001; Jordan 2001). In addition, there are a number of national organizations that focus on human rights, the environment and many other questions relating to the responsibility of corporations (see for example McNichol ch. 17).

Corporate governance in interaction

It should be noted that the four counterparts do not operate in isolation. Instead they interact and put pressures not only on corporations but also on each other. Thus governments, the media and civil society organizations together put continuous pressure on owners to behave in certain ways. Governments still shape, at least to some extent, the rules of the game for the actions of owners, the media and grass roots organizations, i.e. rules of trading in financial markets, rules of publication in the media and rules for expressing opposition. Similarly, the media are not only governing corporations but also owners, governments and civil society organizations and movements. In addition they provide information for these counterparts as well as platforms for communication.

However, it is not enough to establish that the four counterparts put pressures on each other and on corporations. It is also, once again, very important to point out that corporate governance is not a one-way street from counterparts to corporations, with corporations merely being *reactive* to signals from the counterparts. Corporate governance also implies that corporations are *proactive*, i.e. that they express what they think and what they want in relation to their counterparts. The purpose of such vocal expressions is either to communicate a preferred view of the performance of the corporation (presentation) or to influence the rules of the game through lobbying (persuasion).

Presentation has become a very significant feature of modern society (Ginzel et al. 1993; Nadler et al. 1998). There are many examples of how owners are told about the good financial performance and good prospects of corporations; how governments and civil society organizations are assured of high standards of social responsibility; while the media are fed with all sorts of positive information. There are of course limits to the positive pictures that can be delivered. Quoted companies are requested to provide quarterly reports, even if they are not positive. In addition they are requested to communicate information about negative profit trends as soon as they are known. All in all, the communication between corporations and the counterparts constitutes a complicated process where interests clearly differ.

Persuasion is normally directed towards key figures in governments. These lobbying activities have a long tradition in the United States and have more recently become a significant feature within the European Union (Mazey and Richardson 1993; Greenwood 1997; Greenwood and Aspinwall 1998). Large corporations therefore to an increasing extent have chosen to have representation of their interests in Brussels. Persuasion efforts can of course also go through other counterparts, particularly the media. In this instance it is not the performance or the good prospects of the corporation that are communicated, but instead the need to change rules in a direction that is favorable to the whole industry.

Finally, it should be noted that corporations also use threats in their relationship with their counterparts. With governments this is manifested through the movement of production (i.e. the movement of jobs from one country to another) but also through threats or the actual movement of central administrative functions abroad (e.g. the plans, both realized and non-realized, of Swedish multinational firms to move corporate headquarters to London). Similarly corporations may use threats in relation to the media. This can take two routes. One is to blacklist reporters from a particular media company. The other is to threaten to stop, or actually to stop, advertising. In both cases the corporation's threats would generally be in response to negative media reports.

The internal corporate response to corporate governance

As pointed out above, the basic problem in the traditional literature on corporate governance is framed in terms of the relationship between the owner (the principal) and the manager (the agent). The main issue concerns the monitoring of the agent so that he or she acts in the full interest of the principal. This literature does not focus particularly on the organizational arrangements in corporations to handle the relationship to the owner. However, evidence from modern corporations shows that some, particularly those with many owners in various geographical markets, have created special organizational units for their investor relations (Edenhammar et al. 2001). Similar arrangements can be observed for the three other counterparts mentioned above.

An appropriate term for those units is boundary-spanning units. The concept was introduced by James Thompson in the late 1960s in the classical book, *Organizations in Action* (1967). A basic idea in that monograph is that uncertainty constitutes a fundamental problem for organizations. Therefore, under norms of rationality, organizations are likely to protect the technical core from upcoming uncertainties. One means to ensure such protection is to create *boundary-spanning units* in order to handle uncertain external relationships. The basic problem for such units is therefore, according to Thompson (1967: 67), "not coordination (of variables under control) but *adjustment* to constraints and contingencies not controlled by the organization – to what the economist calls exogenous variables."

Thompson does not deal with the corporate governance problem on which we are focusing here, but primarily with units more directly involved in the production of services. As examples he thus mentions sales units in business firms, interviewers in employment agencies, tellers in banks, classroom instructors in schools or universities, caseworkers in welfare agencies or purchasing agents (Thompson 1967: 96). However, the concept appears appropriate for the corporate governance problem as well. Although not directly protecting the basic task of the firm, the boundary-spanning units we are discussing here are created in order to protect the work of top managers. The need for such boundary-spanning units has been underscored by a number of studies of executive behavior. As early as 1951 Sune Carlson showed in a classical study of a dozen executives that their working days were characterized by a large number of very short episodes. His results are therefore often referred to by quoting his own change of views as the study unfolded (Carlson 1991/1951: 46):

Before we made the study, I always thought of a chief executive as the conductor of an orchestra, standing aloof on his platform. Now I am in some respects inclined to see him as the puppet in a puppet-show with hundreds of people pulling the strings and forcing him to act in one way or another.

Studies by Stewart (1967), Mintzberg (1973) and Kotter (1982) later corroborated Carlson's findings. However, a more recent study by Tengblad (2002: 558) indicates that modern managers have a somewhat different working situation:

The frequency of interruptions was consequently less than half that recorded in Carlson's study. The corridor outside the CEO's office was generally quiet, and only his immediate subordinates made any spontaneous visits. The picture of the constantly interrupted top manager thus gains no support from the new study.

A probable explanation for this change is that the above-mentioned organizational units protect present-day top managers from continuous disturbances. Such an explanation is also consistent with the idea of organizations acting upon upcoming problems like a fire brigade (Cyert and March 1963) and in this way creating solutions to more permanent problems.[2]

The concept of boundary-spanning units can also be related to the concept of gatekeepers in studies of communication. In media companies these actors are, according to a concept coined by Kurt Lewin (1947), mostly used for persons who are controlling the incoming information, i.e. those who make decisions on news selection. Similarly, the concept has been used in studies of laboratories (Allen and Cohen 1969) and in studies of organizational decision-making (Pettigrew 1973).

As shown above both Thompson (1967) and the studies of gatekeepers primarily focus on the role of the boundary-spanning units to filter information going into the organization. However, boundary-spanning units are also used for presentation and persuasion (see above), to present the corporation in a favorable way and to influence the rules of performance set up by the four counterparts as well as their future behavior.

Many large corporations have created boundary-spanning units to handle each of the four counterparts. There are units handling investor relations, government relations, media relations and public relations, respectively. These in turn require expertise in the areas of finance, law and politics, journalism and ethics.

Needless to say there are variations in corporations in the extent to which all these types of boundary-spanning units exist. Some corporations may handle all these external relationships through just one boundary-spanning unit related to top management. In any case, the most common, or at least most visible, boundary-spanning unit of the modern corporation appears to be the one dealing with media relations. In many companies, the directors of communication are even members of the top management team.[3]

Furthermore, boundary-spanning units are not created only in corporations. They exist also in many other types of organizations, and in particular they can also be found within the counterparts of the corporations. Press officers and media relations units are thus standard today in ministries, government agencies and political parties as well as among institutional owners and civil society organizations and movements. In this way boundary-spanning units of various kinds in corporations and their counterparts participate in interplay of corporate governance.

The fact that the boundary-spanning units require expertise in the areas of focus for the four counterparts has implied an increasing incidence of a phenomenon that is similar to what the French call "pantouflage."[4] While the original use in France of the term "pantouflage" referred to the move between public service or government and corporations, we see today multidirectional forms of "pantouflage." People formerly employed within investment companies, governments, media companies, or even civil society organizations tend to be hired by corporations in order to deal with their former colleagues. As a result networks of relationships are created between actors in boundary-spanning units and in the four counterparts. Such relationships are to the advantage of corporations for two reasons. First, the former employees of the counterparts have the expertise of their former field of employment and therefore know how their former colleagues reason and work. Second, they are well connected to significant actors in the collective of a particular counterpart. This makes it easier to bridge the gaps and to generate initiatives on both sides.

External corporate response to corporate governance

Intermediaries

Earlier research has shown that corporations to a large extent make use of intermediaries in handling the four counterparts (Engwall et al. 2004). This is the result of the requirement for new forms of decision-making and action in response to constantly evolving conditions and increasingly intertwined governance relations. In organizational terms, the use of intermediaries can be seen as an outsourcing of work from boundary-spanning units or as a substitute for the creation of a boundary-spanning unit.

Intermediaries mediate demands and expectations that are put on corporations, and they interact with corporate executives. In so doing those intermediaries translate interests, demands and expectations, and they translate responses from corporations back to the counterparts (cf. Czarniawska and Sevón 1996). This gives intermediaries a vital role in corporate governance. And, again we should note that relations with the four counterparts are reciprocal. As executives perform for the counterparts, they may use intermediaries as channels or stages for such performances.

Two types of intermediaries can be distinguished: (1) organizations from which corporations are buying services, i.e. consultant organizations, and (2) organizations of which corporations are members, i.e. corporate interest organizations. In the first case the relationship is primarily on a project basis and in principle piecemeal, a circumstance that does not exclude the existence of long-term relationships between a corporation and a particular intermediary. In the second case the relationship is primarily general and long-term, i.e. a corporate interest organization is acting on behalf of a body of corporations to deal with the different counterparts.

Consultants

The consultancy industry has experienced a considerable expansion during the last decades (Micklethwait and Wooldrige 1996; O'Shea and Madigan 1997; Ashford 1998; Kipping and Engwall 2002; Sahlin-Andersson and Engwall 2002). Among the actors in this industry, the consultancy arms of the large Anglo-American accountancies have particularly expanded their activities. They now offer a wide range of different services, including advice on regulatory and legal issues to both private and public organizations (Suddaby and Greenwood 2002). As pointed out by Dezalay (1993) this may mean that the activities of the consultants have a double-dealing nature.

In the same way as global companies have developed, globalization is also having an impact on consultancies. In order to be able to provide their clients with relevant services, in many different countries and of several different types, consultants have internationalized and grown in size (Wallerstedt 2002). Nowadays, globalization discriminates against nationally based intermediaries and intermediating structures and naturally favors internationally operating intermediaries (Streeck 1997). In many cases this is accompanied by the substitution of non-commercial, quasi-public mediation by commercially oriented intermediaries. One very prominent example of this development is the mergers and acquisitions occurring in the auditing industry. Until recently a group of companies known as "The Big Five" (Arthur Andersen, Deloitte Touche Tohmatsu, Ernst & Young, KPMG, and PriceWaterhouseCoopers) dominated it. After the Enron scandal in the United States the concentration process has continued as competitors have acquired different parts of Arthur Andersen (Squires 2003).

Other significant intermediaries are the big management consulting companies such as Accenture, IBM Business Consulting, Cap Gemini Ernst & Young, McKinsey and Boston Consulting Group. However, there are also a number of consultants specializing in media relations, public relations and investor relations. Among the last-mentiond investment banks play a particularly significant role, but rating agencies such as Moody's and Standard and Poor also perform important intermediary functions in relations between businesses and owners.

Corporate interest organizations

One important way to handle the interests of a corporation is to be member of a corporate interest organization. These are numerous in modern society (see Ahrne and Brunsson ch. 4). At the turn of the century there were around 30,000 international organizations, of which more than 80 percent were non-governmental organizations (*Yearbook of International Organizations* 2001/2002). According to Boli and Thomas (1999: 42) the largest group among these – around 25,000 organizations – was made up of organizations oriented towards industry and trade.

These corporate interest organizations have become increasingly important as intermediaries between companies and regulators at local, regional, national, European, and world levels. Although some major transnational firms develop their own relationships with national governments and the European Commission, many work, as before, through industry or employers' associations (on a national and a European level). In particular, there are numerous organizations in specific sectors that influence decision-making processes concerning those sectors. In standardization organizations – like CEN, CENELEC and ETSI – rules are sometimes produced in close relation between government officials and representatives of businesses and industries (Brunsson and Jacobsson 2000). Other significant non-governmental organizations through which executives have sought to influence governmental decision-making and collaboration are business executive organizations such as the International Chamber of Commerce and the European Round Table of Industrialists. The latter has had a major influence on the creation and the shaping of the single market program (Green Cowles 1995), and also on infrastructure projects, at least in the Northern parts of Europe. In addition, an organization called the Transatlantic Business Dialogue, which constitutes a business-to-business dialogue across the Atlantic, has been significant, for instance, in the world trade negotiations (Green Cowles 2001).

Corporate interest organizations thus play significant roles in the formation of regulation as partners in discussions and negotiations. In addition they are important as providers of alternatives to government intervention through various kinds of soft regulations and self-regulation instead of – or closely intertwined with – government regulation (see Jacobsson ch. 10; Jacobsson and Sahlin-Andersson ch. 12; Mörth this volume). In the formation of these regulations corporate governance is, to a considerable extent, a negotiation between corporations with differing interests.

The role of intermediaries

A key role of the intermediaries is to help to form and structure the rationalized images of corporations and hence to establish their legitimacy (Meyer and Rowan 1977). Therefore intermediaries are significant in editing rationalized accounts of corporations. The intermediaries also carry knowledge between settings and situations (Engwall et al. 2004; Sahlin-Andersson and Engwall 2002).

With the growth of intermediaries, the channels to govern corporations and the channels for executives to perform relative to the various counterparts have multiplied. The enhanced demands and the broadened relations between corporations and the counterparts could partly

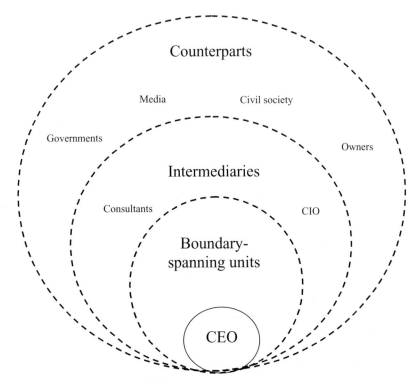

Figure 8.1 A field model of corporate governance.

explain the expansion of intermediaries. However, the dynamics of
this growth of intermediaries appear to be more complex, and not
dependent only on the counterparts per se. Instead the reverse seems
to be partly true: with the expansion of intermediaries, possibilities for
developed corporate governance follow.

The modern governance of corporations

The above reasoning implies that in the governance of modern corporations, particularly transnational corporations, executives are facing
four significant counterparts: owners, governments, the media and civil
society (Figure 8.1). In dealing with these counterparts, corporations
tend to use both internal units (boundary-spanning units) and various
kinds of intermediaries (consultancies and corporate interest organizations).

As illustrated by the figure, interactions between executives and counterparts can take many different forms. They can be handled by using both boundary-spanning units and intermediaries, using only one of these types of organizations or even dealing directly with the counterparts. We can thus identify three fundamental types of interaction between executives and counterparts:

1. *Double-buffered contacts*, i.e. CEOs going through both boundary-spanning units *and* intermediaries.
2. *Single buffered contacts*, i.e. CEOs going through *either* intermediaries *or* boundary-spanning units.
3. *Direct contacts*, i.e. CEOs talking to or performing for top politicians, editors, representatives of popular movements or institutional owners.

In addition, it should be noted that there are many interactions between the different actor groups. The four types of counterparts thus have a number of such reciprocal contacts. Governments, the media and civil society scrutinize owners. At the same time owners feed information of their own interest to the other three types of counterparts. Similarly, the media scrutinize governments and popular movements, report on their behavior and sometimes pass on information. Furthermore, intermediaries may interact between themselves and with counterparts.

All in all, we have thus found the governance of corporations to be a rather complex interaction among various actors and actor groups. This is the result of the argument that the analysis of corporate governance, particularly that of transnational firms, has to take a much wider perspective than is normally done in the literature. This approach implies that corporate governance is not an interaction between just two actor groups, but a series of processes in fields of governance. In these processes the different counterparts in many instances have similar interests in their relationships to executives, i.e. to guarantee the long-term performance of the corporation. For instance, had it been to the advantage of owners, the other three counterparts would have blown the whistle for the owners earlier in relation to the upcoming problems of ABB and Enron.[5] In the former case some even argue that it would have been preferable for the owners of Asea if the merger with Brown Boweri had never taken place (see Carlsson and Nachemson-Ekwall 2003). Similarly, the European Union's halting of the above-mentioned merger plans might very well have been to the advantage of investors. Although this is counterfactual reasoning it underscores the significance of a critical examination of executive actions in multinational corporations – but also national ones for that matter – in order to ensure that executives are not working primarily for their own prestige and well-being.

In addition to pointing to the need to give greater consideration to counterparts in general rather than focusing only on owners, the chapter has also called attention to the use of boundary-spanning units and intermediaries by executives in their interaction with counterparts. In that context it is important to point out that executives are not only reactive – that is, simply reacting to signals from counterparts – but also proactive, communicating their preferred views to outsiders through presentation and persuasion.

The presented approach provides a much more complicated picture of corporate governance than the existing literature. Instead of looking upon the problem as an issue between principals and agents, it emphasizes the need to consider the rules of the game, not only in terms of formal regulation determined by governments but also through diffused norms and soft rules voiced by the media and civil society. This is particularly important in times of globalization and in a context characterized by the growth of multinational firms operating across many different national borders.

Notes

* This chapter is based on research supported by the Bank of Sweden Tercentenary Foundation and by an earlier grant from the European Union.
1. A Swedish example is the strong critical remarks in 1996 from the then Minister of Culture, Marita Ulvskog, regarding the compensation of the Astra CEO, Håkan Mogren. From a strict corporate governance point of view this is an issue for owners only. The debate that followed clearly demonstrated that the views of non-owners are also important in present-day society (Ljunggren 1997).
2. It should be noted that Tengblad (2002) found that the modern executives, instead of a fragmentation in time, experienced an increased fragmentation in space. He also noted "the expansion of space has been accompanied by a change in stakeholder relations, in particular away from nationally oriented stakeholders such as governmental agencies and trade associations and towards a more dispersed pattern in which financial market actors have risen to greater prominence" (p. 559).

3. For a study of the handling of corporate communications, see Pallas (2004).

4. Cf. *Le Nouveau Petit Robert* (1994): "**pantoufler**[. . .] **2.** (1880) MOD. Quitter le service de l'État pour entrer dans une entreprise privée [. . .] N.m. PANTOUFLAGE" and *Lexis* (1975): "Pour un haut fonctionnaire, quitter le service de l'État pour le privé."

5. For ABB, see Carlsson and Nachemson-Ekwall (2003) and for Enron, see McLean and Elkind (2003).

9 The transnational governance network of central bankers*

MARTIN MARCUSSEN

Introduction

Central bankers are the wizards of our time. Pronouncements from a central bank governor are interpreted in the media in much the same way as the utterances from the Delphic Oracle: the fewer, the more secretive and the more futile they are, the more attention they attract and the more discussion they activate. Compared with the average politician, central bank governors are furthermore being treated with respect and even devotion by the media and the public at large. The present *doyen d'âge* among the central bankers of the world, Alan Greenspan, describes his own public statements as "constructively ambiguous" (Woodward 2000: 245). In one case, a Congressman having received a typically long-winded answer to a question at a congressional hearing, thanked Greenspan for his answer and said that he now understood the chairman's position. Greenspan ostensibly answered: "If that's the case, then I must have misspoken" (Meyer 2004: 214).[1]

Today there is no lack of data informing the general economic debate. Private and public, national and international authorities constantly publish analyses about the past, present and future. However, the reports and releases coming from central banks have a special status. They are meticulously studied by market analysts, professional investors, civil servants and politicians alike. The knowledge production of central banks is considered particularly apt, relevant and consequential. Central bankers worldwide have become authoritative producers of knowledge, ideas and standards. Some would argue that, today, central bankers constitute a global knowledge community with a monopoly on the production of authoritative knowledge about economic and financial questions (Dean and Pringle 1994: 1).

This knowledge community has been strengthened by the fact that most central bankers have achieved a legally independent status.

Central bankers are generally not dependent on other public authorities for financing their activities and central banking has therefore become a self-sustained and partly decoupled area of activity. In principle, neither politicians nor anyone else can rightfully and legitimately intervene in the business of central banking. At the same time, central bankers are free, and even expected, to intervene in matters that only indirectly concern monetary policy.

The knowledge community of central bankers has also become consolidated by the fact that most political actors now support the objectives traditionally promoted by central bankers: low inflation, stable financial and currency markets (see Djelic ch. 3). Those objectives are now on the political agendas of both right- and left-wing governments. It is today common practice to think like central bank governors, which means that central bankers do not even have to fight hard to spread their messages.

Finally, this particular knowledge community has been strengthened by the fact that politicians increasingly feel powerless in a world of foot-loose capital, where the scale and speed of capital flows are unprecedented. Still, politicians struggle to establish themselves as "responsible" authorities with the ability to create the domestic conditions for financial and monetary "stability." If the performance of national policy-makers lacks "credibility," financial capital can react much faster than ordinary productive capital. Capital portfolios can be reconfigured from one moment to the next and investment capital can be withdrawn with severe consequences for exchange and interest rates and foreign exchange reserves (Dyson et al. 1995; Gill and Law 1993). In those situations, central bank governors are firefighters and conflict managers because they are part of and actors on financial markets. In times of stability, central bankers furthermore play multiple roles – as advisers, policy analysts, idea generators, supervisors and examiners. Never before in recent history have elected politicians felt so powerless in the face of capital markets and so dependent on central bank governors (Gill 2003: 130).

This autonomous and self-governing knowledge community of central bankers can be depicted as a transnational governance network. In this chapter, a governance network is defined as a group of self-governing actors that interact within a more or less formalized institutional framework with a view to producing public policy (see also Djelic and Kleiner ch. 14).

Three central elements of the definition structure the argument of the chapter. First, we have to know more about the *actors* that constitute the network. How widespread is the central bank as an organizational form and who in fact are these central bank governors? Second, we need to get an overview of the *fora* that structure cooperation between central bankers. How can we characterize these structures and are there some central bankers who are structurally more central than others in the network? Third, we need to understand how this particular transnational network actually works. What kind of public policy is being produced and what kind of governance are we talking about? The purpose of the chapter, therefore, is to describe a particular transnational network with a focus on three dimensions: the network as a group of actors, as connected meeting places, and as producer of public policy.

Network actors

Central banks

Before talking about a global network of central banks, it is necessary to show that the central bank as an organizational form has disseminated on a global scale. National monetary authorities could organize differently than through the establishment of central banks. In the interwar period, for instance, currency boards were common in parts of the world and in some countries the practice was to let a private bank take care of central bank functions (Green 2003). But this is not the case anymore and today the central bank as an organizational form is truly a global phenomenon as Figure 9.1 shows. In 1900 about 33 percent of all states had established a central bank; today more than 90 percent of all states have a central bank. Figure 9.1 also shows that while 20 percent of all central banks were legally independent from other state authorities in 1900, today 65 percent of all central banks are independent.

This figure, naturally, does not show the extent to which existing central banks perform the exact same functions. It is also clear that legal independence is not the same as real independence (Bowles and White 1994). Strictly speaking, the figure shows that an organizational form (the central bank) has diffused to all corners of the globe and that the same is about to happen to a formal, legal standard (independence).[2] The figure also indicates two patterns in the diffusion process. The central bank as a form has diffused progressively over more than a century,

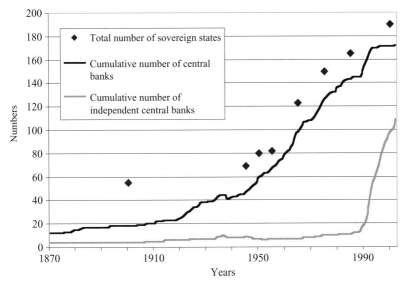

Figure 9.1 Sovereign states and central banks, 1870–2003.
Source: Sovereign states: Freedom House (2000); McNeely (1995: 42). Central banks: The Morgan Stanley Central Bank Directory 2004, www.centralbanknet.com. Legal central bank independence: Cukierman et al. (1992); Jácome H. (2001); Malizewski (2000); Maxfield (1997); McNamara (2002); www.centralbanknet.com; national central bank legislation.

whereas the standard of legal independence has diffused rapidly over less than a decade.

The diffusion process has been going through at least four stages (Marcussen 2005; see also the parallel with Djelic and Kleiner ch. 14) and different mechanisms of diffusion have been decisive across time and space. The first central banks were founded because state leaders were in acute need of capital to finance their war adventures. A central bank could provide the capital either by functioning as private lender or by using its mint monopoly to print money. Another reason for creating central banks in early periods was the occurrence of bank crises. Central banks could function as safety nets, protecting private banks from bankruptcy. Even when private banks engaged in risky investments, financial stability could be preserved if the central bank acted as lender of last resort. The signal sent to ordinary citizens and investors was that they could safely entrust their savings to private banks. The latter could then channel capital towards productive investments thereby benefiting the entire economy (Broz 1997).

These demand-based accounts are sufficient explanations for the early diffusion of the central bank as an organizational form. However, they are not entirely adequate to explain what happened during the interwar period. In order to understand why central banks were established in countries as different as South Africa, Peru and Greece, we need to bring in supply-based explanations, i.e. the fact that somebody and something actively helped central bank diffusion (Finnemore 1996a). Between 1918 and 1930, the legendary Governor of the Bank of England (the British central bank), Montagu Norman, and the Governor of the Federal Reserve Bank of New York, Benjamin Strong, regularly summoned existing central bank governors to international financial and economic conferences within the framework of the League of Nations where they preached the gospel of sound money and central bank independence. Together with the so-called money-doctors they engaged, furthermore, in intensive bilateral dialogue with neighbors, strategic partners and colonies with a view to establishing new central banks modeled on their own institutions (Babb 2001; Drake 1989). To a large extent they succeeded in establishing the same formula everywhere: sound money and finances as well as a central bank. It is possible to see from the data that the number of central banks increased relatively more in the interwar period than just before or after. It is tempting to argue, therefore, that the creation of new central banks in that period reflected both a country's demand and the sustained pressure and persuasion exerted by British and American central banks on these countries.

The next wave of central bank diffusion took place in the 1960s and 1970s, when central banks were established in almost all former colonies in Africa and South-East Asia. In order to understand this wave, we go back to demand-based explanations, although of a completely different nature from the ones that had worked earlier. After securing political autonomy, former colonies immediately established central banks because, in the world society of sovereign states, this was considered a normal thing to do. By the 1960s, the central bank was considered to be an integral part of a modern, progressive and successful nation-state. By then, diffusion had achieved a dynamic of its own and active proselytism by norm entrepreneurs had as a consequence become superfluous (Finnemore 1996b; Meyer 2000). Today, most states have annual budgets, citizenship, financial accounts, bureaucratic structures of governance and central banks. The central bank is part of the package of institutional forms that any state must have to be considered "real," and "legitimate."

The same diffusion dynamics can help us understand the fourth and most recent wave of diffusion that took place during the 1990s. The first thing that new sovereign states from the former Soviet world did was to run up their own flag and create a central bank. As an organizational form, the central bank has now achieved so much symbolic value that it signals freedom and political independence. It is not always the case, though, that these organizational forms work according to the large master plan. Through the 1970s many central banks functioned merely as money machines for local African dictators. In the newly independent states from the former Soviet Union central banks are only slowly starting to act as classical central banks (Dean and Pringle 1994).

Central bank governors

We now turn to central bank governors. Which objective characteristics, if any, do the persons in charge of the world's central banks share? To explore this we use as starting point the Central Bank Directory (J. P. Morgan 2001) that contains the updated personal biographies of almost all central bankers in the world.[3] A first striking conclusion is that an overwhelming majority of central bank governors are men (Table 9.1). In that regard, not much has changed over the years. There has never been a female chairman heading the American Federal Reserve and only one female vice-chairman (Alice M. Rivlin, 25 June 1996–16 July 1999). Furthermore, of the 82 current or former members of the Board of Governors since 1913, only six were women.[4] In the OECD-world, the Danish Central Bank Governor, Bodil Nyboe Andersen is an exception. Only in Central and South America does the number of women reach 10 percent.

There is also remarkable similarity across the global community of central bank governors for the length of tenure. On average, present central bank governors have been in position for seven years. There are central bankers, however, who clearly have distinguished themselves with regard to length of tenure. For instance, the former Danish Central Bank Governor, Erik Hoffmeyer, stayed in position for thirty years (1965–1995) leaving when he reached the age limit for civil servants in Denmark (70 years). Montagu Norman held his position for twenty-four years and Benjamin Strong for fifteen years. Among active central

Table 9.1. *Sex of central bank governors (percentages in parenthesis), 2001*

	Global		West Europe/ USA/Canada/ NZ/Australia/Japan		CEECs/NICs*		Africa		Asia/China/ Pacific		South and Central America	
Males	139	(95.9)	24	(96)	23	(100)	39	(97.5)	28	(96.6)	25	(89.3)
Females	6	(4.1)	1	(4)	0	(0)	1	(2.5)	1	(3.4)	3	(10.7)
Total	145	(100)	25	(100)	23	(100)	40	(100)	29	(100)	28	(100)
Missing**	22		1		1		6		14		0	

*CEECs = Central and Eastern European countries; NICs = newly independent countries from the former Soviet Union.
** "Missing" indicates that it has not been possible to obtain data for these central banks.

bankers, the Central Bank Governor of the Maldives, Maumoon Abdul Gayoom, has been in position for twenty-four years (1981-present). The Chairman of the FED, Alan Greenspan took office on 11 August 1987. Greenspan was reappointed to the Board to a full fourteen-year term, beginning 1 February 1992, and ending 31 January 2006 thus having been designated Chairman by four Presidents: Reagan, Bush Sr, Clinton, and Bush Jr.

On the age of central bank governors, there seems to be more variation. Central bankers in the OECD group (59 years) tend to be older than central bankers in the rest of the world (53 years) and significantly older than central bankers in the newly created central banks in Central and Eastern Europe and the former Soviet Union (48 years). Until March 2003, the oldest central bank governor in post was Masaru Hayami of the Bank of Japan who was born in March 1925. At present, Alan Greenspan, born in March 1926, is the oldest central banker in post. However, age is one of the rare criteria where there is variation; on the whole central bankers are a quite homogenous group.

Turning to education, Table 9.2 reveals interesting findings. The first finding is that there is isomorphism. The large majority of central bankers today have degrees in economics or finance (81 percent). Education in economics seems to be a fairly well-trodden path for central bankers in all parts of the world. Since central bankers on an everyday basis are dealing with economic and financial matters this finding may not be surprising. However, historically, central bankers could have different profiles:

Before, central bankers had degrees in classical history and maybe a career in the army. Today, they are all economists, mathematicians etc. . . economics is probably the best first discipline for them and gives them a common jargon in which to communicate with each other . . . if you ask them for their job description, they will stress that they practice *practical* economics, *practical* monetarism (Dean and Pringle 1994: 311 and 313, emphasis in original).

A second finding is that central bankers are extremely well-educated in economics. No less than 41 percent have a PhD in economics or finance. However, the overall average hides the fact that central bankers from the African region have fewer PhDs (26 percent) and that central bankers from Central and Eastern Europe and the former Soviet Union have more PhDs (57 percent) than central bankers in the OECD region (45 percent). Finally, the third finding is that well over half of

Table 9.2. *Education of central bank governors (percentages in parenthesis), 2001*

	Global	West Europe/ USA/Canada/NZ/ Australia/Japan	CEECs/NICs	Africa	Asia/China/ Pacific	South and Central America
Type of education						
Economics/Finance/Banking	102 (81.0)	20 (80.0)	21 (91.3)	25 (75.8)	21 (77.8)	15 (83.3)
Accountancy	1 (0.8)	0 (0)	0 (0)	0 (0)	1 (3.7)	0 (0)
Law	2 (1.6)	2 (8)	0 (0)	0 (0)	0 (0)	0 (0)
Political science/public policy/MBA	13 (10.3)	1 (4)	0 (0)	7 (21.2)	4 (14.8)	1 (5.6)
Other	8 (6.3)	2 (8)	2 (8.7)	1 (3)	1 (3.7)	2 (11.1)
Total	126 (100)	25 (100)	23 (100)	33 (100)	27 (100)	18 (100)
Missing	41	1	1	13	16	10
Level of education						
Bachelor	12 (10.5)	1 (4.5)	1 (7.1)	5 (14.7)	4 (16)	1 (5.2)
Master	55 (48.2)	11 (50)	5 (35.7)	20 (58.8)	9 (36)	10 (52.6)
PhD	47 (41.2)	10 (45.5)	8 (57.1)	9 (26.4)	12 (48)	8 (42.1)
Total	114 (100)	22 (100)	14 (100)	34 (100)	25 (100)	19 (100)
Missing	53	4	10	12	18	9
International education*						
USA	50 (41)	5 (20.8)	5 (21.7)	18 (56.3)	13 (54.2)	9 (47.4)
UK	20 (16.4)	1 (4.2)	1 (4.3)	9 (28.1)	7 (29.2)	2 (10.5)
France	9 (7.4)	2 (8.3)	0 (0)	6 (18.8)	0 (0)	1 (5.3)
Other	12 (9.8)	0 (0)	1 (4.3)	3 (9.4)	6 (25)	2 (10.5)
Total	122	24	23	32	24	19
Missing	45	2	1	14	19	9

*The sum of 'International education' does not add up to 100 percent since some central bankers have attended universities in several foreign countries.

all central bank governors have studied in the United States or in Great Britain. Central bankers from Africa and Asia are particularly likely to have learned their skills in an Anglo-American context. African central bankers have also often spent some time in France. Central bankers from the former Soviet Union and Central and Eastern Europe, and central bankers from continental Europe, are more likely to have studied in their home countries or in neighboring countries.

Finally, available attributional data tells us something about the career patterns of central bankers (Table 9.3). Only 3 percent had done their full career within the central bank. Governors have actually had quite varied careers: 64 percent have been civil servants before and 47 percent have had an experience in the private sector. Note that 25 percent of all central bankers have had an experience as politicians the number going up to 46 percent in Central and Eastern Europe and in the former Soviet Union. It is also interesting that 32 percent of all central bankers have been associated with the World Bank or the International Monetary Fund prior to taking up their posts as central bank governors and that no less than 70 percent of central bankers in South and Central America have functioned as university professors and/or researchers.

Overall, those findings tell us a great deal about the ecology of the global central bank network. Not only has the central bank as an organizational form diffused worldwide. It is also noteworthy that central bankers share a number of objective characteristics: gender, length in tenure, education and previous career patterns. Similarities clearly overshadow differences. In an almost organic fashion central bankers seem to be each other's pictures. This adds to the impression that there actually exists a distinct central bank community.

It can be deduced from those findings that central bankers have had plenty of opportunities to be socialized in parallel ways so that they look at the world through the same glasses (for parallels see Drori and Meyer ch. 2; Djelic ch. 3; Ramirez ch. 11). An archetypical central bank governor has been studying economics and he has therefore also learned to understand and apply the established terminology and methods within this particular discipline. This proximity is reinforced by the fact that many central bankers got their economics degrees in the same Anglo-American context. This means that, theoretically and socially, they have the same reference points. With regard to the practical understanding of the social world, this is likely to have been influenced by the fact that a surprisingly large share of central bankers has been working within the so-called Washington institutions in which

Table 9.3. *Career patterns of central bank governors (percentages in parenthesis), 2001*[*]

	Global		West Europe/ USA/Canada/NZ/ Australia/Japan		CEECs/NICs		Africa		Asia/China/ Pacific		South and Central America	
Only central bank	4	(3.1)	0	(0)	0	(0)	2	(6.3)	2	(6.9)	0	(0)
Civil servant	83	(63.8)	15	(60)	17	(70.8)	22	(68.8)	17	(58.6)	12	(60.0)
Politician	32	(24.6)	5	(20)	11	(45.8)	6	(18.8)	5	(17.2)	5	(25.0)
Private sector	61	(46.9)	11	(44)	9	(37.5)	19	(59.4)	9	(31)	13	(65.0)
WB/IMF	42	(32.3)	9	(36)	6	(25)	13	(40.6)	7	(24.1)	7	(35.0)
IO-other	32	(24.6)	7	(28)	3	(12.5)	7	(21.9)	5	(17.2)	10	(50.0)
University	52	(40)	12	(48)	9	(37.5)	9	(28.1)	8	(27.6)	14	(70.0)
Other	3	(2.3)	1	(4)	0	(0)	1	(3.1)	1	(3.4)	0	(0)
Total	130		25		24		32		29		20	
Missing	37		1		0		14		14		8	

[*]The sum total does not add up to 100 percent since most central bankers have occupied positions in many sectors before entering the world of central banking.

the so-called Washington consensus has developed and from where it has been diffused to most parts of the world (see Djelic ch.).

In short, on the basis of this analysis, not only will central bankers in the global central bank network look like each other in objective terms but they will also probably look at and analyze the world in very similar ways.

Network institutions

Let us now turn to the institutional framework within which network interaction takes place. Since the Second World War the number of international organizations has exploded (Cupitt et al. 1996; Shanks et al. 1996). This is true also for the field of activity of central bankers: the financial and monetary area.

We identify four tendencies within that area. First, the meeting places of central bank governors have become formalized and organized (cf. Drori and Meyer ch. 2; Ahrne and Brunsson ch. 4). During the heydays of central banks, before the 1930s, international connections between central banks were generally ad hoc and informal in character (Eichengreen 1992; Gallarotti 1995). Today, informal relations remain intense while formal organizations have been built up in parallel, thereby creating an international infrastructure for exchange between central bankers. Second, we can observe that the fora where central bankers can meet have increased in number. Since the 1950s and particularly the 1960s, many international organizations counting central bankers among their members have been set up (Table 9.4). Third, meeting places for central bank governors have become diversified. Today, central bankers meet each other in development banks, in multilateral central banks, in pure central bank fora and in mixed fora that also include members of government. Finally, it is clear that a form of globalization has taken place. Some central bank fora, such as the Bank for International Settlements (BIS), now increasingly invite non-European central bankers to become members. We can furthermore observe that central bankers from the non-Western hemisphere organize themselves in separate fora.

Using data about the membership of central banks in international organizations, we can say something about relational structures within the transnational network of central bankers. We can start to answer questions such as: How are central bankers connected? Are some

Table 9.4. *The gradual institutionalization of the transnational central bank network. (Source: Union of International Associations (2002/2003).)*

	Multilateral central bank fora	Development banks	Mixed central bank – government fora	Pure central bank fora
>1930			League of Nations Financial and Economic Committee (1920–46)	
1930s	BIS – Bank for International Settlements, 1930 (www.bis.org)			
1940s		IBRD – International Bank for Reconstruction and Development, 1944 (www.worldbank.org)	IMF – International Monetary Fund, 1944 (www.imf.org)	SEACEN – South- East Asian Central Banks, 1972 (www.seacen.org)
1950s		IADB – Inter-American Development Bank, 1959 (www.iadb.org)	Monetary Committee, EEC, 1958–1999.	CEMLA – Centro de Estudios Monetarios Latinoamericanos, 1952 (www.cemla.org) SEANZA – Central Banks of South East Asia, New Zealand and Australia, 1956
1960s	BCEAO – Central Bank of West African States, West African Monetary Union (WAMU), 1962 (www.bceao.int)	AFDB – African development Bank, 1963 (www.afdb.org) ADB – Asian Development Bank, 1966 (www.adb.org)	WP3 – Working Party three, OECD, 1960 (www.oecd.org)	G10 – Group of Ten, 1962 Committee of Governors, EEC, 1964–1994 AACB – Association of African Central Banks, 1968

1970s	BEAC – Central African Central Bank, Central African Monetary Union (UMAC), 1972 (www.beac.int)	ISDB – The Islamic Development Bank, 1973 (www.isdb.org)	C-20 – Committee of 20/Interim Committee, IMF, 1972–1974, 1974–1999 G24 – Group of Twenty Four, 1972 (www.g24.org) G5/Library Group – Group of Five, 1973–1986 G7 – Group of Seven, 1975–1998	
1980s	ECCB – Eastern Caribbean Central Bank, Eastern Caribbean Currency Union, 1983 (www.eccb-centralbank.org)	PTA-Bank – Eastern and Southern African Trade and Development Bank, 1983 (www.ptabank.org)	APEC – Asia Pacific Economic Cooperation, 1989 (www.apecsec.org.sg)	
1990s	ECB – European Central Bank, European Economic and Monetary Union (EMU), 1999 (www.ecb.de)	EBRD – European Bank for Reconstruction and Development, 1991 (www.ebrd.org)	Manila Framework Group, 1997 G8 – Group of Eight, 1998 (www.g7.utoronto.ca) IMFC – International Monetary and Financial Committee, IMF, 1999 FSF – Financial Stability Forum, 1999 (www.fsforum.org) EFC – Economic and Financial Committee, European Union (EU), 1999	EMEAP – The Executive Meeting of East-Asian-Pacific Central Banks, 1991 (www.emeap.org) EMI – European Monetary Institute, European Economic and Monetary Union (EMU), 1994–1999 Committee for Central Banks, Common Market for Eastern and Southern Africa (COMESA), 1994 (www.comesa.int) MEFMI – Macroeconomic Financial Management Institute of Eastern and Southern Africa, 1997 (www.mefmi.org) G22 – Group of Twenty Two, 1997–1999 G33 – Group of Thirty Three, 1999–1999 G20 – Group of Twenty, 1999 (g20.nic.in)

Note. Source: Union of International Associations (2002/2003).

central bankers more centrally placed than others in the transnational network of central banks? Does more than one center exist in the transnational network? By way of social network analysis it is possible to describe the relations between agents in a larger population, such as the total number of central banks (Scott 2000). Governors of all existing central banks can be tabulated in a data-matrix, and it becomes possible to produce a sociogram like the one in Figure 9.2. In this figure, square points are international organizations and round points are national central bank governors. The lines between square and round points indicate membership in an international organization. To produce the sociogram, the computer program (Ucinet6) calculates the position of international organizations and national central bank governors: those central bankers with few memberships emerge in the periphery and those with many memberships appear closer to the centre. Furthermore, the program attempts to position the international organizations as close as possible to its members. Thus, the construction of a sociogram actually allows us to identify visually whether there are some cliques of central bankers that are more connected than others in the central bank community (Borgatti et al. 1999). What we should look for are clusters of round points (central bank governors) surrounded by squares (international organizations).

For a start, four observations can be made. First, the International Monetary Fund (although not the International Monetary and Financial Committee of the IMF) has been withdrawn from the list of central bank organizations. The IMF is a global organization and since individual membership status has not been weighted, membership cannot help us understand which members are most centrally located. Second, based on membership in international organizations, we see a global central bank community emerge in this sociogram. Third, it is possible to identify visually at least two cliques of central bankers. One clique includes twenty-five mostly African countries, another clique includes fifteen OECD countries. Finally, the sociogram shows that there is a periphery to the community and that a very large majority of central bankers are located in that periphery.

Social network analysis allows us to calculate which of the two cliques is most centrally located. The so-called centrality score of individual central bankers is calculated on the basis of not only their membership in international organizations, but also on the international connectedness of the other members of these international

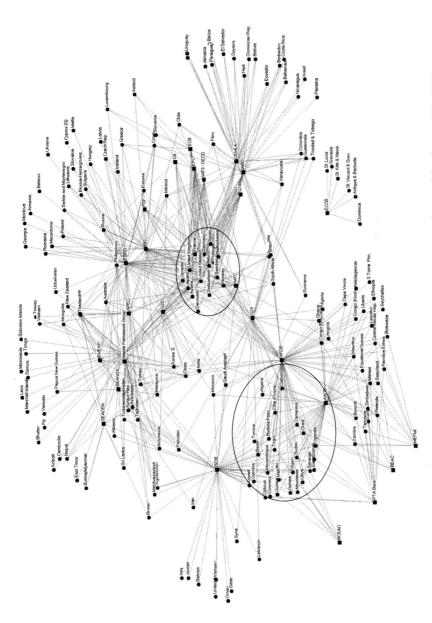

Figure 9.2 Centre and periphery in the transnational governance network of central bankers, 2001–2002.

organizations (the so-called Eigenvector score). For instance, if the Danish central bank is a member of an international financial institution where other members are Haiti, East Timor and Nepal, all relatively unconnected, such membership will not contribute very much to the centrality score of the Danish central bank governor. However, if it belongs to an international financial institution that counts among its members the USA, Canada and Germany this would considerably contribute to the centrality score, because the central banks of these three countries are themselves members of many other international financial institutions. Therefore, by calculating the centrality score of each one of the world's central bank governors based on their membership in international organizations, we are able to rank them and identify which one of the two central cliques is actually *the* center of the global community. Unsurprisingly, that center is the clique that represents the large majority of the world's financial resources – the OECD clique.

Network governance

We now turn to the governance dimension of the global central bank network and its contribution to public policy. The understanding of public policy is broad here. Contribution to public policy does not mean only and necessarily direct involvement in the production of formally binding regulation – regulative governance. Public policy can also be about producing rules of appropriateness, standards and guidelines – normative governance; knowledge and data – cognitive governance; as well as common histories, myths about the past and visions about the future – imaginary governance (see Jacobsson and Sahlin-Andersson ch. 12; Drori and Meyer ch. 2). If we allow all these dimensions to be included in our understanding of public policy, we will be better able to understand what central bankers in their transnational network are actually doing (cf. Djelic and Kleiner ch. 14; Hedmo et al. ch. 15).

The transnational network of central bankers does not contribute to public policy through all those dimensions. So far, central bankers and their organizations have not been particularly apt at developing formal conventions and treaties. Since the final breakdown of the Bretton Woods system, in the early 1970s, the debate has been going on: is it possible and indeed desirable that central bankers engage in the development of a formal framework for monetary and financial policy-making? (Federal Reserve Bank of Boston 1984, 1999). A key point of discussion has been whether markets can and ought to be formally regulated and whether, in crisis situations, heads of state and government are likely to comply with central bank conventions. However, that central bank governors hesitate to formally regulate financial markets does not mean that they are passive with regard to the formulation of public policy. A short comparison of two different international fora for central bankers – the Bank for International Settlements (BIS) and the International Monetary Fund (IMF) – shows that the transnational network of central bankers essentially produces standards, knowledge and identity (for parallels see Djelic and Kleiner ch. 14; Hedmo et al. ch. 15; Jacobsson and Sahlin-Andersson ch. 12).

The Bank for International Settlements is located in Basle, Switzerland. It can be characterized as a "pure" central bank forum since only central bankers are among its members. These central bankers meet regularly on the premises of the BIS, typically to participate in one of the working committees that are supported by the BIS infrastructure. One of the central tasks of BIS is to produce standards for national and international banking. This primarily takes place in one of the most prestigious BIS-committees, the Basle Committee on Banking Supervision, which was established in 1974 by the ten leading central banks. Over the years, guidelines about how banking supervision ought to be organized and implemented were formulated in Basle. In 1988, the committee adopted a whole package of standards – the so-called Basle Capital Accord (Basle I) – that, among other things, contains minimum standards for how much capital private lenders should retain as a percentage of their loans. This accord is currently being updated and an expanded Basel-II Accord will be ready by the end of 2006. Even if the committee does not itself act as a bank supervisor and even if its recommendations do not in any way have legal force, the Basle Accord has become a veritable international standard on the area of banking supervision. In Europe, for instance, the EU has granted the accord the force of law.

The IMF is located in Washington. Since 1974, a small group of IMF members (twenty-four central bank governors and/or Ministers of Finance) have gathered in the International Monetary and Financial Committee (known until 1999 as the Interim Committee). The objective of the committee is to discuss and consider propositions from the executive body of the IMF – the Executive Board – and to counsel the decision-making authority – the Board of Governors. All public policy related to financial and capital markets passes through the International Monetary and Financial Committee. Just like the BIS, this is a place where a series of standards are formulated. The types of standards produced concern the issue of transparency in monetary and financial politics; and also payments systems; insurance; the fight against money laundering and the financing of terrorism; corporate governance; accountancy and auditing standards. In contrast to BIS, the IMF has a number of instruments at its disposal when it comes to diffusing its standards. The IMF can make its loans conditional on compliance with those standards. The IMF also engages in multilateral surveillance of member states' economies, establishing benchmarks and revealing which states actually comply (and which do not) with the agreed-on standards. Over the years a so-called Washington Consensus has developed, which basically is a meta-standard for how to organize and run a stability-oriented macro-economic policy (Williamson 2000; see also Djelic ch. 3). Finally, the IMF offers technical assistance to member states to help them with the practical introduction and implementation of IMF standards.

Within the framework of both the IMF and the BIS, knowledge is being produced and data is being gathered and organized. Both organizations spend considerable amounts of resources on research activities and data collection. Some of that research forms the basis for the annual report from the two organizations and for the many regular analyses of the international financial and capital markets. Personnel in both organizations also produce research papers, organize scientific conferences and contribute to scientific journals. The legitimacy and authority of the two organizations is to a large extent based on their scientific reputation. If those who are supposed to adopt BIS and IMF standards consider the two organizations to be "knowledge" and "scientific" organizations first of all, and not only political organizations, there is a greater likelihood that their standards will be diffused, adopted and complied with (see Drori and Meyer ch. 2).

Finally, a rarely discussed activity of international financial organizations is that they to a large extent reproduce a culture of central banking (see Djelic and Kleiner ch. 14 for parallels). The BIS is repeatedly presented as a secret brotherhood and the mastermind behind a particular central bank culture that characterizes the transnational network of central bankers (Dean and Pringle 1994). It is possible to trace the source of that culture to the very first years of the organization's existence. In the fifth annual report from 1935, for instance, a number of deeds and duties of central bankers are listed. They concern the very *raison d'être* of central banking as well as the standards that a sound, stability-oriented macro-economic policy ought to live up to (Auboin 1955; Clarke 1967; Schloss 1958). Central bank governors who are new to central banking may already have learned the special central bank culture when studying in Anglo-American universities for their PhD in economics or finance or through their previous experience in the World Bank or the IMF. If not, there is a great likelihood that regular meetings with other more senior central bankers in the many central bank fora will teach them the informal rules of the game about what central banking is all about, including the question about how to relate to politicians. The General Manager of the BIS and the Managing Director of the IMF also take advantage of their many public speeches to re-affirm that culture constantly: emphasizing that sound macro-economic policy is about keeping inflation and public deficits low. It is furthermore emphasized now and again that an integral element of a sustainable macro-economic polity is the existence of a truly independent central bank.

In recent years, central bankers tend to present themselves as representatives of objectivity and factual correctness. It is implied to politicians that central bankers do not seek personal gains, power or the realization of an ideological project. As a correlate, international central bank fora and national central banks increasingly seek to assert themselves as scientists in renowned scientific journals (Eifinger et al. 2002). Central bankers are not merely applying science, they have to a large extent started to produce it as well. This movement towards the scientization of central banking is underlined by the fact that an increasing number of central bank governors have previously earned their reputation as university professors. This is the case, for example, for the new Governor of the Bank of England, Mervyn A. King, and the Governor of the Bundesbank, Axel A. Weber. That scientization is a deliberate strategy of central bankers is shown by the fact that most central banks are spending ever larger resources on hiring PhDs in their research departments, making the ECB, for instance, a research power house within the area of monetary and financial affairs. So far, it seems as if the process of central bank scientization is paying off. In 2004, the most prestigious scientific distinction within the area of economics, the Nobel prize, was given, for the first time ever, to a central banker. Edward Prescott was among the leading economists who provided the theoretical building blocks in support of the movement towards central bank independence.

The central bank culture is reproduced inside the transnational central bank network through various meetings, seminars and courses, but it is also diffused to a larger audience outside these narrow central bank circles. This, for instance, takes place in the Joint Vienna Institute (www.jvi.org) in which civil servants from transition economies are being taught by civil servants from the IMF and BIS (Johnson 2002). It also takes place through the public appearance of central bankers (Woodward 2000: 363). Most central bank governors and employed personnel in international central bank organizations spend considerable amounts of time developing their ideas about sound economic and financial policies in public fora. Central bank governors are sought-after and prestigious speakers. Their message is furthermore disseminated through research and annual reports that cover much more ground than purely financial matters. For example, researchers related to the European Central Bank have recently expressed critical remarks with regard to the efficiency of the public sector in various European countries (Afonso et al. 2003). In an American context, Alan Greenspan has earned a notorious reputation for speaking out loud on issues that are far beyond the authority of the Federal Reserve, including those that are politically contentious (Meyer 2004: 215).

Overall, the purpose of these public activities is to exploit the knowledge authority that central bankers have obtained and cultivated since the 1980s with a view to defining what counts as modern, attractive, acceptable and appropriate. In their public utterances central bankers also often exploit the possibility of defining which models in the past and the future we should measure up against and which horror examples – persons, institutions and episodes – we should avoid copying. Theories are being formulated about which role different actors – public and private, central bankers and politicians – ought to play in the formulation, adoption and implementation of economic policies.

Conclusion – network change

We have now gained a clearer understanding of who are the members of the transnational governance network of central bankers. We know more about how they organize themselves and meet in international fora, and about the kinds of public policy produced by this network. We have used data on the background of network members (attributional data), on their mutual relations and patterns of interaction in international fora (relational data) and on the ideas and worldviews shared by network members (ideational data). A general conclusion that comes out of this study concerns the importance of individuals. The core of the transnational network of central bankers is small, coherent and tightly interconnected. Few are the actors that are able to impact decisively on monetary affairs in a globalized economy, but centrally placed central bank governors are among these few actors that effectively can and do make a difference. Thus, worldwide attention is turned towards central bank governors such as Alan Greenspan of the Federal Reserve and Jean-Claude Trichet of the European Central Bank when they convene the international press after committee meetings or make speeches in public. Overall, therefore, the story of central banking is also a story about the power of individuals and their networks in a globalized world (for parallels see Djelic and Kleiner ch. 14).

However, the overall picture we have got is descriptive and static in nature. We have not reported information about whether and under which conditions the network has changed and still does. From a historical perspective, the political authority of central bankers and their position in national decision-making procedures have changed radically. As mentioned, central bankers during the years of the classical Gold Standard at the end of the nineteenth century and the beginning of the twentieth century used to reign supreme when it came to national and international exchange rates and monetary policy. One could argue that the very institution of central banking was constituted in that period (Capie et al. 1994). After the First World War, the Gold Standard was never totally resurrected and the crisis of the 1930s as well as the Second World War formed the basis for an entirely different position of central bankers in macro-economic policy-making. Many central banks were nationalized and, throughout the Bretton Woods period, most central banks were de facto subjugated to national ministries of finance and economics. However, Figure 9.1 illustrated that the pendulum did swing back towards greater authority and independence during the 1980s and particularly since the 1990s. Central bankers have now regained past glory. National as well as international bastions are being constructed on which central bankers can consolidate their power and formulate and implement normative, cognitive and imaginary governance rules. The central bank macro-economic philosophy is now widely accepted and the transnational network of central banks has ample resources at its disposal.

That the pendulum presently is in favor of central bankers does not of course mean that it will never swing back again towards national politicians. One can roughly distinguish between internal and external factors that could bring along change. Internally, replacement on a large scale of central leaders in the most prominent financial institutions could help to alter network structures, procedures and relations. New leaders generally mark their arrival by proposing reforms. This happened when Horst Köhler became Managing Director of the IMF in 2000. He decided to establish working groups and evaluation panels with a view to adapting the IMF to new and pending challenges. The new Managing Director since 7 June 2004, Rodrigo de Rato, continues in the same direction. When Andrew Crockett became General Manager of the BIS on 1 April 1993 one of his priorities was to enlarge membership; he transformed the organization in the process from a narrow European forum to a veritable global central bank organization. His successor since 2003, Malcolm D. Knight, has also started to leave his mark on the BIS. He considers the secretiveness of central banking to be old-fashioned and in direct conflict with the standards that the organization promotes worldwide. The international non-governmental organization One World Trust has recently compared the BIS with other international organizations, both private and public, and it concludes that the BIS is by far the most secretive and inaccessible of all (One World Trust, 2003: v). Among central bankers, the traditionally cryptic and equivocal form of expression has also become a matter for discussion (Blinder et al. 2001; Economist 2003). Small step reforms such as these may gradually change the contours of the network. In the process, the periphery of the network could be getting easier access and more influence over the core. However, we are not talking fundamental reforms and it is unlikely that radical change will be triggered from within the network. Most ordinary members of the central bank network in fact – both in the core and at the periphery – do not explicitly ask for reform, not even for small-scale adaptation.

Hence we propose that network change is more likely to be triggered by outside pressures. Traditionally, the advent of large-scale international crises could seriously challenge the status quo. Historically, world wars also naturally played a role transforming the relationships between central bankers and their standing in national policy-making. Today, global financial crises, such as those in South-East Asia, Russia and South and Central America in the late 1990s, could have the same impact. Neither central bankers individually nor the international central bank organizations were able to act as firefighters during these crises. Politicians could, therefore, start to question the ability and willingness of central bankers to guarantee global financial stability in times of crisis. Yet, this is not what has happened, at least until now. At the level of civil society, however, there is a tendency to express increasing hostility towards an international financial elite that disregards the needs and aspirations of ordinary people. Meetings in the World Bank, OECD, EU and IMF have been criticized by NGOs that call for transparency, democracy, regulation and redistribution. However, we must conclude that so far the transnational governance network of central bankers has been relatively robust in the face of external challenges and that it will take more than diffuse pressure from civil society to change the structures and functions of the network.

Notes

* The author is very grateful for all the continuous help, inspiration and encouragement received from the two editors of this volume.
1. The secretiveness of the central bank community is also emphasized in the classical account of monetary policy-making during Paul A. Volcker's term at the FED (Greider 1987). Tellingly the book has been entitled *Secrets of the Temple – How the Federal Reserve Runs the Country*.
2. Legal or statutory central bank independence is not a binominal either/or phenomenon. More detailed scales of central bank independence have been developed (Cukierman et al. 1992). In the figure central banks are defined as "independent" when such a status is explicitly referred to in the national central bank legislation.
3. J. P. Morgan's *Who's Who* contains information on 130 central bank governors (out of a total population of 160 to 170). Missing countries are the following: Afghanistan, Angola, Bangladesh, Belize, Bhutan, Brunei, Costa Rica, Cuba, Djibouti, East Timor, El Salvador, Ethiopia, Guinea, Guyana, North Korea, Laos, Lesotho, Libya, Madagascar, Mauritania, Morocco, Mozambique, Nauru, Nicaragua, Papua New Guinea, Paraguay, Rwanda, São Tomé and Principe, San Marino, Seychelles, Sudan, Surinam, Syria, Tajikistan, Tanzania, Turkmenistan and Vanuatu.

Information for those countries has been obtained, when available, directly from websites of national central banks.

4. In reverse order of dates of service, the six female members of the Board of Governors of the FED are/were: Susan S. Bies (7 December 2001–present); Alice M. Rivlin (25 June 1996–16 July 1999); Janet L. Yellen (12 August 1994–17 February 1997), Susan M. Philips (2 December 1991–30 June 1995), Martha R. Seger (2 July 1984–11 March 1991) and Nancy H. Teeters (18 September 1978–27 June 1984).

10 Regulated regulators: Global trends of state transformation*

BENGT JACOBSSON

Changes in governance

States are increasingly subjected to numerous forms of regulative, inquisitive and meditative activities. The European Union (EU) is one important example of this expanding governance directed towards states. Structures, processes, and even the policies of European states are typically disciplined by discussions, examinations and rule-making orchestrated by organizations in their environments. As a consequence, these states can be seen less as autonomous rule-making organizations than as organizations deeply embedded in their environments and scripted by wider systems of rules and ideas. This chapter investigates these transformations and the governance activities that define many of the parameters within which states operate. Illustrations are taken primarily from changes in the Nordic states and from the EU as the locus of rule-making, monitoring and discourse. The argument is, however, a more general one.

Despite much talk about globalization and the hollowing out of states, what we see in the world is not that states are becoming less attractive than before: On the contrary, they tend to be more popular than ever. There were 191 states in the United Nations in 2003 compared with 144 in 1975 – and 60 in 1950. Common discussions about a possible "abdication of states" (Ohmae 1995), "retreat of states" (Strange 1996) and "hollowing out of states" obviously have not diminished the desire to create them.

We are witnessing not only a rapid creation of new states, but also transformations in existing ones. To take Europe as an example, membership in the EU went from the original six member states in the 1950s to fifteen by the end of the 1990s. In the spring of 2004 ten more states were added and still more want to join. Membership, however, imposes certain rules. The former Communist states in East and Central Europe have re-structured and re-regulated themselves over the last fifteen years in order to be accepted as members of the EU. Significant changes have been made in structures, policies and activities. However, the older members of the EU have also had to adapt themselves to the emerging policies of the Union. We can observe that European states are not insulated units, but are instead part of fields packed with ideas and rules about how they are to be organized. These ideas and rules influence both state activities and state identities – both what states are able to do and what they are able to be.

A multitude of organizations is involved in the issuing of rules for states and monitoring these rules, as well as in all kinds of consulta- tions, rankings, peer reviews and other discussions concerning states (see Mörth ch. 6; Jacobsson and Sahlin-Andersson ch. 12). The EU is especially relevant for EU states, but among these regulators are also international organizations, such as the United Nations (UN), Inter- national Labour Organization (ILO), International Monetary Fund (IMF) and the World Trade Organization (WTO); non-governmental organizations, such as Amnesty International, the Red Cross, Freedom House, Greenpeace; standardization organizations, such as the Interna- tional Accounting Standards Board (IASB), International Organization for Standardization (ISO), European Committee for Standardization (CEN) and European Communication Standards Institute (ETSI); professional organizations; consultancies corporations and a host of others.

All these organizations are involved in governance activities directed towards states, and governance should here be understood in its broad meaning. These systems of organized governance rarely resemble hier- archies (it is often quite the opposite, there are sometimes strong con- flicts between rule-makers), but are more like loose constellations of different organizations claiming authoritative knowledge about what states should do in specific fields. In this way, states are embedded and enveloped in fields of organized governance.

These systems of governance sometimes take new forms. First, there are regulative activities with formal laws and directives and penal- ties for their violation. EU members, for example, are required to implement the full *acquis communautaire* (that is, the whole body of EU law and practice) while members of the WTO are expected to follow WTO Agreements and accept the Dispute Settlement Proce- dures of that organization. However, there are highly authoritative and influential rule-makers that regulate only through voluntary rules. The

International Organization for Standardization (ISO) and the International Accounting Standards Board (IASB) are examples of this. Standards (Brunsson and Jacobsson 2000) and "soft rules" (Jacobsson and Sahlin-Andersson ch. 12) abound.

We also see this quite remarkable softness in regulation in the EU with its expanded use of an "open method of coordination," for instance in the employment field. Using the open method of coordination usually means that member states have to work towards agreed-upon goals, follow specified procedures, and offer themselves to be critically examined by the Commission and other member states. However, they retain the right to decide about the content of their activities (Jacobsson 2004). The open method of coordination has been a way for the EU to govern without using the traditional community method, which is based on obligatory rules, and it has been used in areas where disagreements about the scope of harmonization preclude more conventional "hard" regulation (Mörth ch. 6).

Second, there are inquisitive activities. This is certainly the case in the above-mentioned open method of coordination. Member states are not obligated to follow certain specific policies, but they are required to "open up" for others to examine and critically judge what they are doing. Generally, we see lots of auditing, comparisons and rankings of state practices. Sometimes the inquisitors evaluate according to rules that they themselves have previously produced (thereby connecting inquisition with rule-making); sometimes they evaluate according to rules produced by some other organization, and sometimes inquisitory activities themselves produce the rules/standards that are used by the scrutinizers.

Several templates have been developed for how to assess, organize and develop states and these are propagated and diffused in the world by organizations such as the OECD, the World Health Organization (WHO) and Transparency International. Some of the organizations that monitor states often have to generate media coverage for their rankings in order to exert any meaningful influence and people in state organizations are often very conscious about the position of their own state (and of other states) in these rankings. All leading politicians in Estonia, Latvia and Lithuania, to take an example, know the exact position of their own state and its neighbors in the corruption ranking developed by Transparency International (Dahl 2004).

Third, there are meditative activities. There are many organizations that function as arenas where state activities are discussed. These organizations do not always claim to have rule-making or enforcement authority. Instead, their activities are more focused on discussing, probing and penetrating. They function as arenas where all kinds of experiences can be transmitted and compared, where ideas are generated and shared. Of course, meditative organizations may sometimes function as arenas where specific ideas are proposed and disseminated, but the implication here is that meditating activities are mainly framed as discussions among experts about what is the best way or ways of doing something. Such discussions can be quite influential.

Meditation could be seen as one specific process, but it can also be seen as one that conditions and envelops other processes. Evaluators and monitors need standards and rules as benchmarks. Rule-makers such as the EU need fora and arenas where logics and consequences of regulation are discussed. Imitation requires activities where potential good examples are produced. And those that want to be seen as innovators always need to have a supply of good stories and reform proposals to collect from as they bring together and promulgate their own innovations. All these processes are embedded in discourses about what kinds of structures, policies and activities modern states should have. The EU often functions as an arena where ideas and models are presented and discussed.

Why would states and other organizations follow rules without being formally required to? In some ways, the would-be rule-maker has to create an authoritative position for itself. This is frequently done, for example, by claiming special expertise (Jacobsson 2000). Experts often claim a scientific basis for their knowledge (see Drori and Meyer ch. 2). Another strategy is to borrow authority from other rule-makers who are perceived as legitimate. Here we can talk of governance clusters – complexes of rules and rule-makers that may be extremely difficult for states and other organizations to forget about. Concerning financial markets, for instance, the International Monetary Fund (IMF) is the central actor in a cluster consisting of a variety of organizations (both public and private) working for macro-economic and financial stability.

Some aspects of the governance dynamics in the world have changed towards more voluntary abiding and partnership – towards a form of regulated autonomy (Knill and Lehmkuhl 2002). In various fields, extensive discussions are going on about how states need to act to be considered progressive and modern. In the EU, enlargement has clearly bolstered such discussions along with the multiplication of assessments, audits and certification activities. The so-called "candidate states" were forced to present themselves in accordance with the common official values of the European society in which they wanted to participate. This has necessitated both idealized presentations and some decorous ceremonies (cf. Goffman 1959).

The overall picture presented here shows that there is a fair amount of governance activity directed towards states, combining traditional instruments with softer forms of regulation. The question explored in the next sections of this chapter is: what impact do these changes in governance practices have for the operations of states? The discussion is based on the experience of four states in the European "periphery" – Denmark, Finland, Norway (not a member of the EU) and Sweden – and how these comparatively resourceful states with vast capacities adapt to rules and ambitions in the EU. These examples are more than special cases, though; they say something general about the transformation of states.

Europeanization and the transformation of states

The forms of governance discussed above can be observed in Europe – mostly in connection to the EU. Since large portions of the populations of European countries have been quite skeptical about being controlled from Brussels, Strasbourg and Frankfurt, attempts at coordinated action have frequently been carried out rather cautiously. The ambition has been to strike a balance between the perceived necessity for harmonization, on the one hand, and the desire for autonomy and celebration of national cultural differences, on the other. Subsidiarity has been both a catchword and an organizing principle, although its precise meaning has been a subject of dispute. These tensions have given rise to rule-making that combines legally binding forms with voluntary elements.

In this section I try to make sense of some of the transformations that have taken place as Nordic state administrations have increasingly become integrated in the European polity (see Jacobsson et al. 2003). Note that the focus here is not primarily on "policy changes" but on the administrative aspects of Europeanization: how issues are organized and controlled; how relations between politicians, civil servants and experts are affected; how national actorhood is created etc. I emphasize three important changes: the first is an increase in embeddedness within the European spheres; the second a development where states to a large extent become rule followers in Europe; and, third, a tendency towards the fragmentation of states. I discuss each of these tendencies in turn.

Embedded states

Nordic state administrations have become increasingly embedded in European networks – to such an extent that we now may speak of the emergence of a transnational administration (Jacobsson et al. 2003). Central administrations have undergone significant changes and Europeanization has led to major alterations in both the structure and mode of operation. In fact, few of the important administrative units in the Nordic states have been wholly unaffected by the EU within their respective fields of activity. The administrative units within the Nordic states devote a considerable proportion of their time to EU affairs and they are significantly affected by the EU within their various fields of activity. Many administrative units have cultivated extensive involvement in Brussels, especially in connection to the Commission and its subsidiary bodies.

One may question the extent to which elected national politicians control these expanded transnational activities. Contacts between the political and administrative levels are not particularly intense, although there are exceptions (especially Sweden). These contacts are largely informal and when taking part in EU activities, many units have to manage either without political guidelines or with only general indications. For many, tight time schedules make it difficult to refer questions to the political leadership. The overall impression is that elected politicians are relatively passive in relation to EU affairs. Many issues are entrusted to specialists and experts, and most state units have no major difficulties getting their views accepted by their government and in political circles.

In a sense, this is the organizational version of the democratic deficit. Compared with the elected politicians in their countries, citizens in the Nordic countries have been hesitant about European integration. It is also apparent that civil servants in the central bureaucracy are even more enthusiastic about the EU than politicians. This may of course be a result of private factors (such as increasing opportunities to enjoy Belgian beers and Gaudian architecture) but it is also a result of the new possibilities to discuss problems and compare similarities and differences in administrative traditions.

We observe numerous interactions across national borders and there is considerable travel to and from Brussels – enough that we could almost talk of the Nordic states as traveling states. Many organizational units in the Nordic states have seconded staff to EU organizations as national experts. Participation in networks with EU organizations is high (Kohler-Koch and Eising 1999). This networking also seems to reinforce contacts between state bureaucrats on the one hand and representatives from interest organizations, private companies, NGOs, etc. on the other. Effects of this networking are felt by elected politicians and civil servants in senior positions, but also further down in the hierarchy, by agencies and relatively low-level specialists (Mörth 1996).

Embeddeness is partly about increased interaction and contacts. It also has to do with the fact that states are becoming integrated in and enveloped by wider European and global schemes of rules and ideas. The organization and governing rules of the Swedish competition authorities are copied from the European organization (see Djelic and Kleiner ch. 14). The Swedish finance inspectorate is influenced by developments in the global financial regulatory fields – that is, in the International Organization of Securities Commissions (IOSCO). The national audit office in Sweden learns about how auditing should be carried out in relation to ideas and rules developed by the International Organization of Supreme Audit Institutions (INTOSAI). It is easy to multiply these examples. Below, I return to this point as an illustration of the increasing scriptedness of states.

A puzzling feature is that embeddedness tends to re-create states as important actors. More than ever, there has been a production of national strategies, interests, positions, etc., and Europeanization seems to be an important factor in this. In the early phase of membership, Swedish national administrators were facing strong demands to present, for instance "the position of Sweden" (even concerning issues where nobody before ever had been thinking about such things as Swedish positions). As a result, formal and informal groups were formed in the state organizations, and national positions and strategies were produced.

Europeanization in this way seems to raise strong demands on states to become "real" organizational actors. And we have never seen such an expansion of state strategies and activities as has occurred during the past decade. However, the other side of the coin is that to a large extent, state organizations learn about "what to do" and "what to be" in the wider European systems that they are now part of. On the one hand, Europeanization puts strong demands on states to present themselves as coherent and coordinated national actors. On the other hand, it is within the wider European environment and its structuring scripts that states learn how to present themselves as such actors.

Scripted states

The second argument was touched upon earlier. We can speak of the increased scriptedness of states in that states may act less as autonomous rule-makers and more as embedded rule-followers or rule enforcers. As mentioned earlier, states and their component parts are connected to broader environments of organized rule-making. The EU is obviously important in all this. In exchange for the anticipated benefits of joining an organization such as the EU, a state promises to comply with the rules and accept the enforcement procedures of the Union. In this way, membership becomes one strong regulative mechanism (see also Jacobsson and Sahlin-Andersson ch. 12; Ahrne and Brunsson ch. 4).

The enlargement process provides a useful illustration. Many activities of the candidate states to the EU focused on how to (re-)construct themselves as legitimate states in the framework of the Union. Since the candidate states wanted to become members of the EU, they had to prove that they were able to live up to the full *acquis communautaire*. There are also other rules that need to be followed for states to qualify as members. States should be market economies, democracies, ruled by law, non-corrupt and they should have organizations and administrative systems that make it possible to implement EU rules.

The EU created numerous mechanisms to facilitate this process of (re-)creation by candidate countries. In so-called twinning projects one or more of the "old" members helped candidate states to create a more efficient organization or an acceptable policy program. Twinning projects were organized in diverse fields of activity, generally involving some form of imitation and/or learning processes organized around

EU rule systems. Sweden, for example, was involved in seventy-three twinning projects with ten of the candidate states (Svensson 2003).

Another mode of governance entails various forms of scrutiny (Boli ch. 5; Jacobsson and Sahlin-Andersson ch. 12). As discussed above, audits, evaluations, reporting and accounting systems and more general assessments, comparisons and rankings directed towards states have expanded and become widespread. It has become part of everyday life for states and separate state organizations to be scrutinized by the EU. According to the European Employment Strategy and the so-called Luxemburg process, the Commission and the Council jointly scrutinize the national actions plans of member countries. The Council may also, on the basis of this, issue country-specific recommendations intended to bring attention to an issue or to suggest corrective action. Such recommendations can be seen as standards – that is, as soft rules that may or may not be followed. This is an example of "the open method of coordination" where common objectives are set in the EU, but the means to carry out the implementation necessary to achieve these objectives is left to member states. The success of the strategy is said to rely on the use of quantified measurements, targets and benchmarks that make it possible to allow for ". . . proper monitoring and evaluation of progress." Through the use of targets and indicators, the results of policies are made transparent and therefore open to public scrutiny. This is the idea of the employment strategy and of the Lisbon process, but it is also the favored working method in other fields.

So, the EU consists of different governance mechanisms. With respect to the internal market there are mandatory rules. In community legislation, states are required to follow the rules. Community law has priority over any conflicting law of the member states and national courts (if they are involved) have to give effect to EU legislation. There may be penalties for non-compliance. The open method of coordination is an example of less coercive forms of rule-making. There are even softer and more meditative forms. In health policy (which is still seen as primarily a national responsibility) there are processes that do not fall under the open method of coordination but allow open consultation and shared reflection. In consultation processes, states agree to talk and reflect together with others, but not necessarily to follow up with action.

Hence, EU states are scripted actors and scriptedness comes in different forms. It is also necessary to point to the coevolution of states and rules. States are part of the processes where rules are produced according to the community method. They are very much involved in benchmarking and scrutinizing processes connected to the open method of coordination. And they are the central actors in reflection and consultation processes. So, the situation is not one where states are following rules produced by "outside" actors. Quite the contrary: states are following rules they themselves have produced, at least in combination and discussion with other states.

Fragmented states

A third observation is the tendency toward fragmentation within states (cf. O'Riain 2001). Organizations in the Nordic states sometimes seem to be closely connected to actors, arenas and discussions in "their own" specific sector environments in other states and in European organizations, while less connected to actors, arenas and discussions in "their own" state. This tends to disrupt the established hierarchies within the states and raises questions about the relevance of the formal organizational structures.

One example of this fragmentation is the development of competition agencies in individual member states. Those agencies are set in a field where there are mandatory rules that all member states are expected to follow, and national competition agencies in all EU states have become advocates of EU rules and of the ideas sustaining the rules – in particular markets and competition (see Djelic ch. 3). Since 2001, all European agencies work together in an informal network called the European Competition Authorities (ECA). ECA is a forum for discussion between competition agencies relayed and reinforced by a parallel global network, the International Competition Network (ICN) (see Djelic and Kleiner ch. 14). This is an example where national competition agencies may have more in common with national competition agencies in other states than they have with other agencies in their own state.

In areas where national agencies are highly embedded in transnational and European networks and in systems of rules and ideas, there are clear risks (or possibilities, some may say) that identities and loyalties will develop in these sector networks. This may be especially important in fields where ideas and systems of rules dominate that put strong emphasis on markets and competition (and stigmatize state intervention). But it may also be the case in fields where there are strong professional traditions, epistemic communities or belief in expertise (cf. Marcussen ch. 9).

These fragments of states do not always consist of a single specific organization. There are instances where, for example, one section in one agency, two sections in another agency, one section in a government ministry, together with people from private corporations, could form the national node in European exchanges. Here one may speak about enclaves in the states (Vifell 2002) where people cooperate, discuss issues, form national positions and meet officials in their specific field in other countries. These informal networks are important in policy formation processes within the EU.

The described embeddedness, scriptedness and fragmentation of nation-states stand in sharp contrast to conventional conceptualizations where states are typically conceptualized as sovereign, autonomous and coherent actors and as the only authoritative rule-makers in their own territories. The picture presented here is more one in which states function in environments that are organized and regulated in ways that exert enormous influence on both their activities and their identities. Organizations in the environment of states have different functions. Classical rule-making directed towards states is only one of them. Other such functions include the inquisitive activities performed by organizations involved in the certification, monitoring and ranking of states. Still others include the meditative functions where organizations serve as arenas for discussions, dialogues, problem solving, learning, etc.

Understanding scriptedness

Above, I have outlined three tendencies that can be observed in the Europeanization of the administrations of Nordic states. I have emphasized that states (or parts of states) are situated in different kinds of regulatory fields (cf. Hedmo et al. ch. 15) and that activities in these fields influence state practices (both what states say and what they do). I have claimed that states are scripted. They follow rules (and rules should, of course, here be understood in the widest sense). In this section I will develop the discussion of this scriptedness of states.

Rule-following obviously is not a straightforward process with a one-to-one relationship between the content of the rules and the form of implementation. As we know from studies on reforms and changes in all kinds of organizations, lots of things may happen on the road from talk to action. First – and this may be obvious – the nature of the rules will be likely to have an impact on the degree to which they are followed. Establishing new rules is easier if those rules are general and no sanctions are involved. And as we have seen, rules come in different forms in the EU: regulations, frameworks, directives, guidelines, recommendations, co-regulatory mechanisms, etc.

A special feature of rule-making in the EU is the comparatively tight links that exist between rule-makers and rule-followers. Those who produce the rules are also largely those who have to implement the rules. There is a reciprocity here that sometimes is missing in other instances of rule-making. If there is large variation among potential rule-followers (differences in ambitions, strategies, capacities etc.), we will probably also get rules that allow for differences in implementation. For instance, as the number of members in the EU grows, we will probably see changes in rule-making favoring rules that focus more on procedures than content, more on objectives than specific means, etc. In other words, we are likely to see more rules that allow for variation in implementation.

Following scripts always involves some degree of translation (Czarniawska and Sevon 1996). There is never any form of automatic compliance with rules. Even as we talk about the directives concerning the internal market, there are systematic differences in rule-following. Some countries are consistently worse than others in contributing to this "transposition deficit." According to the scoreboard from July 2004 from the European Commission, France had the worst record followed by Greece, Germany, Italy and the Benelux countries. There are also infringement cases where states are, according to the Commission, incorrectly applying the directives, and here Italy tops the list, closely followed by France.

As we move to softer forms, we have even more leeway for translation. It is also important to stress that these translations take place in specific historical and institutional contexts (Sahlin-Andersson 1996; Djelic 1998). Factors such as different administrative traditions, state capacities and strategies may influence the way in which rules will be followed. It seems to be the case – if we judge from the Commission scoreboard – that those countries that have been quite critical of the integrative ambitions in the EU (the UK, Denmark, Sweden) actually seem to follow the rules more carefully than some of the EU enthusiasts.

Following a rule usually means establishing some degree of consistency between what the rule prescribes and what one actually does. This consistency can be created in two ways: either by changing practice to fit the rule, or by changing the presentation of practice in accordance with the rule. In the first case the rule is said to be implemented. This means, first, that the rule is translated into what the follower does (translation from talk to action) and, second, that the general requirements of the rule are translated into the follower's own specific practice (translation from the general to the specific). However, implementation as it is talked about in the EU often means that the European rule has been transposed into a national rule, which may or may not have any effect on actual practices.

When we talk about softer rules (such as in the open method of coordination), the question is not whether or not the rule is implemented, but in what ways the rule-follower makes sure that the common objectives are met. In this case it is important how state organizations present what they are doing. They may not have to change their practices at all, but only make sure that activities that may have been going on for a long time are reported in accordance with the rule. Practices can be generalized in ways that make it possible to present the organization as a serious rule-follower.

Since it is often unclear what kind of practice may be presented as conforming with a rule, states may have considerable freedom to decide whether or not to change existing practices or how much to change them. This freedom grows with the softness of regulation. Often a stepwise approach is used: first testing whether an existing practice can be translated into the rule and then – only if this translation is not credible enough – taking the trouble to change existing practice. The possibilities of such strategies are dependent on the degree of openness. People outside the specific organization may have a poor insight into the actual activities of the organization.

This raises the question of to what extent the expansion of rules in the EU will lead to increasing homogeneity between the different states. To some extent, this seems to be obvious. Rule-following concerning the rules connected to the internal market is not something that can take place in secret. The European Commission is eager to monitor, measure and announce both to what extent different countries follow the rules and whether they do it in the proper way. This will increase homogeneity to some extent at least, not only in structures and procedures but also in actual operations and practices.

Reflections on states in complex regulatory fields

What can be said about the position of states with these observations in mind? How can we depict the role of states in these emerging fields of regulation in Europe and in the world? Arguments about a retreat or abdication of states clearly miss the point. States are still important actors, but not in the way usually understood. Most perspectives (especially within the international relation tradition) see states as purposive and rational actors that know what they want. Those perspectives are based on the idea that states "have" interests and use their power to pursue or safeguard these interests. Sometimes, networks and interdependencies between states are stressed and sometimes, in more elaborate versions, it is also acknowledged that these actions and interactions take place in institutional frameworks that form constraints (but constraints previously created by purposive actors).

Such a perspective, however, makes little sense if we want to understand the processes where states adapt to the EU. If we take, for instance, the work with the employment strategy in the new member states, it is obvious that it was the involvement in the EU that in the first place created the specific strategies and all the structural and procedural arrangements. Goals and strategies (in this specific field normally phrased in terms such as employability, entrepreneurship, adaptability, equal opportunity) were quite easily imported and used. But they did not exist as a concrete framework until integrative processes started to reshape the goals and preferences of the respective state organizations. More than as a process where states' interests are articulated and played out, what could be observed was a process where interests were constructed along the way.

Conceptualizing and understanding states as complex organizations (like other complex organizations) as is done in this chapter makes it possible to relate to some significant thought in organizational theory (March and Simon 1958; Cyert and March 1963; March 1981, 1994). Ever since the late 1950s, studies have repeatedly challenged the view of organizations as units that make rational decisions that are implemented in a straightforward way (which is quite a common way to understand the role of states). A more complex image of organizations has emerged where processes may be solution-driven more than problem-driven, and where search and attention are important concepts. As we have seen, solutions in terms of strategies, goals, structures, procedures have in the European context been quite easy to demand and import.

To say that organizations learn what they want (preferences) as well as what they are (identities) in these processes (March and Olsen 1989), challenges the rationalistic view where leadership knows what it wants and tries to act to realize these interests. In cases where preferences are ambiguous, non-stable and changing, it is more useful and interesting to find out how such preferences are formed and shaped. And for the new as well as the older member states of the EU, there are lots of arrangements that drive preference-formation. As outlined above, states are embedded actors and they often learn both what is reasonable to think and what is possible to present in terms of strategies through this wider European environment and its associated scripts.

To use this perspective to understand the transformation of states seems like a promising path to pursue. States or parts of states could be seen as boundedly rational (rather than perfectly rational actors), as entities that learn what they want and what they are over time (rather than keeping preferences and identities stable), as rule-following actors (rather than as actors choosing on the basis of estimated consequences), as full of conflicts (rather than as actors where there is agreement around goals), as actors that are embedded in relations both to other organizations and to a wider environment of rules and regulations (rather than being independent).

De-coupling may be a common way to handle conflicting demands in state organizations. We could portray states as attending to goals sequentially (Cyert and March 1963) or in parallel (Jacobsson 1987); we could portray them as consisting of different units with local rationalities (that may be European and global). And we may see lots of de-coupling not only between organizational units in the state, but also between how states actually perform their daily activities and how they present themselves. Since the states accepted as members of the EU are very different from each other in terms of capacities and administrative traditions, we could expect more than a modest amount of de-coupling.

This is surely not to say that states are no longer important, but rather that their importance could be interpreted somewhat differently than is usually done. Basically the argument here is one that stresses logics of appropriateness (March and Olsen 1989, March 1994). States as well as specific parts of states are connected to wider environments of organized rule-making. EU member states adapt to different kinds of European scripts, but, as was pointed out, this adaptation also typically involves some reformulation and amendment of the script by the designated rule-follower. The EU is obviously important in all this, but the argument is a general one.

States are complex organizations that want to live up to obligations and rules in their complex environments. And as they try to fulfill their identities ". . . they follow rules or procedures that they see as appropriate to the situation in which they find themselves" (March 1994: 57). If the state in question wants to be perceived as modern and legitimate, then there are rules governing how one should go about achieving that. These processes can be complicated but the basic features are, first, one of establishing identities (for instance as a modern European state) and, second, one of matching rules to recognized situations. These rules (remember that rules are defined in a very wide sense) should not be seen as located somewhere "outside" the micro processes of adaptation. They are not merely a context for behavior – a result of micro processes on a "higher level."

Rules are produced in organizations and they are communicated, supplied and legitimized in processes where organizations and individuals take part. These processes of rule-making may take place in many different kinds of organizations. One should not make too sharp a distinction between rule-making, rule-monitoring and rule-following. Organizations can sometimes be involved in all these processes. Take for instance the EU where states obviously are rule-makers (together with other member states) but also rule-followers and involved in rule-monitoring. To frame all states as scripted and the processes as permeated by logics of appropriateness does not mean that actors are in any way predetermined in how they will do things. They should not be seen as cultural dopes, but as intentional, willful and sometimes even quite capable of strategic maneuvering. There is room for agency – or as March said: ". . . since identities and rules rarely specify everything unambiguously, motivational, cognitive, and organizational factors play a role in determining behavior within the identities and rules evoked" (March 1994: 68).

The idea of a logic of appropriateness has very little to do with any thoughtlessness on the part of those following the scripts. But the thinking in the processes studied is more related to identities and rules than to preferences and expectations. This perspective highlights the regulative activities and it clearly relates to basic ideas in sociology that there are strong institutional structures – rules and norms – that make exchanges between organizations possible (Meyer et al. 1997). Exchanges between states and in markets are seen as legitimated by a wider cultural system that justifies exchanges, by claiming for example that they are fair, progressive and beneficial (cf. Djelic ch. 3). This cultural system also defines actors (individuals and states), contributes to and justifies exchanges that otherwise would not have taken place.

In this line of thinking, Boli and Thomas (1999) described the expansion of a political community in the world, where international non-governmental organizations function to a large extent as carriers of a world culture. Changes happen since ". . . all sorts of actors learn to define themselves and their interests from the global cultural and organizational structures in which they are embedded" (Boli and Thomas 1999: 4). This means that states do not wither away but are instead reconstituted as important actors. Or, as Meyer and his associates phrase it:

A considerable body of evidence supports our proposition that world-society models shape nation-state identities, structures, and behavior via worldwide cultural and associational processes . . . As creatures of exogenous world culture, states are ritualized actors marked by extensive internal decoupling and a good deal more structuration than would occur if they were responsive only to local cultural, functional, or power processes. (Meyer et al. 1997: 173)

Meyer and his colleagues argue that ". . . the culture of world society allocates responsible and authoritative actorhood to nation-states" (1997: 169) and that states in their actions and activities incorporate general principles that to a large extent are worldwide. States may pursue their own "interests" but those interests are defined in a context of values and models that are more universal, resulting in more similarities between states than would be expected if all states chose on the basis of their own local traditions and interests.

Conclusions

States are often presented as autonomous – as organizational units that decide for themselves and form their own preferences, strategies and positions. They are presented as actors that are coordinated and coherent. Some kind of aggregation of preferences and goals is assumed to take place. And states are described as regulatory actors – as organizational units that with the help of rules and rule-enforcement procedures are able to decide about the lives of those individuals within a particular geographical area. This "command-and-control" model of states is still popular, and it certainly dominates the reform agenda in states. There are also some elements of truth in this image of states. From what we have learned, however, we may also describe states in a different way.

A more complex picture has emerged that stresses states as both autonomous *and* embedded. States do produce strategies and national positions and in fact at an increasing rate and speed in Europe during the 1990s. The ritualistic presentation of sovereign and autonomous states is everywhere to be seen. Still, strategies and positions are not created in isolation, but in exchanges with others (EU organizations, agencies in other states, interest organizations, corporations etc.) and they are embedded and enveloped in wider systems of discourse, examinations and rule-making. States and their organizational sub-parts are set within fields that condition the development of wishes, strategies and worldviews.

States are both coherent *and* fragmented. Over the last decades, we have seen significant attempts to create consistency, coordination and common positions across European states. Much effort has been put into the creation of coordination and control in state administrations. Simultaneously policies are formed in segments that transcend national borders. Policies emerge and are formed within transnational networks. This is a challenge for governments. We get more fragmentation, and the gap widens between what state politicians are held responsible for, on the one hand, and what they actually are able to influence, on the other. Another problem is that these transnational networks are frequently less transparent than most of us would like.

States are both regulators *and* regulated. States still produce rules. More than ever before, however, their work seems to be to make sure that rules issued by other organizations (EU, UN, WTO, IASB etc.) are followed inside their own territory. This does not mean a withdrawal or hollowing out of states. In many fields, it is through states that global rules are implemented and legitimized. For member states in the EU, it is a necessity to have the capacity to implement the full *acquis communautaire*, but it also necessary to follow other kinds of rules, to be monitored by others and to take part in reflections about all kinds of policies and problems.

Thus, despite much talk about globalization and the retreat of states, we see that states are not becoming less attractive than before. Nevertheless, the role of states is in flux. In order to understand what this means, I have argued that it is necessary to consider the organizational fields that states are part of: involving regulative, inquisitive and meditative activities. I have also argued that instead of autonomous and coordinated rule-making organizations, states should be seen as organizations (a) deeply embedded in their environments, (b) severely fragmented; and (c) scripted by wider systems of rules and ideas.

In a way, this idea about the scriptedness of states resembles society-centered traditions where states are interpreted as mainly responding to the demands of powerful societal interests. However, as I argued above, scriptedness does not mean that states should be seen as largely passive and unassuming agents. States (or parts of states) also seek to influence rule-making, examinations and discussions. European scripts are a collective product of all the states in the EU, even if some exercise greater influence than others – and even if they individually become subject to the parameters that emerge from such processes. If other organizations such as corporations, interest groups, NGOs, etc. really want to influence European rule-making, sometimes the only way to do this is through their own state. The path into policy formation processes in the EU, quite frequently, passes through state organizations and state officials.

States also matter because they remain one of the most important sources of authority. What we see is the emergence of new forms of governance in combination with the old. We see new types of rule-makers as well as, at least partly, new types of rules. But it is not at all obvious how such forms of governance are to be legitimated. The IASB, which is a (private) standards organization that has become one of the most important rule-makers for financial accounting, has created its position partly as a result of its expertise (see Botzem and Quack ch. 13 for an extended analysis). However, the IASB's legitimacy and position are also a function of the fact that it has been able to connect to organizations such as the IOSCO and the EU. The IASB has in this way been able to borrow legitimacy from organizations consisting of states. States matter because it is difficult to expand such forms of governance if these are not in some way legitimated by states (see also Engels ch. 16; McNichol ch. 17).

Thus, states do not wither away. Instead, they are transformed and re-constituted as important actors through Europeanization and transnationalization. States are generally part of rule-making, examination and meditation processes. They guarantee that rules are implemented (not always perfectly but at least to some extent). And they are crucial actors when it comes to legitimizing new forms of governance. States ought not to be undervalued in the discussions about new forms of governance. However, the main argument in the paper is that states are themselves subject to various forms of governance. State identities, structures and behavior are shaped via processes of supranational and transnational rule-making, inquisition and meditation. The preferences and strategies of states are to a large extent constructed within a context conditioned by these wider systems of governance. Of course, states still have ambitions to govern and sometimes they can do this successfully. More than ever before, however, states have become regulated regulators.

Note

* The author thanks Marcus Carson, Per Lægreid, John W. Meyer, Ove Kai Pedersen, Göran Sundström and the two editors of this volume for comments on earlier versions.

11 The rationalization of universities

FRANCISCO O. RAMIREZ

Introduction

Universities are increasingly influenced by a common logic of mass higher education suggesting they become broadly inclusive, socially useful,[1] and flexible organizations. For European universities this common logic is most clearly expressed in the Bologna Declaration and resonates with the European Union as a source of legitimate university identity. This logic emerged earlier in America, can be traced back to at least the late nineteenth century, and persists in the present. Not surprisingly a number of scholars comment on the Americanization of European universities (e.g. Rupp 1997). More indirectly the coming of the entrepreneurial (read American) university to Europe is hailed as salvation in some analyses (Clark 1993) and in others as tantamount to the university losing its soul (Readings 1996).

This chapter is agnostic on the deeply normative character of the debates on the future of the university. Its goals are as follows:

1. To demonstrate that universities are changing towards greater inclusiveness, usefulness, and flexibility.
2. To contend that these changes are driven not solely by rational adaptations to environmental changes but require and are propelled by general rationalizing accounts; and lastly
3. To suggest that these changes are further enhanced by the rationalization of universities as organizations and the corresponding decline of tradition and charisma as legitimating sources of university identity.

Throughout this chapter a core idea is that the logic of mass higher education is rooted in universalistic models of progress and justice that transcend the national ecologies of universities.

These universalistic models are transnational in character and parallel the transnationalization of the authority of science and the professions on the one hand, and on the other, the authority of the person and the value of individual choice and participation (see Drori and Meyer ch. 2). The emphasis on broad inclusion is no doubt linked to the triumph of democratic ideals (see Mörth ch. 6). These ideals emphasize the value of higher education for all and make earlier elite forms of higher education morally suspect. The logic of mass higher education calls for broad inclusion with respect to the "personnel" in universities but also as regards its curricula. Satisfying this logic should result in increased access and diversity with respect to the composition of the university and increased diversity and flexibility as regards what constitutes university knowledge.

The transformation of university knowledge reflects market forces. The latter may in part account for the rise in the "practical arts" but not for the increase in identity focused subject matter. Both changes, we contend, are driven by the rise of the socially useful university ideal. This ideal fosters a more open university where new forms of knowledge are readily imaginable and their scholarly pursuit is highly legitimate. Within this ideal universities look to the future to rationalize and justify their persistence and maintenance. To become more broadly accessible and socially useful, universities are increasingly expected to become more organizationally flexible. What these changes undercut is the university as the institutional embodiment of high culture and canonical knowledge.

These universalistic and transnational models increasingly operate as "soft law" and become an important feature of the institutional governance of universities. (see Jacobsson and Sahlin-Andersson ch. 12; Mörth ch. 6). Soft law can start with a declaration of principles by ministers of education and then become a standard for monitoring and assessing national systems of higher education. The Bologna effort to institutionalize a European higher education area has been analyzed along this line (Tomusk 2004; Baert and Shipman 2005). Soft law can be formalized through accreditation bodies but it can also operate informally through rankings of universities that convey both diffuse and specific reputational pluses and minuses. Though they obviously lack bureaucratic teeth, these rankings foster standardization, as universities become more aware of where they stand relative to peers and "competitors" and what they can do to upgrade their reputation.

In what follows I reflect on each of the three core elements of the changing university profile: broad accessibility, social usefulness, and organizational flexibility. I contrast this profile with an earlier one which favored the university as a more restricted or specialized, socially

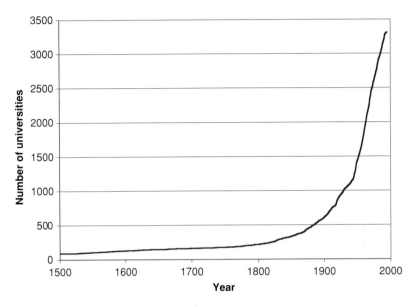

Figure 11.1 The global expansion of universities.

buffered, and more rigid or coherent institution. The rationalization of the university, I conclude, is further enhanced by its emergence and development as an organization. (see Ahrne and Brunsson ch. 4). This dynamic is linked to transnational trends in organizing, trends that often lead universities to engage in planning, data gathering about themselves, and advertising.

The broadly inclusive university

The most striking fact about higher education is its phenomenal growth after the Second World War. Although the United States attained much higher enrollment levels earlier on, it is no longer an outlier. Between 1965 and 1995 among Western countries the growth in national average tertiary enrollment ratios soared from 10 to nearly 45 percent (Ramirez 2002). True, some of the expanded enrollments are found in two-year community colleges in the United States and in new post-secondary institutes in other countries. But university enrollments have also sharply increased (Schofer and Meyer 2004). Moreover this world-wide phenomenon has clearly involved the expansion of universities, not just the enrollments therein. Figure 11.1 traces the worldwide growth of universities from 1500 to the present. There is steady though modest growth until the middle of the nineteenth century where a first spike becomes evident. The movement is from fewer than 500 universities worldwide to over 1,000 by 1950. A second and more dramatic spike results in close to 3,500 universities by 2000. Most universities in the world today were in fact founded after the Second World War (Riddle 1989). So, what started as a medieval undertaking in Western Europe initially legitimated by papal decrees, is today a worldwide phenomenon in part legitimated in organizational density or structuration terms.

Between its medieval roots and its current forms, universities in Europe were unabashedly elitist. Moreover, exclusivity in some of the leading universities could be explicitly defended on social class grounds, not merely on the premise that very high standards weed out all but the most talented scholars. The dual admissions system at Oxford, for example, where some men were admitted because they were promising scholars and others because they were promising gentlemen, could be explicitly articulated on those grounds. Well into the twentieth century the literary luminary T. S Eliot would write:

The idea of an educational system which would automatically sort out everyone according to his native capacities is unattainable in practice; and if we made it our chief aim, would disorganize society and debase education. It would disorganize society by substituting for classes elites of brains, or perhaps, only of sharp wits. (1968: 177 cited in Soares 1999: 49)

For Eliot and others, universities would be foolish not to facilitate class reproduction and the reproduction of social order itself by admitting promising gentlemen. The latter had already undergone the kinds of familial socialization experiences that would enable them better to appreciate what universities had to offer. In modern parlance investment in gentlemen would yield a higher socio-cultural rate of return to the national society. Destined to be its future leaders these gentlemen needed Oxford and Oxford needed them.

This elitist perspective manifests itself anew in the thesis that too many Americans act as if there were "no salvation outside higher education" (Shills 1971). Notions like the "diploma disease" (Dore 1976) or the "overeducated American" (Freeman 1976) or more recent efforts to curb higher education in the former Communist countries (Lenhardt and Stock 2000) already imagined a higher education/occupation link. But it was a manpower planning logic in which a finite set of jobs required a finite set of skilled personnel. Too many educated people were a problem because it was economically inefficient, not because it was a cultural or social disaster. The current and dominant logic rejects the naturalness of class-based leadership as unjust and reaches the conclusion that everyone can benefit from higher education and that societies everywhere benefit from expanded higher education. There is indeed much evidence that raises questions about the utility of higher education especially at the societal level (see Chabbott and Ramirez 2000 for a review of the evidence), but the massification of higher education is indisputable (Altbach 1999). Massification is not just an observable phenomenon, but one subjected to a contemporary rationalizing account emphasizing justice and progress.

Nowhere is this worldwide rationalizing account more evident than when dealing with the issue of women in higher education. The failure of universities to admit more women is critiqued both on the ground that this is a waste of human capital and that it is a violation of women's human rights. This two-pronged account is found in self-examinations in universities, national reports, and quite prominently in cross-national assessments (e.g. European Technology Network on Women and Science 2000). But in fact women have made significant strides in higher education. Among Western countries between 1965 and 1995 women's share of higher education increased from less than 33 percent to some 45 percent of total enrollments (Bradley and Ramirez 1996). Between 1972 and 1992 women's share of science and engineering enrollments among Western countries increased from 17.2 percent to 24.8 percent (Ramirez and Wotipka 2001). Even at highly prestigious universities the trend is towards greater gender parity: Soares (1999) finds that fewer than one out of five Oxford undergraduates were women in 1923 in contrast to more than four out of ten by 2000. The massification of higher education has also meant feminization, at least, with respect to student composition.

The composition of the university, however, once limited to the clerical estate, was no trivial matter. Just as one could imagine the university as a socially exclusive club and worry about the erosive effects of an aristocracy of brains or wits, so too universities could be imagined as exclusive enclaves for men. The German variant strongly linked academic citizenship with masculinity. As late as 1897 a law professor would express a common fear among German academics: "We are at a critical time. The German people have other things to do besides undertaking risky experiments with women's higher education. Let us ensure above all that our men remain men!" (cited in Mazon 2003).

Not only was it feared that scholarship standards would be diluted to accommodate women; worse, it was feared that the transition from gymnasium boys to university men would be compromised. Note that at this time women were also barred from the Ivy League and from universities in other Western countries. A century later not only are women a commonplace across Western universities but nowhere do exclusionary rationales command much serious attention.

It is difficult today to think of universities as elite institutions given their ever-increasing numbers. This is not to argue that every Western university is as accessible along class and gender lines as every other Western university. The point is that all universities act as if the changing class and gender composition makes sense and reflects justice and progress ideals. University laggards along these dimensions commission studies and make plans to catch up and look like legitimate universities. The detection of old and the discovery of new barriers to equality owes much of its success and momentum to the triumph of highly theorized egalitarian standards (Ramirez 2002).

In an earlier era one could straightforwardly discuss access barriers and these still exist in some prestigious universities. But for the most part the barriers are cast in curricular terms and here there are fundamental questions: What counts as knowledge in the university? Who are to be its producers, caretakers, and teachers? Under what conditions will production, conservation, and transmission take place?

These questions are raised within a broader culture in which assessments and comparisons can function as governance and regulatory mechanisms (see Hedmo et al. ch. 15) Within the United States for example, federal funds can be withheld from universities that fail to demonstrate a commitment to providing women with equal opportunities to engage in competitive athletics. There are lively debates on what constitutes sufficient evidence of commitment and experts on both sides present their scientific views. Access to the university thus means access to a range of activities within the university and this leads to more specialized quantification than simply overall enrollment counts. These assessments and comparisons need not involve government bureaucracies but could stem instead from the organizing activities of professional associations. By means of a rating system professional associations can thus also become part of the broader governance structure.

The Sociologists For Women in Society, for example, seek to rate sociology departments for their gender and for their woman-friendliness by reporting on the percentage of full-time faculty who are women and the percentage of full-time faculty with research and teaching specialties in the areas of gender and inequality (Footnotes November 2004). Within the European Union the European technology assessment on women and science offers many cross-national gender report cards along different educational and occupational dimensions.

The socially useful university

Let us start here with the distinction between the socially buffered and the socially embedded university (Ben-David and Zloczower 1962). The socially buffered university in many ways corresponds to a European ideal type: a community of masters and scholars pursuing knowledge for its own sake without consideration of its uses or applications. These communities were sponsored and funded by religious, and later, state authorities. These authorities and the authority of the professorate buffered the university from the influence of a myriad of interest groups. The value assigned to the activities of the university was cultural and political, not technical nor economic. These activities largely consisted in the pursuit of the humanities, the study of the liberal arts. In the early nineteenth century this ideal type is associated with Humboldt and the founding of the University of Berlin and later in the century with Newman and the reform movement in Oxford. The national heritage would be affirmed through the study of philosophy in Germany and literature in England (Readings 1996). These studies in philosophy and literature presupposed a canon and the canon presupposed a bounded, coherent, and differentiated national identity.

By contrast the curriculum in American higher education has never been as strictly canonical. This is not to say that this or that university has not sought to cloister itself and proclaim its virtue via commitment to disinterested scholarship. But then it would have to confront the much larger number of universities and institutes of higher education that were less committed. This has meant that canon building efforts have tended to be university specific rather than widely shared and systemic. As a result there has been great instability in what constitutes canonical knowledge and much innovation in what gets taught and how it gets taught. This situation in turn makes it possible for an early twentieth century critic to pick on top-notch universities like Columbia or the University of Chicago and poke fun at what passed for university knowledge in their curricula (Flexner 1930). The main thrust of the criticism is that what is taught and what gets done by way of dissertations is too narrow and too practical to merit the status of university knowledge. This is, of course, the same University of Chicago which would later take great pride in its commitment to the Great Books (i.e. the Humanities) but which owes its beginnings to the largesse of John D. Rockefeller (Kirp 2003; see also Djelic ch. 3).

At least two kinds of evidence suggest that just as universities are becoming more broadly inclusive they too are moving in the direction of a more socially useful profile. In practice this often entails curricular changes that foster the "practical arts" and identity focused subject matter. Professional curricula emerge and expand in universities across Europe. You may get a first degree in business at the University of Frankfurt and at the Humboldt University you may encounter Faculties of Agriculture and Horticulture, of Education, Rehabilitation, and Sports, and of Economics and Business Administration (Humboldt-Universitat Zu Berlin 2000 (a published list of courses)). There are distinguished business schools in Sweden, France, Spain, and other European countries (Moon 2002); you may even get an MBA at the Said Business School in Oxford. At Oxford University you may also get a first degree in engineering and materials, engineering and computer science, engineering, economics, and management, or metallurgy (University of Oxford Undergraduate Prospectus 1998–99). And indeed, contrary to the popular impression of Oxford as a bastion of the humanities, the historical trend is in the direction of greater proportions of students opting to read the natural sciences and technology and the social science and a corresponding decline of students reading humanities. A similar trend is observable if one focuses on the faculty: there are losses in the humanities and gains in other fields of inquiry (Soares 1999).

The "practical arts" are on the rise in European universities. The line between basic and applied research is dismissed as an outdated fiction by the Director of the Max-Planck Society (Krucken 2003) Even at the helm, there are changes in this direction. The new vice chancellor of Oxford, Dr. John Hood, for example, has an academic degree in management studies, has taught civil engineering at the University of Auckland in New Zealand, and has even served as a senior manager of a business corporation, the Fletcher challenge company. In this regard Dr. Hood would fit in nicely with the leadership of American universities. The leadership at Stanford, for instance, has included geologists, medical doctors, engineers, and at present, a computer scientist who personifies faculty entrepreneurship. The line between basic and applied research is of necessity weak in a university that boasts:

Let us not be afraid to outgrow old thoughts and ways, and dare to think on new lines as to the future of the world under our care. Let us not be poor copies of other universities. Let us be progressive (Jane Stanford 1903. Cited in the Message from the President in the 2001 Annual Report of Stanford University).

Working more formally with longitudinal cross-national data, Frank and Gabler (2006) show the diminished influence of the humanities among university students. The big winner, particularly in recent decades, is the social sciences. This is not merely the triumph of the practical but also the victory of the personal. Students choose to study that which they find relevant and much of this involves not just business and engineering but also human biology, environmental studies, ethnic and women's studies. Students choose because universities increasingly provide students with expanded menus of courses and expect students to make choices.

The American pattern maximizes student choice and minimizes canonical requirements. If this pattern adds up to the "closing of the American mind" (Bloom 1987) one could contend that the European mind is also closing. To cite but one example of inter-disciplinary curricular innovation in Europe, note the steady increase of countries that offer courses in women's studies, from seven pioneers in the 1970s to twenty-one by the 2000s. Moreover, a country is "at risk" of offering its first women's studies course as a function of having a less elitist or broadly inclusive system of higher education (Wotipka and Ramirez 2004). This finding suggests that there is an association between the broadly inclusive and socially useful dimensions of the rationalizing models. As more people enter universities more universities opt for a more popular curriculum. This is clearly good news if you welcome the demise of donnish domination (Tapper and Smith 1992) or the decline of German mandarins (Ringer 1969).

On the other hand, this is bad news if the marketization of higher education and universities as shopping malls offends your sensibilities

(Gumport 2000; see Djelic ch. 3). Some critics lament the fact that the credential is no longer a preparation for a life journey but merely an insurance policy against unemployment and downward mobility (Kivinen and Ahola 1999). In search for the proverbial middle ground academics are likely to rally around the statement "There is a place for the market but the market must be kept in place" (Okun 1975: 19).

The search for the middle ground is at once easier and harder for academics in the United States. Market forces and private monies have always played a greater role in the formation and expansion of universities in the United States and university industry ties are more likely to be imagined as opportunities rather than risks (Ramirez 2002, 2005). This greater familiarity with university industry ties should be a plus in finding the middle ground. But some critics may contend that it will be harder, given the greater thoroughness of the marketing of higher education in the United States.

In the following section this issue is explored within the broader context of the call for more organizational flexibility on the part of universities. To communicate its social usefulness effectively to a broader audience, universities need to appear to be user friendly. This is sometimes called advertising. Universities also need to display organizational flexibility with respect to funding. This is sometimes called entrepreneurship.

The organizationally flexible university

Almost by definition elite institutions are not user friendly, not if the potential users are the masses. As the logic of mass higher education diffuses, changes in university composition covary with changes in curricular content. Whether one is an ordinary university that intends to endure or an extraordinary one intent on prevailing, advertising is an important tool. It is a tool through which the social charter of the university (Meyer 1971) – who are we and who are our graduates – and its organizational saga (Clark 1972) – how did we get to become who we are – can be dramatically narrated to potential enrollees. In the American scene this narration used to be informal, associational, and relatively low-keyed. Much personal enthusiasm and little professional expertise were brought to bear on this process. This is no longer the case. Admissions directors (now often called enrollment managers) are increasingly involved in creating a favorable brand or identity for their universities and in working the numbers to sustain the claims associated with the brand (Kirp 2003; Ventresca and Kratz 2004). Because they were mostly embedded in and responsive to varying social groups, American universities have been in the advertising business for a long time.

Until very recently, however, universities and advertising were an incongruous pair in the European landscape. In continental Europe the universities were not breeding grounds for alumni associations and the networking and advertising activities that are often initially channeled through them. In England the dominance of Oxbridge precluded the need for advertising though alumni have been very influential. But things have changed. Universities seek to appeal to a broader audience and organize themselves accordingly.

The Humboldt University of Berlin displays a very colorful brochure printed in several languages. The brochure is user friendly informative: the university has moved up forty-eight places and is now in sixth place in the "league tables" of German universities. And it is user friendly playful: a reference to the camels in the possession of the Faculty of Agriculture and Horticulture, jesting about the Union Jack flying over the Humboldt (Centre for British Studies), etc.

Not to be outdone, Oxford advertises through the pictures and words of a sample of students that includes women, ethnic minorities, and state comprehensive graduates. To illustrate user friendliness, consider what one student had to say:

I thought there would be a lot more "tradition" – formal dinners, old boys at High Table, prep school manners – but it hasn't been like that at all. There's such a wide diversity of people here, from all sections of the community. Whatever you're into, you'll find someone who shares your interest. I had friends who were scared to apply – scared of the aura of the place, all those impressive buildings – but it's the people who make the experience. If you're not sure about Oxford come here and talk to as many people as you can.

No one argues that this and other featured student views constitute a random sample of student views. On the contrary, these are the views and the profiles put forward by Oxford in its undergraduate admissions brochure. The search for a democracy of brains (or wits) tilts Oxford in the direction of user friendly advertising. How much Oxford moves in this direction and to what extent this and related organizational developments collide with its institutional ethos remains to be seen.

What is evident is that Oxford is no exception to the growing tendency among Western universities to advertise themselves as friendly places for a broader range of students.

Much of this friendliness goes hand in hand with the idea that universities are places where students develop by making choices about the curriculum and related matters. Universities should as a consequence maximize the diversity of options and for that they need to be organizationally flexible. They also need to be well funded as they will thus be in a much better position to recruit diverse faculty, offer diverse curricula, and in many other ways maximize the range of student choices. Much of this flies in the face of canon lovers who favor classical foundations for character development instead of academic smorgasbords for personality enhancement.

But how is the expanded and user friendly university to be funded? Public monies typically funded the nineteenth century European university, and as noted earlier, it was buffered from all sorts of social groups and interests. Universities in the United States were both more socially embedded and more likely to receive private funds. Fear of the corrupting influence of economic power was (is?) more European; a Lockean distrust of state control is more American. Today most of the major universities in the United States actively seek both public and private funding. This is true whether the university is legally regarded as a public or private institution.

University–industry ties have always had their critics in the United States, both from the left (Noble 1982) and from the right (Nisbet 1971). But these criticisms have had little impact on university developments in the direction of expanded research and development facilities, technology patent offices, and industrial parks that symbolize and foster collaborations between scientists and engineers in industry and their counterparts in the universities. Some developments in the same direction have also emerged in Europe but on the whole the greater interdisciplinary character of research teams within the United States fosters more product development efforts than in Europe (Powell and Owen-Smith 1998). It is no accident that multidisciplinary joint activities are more likely in universities where the line between basic and applied research was bridged earlier and more extensively. It is also no accident that general university openness to social interests increases the likelihood of interpersonal ties and interaction patterns across university and industry domains. From a European perspective the question may continue to be the old one: how is it that professors and entrepreneurs are able to collaborate effectively, despite differences in their training (and background) and in the reward structures of their fields of endeavor? From an American perspective what is emerging is the concrete reality of *the faculty entrepreneur*

To examine this phenomenon I briefly consider the case of Stanford University. Stanford's ascendancy as a premier university is closely connected to its successful forging of ties with both industry and government. This forging was characterized by one of its leading architects, Fredrick Terman, as a "win-win-win situation" (Lowen 1997). Terman was also an early proponent of the Matthew effect in university development. Those units, programs, and departments which showed the greatest promise, the "steeples of excellence," would be most rewarded. As Dean of the School of Engineering and later as Provost, Terman fostered an entrepreneurial spirit which in many ways is the foundation of what now is recognized as the faculty entrepreneur. Simply put, the latter is a professor who engages in research, which leads to a product that has commercial value. Faculty entrepreneurs typically emerge from professional schools such as engineering and business but also from medicine and even law. In fact even social scientists and educational researchers can become faculty entrepreneurs.

The reaction of the American academic to the idea of the faculty entrepreneur is likely to be a bag of awe and suspicion that very quickly will come back to "There is a place for the market, but the market needs to be kept in place." There is a place for the market because faculty entrepreneurship in American universities is more likely to be viewed as a new development in an old effort to secure funding. Much of this may still be anathema in European universities where support for research was not typically acquired through competitive proposals. Research funds came to universities in the form of block grants at Oxbridge (and somewhat similar arrangements elsewhere) distributed by committees headed by senior faculty. Under the banner of greater transparency and accountability the rationalization of academic work in Europe has commenced. This has led to a sense that an audit culture is on the rise with trust and conviviality within the academy as its immediate victims (Baert and Shipman 2005). But American professors have much earlier been subjected to these rationalizing processes: the modern faculty vita includes a section called grants and faculty dutifully list the number and magnitude of their grants. Universities benefit from the indirect costs that these grants yield. Faculty also benefit in the form of summer salaries. And, student research assistantships are often underwritten through these grants. University organizations and their faculty personnel have much experience in courting and garnering financial rewards as part of their everyday life. Founding a company is different from launching an institute or center but entrepreneurship is required for both enterprises.

Rationalizing accounts and the rationalization of the university as organization

Much of the literature on the rationalization of universities emphasizes the economic dimension underlying the observable changes. The basic argument is clear and compelling: A decrease in public funds for higher education has led to policy changes designed to allow the university to endure. Curricular and other organizational innovations are dictated by the logic of the market as are university–industry links. Both supporters and critics of the entrepreneurial university often imagine its rise and expansion as driven by economic considerations.

More recently the idea of academic goods and services as exports is discussed in international competitive terms; education has been a feature of the World Trade Organization's Global Agreement of Trade in Services (GATS) since 1995. Foreign students now constitute additional revenues; foreign student enrollment in OECD countries has increased by over 30 percent between 1995 and 2001 (Koch-Weser Ammassari 2004) Furthermore, a number of OECD countries have universities engaged in for-profit educational activities in other countries. To compete successfully in a national, and subsequently, an international market, universities become more broadly inclusive, socially useful, and organizationally flexible. But is the socially embedded university really nothing more than the economically entrepreneurial university?

There are indeed some changes that can be accounted for by this line of reasoning. But, as I have sought to demonstrate earlier in this paper, many of the curricular and related changes are many steps removed from a solely economic perspective. The ongoing preoccupation with diversity has its roots in anti-elitist notions. The incorporation of women, ethnic minorities, and working class students within higher education is driven by a broad view of progress and justice, not merely a narrow calculation of payoffs to the university. This inclusive view is the antithesis of the Eliot perspective identified earlier. And, it is an optimistic view: in the knowledge society all sorts of people can benefit from a university education and all sorts of countries can likewise benefit. Never mind that the societal rate of return to higher education is not as straightforward as is often imagined (for a review of the evidence, see Chabbott and Ramirez 2000). Without this institutionalized view of progress and justice in place the phenomenal growth of universities would be unimaginable. But the issue is no longer whether categories of people historically excluded from the university should be included. Instead the terms of inclusion have become a central issue throughout much of the world. Broad accessibility requires not merely dismantling barriers but becoming user friendly. The latter in turn pushes the university in the direction of social usefulness and organizational flexibility. Universities change not only to remain solvent in the short run but also to become or to continue to be legitimate in the longer run. Net of other factors, the more universities embody broad views of progress and justice the more legitimacy they enjoy.

The historical shift in the constitution of universities is a movement from institutions authorized by religious, and later, social class elites to institutions that aspire to meet meritocratic, and most recently, multicultural standards. The corresponding shift in the composition of the university is from a taken for granted faith community (the medieval university) to one characterized by good family background (Oxbridge in the nineteenth century) to an "aristocracy of brains" association (Conant's meritocratic ideal for elite American universities) to one engaged in the celebration of multiple intelligences, tastes, interests, etc. (the contemporary rationalized and user friendly ideal). The now common university emphasis on both excellence and equity clearly reflects the triumph of broad views of progress and justice. Universities increasingly act as if they know they are expected to emphasize human development goals along multiple dimensions. And it becomes harder to justify a rank ordering of these human development goals by appealing to an authority based on tradition or charisma. Who is to say whether the study of human biology is more edifying than the study of Latin? Whether the pursuit of the practical arts or the new identity focused courses should be assigned less value than the pursuit of the liberal arts? Whether career-related skills or more diffuse self-fulfillment experiences constitute the high ground in human development goals? What Humboldt, Newman, or Hutchins had to say about true university education is less consequential in practice than the imperatives of accessibility, usefulness, and flexibility. The idealized university in the twenty-first century is the socially embedded one.

The socially embedded university is more than a profit maximizing entrepreneurial one. Expanded accessibility often turns out to be fiscally costly. Organizational flexibility often means new budget lines reflecting the need for new experts in the management of higher education. Of course, universities will take into account the economic impact of this or that change. This has led some observers to contend that increasingly new managerial logics have replaced the old social institutional ones (Gumport 2000). There is indeed evidence of the increased uses of managerial logics in higher education. In general these logics are more likely to be displayed in American rather than European universities and in newer rather than older ones. But change in the direction of more managerial discourse is found in both older universities and in European ones.

These changes reflect the degree to which the university is rationalized as an organization. This does not mean that universities are just like any other organization: not all organizations have human development goals and link these to knowledge production, transmission, and conservation. But all organizations are expected to have goals and plans for attaining these goals. Not all entities concerned with human development are readily imagined as organizations. Families, for example, are presumed to foster human development and may even consult organizations to do so but families are typically less formally organized. Throughout much of their history, many universities have been less than formally organized, but increasingly universities are becoming more formally organized. This means that universities are more likely to state their goals (with or without mission statements) and to engage in planning activities to attain these goals. This is true not only with respect to overtly financial matters, such as the American penchant for fundraising campaigns, but also as regards faculty recruitment and retention processes. Older, more casual, and more idiosyncratic arrangements give way to more transparent and more standardized ways of organizing faculty searches and promotion procedures. But note that in this and in other instances the guiding principles have to do with fairness, not with economizing. The old boy network that went hand in hand with the older institutional logics was a cheap mode of operating. The erosion of the clout of the network is brought about by the standardization of organizational policies and practices including those directly affecting recruitment and retention. This is a standardization that undercuts local custom and informal practice, but also generates costs in terms of adding legal and managerial staff to the university.

The core idea is that the rationalization of the university as organization, influenced by broad models of progress and justice, paves the way for a managerial discourse that involves more than transforming the university into a business. The university proceeds as if it were a rationally managed organization attuned to those organizational goals that follow from an increasingly standardized organizational identity, *university*. Standardization is more likely in entities that are more formally organized. The idea that an entity should be influenced by the "best practices" of other similar entities is more likely to take place if the entities are imagined as formal organization rather than as historically rooted social institutions. Furthermore, the idea that there is some abstract expertise that should be consulted is more likely the more the university is formally organized. The more abstract the formal expertise and the "best practices" the greater their portability and the likelihood that these general principles will result in organizational isomorphism among universities. Needless to say a significant degree of loose coupling will also be evident.

Broad models of progress and justice privilege the socially embedded university directly but also indirectly via the rationalization of the university as an organization. Commitments to accessibility, usefulness, and flexibility are displayed through formal organizational decisions that enact legitimate university identity. The decisions will vary with respect to details but there will be enough general overlapping elements to indicate that these are not triggered by local exigencies. In some instances the same consulting firm was hard at work in different universities in different countries, thereby generating commonalities in decision-making outcomes. In other cases informal learning takes place as universities eagerly share success stories with one another. Which American university administrator has not heard of the wonderful ways in which the Massachusetts Institute of Technology seriously addressed its gender equity issues? Or, more recently, which American university administrator has not heard of the less than wonderful ways associated with presidential leadership at Harvard? Most American universities will never remotely be Harvard or MIT but there is nonetheless a sense that there are lessons to be learned. Why? Because the issues are couched in portable organizational terms such as leadership training, commissioning a study, goal setting, monitoring progress, etc.

More formally the Bologna Declaration of 1999 sets the year 2010 as the year in which the ideal European university will be in place. This university will adhere to a European model of higher education characterized by a comparable degree system, harmonized organization of undergraduate and post graduate education, a compatible credit transfer system, quality assurance strategies, and an end to obstacles to student and staff mobility (Koch-Weser Ammassari 2004). A standardized Europeanization of the university along these organizational dimensions will parallel the more informal but nonetheless fairly standardized organization of higher education in the United States.

On both sides of the Atlantic, models of progress and justice are invoked to justify the rationalization of the university as an organization. The managerial discourse that these developments generate is pervasive precisely because it is not limited to bottom line issues but affects the university as a whole. It is an oddly optimistic discourse: with better management of time and resources all university players can upgrade themselves and in the process the university itself. Not just administrators but students and even faculty can do better with better management. It is also an oddly offensive discourse, reeking of academic capitalism and of anti-humanism from the perspective of its left-wing and right-wing critics respectively. The latter critics often forget that the humanism which the managerial discourse disturbs often lacked a democratic sensibility while the former critics have yet to come to terms with the complex relationship between capitalism and democracy. Why may a university not be both inclusive and committed to good management.?

What constitutes a well-managed university? This would be a relatively simple question if only the bottom line counted. But the socially embedded university involves a set of complex progress and justice goals for which efficacious technologies are not evident. Much of the energy expended on the rationalization of the university needs to be understood as energy invested in the management of proper identity. Without a clear chain of means-ends ties, university identity enactment through proper organizational displays is likely to be rampant. Through both more soft law mechanisms in Europe and informal networking in the United States, universities will learn how to commit themselves to the principles of broad accessibility, social usefulness, and organizational flexibility. Much of this display of commitment will involve a user friendly managerial discourse. The rationalization of the university has become both a means and an end. *The rationalization of the university has become the bottom line.*

The socially embedded university is not unlike the socially embedded individual that is the object of Goffmanesque social psychology (cf. Goffman 1959). This individual cannot rely on stable cultural categories to negotiate reality, but must instead be actively engaged in presentations of self that require both interpersonal advertising and entrepreneurial interaction. There is much professional discourse to assist individuals to communicate their persona effectively and there is much agreement on the abstract virtues of personhood. Likewise the socially embedded university rationalized as an organization is obliged to go the advertising and entrepreneurial route. How else is one to know and let others know that one is doing the right thing? As with individuals, some of these efforts result in differentiation and much of the literature on universities emphasizes these differences. What is overlooked with respect to both individuals and universities is the degree to which there are standardized and standardizing models of personhood and organization. It is precisely this standardization that makes the university as organization highly portable across local and national boundaries. In search of "deep structures" one can imagine, and even celebrate the distinctiveness of this or that university. Much educational policy proceeds, however, as if the socially embedded university is here to stay and its main characteristics are both well known and desirable. That is why universities can proclaim that they favor broad accessibility, social usefulness, and organizational flexibility. Adherence to these goals and the broader virtues that inform them (progress and justice) is first and foremost a display of proper university identity.

Concluding reflections

In principle and to a large degree in practice the socially embedded university has triumphed worldwide. This triumph reflects a world which increasingly is not just an interstate system nor a world market. There is little evidence of either state bureaucracies or market efficiencies molding the socially embedded university. So, what are the mechanisms through which the socially embedded university diffuses worldwide?

First, the socially embedded university is identified with America, and American ideas and institutions have outcompeted alternative ones in the last two decades (see also Djelic ch. 3; Djelic and Kleiner ch. 14) Furthermore the core elements of the socially embedded university – broad inclusiveness, social usefulness, and organizational flexibility – are associated with recent waves of democratization and marketization. In an era where all sorts of institutions should demonstrate their value and not be buffered from external scrutiny, the earlier more restricted, more distant, and more "timeless" university profile is increasingly de-legitimated. Secondly the socially embedded university has become the subject of much positive theorization in the last two decades. All sorts of epistemic communities have lionized the learning society and the socially embedded university is often imagined to make direct contributions to the learning society. Higher education for all and all for higher education are intertwined themes that privilege the user friendly university. The positive theorization is found in the work of a growing army of experts and consultants whose professional and scientific views carry much practical weight despite the occasional critique of the learning industry.

Finally, as more universities move in the direction of a socially embedded university, they add up to a dense global network that further carries and articulates the logic of mass higher education. Resistance to this aspect or that dimension of the socially embedded university becomes more difficult when at the global or regional level more and more universities present themselves as socially embedded organizations. At that point university specific traditions or highly historicized national university profiles are undercut by the normalization of the rationalized university. The latter allegedly serves all. Not surprisingly mass support is expected for the organizational flagship of the knowledge society, the socially embedded university.

Note

1. By a socially useful university I mean one that directly or indirectly proclaims social usefulness or relevance as a goal. Whether in fact this university really functions in the best interests of society is irrelevant from this perspective. This paper argues that a commitment to the goal of social usefulness is increasingly a constitutive element of university identity.

PART III

Transnational governance in the making

12 Dynamics of soft regulations

BENGT JACOBSSON AND KERSTIN
SAHLIN-ANDERSSON

Introduction

In a speech given in Uppsala on 6 September 2001, in memory of the fortieth anniversary of the death of the late UN Secretary-General, Dag Hammarskjöld, UN Secretary-General Kofi Annan argued that today, in many respects, the activities of the UN follow an agenda established by Hammarskjöld. However, towards the end of his speech, Annan pointed to a fundamental difference between today's world and the one in which Hammarskjöld lived and worked.

So if we go back to the things about today's world that we would have to explain to him, if he unexpectedly joined us now, probably the most difficult for him to adjust to would be the sheer complexity of a world in which individuals and groups of all kinds are constantly interacting – across frontiers and across oceans, economically, socially and culturally – without expecting or receiving any permission, let alone assistance, from their national governments . . . From this he might well conclude that we should not rely exclusively on state action to achieve our objectives on the international level, either. A great deal, he would think, is likely to depend on non-state actors in the system – private companies, voluntary agencies or pressure groups, philanthropic foundations, universities and think tanks, and of course creative individuals. And that thought would surely feed into his reflections on the role of the United Nations (Annan 2001: 10–11).

Annan described a fundamental reordering of the world, a world in which boundaries between levels and nations are blurred and in flux. However, this is not an anomic or chaotic world, but one filled with governing efforts that transcend the boundaries among levels, sectors and territories. Levi-Faur and Jordana (2005) characterized the present times as the Golden Era of Regulation. Although traditional notions of regulation are largely associated with the state, much regulation in our contemporary world is formed and pursued by actors other than states or in constellations of public and private actors, including states, international organizations, professional associations, expert groups and business corporations. Hence, governance capacity is dispersed among and shared between many actors (Knill and Lemkuhl 2002). The emergent transnational regulation displays patterns of fragmentation and relations among those who regulate, and those who are regulated are characterized more by reciprocity than by coercion and the threat of sanctions.

Not only do actors differ in contemporary patterns of regulation. Modes of regulation are also quite different. Coercive rules are common and expanding around the world. We find, however, that the most profound change is the expansion of "soft rules" – non-hierarchical rules that are not legally binding (Mörth 2004; Mörth ch. 6). The domain and applicability of soft rules and the conditions for compliance are being defined together with the rules themselves. Authority is not predefined in the relationships between those regulated and those regulating, but must be built into each governing relationship.

Although the regulatory actors may seem to be diverse, what appears is a striking convergence across sectors and across territories. Fields as diverse as the defense industry, labor markets, higher education, health care, public management and the social responsibility of corporations are increasingly governed in similar ways – transnationally.[1]

In a world so clearly displaying patterns of transnational interlinkages, we cannot conlude that certain areas in society are governed and regulated in certain ways. Rather what seem to be the basic building blocks from which to begin an analysis is an examination of the processes of organizing and the patterns of organization that emerge. Regulation does not just happen; it is produced by organizations, and is often directed towards other organizations. Hence regulation and its dynamics need to be understood through studies of specific organizational settings; and in order to further our knowledge about the present re-regulation, we must conduct empirical studies of individual processes of regulation.

This chapter pictures the emergence and convergence of transnational regulations. We depict transnational regulation as an organized activity and we use accumulated lessons and experiences from organizational and institutional theory to understand how this form of governance is organized. We analyze modes of regulation and how and why regulations appear authorized and reasonable – even attractive – to follow. This analysis points to important dynamics in the development of transnational regulation: regulations and regulators compete and collaborate with each other, regulations evolve incrementally and emerging transnational regulations seem to spur extended regulations. We conclude the chapter with a discussion about these dynamics. Before turning to our analysis and proposing our framework, we provide a number of brief examples of regulations and their development.

Development of regulations: seven examples

In the European Union (EU), the realization of the Single Market was made possible by the increasing use of standards as rules (Bundgaard-Pedersen 1997). Instead of trying to reach agreement at the European Council level, rule-making in major fields was delegated to private expert organizations such as the European Committee for Standardization (CEN), the European Committee for Electrotechnical Standardization (CENELEC) or the European Telecommunications Standards Institute (ETSI). The rules produced in these organizations are voluntary standards. Such standards can be extremely important as means of regulation (Morgan 2001) and conforming to those standards is also likely to imply that EU directives will indirectly be followed.

The EU is increasingly using what is called an open method of coordination (see Borrás and Jacobsson 2004; Mörth ch. 6; Jacobsson ch. 10). Member states promise to work towards certain goals, to follow specified procedures and to accept being critically examined by the Commission and other member states but they preserve the right to make their own independent decisions about the content of their activities. The open method of coordination has been a way for the EU to govern without using the traditional community method based on compulsory rules, and it has been used in areas such as the labor market, in which there has been considerable disagreement on the acceptable scope for harmonization.

The United Nations Global Compact initiative was announced by Kofi Annan at the World Economic Forum in Davos in January 1999 and is directed towards corporations. The Global Compact is based on ten principles derived from the Universal Declaration of Human Rights, the International Labour Organization's Fundamental Principles on Rights at Work, the Rio Principles on Environment and Development, and the United Nations Convention Against Corruption. Corporations that participate in the Global Compact promise to support the principles, make them part of their strategy and day-to-day operations, publicly advocate the principles and describe the ways in which they are supporting the ten principles. The Global Compact is based on the idea of forming a network in which norms will be diffused and where corporations and their stakeholders will monitor and discipline each other.

The most important global regulator concerning accounting standards is the International Accounting Standards Board (IASB) (see Tamm Hallström 2004; Botzem and Quack ch. 13). This is an independent, privately funded accounting standard setter based in London. The IASB is committed to developing, in the public interest, a single set of high quality, understandable and enforceable global accounting standards. The IASB co-operates with national accounting standard setters to achieve convergence in accounting standards around the world. Although it has no authority to require compliance with these global standards, many countries require the financial statements of publicly traded enterprises to be prepared in accordance with them.

The Public Governance and Territorial Development Directorate (GOV) is an OECD committee that was established in 1990 under the title Public Management Committee (PUMA). The mandate of GOV is described as being the support of improved public sector governance through comparative data and analysis, the setting and promotion of standards and the facilitation of transparency and peer review. GOV's predecessor had developed a number of principles to direct the work of member countries on accountability, transparency, efficiency and effectiveness, responsiveness, forward vision and rule of law. GOV regularly arranges networks and meetings in which ideas and experiences are exchanged and publishes overviews of the public sector reforms of member countries.

A number of initiatives have been developed for assessing, ranking and accrediting management education programs worldwide. Professional associations, the media, states, expert groups, international organizations and many other actors and bodies, perform and carry out these monitoring and assessment activities. Assessments are done on the initiative of both those being assessed (management education providers) or those performing the assessments (such as professional organizations and the media). Such activities are not merely ways of assessing and spreading information about management education. Rather, they have taken the form of new modes for regulation, and their emergence has had an impact on other forms of regulation and on the development of management education in general (see Hedmo et al. ch. 15).

Worldwide discussions in the field of health care have focused on the establishment of priorities and ways to make curing and caring better and more transparent processes. In this context evidence-based medicine (EBM) has been pursued as a way of strengthening the scientific base for clinical practice. Several national and international bodies that are more or less directly supported and controlled by states have pursued EBM. These bodies search scientific journals in order to find the best scientific evidence available for treatment and care of various health problems and develop guidelines based on these overviews for individual clinical doctors to follow. Guidelines are distributed and, in some places tied to financial schemes, strategic policy developments and the organizing of health care.

These examples are cases of regulations that are partly, but not entirely, new. We suggest, however, that transnational regulations are becoming increasingly important and expansive. Moreover, we suggest that these changes also call for new theoretical developments. There is a need, in other words, to re-visit and critically examine dominant theories about rule changes in the world.

Theoretical challenges to a state-centered world view

In theories of international relations, the world is primarily seen as being structured by nation states and the focus has been on states as the principal actors, power holders and regulators on the global scene. Such a view is featured in intergovernmental theories about European integration (e.g. Moravcsik 1993). The basic argument is that states or coalitions of states are the driving forces of integration, so that if one wants to know what will happen in specific fields, one should analyze the strategies, capacities and resources of national governments. Theorists in the area of globalization have, however, questioned such propositions, claiming that borders are becoming less important in a world where transnational corporations and financial capital constantly cross state borders and often seem not to reflect much concern about territorial limitations. It has been argued that there is an increasing hollowness in state power: a "retreat of the state" (Strange 1996).

As a result, attempts have been made to "bring society in," by pointing, for instance, to the importance of international organizations per se (Jönsson 1990), regimes (Krasner 1983), epistemic communities (Haas 1990), transnational corporations (Friedmann 2000) and non-governmental organizations (Boli and Thomas 1999). This societal perspective has sometimes been placed in opposition to state-centered approaches (see also Mörth's discussion about governance and government in ch. 6). Risse-Kappen claimed that there was:

a bifurcation in the international relations literature. Those who theorize about international relations and about domestic politics tend to ignore the linkages between societies and societal actors across national boundaries. Those who study transnational relations mostly neglect structures of governance, in particular the state (Risse-Kappen 1995: 16).

We also believe that it is necessary to study the interconnections between states and other actors. States exist and still play an important role, even if it is a changing role (see Jacobsson ch. 10). From this follows that one should not make any a priori assumptions about a neat differentiation between state and non-state actors or state-centered or society-centered explanations. Moreover, the many organizations that are often lumped together as non-state actors, display a great variety, which makes it necessary not to group them together into one coherent category. Instead, the ongoing relationships among and reciprocal interactions between states, international organizations, non-governmental organizations, private companies and others should be studied. Such an analysis is a beginning towards explaining the nature, emergence and effects of a re-regulated world and it should help us see how the strategies and resources of states emerge in connection with other organizations. It also illustrates how the governing efforts and powers of non-governmental organizations and companies are affected by state policies and actions. States interact with and are embedded in complex multisectoral and multilateral networks of actors (e.g. Higgott et al. 2000; O'Brien et al. 2000; see also Jacobsson ch. 10; Marcussen ch. 9). As Rose and Miller (1992) have claimed, this requires us, as analysts, to relocate the state and to focus on governmental problematics and technologies beyond states. Regulation in the modern world, claims Moran (2002), is about steering networks, and therefore, we, as scholars, must think in global rather than national terms. Just as studies of organizational practices and devlopments have illustrated the importance of combining studies of individual actors, organizations and fields (e.g. Scott et al. 2000, DiMaggio 1983; Martin 2003), we believe that in order to explain the emergence and impact of various types of regulations, we need to analyze how individual processes, relationships and organizations are shaped in the context in which they evolve.

Three modes of regulation

Three different and intertwined modes of regulation serve to structure the transnational world: rule-setting, monitoring and agenda-setting. We characterize and exemplify these three modes below.

Rule-setting

The type of rules that dominate the transnational world are soft rules (Mörth 2004 and ch. 6): standards, codes of conduct, recommendations and guidelines. Formally, at least, standards and other types of soft regulations are voluntary and include large elements of self-regulation and co-regulation (Brunsson and Jacobsson 2000; Ahrne and Brunsson ch. 4). Soft regulations tend to transcend the regulation–de-regulation divide. What is often termed de-regulation certainly involves new types of regulations: a line of thinking that has been pursued with the concept of "responsive regulation" (Ayres and Braithwaite 1992, see also Moran 2002). With this concept, the dialogue between the regulator and the regulated has been emphasized. In such dialogues, common norms and understandings develop, and possibilities for voluntary compliance are formed. Again, the importance of the organization of regulatory processes is illustrated, pointing to the significance of understanding what have been termed "subtle" or "non-formal" regulations (Moran 2002); we prefer to call them soft regulations, because they are not always non-formal. Soft regulations often include highly formal types of reporting and coordinating procedures (for instance, the use of the open method of coordination in the EU), and, from a coordination or administrative point of view, those regulations are often far from subtle.

What we term "soft regulations" display similar patterns to what Knill and Lehmkuhl (2002) have called "regulated self-regulation." This type of regulation leaves plenty of space for those who are being regulated to edit the rules – they choose parts of the rules and display their compliance with them or translate rules to fit their own expectations. Moreover, the regulatees themselves often report compliance with the regulations, editing their practice to fit the expectations. The regulations evolve incrementally in a dialogue between the regulator and the regulatee and partly through the process of regulation (cf. Botzem and Quack ch. 13; Hedmo et al. ch. 15; McNichol ch. 17). In this way it is not clear who is regulating whom. The realm of regulation, in other words, is highly ambiguous. Adding to the ambiguity is the fact that many new regulations come in packages or clusters and are connected to existing regulations. The regulations often build upon each other and are combined differently in different settings. This is why it is difficult to measure compliance to, or the impact of, single rules.

Soft regulations are not connected to sanctions – at least not sanctions issued by the regulator. They tend to be motivated by the need for coordination and comparability (Jacobsson et al. 2002; Ahrne and Brunsson ch. 4) and, in this sense, are often seen as administrative issues rather than issues of control and command. This also means that it is difficult to allocate responsibility for developments and operations.

Monitoring

Several examples in the introduction pointed to the widely used forms of monitoring: the EU's open method of coordination, the global compact, the OECD, and rankings and accreditations of higher education (see also Boli ch. 5; Botzem and Quack ch. 13; Hedmo et al. ch. 15; McNichol ch. 17). Monitoring activities are often coupled with rule-setting and serve to assure rule-following. Sometimes the monitoring bodies evaluate according to rules that they themselves have produced. However, compliance with many soft rules are not monitored by the rule-setting body; rather other organizations may be allocated the task of monitoring or may take initiatives to start monitoring the compliance with rules that have been produced by some other organization. Monitoring activities also begin in cases in which no rules have been issued beforehand. We find examples in which monitoring activities lead to the setting of new rules. Monitoring activities also appear independent of rule-setting activities and are announced as ways of informing rather than as means of controlling.

Several of the monitors mentioned above are private, non-governmental organizations. Another example of a renowned international non-governmental organization is Transparency International.

This organization is ". . . devoted to combating corruption, [and] brings civil society, business, and governments together in a powerful global coalition." Transparency International tries to raise awareness and advocate reforms, but mainly works through the monitoring of compliance by governments, corporations and banks. In contrast to Amnesty International, which also is a non-governmental organization that monitors compliance (with UN rules concerning human rights), Transparency International has a policy not to expose individual cases. It does, however, publish rankings about the amount of corruption in various countries and functions as an auditor of conventions and standards concluded within the frameworks of the OECD (especially the Convention on Combating Bribery of Foreign Public Officials), the Council of Europe, the Organization of American States and others. Transparency International, in its annual Global Corruption Report, evaluates the state of corruption around the world. Monitoring efforts in many areas have expanded with an increasing interest in transparency; one common argument for expanded monitoring activities is, in fact, that they will serve to enhance transparency and result in improved practice (see Sahlin-Andersson 2003).

The monitoring, auditing and scrutinizing of bodies, activities and policies have expanded to such an extent that it has been suggested that the present society can be characterized as an audit society (Power 1997, 2003). This audit society is not only a society in which auditing is commonplace, but one in which activities are formed in such a way that they can be audited and auditable. Monitoring activities not only picture the world in certain ways, but have a regulating impact. We find monitoring activities that are conducted with the expressed intention of affecting and regulating the assessed activities. Scrutinizing procedures, reporting requirements and classification schemes for reporting are introduced, not only in order to highlight certain features of monitored operations, but also as a way of improving or influencing these operations (Bowker and Starr 1999).

Agenda setting

Our introductory examples point to several organizations that function as arenas in which activities and organizational reforms are discussed. These organizations do not always claim to have a rule that must be followed. Instead, their activities are less actor-oriented and more a case of discussing, probing and penetrating, that is to say meditative (see also Jacobsson ch. 10). Sometimes they function as arenas in which specific ideas are proposed and disseminated (see Sahlin-Andersson 2000). The arenas serve as places where agendas are set for what is good and desirable practice.

For example, GOV, a committee of the OECD, serves as an arena in which representatives of the OECD countries can share ideas and experiences concerning the development of new public management reforms (Sahlin-Andersson 2000; Marcussen 2004). An agenda is set through the collection, comparison and dissemination of information. For instance, in November 2001, PUMA convened a forum on Modernizing Governments, a meeting that, according to the organizers themselves ". . . reflected the recognition that there was a common and widespread interest in the lessons that can be learned . . . Members and non-members both have useful experience to share and can learn from each other."

Agenda-setting has been discussed in a similar way by Kingdon (1984). We find agenda-setting to be a form of regulation in cases for which there are no binding rules, but for which organizations, like the OECD, may issue recommendations and advocate policies taken by specific countries. PUMA, for example, collected information about the public management policies of the member countries, and compared and disseminated that information. When doing so it edited the collected information into a policy agenda for preferable and necessary public management reforms, but it did not – at least not directly – audit or certify the policies of the member countries.

Combined modes of transnational regulation

The three modes of regulation appear as alternatives to each other, but they are also interrelated. Sometimes one regulation mode paves the way for others and sometimes one mode of regulation serves as a means of authorizing and strengthening other modes. We find many networks that are originally set up with the primary aim of coordinating or sharing knowledge. Over time they develop the idea of sharing not only knowledge or experience, but also "best practices," seeking to formulate and assess local practices in order to find and spread them. And they develop scrutinizing or accrediting procedures in order to distinguish those whose practices are of good quality from those whose practices are less valuable. PUMA is one example of a network that followed this line of development (Sahlin-Andersson 2000). In the area of higher education, we find professional member organizations that have followed a similar line of development: from an arena for sharing knowledge to hosting organizations for accrediting and standardizing programs and thus developing extended systems of monitoring and rule setting (Hedmo 2004).

Another example is the Global Compact. The proponents of the Global Compact argue that it is not a legally binding code of conduct complete with performance criteria and the monitoring of compliance (Ruggie 2002) for three reasons:

(1) it would be impossible to agree upon binding rules;
(2) the UN lacks the capacity to monitor global companies and their supply chains; and
(3) the business community would oppose such an initiative.

However, the intellectual claim is that agenda-setting activities such as the forming of networks and the pursuit of a common discourse is more than a second-best solution. The idea is that the accumulation of experience is likely to ". . . lead gradually to a desire for greater codification, benchmarking and moving from 'good' to 'best' practices" (Ruggie 2002: 32). Clearly, we have a case in which the soft approach could be seen as a stage in a development, the end-point of which may be that all actors agree about best practices. The UN also claims that more and more organizations should become involved in the Global Compact; the latter is seen as an expanding set of nested networks.

This form of regulation does not replace other forms of regulation. Voluntary initiatives are no substitute for actions by governments, the Compact proponents argue. Instead, they contend that governments alone cannot achieve the amount of regulation that is necessary in the evolving global economic space. It is also clear that the achievements of the Global Compact have been made possible through the authority of the United Nations. Critics claim that the UN takes part in "bluewashing" activities, and that companies may wrongfully borrow authority from the UN. The UN, on the other hand, is quite clear that the underlying "bargain" is that the UN provides legitimacy, but that companies have the capacity to provide desired changes.

The EU too is working with agenda-setting in addition to extended rule-setting and monitoring activities. For example, in the field of employment policy, the key elements as defined in the Lisbon summit were:

(1) definition of guidelines from the Union;
(2) translation of these guidelines into national policies by setting specific targets;
(3) establishment of indicators and benchmarks as ways to compare best practice; and
(4) periodic monitoring, evaluation and peer review of states (Jacobsson 2001).

Just as the UN claims that it would be impossible to agree on common policies of corporate behavior, the EU has found it increasingly difficult to achieve its goals using only the traditional methods of rule-making. In its Employment Strategy, the EU instead used what could be seen as self-regulation. Member states are expected to take the EU guidelines into account in their policies when they write their National Action Plans, even if the guidelines are not legally binding. These plans are then compared and evaluated and "best practices" are identified. The Council supervises the implementation in the member states and it can recommend that specific states modify their policies according to the EU guidelines (Jacobsson 2001). The role of the Commission is less that of a rule-maker setting guidelines and engaging in monitoring activities than that of a mediator working with member states, with social partners and with experts. Employment policies are at the heart of welfare systems, and it may be difficult to convince member states to give up their own strategies. With this form of regulation they need not do so, but there may be strong forces towards policy convergence. As Ruggie claimed concerning the Global Compact, ". . . laggards will have a harder time opposing actual achievements by their peers than by a priori standards" (Ruggie 2002: 33).

Authority and compliance

In traditional forms of regulation, there is an authoritative center (a state or a super-state) that produces rules and directives that others must follow. This is a system in which conflicts or potential conflicts are likely to be spurring regulations; regulations are formed when agreement cannot be formed in other ways. The reason for following directives is that those who issue such rules are looked upon as legitimate or because those who do not follow the rules risk some type of sanctions.

The forms of regulation we have discussed above do not follow this pattern. It is far from obvious that some of the rule-makers that we listed above should be seen as authoritative. In many cases, there are no explicit sanctions or territorial specifications connected to deviations in rule-following. And many of the new rule-makers have far-reaching claims. In a globalized world, we find that even those rules issued by states cannot be assumed to have a monopoly or to be built on an authority structure of nation-states. Why then do many organizations (including states) voluntarily adhere to these rules? We will elaborate on how rule-makers create authority around themselves and around their rules. In the previous section, we mentioned that the various modes of regulation – rule-setting, monitoring and agenda-setting – may serve to authorize and strengthen each other. We have observed three additional ways in which the authority of soft rules is attained. The first is to organize, and in doing so the organizer and the organization gains authority over members of the organization. A second way is to claim expertise: those regulated should follow rules, not because, as members, they must, but because these are the best rules and models available. A third way is to support one's own claim with other, authorized, rules and rule-makers. This approach is attained as regulatory constellations are formed. This may not be an exhaustive list of authorization means. Nor may it be easy, in practice, to separate them. Below, we provide examples of the three types.

Organizing

By voluntarily joining an organization, members bind themselves to following the rules issued by that organization (see Ahrne and Brunsson ch. 4). A decision to join the EU, the World Trade Organization (WTO), the North Atlantic Treaty Organization (NATO) or virtually any other type of organization is a voluntary act, but those states that join are obliged to follow the rules of that organization. As in the case of the EU, there may be exceptions for some members and transitory rules for new members, but the principle is that a state joining an organization accepts an obligation to follow the rules and accept the mechanisms for handling conflicts in that organization. This is also the case for companies that are members of various industry organizations.

So, the creation of organizations may be a way to achieve authorization of a regulatory measure. In the area of free trade, it was seen as a great success finally to be able to establish the WTO. It is argued by the WTO that ". . . a system based on rules rather than power makes life easier for all." It is a system, it is argued, that gives voice to smaller countries, but also a system which frees ". . . the major powers from the complexity of having to negotiate trade agreements with each of their numerous trading partners." The creation of WTO has clearly been beneficial for rule-following (partly by reducing transactions costs), compared with the looser cooperation in GATT (General Agreement on Tariffs and Trade) and, especially, in relation to a state of non-organization.

We know, of course, that the implementation of rules does not automatically follow organizational membership. Things can happen between policies and actions as shown in studies about implementation (e.g. Pressman and Wildavsky 1973, Bardach 1977, Hogwood and Gunn 1984), and organizations do not necessarily work with mandatory rules. Organizations like the OECD have members but rule-making is organized primarily around voluntary rules and agenda-setting activities. The EU also works to a large extent with soft law and with rules that are concerned with procedures, documents and arenas for discussions rather than with the specific contents regarding what policies to pursue.

Expertise

Rules may also be authorized and attractive to follow because they appear to be sensible or because the activities of the rule-maker are based on expertise, science or similar authoritative knowledge (see Drori and Meyer ch. 2). In the EU, standardization organizations like CEN, CENELEC and ETSI have been decisive in the creation of the internal market. Like all standards organizations, such as the International Organization for Standardization (ISO) and the International Accounting Standards Board (IASB) (Tamm Hallström 2004; Botzem and Quack ch. 13), they issue rules that are made by experts and that aim to satisfy the common good (see also Boli ch. 5). The Dispute Settlement Body in the WTO usually makes a rule by adopting the findings of a panel of experts.

In the field of health care, EBM is an interesting example; its work clearly indicates that there are best solutions (that is, scientifically based best practices) that can be identified and offered to everyone. With the expansion of voluntary rules, we have seen an expansion in proclaimed expertise (Jacobsson 2000). These experts often claim a scientific basis for their knowledge and derive their legitimacy from an association with academia, however tenuous it may be at times. Or they claim that their expertise is "technical" and instrumental, even though it may be based primarily on politics, as happens when companies try to increase their competitiveness by getting their own standard as *the* standard. The technical argument has been the rationale for delegating rule-making to standardization organizations, which has happened to a great extent in the EU in the context of creating the Single Market. The claims about expertise have been made in the context of regulation, and we find it necessary not to take these claims of expertise at face value. Experts are sometimes in positions to exert substantial influence, but often need not take responsibility for the consequences of the application of their expertise by others.

Authority through association

A third way to authorize soft regulations is to associate them with other rules, regulations or rule-makers that are perceived as being legitimate. IASB borrowed authority from both the EU and the International Organization of Securities Commissions (IOSCO), through an agreement whereby IOSCO stated that it favored IASB standards (Tamm Hallström 2004). Thus IASB managed to become the major authoritative rule-maker in that field (see also Botzem and Quack ch. 13). IOSCOs member agencies (state organizations in different countries) have agreed to cooperate in order to promote high standards of regulations that maintain just, efficient, and sound markets; and to establish standards and an effective surveillance of international securities transactions. IOSCO has become an authoritative rule-maker by connecting to IASB and other organizations in the field. In a joint venture sponsored by IOSCO, the Basle Committee on Banking Supervision (BCBS), the Committee on the Global Financial System of the G-10 central banks (CGFS) and the International Association of Insurance Supervisors (IAIS), recommendations were launched regarding public disclosure practices of financial institutions. These rule-makers do not all compete with one another; in fact, they cooperate. By connecting to each other and by establishing regulative networks, they borrow authority from each other.

Thus, we observe a development of regulatory constellations – packages of regulations and rule-makers – that may be extremely difficult for states and other organizations to forget (see also Hedmo et al. ch. 15). Both private and public organizations are involved in these regulatory constellations, and national, regional, and global organizations are involved. Clearly, rule-making is simultaneously global and national.

In this section we have illustrated how regulations are being authorized as regulators build authority around themselves or around the regulations they issue (cf. Hall and Biersteker 2002). Three modes of authorizing were identified: organizing, reference to expertise and the association to other rules and rule-makers. In practice, these modes are not mutually exclusive, but are often combined. We have tried to illustrate the complexities of transnational regulation and the degree of authorization that such organizations have achieved.

Dynamics of transnational governance – extended webs of regulation

Based on a broad collection of studies of emergent forms of transnational regulation, we have portrayed three modes of regulation and three modes of authorizing regulations. All these measures are characterized by reciprocity; it is not always clear who is governing whom. These regulations evolve incrementally with interaction among participating actors, enrollment of additional actors and in interaction with related regulating and authorizing endeavors. Our empirical data provide a basis for characterizing dynamics of present modes of regulation and re-regulation. Before turning to these dynamics, we emphasize again some of the main characteristics of soft regulation identified at the beginning of this chapter. We note a large supply of regulations, and the emergence of multiple regulators. In addition we point to blurred distinctions between coercive and voluntary rules (especially in regulatory constellations) and blurred distinctions between widely spread management ideas and regulations (especially in regulation through agenda-setting).

Our examples illustrate the seemingly continued broadening of transnational rules and rule-makers. The Global Compact is one example of how regulation extends both to new aspects of society and corporations and to new types of activities and developments. The targets as well as the boundaries for this particular initiative are far from clear.

This initiative can be viewed as an effort to strengthen state control over business corporations. When business goes global, state regulations are supplemented with international ones. And international law tends to be soft (see Mörth 2004 and ch. 6), so that accompanying changed boundaries of regulations are changed modes of regulation. However, corporations are asked not only to comply with the established principles in their own domain, but to support and spread these norms to broader groups. They are encouraged to form partnerships with companies, public bodies and civil society organizations. Regional and local networks in which company representatives are partners have been formed around the world. From this perspective, the Global Compact is a means for the United Nations to build on and use globally organized and influential corporations to spread human, social and environmental norms to states and societies. Ccorporate actors are enrolled in this effort, both as targets for regulation and control and as channels for amplifying UN governance over societies and states.

The Global Compact exemplifies the expansion of transnational regulations. Soft rules are framed by modes of regulation that emphasize networking and learning. These networks are formed and framed in a manner that results in low barriers to entry; networks are formed through principles of inclusion. This mode of regulation tends to give rise to dynamics that spur further regulations based upon initial efforts, and this organic growth occurs within the same network and by adding new groups and networks to the ones initially formed. In the case of the regulation of higher education, we also find that the expanded regulation leads to the quest for greater regulation, not only because new actors are being enrolled, but because competing regulatory schemes have been established (see Hedmo et al. ch. 15).

Participating actors in transnational regulation relations are intertwined and tend to adopt ideas and identities from each other; thus the boundaries between the various categories of international organizations are becoming blurred. Regulatory systems that emphasize soft rules, monitoring, and agenda-setting are held together by common norms and procedures. Those in conflict or unlikely to adhere to the regulations are often not punished within the system. The current mechanism for compliance in monitoring and agenda-setting activities is to include participating actors in a group and persuade them that it is of great importance to preserve their good name within the group. In this respect, it is apparent that soft regulations presume the existence of common norms and a will among those joining networks and watching each other to share common norms and to judge each other relative to these norms. It is a way of regulating by building communities that foster development of common norms and that exert social control on each other (cf. Boli ch. 5).

Although common interests may not be present at the outset, this inclusion dynamic serves to shape common interests, so that those included in the network come to share common norms. Instead of sanctions, the entities that do not follow principles or do not engage are singled out for blame and shame. This is an order in which no one has clear authority over any other; each unit is seen as sovereign, at least in part. In short, it is a mode of regulating an organized society. The present is not only "the golden era of regulation"; it is also a golden era of organization, evidenced by a steady and dramatic growth of organizations (e.g. Perrow 1979; Boli and Thomas 1999; Drori and Meyer ch. 2; Ahrne and Brunsson ch. 4). Modern organizations tend to be treated and thought of as social actors who are in control of their own interests and activities (Brunsson and Sahlin-Andersson 2000) and, hence, rather than being obliged to follow a rule, they are persuaded that it is in their best interest to follow issued regulations. Expertise and rationalized norms – a generally assumed idea of the right way to be – provides the grounds for such regulation. It is a matter of co-regulation rather than self-regulation. Our analysis demonstrates that soft regulation does not seem to be capable of handling genuine conflicts – it assumes some basic agreement among members and the existence of a community before which the regulated can demonstrate their willingness and their performance in line with the regulations. Moreover, this brief discussion indicates that the two trends of the expanded transnational approach – soft regulations and organizing – are interrelated and mutually shape each other.

Concluding remarks

In this chapter we have taken a transnational approach to the emergence of new regulations. This does not mean that a national approach has been rendered unimportant, but the national is sometimes fragmented, and always embedded in wider societal settings. We have combined insights from various theoretical areas in an attempt to demonstrate that such an approach is needed in order to find out how the complicated ecology of transnational actions and interactions proceed (cf. March and Olsen 1998: 329). The very term "transnational" shows that nations – and states – are still important (cf. Katzenstein et al. 1998), but that states must be understood to be other than coherent bodies, and not the sole or most important bodies that make up the world.

As organizational scholars, we find it especially important to point to the many organizations and their interactions, in which new forms of regulations are formed and pursued. New regulations do not develop at a superficial policy level, but in the activities and interactions of organizations. These organizations develop, as all organizations do, their own policies, interests and procedures. Because such micro organizational processes may be as important as sector-wide logics and regimes, we cannot take as a given what interests and activities are or will be pursued by single organizations or individuals operating in specific societal sectors.

Organizations and individuals play profound roles in our transnationally structured world, partly because of the sheer complexity of the transnational connections that may leave space for individual agency. And as boundaries between societal sectors blur and simultaneously separate, particularly in the allocation of responsibility and attention, it is possible for an individual or an organization to operate in parallel in different societal settings and roles. Micro studies of individual actors and individual interactions can display such processes, while revealing how individual interactions are permeated and fashioned by the context in which they evolve. When taking a micro organizational approach to the issues of the re-regulation of the world, we see how and why actors with seemingly very different and sometimes opposing interests merge into constellations that often result in the issuing of soft regulations.

Note

1. This chapter is based on comprehensive empirical studies in what at first may seem to be vastly different settings: the European Union, WTO, the UN Global Compact initiative, a transformed regulation of European management education, and attempts to re-regulate professional health. These studies were conducted in the research program, "Transnational Regulations and the Transformation of States," headed by Bengt Jacobsson and Kerstin Sahlin-Andersson and financed by the Swedish Research Council.

13 Contested rules and shifting boundaries: International standard-setting in accounting*

SEBASTIAN BOTZEM AND
SIGRID QUACK

Introduction

In this chapter we set out to investigate the emergence and development of international standard-setting in the field of accounting, with particular reference to financial reporting. Beyond technicalities and dry figures, financial reporting standards shape the categories through which corporate governance actors evaluate each other; thereby also influencing strategies and decision-making (Power 1997).

Historically, the meaning and understanding of accounting standards has been contextualized in national accounting traditions and systems. However, the last decades have seen a proliferation of activities and initiatives to make financial reporting standards comparable across national borders. Developments in accounting are part of a broader movement towards global ordering by means of standardization (Ahrne and Brunsson ch. 4; Drori and Meyer ch. 2). One common characteristic of international standardization is the lack of sanctioning power (cf Jacobsson and Sahlin-Andersson ch. 12). Thus, standard-setting organizations have to struggle for voluntary recognition of their rules. A second common feature is the degree of translation (Czarniawska and Joerges 1996) involved in international standard-setting. Actors that engage in international standard-setting contribute their contextualized interests, perceptions and strategies. The outcome of the standard-setting process is a set of highly formalized rules that need re-contextualization to be implemented. In consequence, struggles around international standards are expected to be quite significant (Brunsson and Jacobsson 2000; Tamm Hallström 2004).[1]

The neoinstitutional literature has so far paid little attention to issues of contestation, conflict, power and influence in international standard-setting processes (as notable exceptions see Schmidt and Werle 1998; Mattli and Büthe 2003). We see three main reasons for that. First, standardization is predominantly understood as a technical and rational process driven by the worldwide spread of consensual universalistic principles and cognitive routines (Loya and Boli 1999) or, in institutional economics, by functional needs of coordination (David and Greenstein 1990; Abbott and Snidal 2001). Secondly, the neoinstitutional literature deals mainly with formal rule-setting and diffusion. It does not investigate the development and appropriation of standards by actors from different contexts – a potential area for conflict (Heintz et al. 2001). Thirdly, neoinstitutional contributions have focused more on the diffusion of existing standards than on the emergence of new standards (Finnemore 1996b). Process models of institutionalization, however, suggest that the early phases of rule-setting are likely to be conflictual and contested with actors promoting different rule sets (Tolbert and Zucker 1996; Finnemore and Sikkink 1998; Lawrence et al. 2001).

In this chapter we aim to highlight the ongoing political nature of international standardization. Hence we draw on theoretical approaches that emphasize contest and conflict in rule-setting. As Bourdieu (1989; see also Stinchcombe 1965) has pointed out, the opening up of new social spaces – and international standard-setting arenas are such spaces – is likely to generate conflicts over the material and symbolic occupation of this space. Actors from different backgrounds enter the game with specific interests, perceptions, strategies, resources and goals (Djelic and Quack 2003). Interactions also involve symbolic struggles over the perception of who the appropriate actors are, what the boundaries of the space are and what the dominant logic of coordination should be. Those struggles are part of an ongoing process of re-negotiation of power relations, both at the material and symbolic level (see Dezalay and Sugarman 1995; Dezalay and Garth 1996; 2002a).

We apply this approach to a longitudinal analysis of the emergence of the international regulatory field of financial reporting since 1945. We want to build a dynamic perspective into the analysis of regulatory spaces. So far, the concept has been predominantly used to describe an outcome. Hancher and Moran (1989), for example, refer to a regulatory space as determined by a range of regulatory issues that are subject to decision by a population of organizations (see also Crouch 1986). The same applies to the notion of organizational field (DiMaggio 1983; DiMaggio and Powell 1983: 148) that refers to "organizations that, in the aggregate, constitute a recognized area of institutional life." We concur with Hedmo et al. (ch. 15) on the importance of a more process-oriented approach (for an example of dynamic analysis see Young 1994).

Therefore, the following analysis focuses on the evolving interrelationships between various actors that engage in international standard-setting, how their struggles and cooperation contribute to the emergence of an international regulatory field of financial reporting, and how they continue to shape the logics and boundaries of this field over time. The main argument presented here is that contest and conflict, instead of an impediment to successful standardization, can become a driving force of international standardization if organized within a commonly accepted procedural framework.

The point of departure: National diversity in accounting

Accounting standards are guidelines for preparing annual reports, defining the necessary information and formal rules of presentation. Accounting standards also influence the procedures for auditing financial reports. Since the emergence of the nation-state and well into the second half of the twentieth century, accounting rules have been drafted, implemented and enforced within national jurisdictions. They became necessary as a tool for national governments to help prevent corporate failure and financial crisis. National accounting systems evolved in close interconnection with other important features of national business systems (Whitley 1999; Maurice and Sorge 2000; Quack et al. 2000; Hall and Soskice 2001).

At the end of the Second World War, national accounting standards differed considerably in substance and procedure between countries. One major split was that running between the liberal economies of the Anglo-Saxon world and the coordinated capitalism found in continental Europe and Japan. In the first group of countries, accounting rules aimed predominantly at providing investors with information, while in the latter they focused on the protection of creditors' interests (Morgan and Quack 2000; Nobes and Parker 2004). As a result, relevance and reliability of information dominated accounting principles in Anglo-Saxon liberal economies whereas the principle of prudence became more salient in coordinated economies (Whitley 1999; Glaum 2000; Hall and Soskice 2001).

The second, related, split was between common law and Roman law regimes (Rheinstein 1974; Kagan 2000). Most continental European legal systems have origins in Roman law. There, accounting rules were often part of the code law system and could be changed only through legislation. In contrast, the case law system in Anglo-Saxon countries has meant that court rulings have been more significant while the development of standards was delegated to professional bodies. The US exemplifies a particular regulatory approach (Nobes and Parker 2004) to which we return later.

A third important difference between national accounting systems in the period after the Second World War was whether and how closely financial and tax accounting were linked to each other (Glaum 2000; Nobes and Parker 2004). In some countries, like Germany, annual accounting reports were used to determine company tax; in other countries, like the US, financial accounting became entirely separated from tax accounting (Bratton et al. 1996).

Those important variations naturally reflected upon the cognitive and ethical frames of those private and public actors who were developing, applying and enforcing accounting standards in the different countries. During the first half of the twentieth century, exchanges at international accounting conferences remained limited and highly academic. Cross-border transfers of practices and ideas occurred in the context of individual and organizational migration as well as through mutual exchange of publications (Loft et al. 2004; Samuels and Piper 1985: 24f). Despite the undeniable influence of such cross-border transfers and exchanges, the majority of accountants at the end of the Second World War still regarded the nation-state as their primary reference system.

The early post-war period: Expeditions into uncharted territories

Intergovernmental initiatives

The launching of the Marshall Plan in 1947 and the foundation of the Organization for European Economic Cooperation (OEEC) in 1948 set the scene for intensified discussions among politicians and accounting professionals about national accounting harmonization. Fostering economic cooperation on a transatlantic and European scale required a minimum of comparable statistical figures on economic development and public expenditure. The European Recovery Program, in particular, needed such data for the coordination and distribution of Marshall aid. In parallel, national governments across Europe adopted national planning to accelerate the reconstruction and modernization of national economies. This trend was supported by the Keynesian revolution in macro economics (Suzuki 2003) that underlined the importance of coherent public accounting for policy-making.

In consequence, the harmonization of national accounting standards – an issue already discussed in the interwar period – came on the agenda of intergovernmental organizations. The OEEC elaborated a standardized system for national income accounts and began to publish data using those standards in 1953. At the same time, the United Nations proposed a standardized system of its own in order to produce comparable national income accounts. The two systems were merged in 1956 (Samuels and Piper 1985: 56).

The Technical Assistance Program of the Marshall Plan created further pressure for cross-border harmonization. With a view to stimulating European economic reconstruction and modernization, visits and expert exchanges across the Atlantic were organized and combined with intensive dissemination of information on American rationalization methods (Djelic 1998; Zeitlin and Herrigel 2000). Exchanges involved politicians, managers and professional experts, including accounting experts. American accounting ideas and techniques such as budgeting and costing methods traveled as part of the wider transfer of US business models. Although they were adopted only selectively, this transfer raised sensitivity for issues of international comparability (Loft et al. 2004).

Soon, suggestions were made to form an International Institute of Accountancy under the aegis of the United Nations Educational, Scientific, and Cultural Organization (UNESCO) (Samuels and Piper 1985: 64). This Institute, however, never materialized, partly due to the skepticism and resistance of European professionals. In 1951, the *Union Européenne des Experts Comptables, Economiques et Financiers* (UEC) was founded as a European professional body. Members were accounting associations from more than twenty countries (Samuel and Piper 1985: 65). Compared with what intergovernmental organizations had managed to achieve in the post-war years with respect to harmonization of national income accounts, the ambitions and realizations of the UEC remained limited.

The European Community project

The next development came again in Europe through public rather than private actors. The founders of the European Economic Community (EEC) regarded comparable financial statements of companies as a cornerstone of a future common market.[2] The harmonization of accounting standards emerged from the beginning as a significant step to an economic level playing field (Haller 2002), with the Fourth and the Seventh Council Directives becoming the cornerstones of European accounting policies.

In the mid-1960s the European Commission launched an initiative to harmonize national regulation and improve the comparability of financial statements. Under the leadership of a German, the expert committee produced the so-called Elmendorff Report. That report shaped the first draft of the Fourth Company Law Directive submitted in 1971. This draft was strongly influenced by German company law: valuation rules were conservative, formats were described in rigid details and disclosure by notes remained limited (Nobes 1985: 348). The negotiations that followed in the Council were heated, focusing on national strongholds that politicians and business leaders were not ready to abandon. In particular, the determination of income and corporate tax and the incorporation of the principle of prudence remained controversial (Haller 1992; Evans and Nobes 1996).

The accession of Denmark, the UK and Ireland to the EC in 1973 complicated matters further. The UK and Ireland required that the Anglo-Saxon accounting philosophy be reflected in the Directive. The Danish, Dutch and UK delegations insisted on the inclusion of true and fair view principle (Nobes 1985: 346). The following negotiations, in technical committees and in the Council, had to bridge divergent accounting perspectives and conflicting political interests. Finally, the Fourth Accounting Directive was approved in 1978.[3] It laid down requirements for format and valuation and requested limited liability companies across the EEC to prepare annual accounts that provided a true and fair view of the company's assets, liabilities, financial position and profit or loss. It contained substantial requirements on information that had to be provided by means of notes (Haller 2002). In 1983, the Seventh Directive on consolidated accounts[4] was adopted, again after long and cumbersome negotiations. It determined the identification of groups, the scope of group accounts, the obligation to prepare, audit and publish consolidated financial statements and the methods to do so.

Both Company Law Directives compromised between conflicting political interests and accounting views. They did so through the incorporation of a considerable number of optional treatments. The resulting vagueness meant considerable confusion and diversity in national implementation. In particular, differing national accounting traditions implied varied interpretations of the true and fair principle set forth in the Fourth Directive (Haller 2002: 157).

Overall, the Fourth and Seventh Company Law Directives introduced a degree of rationalization and comparability across member states, in particular with regard to balance sheet formats and disclosure aspects (Thorell and Whittington 1994: 219), the obligation to provide consolidated statements and the methods to prepare them (Haller 2002: 159). Up until the 1980s, the requirement of the European Council to reach a unanimous decision blocked further progress towards coherence and harmonization. The problem was not only that rule-setting was fraught with conflicts but also that EEC political institutions did not provide mechanisms that could productively transform conflicting views into generally accepted standards.

In sum, the European Community project of harmonizing financial accounts was primarily driven by public actors and mostly faced political obstacles. Still, the project would not have been possible without the involvement of professionals from member countries who provided expertise. In 1966 the Commission set up a *Groupe d'Etudes* as an advisory body, which also provided accounting experts with opportunities for cross-border professional discussion and cooperation.

The Anglo-Saxon counterweight

In the same year, 1966, Sir Henry Benson of the Institute of Chartered Accountants of England and Wales (ICAEW) proposed the creation of the Accountants International Study Group (AISG). The Study Group brought together representatives of British professional accounting associations, the Canadian Institute of Chartered Accountants, and the American Institute of Certified Public Accountants. In practice, the Study Group consisted of a small elite of high profile practitioners from international accounting firms representing their national accounting associations (Thomas 1970: 63). The proclaimed purpose of the AISG was to develop comparative studies of accounting in the three nations (DeloitteToucheTohmatsu 2003). From 1967 until its dissolution in 1977, the Study Group met twice a year and published a total of twenty reports on issues of accounting thought and practice in the three countries.

The aim of the Study Group was to strengthen private standard-setting as an alternative to supranational regulation. Its work reflected the influence of Anglo-Saxon professionals and a liberal tradition of self-regulation (cf. Jacobsson and Sahlin-Andersson ch. 12; Mörth ch. 16). The initiative was also in the interest of Anglo-Saxon auditing firms trying to open up new markets in continental Europe. The political dimension of the project became apparent when, in 1972, at the Tenth International Congress of Accountants, the chairman of the AISG, Sir Henry Benson, invited professional bodies of six other nations to join in the initiative to set up an International Accounting Standards Committee (IASC).

Seizing the opportunity: Private actors structuring the field

On 29 June 1973, the IASC was created in London by representatives of national professional accounting bodies from nine countries: Australia, Canada, France, West Germany, Great Britain (with Ireland), Japan, Mexico, the Netherlands and the United States of America. Sir Henry Benson was elected chairman (Haller et al. 2000). The establishment of the IASC at that particular moment in time can be linked to the accession of Britain and Ireland to the European Economic Community and to the opposition of the British accountancy profession to the EEC draft for an accounting directive. Anthony Hopwood (1994: 243) described the situation as follows:

. . . the British accountancy bodies . . . were worried by the potential consequences of what they saw as the imposition of continental European statutory and state control on the much more discretionary relationship between corporate management and auditor in the UK . . . Wanting to have a more institutionalized manifestation of British commitment to a wider transnational and

Commonwealth mode of accounting, with the cooperation of its partners in the primarily English language audit community, the IASC was established. Its creation was intended to give a strong signal of Britain's role in what no doubt was perceived as a global accounting community rather than a more narrowly circumscribed European one.

The foundation of the IASC thus marked a significant shift in the development of the nascent international regulatory field of accounting. First, the work of the IASC focused on developing financial accounting standards for companies and thereby stood in contrast to earlier macro level approaches. Secondly, the IASC aimed at developing standards with an international, not just a European reach. Thirdly, and most importantly, private actors previously advising in the shadow of (inter)governmental decision-making bodies now claimed the centre stage of the international standard-setting arena.

Collecting standards: The early years of the IASC

With the IASC, Anglo-Saxon accounting professionals and in particular large accounting firms had an organizational platform from which they could actively pursue the aim of private international standard-setting. Furthermore, they managed to mobilize professional bodies in important industrialized countries. For the latter, participation in the IASC allowed professional dialogue and communication without any immediate repercussion on home country regulations.

The IASC was both a standard-setter and a meta-organization, with national accounting bodies as members (Ahrne and Brunsson ch. 14). Work relied predominantly on the use of members' resources[5] and the Board constituted – at least in the early period – only a weak central authority (for a parallel see also Djelic and Kleiner ch. 14). The primary purpose of the IASC was to develop basic standards that would improve the quality and comparability of financial accounts and could be rapidly accepted and implemented worldwide (Samuels and Piper 1985: 70). Therefore, it needed to take into account different national accounting traditions.

In its early years, characterized by Thorell and Whittington (1994: 224) as the "descriptive period," the IASC was issuing "consensus standards" – essentially inventories of practices accepted in various countries. Though there is little evidence of open conflict in the documented history of the IASC, there was a hidden agenda of contestation going on behind the apparently neutral and expertise-based deliberations (see e.g. Schmidt and Werle 1998; Tamm Hallström 2004). National accounting traditions and the interests of different actors were too distinct to be easily absorbed into one coherent framework. The most ostensible indication of underlying struggles is the wide range of options included in standards published at this time. The twenty-six International Accounting Standards (IAS) published during the first fifteen years of the IASC's existence allowed a wide choice of principles in application and could be used to report under such different financial reporting systems as the US-American Generally Accepted Accounting Principles (US-GAAP) and the German Commercial Code (HGB) (Daley and Mueller 1982: 45).

To sum up, during this early period the IASC allowed an exchange of information and knowledge on practices and standards in different countries, and was also of value to countries that did not have any standards in place, in particular some developing countries. The work of the IASC structured a small community of accounting experts from different national backgrounds who became wanderers between accounting worlds and developed gradually an identity as experts of international accounting standards (for expert communities see also Djelic and Kleiner ch. 14; Marcussen ch. 9).

Linking up with other collective actors: The transformation of a meta-organization

In parallel, the EEC persisted in trying to harmonize financial reporting through directives. During the 1970s, several other international, mostly intergovernmental organizations, also turned their attention to comparability issues in financial reporting. The most prominent among them were the Bank for International Settlements (BIS), the Organization for Economic Cooperation and Development (OECD) that superseded the OEEC, and the United Nations Conference on Trade and Development (UNCTAD). Their activities in the financial reporting field reflected an increasing internationalization of business, the rise of multinational companies and the growth of international capital markets.

In 1976 the IASC linked up with the "Group of Ten" bank governors at the BIS who were interested in developing financial reporting rules for their internationally active banks. The "Group of Ten" agreed to cooperate with the IASC and to fund an IASC project on bank financial statements. Three years later, the IASC met with the OECD working group on accounting standards that had started to publish Guidelines for Multinational Enterprises (Hopwood 1994: 252). In 1980, the IASC presented a position paper on cooperation at the first United Nations Intergovernmental Working Group on Accounting and Reporting and thereby entered into a working relationship with UN officials in charge of developing rules for corporate enterprise accounts (Daley and Mueller 1982).

In the meantime, many (public) national standard-setters remained highly skeptical of the IASC initiatives. To improve relations, in 1981, the IASC launched joint projects on deferred taxes with national standard-setters from the Netherlands, the UK and the US and started a series of visits to national authorities. The first formal meeting with the American Security and Exchange Commission (SEC) took place in 1984. The IASC also established contacts with the American standard-setting body, the Financial Accounting Standards Board (FASB). In the second half of the 1980s, the IASC particularly targeted national regulators of security markets and approached the International Organization of Securities Commissions (IOSCO) with the aim of establishing IAS as a recognized set of standards for company access to stock exchanges.

The IASC Board followed an explicit policy of cooptation, offering membership status to other organizations. This had an impact in time on the structure and decision-making processes of the IASC. Constitutional amendments in 1977 and 1982 enlarged the board to a total of seventeen members. Four of the additional seats were reserved for representatives of organizations with an interest in financial accounting like the Association of Financial Analysts (joined in 1986), the Federation of Swiss Holding Companies (1995) and the Association of Financial Executives (1996).[6] Furthermore, a Consultative Group was formed in 1981 to advise the IASC on strategic projects and priorities (Kleekämper 1995: 420). Over the following decade, the Consultative Group expanded continuously. Intergovernmental and private international organizations such as the International Chamber of Commerce, International Federation of Trade Unions, International Banking Association, World Bank, the OECD, and United Nations bodies became affiliated. Of particular importance was the entry of the European

Commission and the entry of the US American standard-setter FASB (Kleekämper 1998).

In 1988, the IASC introduced yet another institutional innovation, the observer status. This opened the board further still. The FASB (1988), the European Union (1990), the IOSCO (1996), and the Republic of China (1997) were all granted observer status. While they had no right to vote, they could participate in the discussions, thus inserting ideas and requirements into the debate over accounting standards.

A complete overhaul of the organizational setup took place in 2001 when the IASC was transformed into the International Accounting Standards Board (IASB). The process was initiated by the IASC Board in 1997, when it appointed the Strategic Working Group to draft a new structure. The aim was to create closer ties to national standard-setters and to limit the direct influence of professional associations. The IASB differed from its predecessor in a number of ways. Instead of being under the formal control of the worldwide association of professional bodies, the International Federation of Accountants (IFAC), international accounting standardization is now run by a non-profit foundation incorporated in the USA, the International Accounting Standards Committee Foundation (IASCF). Users and preparers (i.e. representatives of large companies) have in parallel gained increased influence.

Over time, the international accounting organization thus proved organizationally inventive and flexible. Organizational reforms in the late 1970s and early 1980s marked the departure from the principle of territorial representation. As Kristina Tamm Hallström (2004) has shown, diverging and potentially conflicting principles and goals were part of a sub-text that was underlying official rhetoric. The IASC became a platform for contest between the conflicting principles of (national and functional) representation, expertise, user needs and interests of financiers.

Shifting field boundaries and logics: From professional to financial market governance

Those organizational changes should be seen in the light of changing economic and business conditions. From the 1980s onwards, foreign direct investment increased steadily and cross-border merger activity became more frequent. The most important factor, however, was the growth of international equity markets, and particularly the centrality of US stock exchanges for global capital flows. The volume and liquidity of American capital markets made them increasingly attractive for foreign investors. In turn, American accounting rules (US-GAAP) gained global significance. As guardians of the financial reporting standards that enabled access to the world's leading capital markets, the American standard-setter, the FASB, and the SEC became key players in the regulatory field (Haller 2002). Those two agencies did not consider IASC standards an acceptable alternative. They viewed US GAAP as superior in terms of coherence and transparency, and were not ready to list foreign companies at US stock exchanges unless these fulfilled the reporting requirements as defined in US GAAP.

Through its worldwide dominant position, the SEC was able to influence the International Organization of Securities Commissions (IOSCO). Created as an inter-American organization in 1974, the IOSCO supervised securities exchanges to foster and maintain efficient and sound securities markets (Lütz 1998). In 1983, the organization opened up to foreign securities regulators and subsequently developed into a powerful global player. Like the FASB and the SEC, the IOSCO was critical of IAS on grounds of incoherence and lack of transparency. Within the IOSCO, however, some national securities regulators were more favorable to IAS.

In the second half of the 1980s, the IASC and the IOSCO entered into discussions that led to the joint Comparability and Improvements Project in 1987 and the affiliation of the IOSCO to the Consultative Group of the IASC. The objective of the project was to reduce or eliminate alternatives within standards and to make standards more detailed and prescriptive. The involvement of the IOSCO meant a shift of the international regulatory field. Until then, it had been dominated by national accounting bodies and their logic of professional clarity and coherence; financial market actors now entered the scene, bringing with them a strong logic of investor transparency.

As part of the Comparability and Improvements Project ten out of thirty-one IAS standards published before 1987 went through revision with a view to reducing the number of options. The IASC entered a new stage, described by Thorell and Whittington (1994: 225) as the "normative period." Representatives from those countries that diverged from the Anglo-Saxon model came increasingly under pressure to give up their accounting principles so that IAS would become more acceptable to financial market actors. Above all, the precautionary measure aiming at protecting creditors was perceived as incompatible with financial market expectations. In many cases, continental European options were subordinated and only treated as second-best alternatives to Anglo-Saxon benchmark options or eliminated altogether (Nobes and Parker 1985; Kleekämper 1995).

Throughout the process, the IOSCO remained a tough veto player. It supported the Comparability and Improvements Project but still was not ready to endorse the revised IAS in 1993. The decision not to approve IAS reflected internal quarrels within the IOSCO and pointed to a clear US predominance. While most European members were in favor of instant endorsements of the fourteen standards considered acceptable in 1993, the SEC wanted to recognize and endorse IAS only with a complete set of core standards.

This led to a second round of revisions. In 1993, the IASC and the IOSCO identified a list of core standards, to be revised by 1998. In 2000, the IOSCO recommended its members to allow the use of IAS in cross-border offerings and listings. Many European stock exchanges had allowed the use of IAS before 2000. Some European exchanges, like Germany's Neuer Mark, even required the use of non-local Generally Accepted Accounting Principles (that is IAS or US-GAAP) from 1997 onwards.

US exchange regulators, however, continued to insist on the use of US-GAAP. To tackle differences of opinion between Anglo-Saxon-standard-setting authorities, a sub-group of the IASC was established in 1993, called the G4+1 group (Kleekämper 1995: 422). The group brought together members of standard-setting bodies from Australia/New Zealand, Canada, the UK and the US, and representatives of the IASC. Between 1993 and 2001, the group met regularly and published several studies, further paving the way for an Anglo-Saxon accounting logic.

This process enabled the IASC and the American FASB to clarify a number of issues and led in 2002 to a memorandum of agreement between the two organizations to foster convergence between US and international accounting standards (Norwalk Agreement). In spite of everything, though, the SEC still required financial reporting to be in accordance with US-GAAP or a reconciliation of other reporting standards with US-GAAP.

One implication of the changing logic in favor of capital market requirements was that the conflicts between IAS and national accounting rules became more acute. This was particularly so for countries that had given priority to the prudence principle. While in 1991, the *Fédération des Experts Comptables Européens* (FEE), the European professional association of accountants, still claimed that there were no serious conflicts between IAS and EC Accounting Directives (FEE 1992), the gap increased in the following years as IAS were being revised.

The European Commission itself faced a complicated situation. On the one hand, negotiations between the EU, member states and the SEC, during the late 1980s, to accelerate mutual recognition of European and US accounting standards had essentially failed (Cairns 1996; Haller 2002). On the other hand, large European companies wanted access to US capital markets for both financial and symbolic reasons. Company representatives and industrial associations were lobbying for European accounting rules that would facilitate this access. The FEE that had advised the EC on several occasions favored a policy that would support IAS over the development of European directives.

Through involvement with the IASC, the European Commission took part in discussions related to the Comparability and Improvements Project and associated revisions of standards. In parallel, it established an Accounting Advisory Forum with independent experts. In 1995, the Commission came to the conclusion that although the Fourth and Seventh Directives had had a positive impact on cross-border business and financing activities within the EC, existing accounting rules did not meet the demands of preparers, users of accounts, and important standard-setters, particularly the FASB. Instead of revising the Directives, the European Commission decided to participate actively in the development of IAS. This new strategy marked an important shift away from developing genuine European accounting rules (Commission of the European Communities 1995).

In the following years, the European Commission undertook two conformity projects looking at possible conflicts between EC directives and IAS. The conclusion was that EC directives were on the whole compatible with IAS provided that the options included in the directives were exercised in line with IAS. Minor conflicting cases were discussed in the IASC Board and led to revisions of IAS. Thus, the EC was gradually moving towards acceptance of revised IAS. This movement reflected the shifting priorities of member states and the European Commission. It was also a reaction to increasing numbers of big European corporations opting for US-GAAP. Rather than having nothing to say about accounting rules, the Commission preferred to jump on the bandwagon of IAS, or International Financial Reporting Standards (IFRS) as they were labeled from 2001 onwards.

In 2001, European accounting directives were revised to ensure conformity with IAS. The European Financial Reporting Advisory Group (EFRAG) was founded as a private sector institution with an interest in financial reporting. The task of the EFRAG was to influence the IASB's standard-setting process proactively, check new drafts and standards for their compliance with European rules and advise the Commission. The formal decision to make IAS/IFRS the only acceptable international accounting standards for European consolidated companies was passed in 2002, thus ruling out US-GAAP as a tolerated alternative. From January 2005, IAS become mandatory for the consolidated accounts of publicly traded companies in the EU (Regulation (EC) 1606/2002). The EFRAG continues to serve as a bridge between the Commission as a public standard setter and the IASB as a private one (Haller 2002: 168).[7] Conflicts that arose in 2003/4 related to the endorsement of IAS 39 on financial instruments indicate that tensions between different accounting approaches do still exist. In the end, the EU accepted only a reduced version of IAS 39.

The dynamics described here point to considerable transformation of the regulatory field of international financial reporting since the early 1980s. The types of actors involved, the logics dominating the harmonization process and the definition of the field's boundaries all changed. In the early 1980s, professional accounting associations, with their attempt to establish a privately organized international standard-setting process, created a regulatory field characterized by professionalism, expertise and non-governmentalism. Towards the end of the 1990s, we find the regulatory field of financial reporting populated by a variety of organizations, both of private and public nature. On the private side, financial market actors (users) and corporations (preparers) have clearly gained influence, displacing in part accounting professionals. In consequence, the professional logic of coherent and encompassing standards for companies with limited liability has been replaced by a logic of capital market efficiency for a few large companies listed on the world's largest stock markets.

The shift from professional to capital market governance, however, has paradoxically brought intergovernmental actors back in because they are otherwise in charge of capital market supervision. The driving force behind changing boundaries and logics of the field have been struggles of influence between different groups of actors claiming to have the interest, expertise and legitimacy to participate in developing international financial reporting standards.

Providing contest with a home: Due process as a means of regulation

The process of international standard-setting in the field of financial reporting, as outlined above, has been characterized by a complicated and shifting balance between contest, competition and cooperation. Actors from different national, sectoral and functional constituencies with diverging and often even opposing interests have been struggling to influence the rule-setting process (cf. for parallels Engels ch. 16; Hedmo et al. ch. 15; McNichol ch. 17). There were open conflicts of interest but also more subtle underlying differences in understanding, interpretation and evaluation of accounting principles.

Given the variety and diversity of actors involved, the multiplicity of interests, traditions and languages, it is surprising in fact that the process of standard-setting did not simply break down. It has been argued elsewhere that resilience was the result of Anglo-Saxon dominance and capital market pressures (Flower 1997; to some degree also Haller 2002). As shown in this chapter, these factors have definitely played a role in the latter stages but cannot account for the continued participation of continental European professional bodies in the IASC.

Another explanation refers to de-coupling, compromise and systemic dominance of expertise as three key mechanisms of organizational conflict resolution within the IASC. According to Tamm Hallström (2004) de-coupling occurred in that a logic of expertise and professional discourse was predominant in the workings of technical committees while a logic of national representation remained legitimate at the Board level (see also Schmidt and Werle 1998). Compromise was favored and standards included alternatives or allowed options. Systematic dominance was given to the principle of expertise. Our view of the story, however, suggests that expertise was a rather ambiguous and contested concept and that the way to compromise changed over time. There was definitely a considerable degree of de-coupling within the IASC but it cannot account for the continued coexistence of contest and cooperation at the field level beyond the IASC as organization.

We would argue that the institutionalization of a specific procedure, commonly referred to as due process, provided a coordination mechanism for actors with conflicting interests and strategies to collaborate in a broad common venture. A due process was first introduced in accounting by the American standard-setter, the Financial Accounting Standards Board (FASB). From there it spread across the international regulatory field of financial reporting.

The FASB was founded in 1973 in response to criticisms from users and preparers of financial statements. These actors argued that their needs had been neglected by earlier Commissions in charge of developing US-GAAP in favor of auditors' interests. The FASB incorporated many different constituencies, ranging from financial executives of companies (preparers), financial market analysts and investment managers (users) to certified public accountants (auditors). To deal with divergent interests, the FASB introduced a procedural framework in three stages. Once an accounting issue was identified as calling for regulation, the Board and technical committees prepared a discussion memorandum as a first stage. The memorandum was published and the public invited to comment within a fixed time period. As a second stage, the Board developed an exposure draft and made it available to the public for further comments. As a third stage, the Board voted on the exposure draft which was then either adopted or withdrawn to develop a new draft (Ballwieser 1998; Vorwold 2000).

The IASC was founded the same year as the FASB. Although its membership was limited to the accounting profession, it nevertheless adopted from the beginning a due process modeled closely on that of the FASB (the compatibility between due process and soft regulation is evident; cf. Jacobsson and Sahlin-Andersson ch. 12; Jacobsson ch. 10; Mörth ch. 6). This due process has naturally generated reactions and criticisms, mainly on the grounds of lack of transparency and for being biased in favor of Anglo-Saxon actors and logics (Larson 1997). The IASC revised its due process several times and following the organizational reform of 2001, the IASB is currently reviewing its organizational procedures, using the same mechanism of public participation.

More recently, the due process has been diffused to national and European arenas. National standard-setters have adopted it for the corresponding national standard-setting committees that were established in the course of the 2001 IASB reforms. The European Financial Reporting Advisory Group, advisor to the European Commission, established a modified version in 2001. To avoid duplication of consultative processes within the IASB and national standard-setting bodies, the EFRAG limits its invitation to comment primarily to its own consultative network – European national standards-setters and other appropriate organizations. Comment letters from the public are considered but not explicitly invited.

The successful diffusion of due process as a means of mediating contest and conflict within the international regulatory field of financial reporting would deserve more detailed analysis. From an ex ante perspective, it appears plausible that this procedure gained legitimacy within the field despite some of its shortcomings (i.e. unbalanced participation rates) because it provided a formal framework for the mediation of different interests and approaches. The formal framework has been supported, and to some extent filled with content, by a gradually emerging international community of experts. This community developed not only a dedication to the task of international harmonization of financial reporting standards, it also strengthened the due process as a legitimate means to deal with divergent interests.

Conclusions

In this chapter we have analyzed the emergence and development of the international regulatory field of financial reporting. We have described how different groups of individuals and collective actors have become involved in the standard-setting process, how they struggled over the directions that this process should take, and how the nature of actors, logics and boundaries of the regulatory field changed over time. The dynamic development of the regulatory field has meant that the form and content of financial reporting standards have gone through numerous re-negotiations and revisions. The process is still ongoing.

In conclusion, we would like to draw attention to three findings that can be of general interest for research on standardization as a means of building global order (cf. Ahrne and Brunsson ch. 4). First, international standard-setting is a political process in the sense that it involves struggles around decision-making and symbolic power between different groups of actors. In the case discussed here, this did not necessarily mean open conflict or clear-cut negotiation. Tensions between conflicting interests, perceptions and strategies were often dealt with at a more subtle level and appeared as hidden sub-text of official rhetorics.

This applied particularly when the standardization work was done by experts cultivating their own technical language, modes of communication and contestation (cf. Drori and Meyer ch. 2).

Secondly, the analysis demonstrates the value of a research design that focuses on regulatory fields instead of individual standard-setting organizations (cf. Hedmo et al. ch. 15). Standardization activities moved out of one area and into another. Actors were coming and going: Intergovernmental actors were pushed aside by professions, but with the shift towards capital market efficiency they came back again in their function as financial market regulators. Governance shifted from professional to financial market logic (cf. Djelic ch. 13). The boundaries of the field were stretched in this or that direction depending on the evolution of interests and power interactions. The analysis, thus, points to the need to make actor constellations and field boundaries themselves the object of a historically sensitive empirical analysis.

Thirdly, the results indicate that contestation between different standard-setters may not necessarily block regulation, provided that procedures exist to handle opposing and conflicting approaches in a way that generates procedural and/or output legitimacy. We propose that contest and conflict, if organized within a commonly accepted procedural framework, can become a driving force of international standardization. We have identified due process as such a mechanism and pointed to the emergence of a community of shared meaning as a supporting element (cf. Djelic and Kleiner ch. 14; Marcussen ch. 9). Though members of that community might still disagree on particular issues, they nevertheless developed a shared reference to the international field of standard-setting and its due process procedures.

As a final note, the study raises questions about inclusion and exclusion from international standard-setting. Actors, we saw, moved in and out and continuously redefined the boundaries of the regulatory field. While our research design makes it possible to detect actors and organizations that were engaged over time even briefly, it ignores groups and organizations that never entered the regulatory field as defined by the dominant actors.

Notes

* Authors are listed in alphabetical order. Special thanks go to the editors of this volume for their constructive comments. We also would like to

thank the participants in the workshop on "The Multiplicity of Regulatory Actors in the Transnational Space" held in Uppsala in May 2003 and in the EGOS Standing Working Group on "Comparative Studies of Economic Organisation" at the 2004 Colloquium in Ljubljana.

1. International standard setting refers to the processes of standardization that take place beyond the nation-state through the interaction of private and public actors. This goes further than traditional intergovernmental standard setting.

2. The Treaty of Rome, signed in 1957, commissioned in Art. 54, para. 3g the Council and the Commission to undertake the necessary steps to coordinate the "safeguards [. . .] required by Member States of companies and firms" with the view to make them equivalent throughout the Community. (The Treaty of Rome as published under http://europa.eu.int/abc/obj/treaties/en/entr6d03.htm.)

3. Fourth Council Directive 78/660/EEC of 25 July 1978, based on Art. 54 (3)(g) of the Treaty, on the annual accounts of certain types of companies.

4. Seventh Council Directive 83/349/EEC of 13 June 1983, based on Art. 54(3)(g) of the Treaty, on consolidated accounts.

5. Up to 2001, board members and experts were delegated and continued to be paid by the auditing firms or other organizations to which they belonged (Tamm Hallström 2004: 129ff.).

6. The fourth seat remained vacant.

7. The case of accounting regulation displays some similar features to technical standardization where Mattli has coined the term "joint standards governance" to describe the interdependence of private and public actors (Mattli 2003: 217ff.).

14 | *The international competition network: Moving towards transnational governance*

MARIE-LAURE DJELIC AND
THIBAUT KLEINER

Introduction

In 1945, antitrust was an American legal tradition with no impact beyond the national borders of the United States. American antitrust reflected the double belief that competition should be the highest organizing principle and that the economy functions best when competitors have limits for permitted activities. Outside the United States, competition was feared rather than fostered for its potentially disruptive and chaotic consequences.

Sixty years later, we can see that a major reversal of trend has taken place. Competition has become the name of the game, both in national and international economic spaces. About one hundred countries have today a competition policy and competition institutions that seem quite compatible, at first sight, with the American antitrust tradition. The last few years have also seen multiple attempts at fostering antitrust principles and institutions within the transnational space as well as initiatives to spread a "culture" of antitrust. Those have culminated in 2002 with the creation of the International Competition Network (ICN). The ICN is a virtual network organization where national and regional antitrust agencies collaborate in their fight for competition. It is quite open to inputs from experts, consultants, academics or even firms and industries and the principal aim of that network is to push along and further the establishment, the implementation and the monitoring of global and "seamless" practices and standards.

The object of this chapter is to try to follow the genealogy of this "community of interests," as the founding fathers of the ICN like to call it. How does one go from a peculiar and quite isolated national regulation to a transnational system of governance? Understanding the process by which emerging transnational actors have been and are being constructed is a necessary first step, we believe, to understanding the ways in which they function and the modes of governance they reveal (see also Marcussen ch. 9). After telling rapidly of the American origins of antitrust, we focus in turn on two important stages. First, we recount how antitrust crossed the United States borders after 1945 and was transplanted in a small number of countries and supranational bodies. This was a double story of exportation and importation. Secondly, the scale and scope of transfer accelerating significantly in the 1990s, we identify the steps that were taken during that decade to overcome simple internationalization and to move towards global or transnational governance. The setting-up of the ICN embodies this evolution and reveals this ambitious project. In the discussion, we look at the ICN as an important actor of global or transnational governance. As such, we identify its constitutive features and wonder about similarities and differences with other types of transnational governance spaces and actors.

A national legislation goes abroad

Throughout the first half of the twentieth century, the emergence of an antitrust tradition was one element of American exceptionalism.[1] The American take on issues of competition and interfirm collaboration was then unique and quite peculiar. After 1945, the consequences of the war and a redefinition of the geopolitical context led to the first attempts at exporting – and importing – the American antitrust tradition, to Germany and Japan for example, to the European coal and steel community and to international spaces such as the General Agreement on Tariffs and Trade (GATT).

An island of antitrust in a sea of interfirm collaboration

In the United States, collusion and cooperation between independent firms became legally impossible and morally unacceptable towards the end of the nineteenth century (Djelic 2002). Following the Civil War and its many disruptions, cartels and other forms of loose networks and agreements had proliferated as a strategy to achieve control and market stabilization. In 1890, the United States passed the Sherman Antitrust Act, with the intent to curb the threat that those aggregates of economic power represented and to re-establish the conditions for free and fair competition. The unique set of conditions, however, in which the Sherman Act was enacted limited its domain of applicability and had unintended consequences of significance (Peritz 1996). Tight combinations seemed outside its reach, at least as long as they remained within the legal frame of particular states (Roy 1997; Djelic 1998). Corporate lawyers identified mergers as a legal alternative to cartelization and the first American merger wave (1895–1904) was soon in full swing (Sklar 1988; Fligstein 1990). In 1914, the Clayton Act confirmed a "rule of reason" argument for size and mergers, thus institutionalizing an oligopolistic understanding of competition (Peritz 1996). By the 1920s, both the per se prohibition of cartels and the "rule of reason" with respect to mergers had become trademarks and defining features of the American antitrust tradition.

In Europe, by contrast, a tradition of interfirm collaboration was clearly dominant. The move to cartelization had started during the 1860s and 1870s. It was triggered by disruptions and uncertainties – stemming from technological developments, market cycles and political turmoil. But it also benefited from an institutional context that was tolerant of interfirm collaborations if not actively fostering them. In most European countries, competition and price wars tended to be negatively valued as essentially disruptive both of the economy and of social order. Agreements and cartels, because they set limits to competition and its associated disruptions, were identified as progressive steps away from chaos and towards orderly and rational economic development (Michels 1928; Dussauze 1938).

At the international level, interfirm collaboration also prevailed. By the 1920s and 1930s, international cartels had become very powerful and they had significant reach – different estimates show the share of international trade under cartel control at somewhere between 40 and 50 percent during that period (Kudo and Hara 1992: 2ff; Haley 2001). Interestingly, American firms were also involved in international cartels, without US antitrust authorities objecting too much (Kleiner 2003b). During the 1920s and 1930s, the most famous – because they were soon judged infamous – such involvements were those of General Electric in the Phoebus cartel, and those of Dupont, Allied Chemicals or Standard Oil in cartels that were dominated by the German firm IGFarben (Maddox 2001).

Engineering a German revolution

Things changed radically after the Second World War when the peculiar American tradition of antitrust was revived and crossed national borders. An important destination was Germany where the United States

loomed large both as a model and as an architect in the process of reinvention that country was going through (Berghahn 1986; Djelic 1998).
A widely shared conviction that cartels had played an important role
in the economic and military build-up of Nazi Germany led Western
Allied forces to introduce decartelization measures.

In February 1947, the American military government imposed a
decartelization and deconcentration law that set itself within the long-
standing American antitrust tradition (Damm 1958). How far should
deconcentration go was a question that led to heated debates (Martin
1950; Djelic 1998: 81ff). In the treaty allowing Germany to return
progressively to sovereignty, the American government demanded that
German agencies prepare their own competition law.

This did not prove an easy task. Difficulties stemmed mostly from
the powerful and sometimes violent resistance of business communities
to the grafting in Germany of the American antitrust tradition (Damm
1958; Braunthal 1965; Djelic 1998). It took ten years, a protracted
fight and strong American pressure all along for the Germans finally to
agree on a bill. The Federal Law against Restrictions of Competition
was enacted in July 1957 and came into force on 1 January 1958.
Antitrust had been transferred to Germany, but it had been partially
translated and adapted in the process in response to powerful resistance
and to fit the local context (Djelic and Quack 2005).

Seeding antitrust in the European space

While the United States was encouraging or imposing bilateral transfers
of its antitrust tradition, it was also pressing for initiatives with a cross-
national dimension. When the French – under the initiative of Jean
Monnet – proposed in May 1950 a plan for pooling European coal and
steel industries, Americans expressed fears that this project might lead
to the emergence of a European-wide cartel. Monnet however insisted
that the goal was to create a competitive space, to stimulate production
and productivity. He had American experts such as Robert Bowie, a
Harvard antitrust lawyer, prepare antitrust provisions (Monnet 1976;
Djelic 1998).

As in Germany, resistance was strong, notably amongst French,
Belgian and German business communities. But the final ECSC treaty
endorsed anticartel and antitrust objectives and Articles 65 and 66 were
incorporated as a major dimension of that treaty. Article 65 dealt with

cartels and loose agreements, prohibiting them in principle. Article 66 dealt with abuses of market power due to concentration. Those two Articles gained particular historical significance when they were transferred in 1957 to the Rome Treaty, extending antitrust principles to most sectors of Western European economies. Here again, however, the transfer of an American antitrust tradition had come with a degree of translation and adaptation.

From a handful to an "epidemy" – the spread of antitrust

Until the late 1980s, antitrust was contained within a few Western countries. US-led initiatives and codes of conduct against anticompetitive practices within the GATT in 1944, within the OECD in 1967, and within UNCTAD (United Nations Conference on Trade and Development) in 1980 did not prove effective. There were no mechanisms associated to allow for the monitoring of those codes of conduct, to ensure that they were being adopted, followed and implemented.

Europeanization, the extension of the West, globalization . . .

Three developments in the second half of the 1980s were to give a new and significant impetus to the spread of antitrust across borders.

First, in chronological order, came the revival of the European construction effort. After some difficult years, the EEC moved under the impulse of Jacques Delors to deepen and solidify its integration. The European Single Act was signed in 1986, paving the way to the 1992 Maastricht Treaty. This process clearly boosted activity around antitrust at the community level. One of the more direct and significant consequences was the enactment of a European Merger Regulation in 1989 giving the European Commission the exclusive power to investigate mergers with a community dimension. Then, in turn, such activity and activism at the European level trickled down to the level of member states. Both old and recent member states developed and/or modernized their antitrust regimes in the late 1980s and early 1990s to follow evolutions at the European level.

A second important development was the fall of the Berlin Wall and the "extension of the West" as a direct consequence. With respect to antitrust, this triggered a wave of international missionary activity on a scale and scope much greater than had been the case in the early

Table 14.1. *US antitrust authorities technical assistance missions worldwide*

Period	Expenditures	Total missions	Total advisors	Foreigners trained in US	Areas
1990	N/A	6	5	N/A	CES
1991–92	N/A	68	64	19	CES, former Soviet Union (CIS), Latin America and Caribbean
1993–94	$2.72 billions	118	95	65	CES, CIS, Latin America and Caribbean, Africa, East Asia and Pacific
1995–96	$3.84 billions	110	104	92	CES, CIS, Latin America and Caribbean
1997–98	$2.03 billions	88	82	57	CES, CIS, Latin America and Caribbean, Middle East, Australia
TOTAL	Over: $8.59 billions	390	350	233	

Notes. Includes both the Federal Trade Commission and the Antitrust Department, Department of Justice.

Compiled from the ICPAC Final Report, 2000, Annex 6-A, to be found online at: www.usdoj.gov/atr/icpac/finalreport.htm

1950s. Both American and European antitrust authorities were actively involved in the process of trying to "export the rules of competition regulation" to Eastern and Central Europe but soon also to many other areas in the world (Rouam et al. 1994; Pittman 1998; Muris 2002). Specific efforts were made through UNCTAD to expand and increase technical assistance efforts in antitrust related matters.[2] As an illustration, Table 14.1 shows the rapid explosion of missions from the United States to the rest of the world since 1990.

In part as a consequence of this missionary activity, competition laws were prepared and enacted rapidly in many countries. In the field of merger control, for example, there are more than sixty jurisdictions with merger notification regimes today when there were only about twelve in 1990. In the process many countries translated and adapted antitrust principles and institutions to their local context. Thus, even though most competition regimes in the world today can be traced back to the American antitrust tradition, the multiplication of antitrust regimes first in Europe and then in other regions of the world, including developing countries, has not resulted in pure and simple convergence and homogeneity of rules and institutions (cf. also Morgan ch. 7).

A third important development, finally, is the episode of economic internationalization – or globalization – that gained momentum during the 1990s. A few figures can give a sense of its significance. The number of multinational firms increased – in 15 developed countries – from around 7,000 at the end of the 1960s to somewhere around 40,000 at the end of the 1990s. Sales of foreign affiliates worldwide now represent $14 trillion – up from $3 trillion in 1980 – and this is nearly twice as high as the total amount of global exports (UNCTAD 2000). Another important figure has direct relevance for antitrust – particularly when it comes to merger control activities. In 1990, cross-border mergers and acquisitions amounted to around $150 billions worldwide. In 1999, the amount was more than $700 billions.

... And their problematic consequences

Globalization and the multiplication of jurisdictions with competition law systems have undeniably created new constraints and challenges. In that context, the risks of inconsistent and/or conflicting regulation and decisions have become particularly salient (Monti 2001; Jalabert-Doury 2003). There are also practical consequences for companies operating internationally, notably for merger control compliance in transnational deals (see also Morgan ch. 7). First, it may be difficult to identify where notification is necessary, given some discrepancies between threshold tests.[3] Secondly, many countries require that filings be submitted within a short period after a transaction emerges (typically less than two weeks). Thirdly, the costs of filing may be high because of burdensome information gathering and high filing fees (Rowley et al. 2000).[4] Finally, national authorities may have different views on an international operation and may therefore impose conflicting solutions on the same parties, leaving them in an awkward position and creating legal uncertainties (Abdelgawad 2001: 167). A new challenge for the antitrust world has therefore emerged – to create the conditions for a better coordination of existing regimes and jurisdictions.

A first strategy: The multiplication of bilateral agreements

The first strategy initially was to develop bilateral agreements as a forum to ensure reciprocal understanding. The main case of such bilateral agreements was signed between the United States and the European Union in 1991 and renewed in 1998. The agreement provided for an alert notification system. Each party notified its partner when a case was likely to affect important interests of the latter. Cooperation meant exchange of information and synchronization of investigations, notably in relation to international cartels, and coordination of enforcement activities. The "Positive Committee" provisions enabled the side adversely affected by anti-competitive conduct carried out in the other's territory to request the competition authority of the other side to take enforcement action. Those have rarely been formally activated but they are an inspiration for daily cooperation.

Similar bilateral agreements have been signed between the EU, Canada and Japan. The US has also multiplied bilateral agreements in the 1990s – notably with Canada, Israel, Australia or New Zealand. In fact, by the end of the 1990s, bilateral agreements linked together the most developed antitrust authorities in the world. A number of bilateral agreements have also been concluded with less developed countries, and notably the future members of the EU in Central and Eastern Europe and other associated countries (Van Miert 1998).

Undeniably, bilateral agreements have had positive results (Melamed 2000). This is particularly true of the EU/US connection (Schaub 2000). However, bilateral agreements have also shown their inherent limitations. It became clear in some cases that different legal systems, different procedures, different analyses of the same facts, and possibly different political perspectives could lead to different appraisals of the same operation by two authorities, in spite of the existence of bilateral agreements.

This was strikingly shown in three high-profile cases of EU–US divergence. The first case was the attempt by Boeing to buy MacDonnell Douglas in 1998. Boeing rapidly got clearance from American authorities while the European Commission strongly argued that this merger could jeopardize the competitive process in the world market for large commercial aircraft. In the end, the merger was cleared after the Commission accepted a package of commitments, both structural and behavioral. A second case to make the headlines was GE/Honeywell in 2001. The tension between the EU and the US reached a high point when the European Commission ruled against this all-American merger, after it had been cleared by the US authorities (cf. Morgan ch. 7). A third case was Microsoft. After many developments, the US Department of Justice reached an agreement in 2001 with Microsoft and the case was closed in November 2002. By contrast, there was no settlement in Europe and the Commission fined Microsoft € 497 million for abusing its market power in the EU. The EU concluded, after a five-year investigation, that Microsoft Corporation broke EU competition law by leveraging its near monopoly in the market for PC operating systems onto the markets for work group server operating systems and for media players. The case led to another stretch in transatlantic relationships and was then put to the European Court of Justice.

Much has been said around these EU–US clashes; some have insisted about differences in legal systems or economic approaches, others have pointed at diverging commercial interests or philosophical differences (see e.g. McKenzie 2000; James 2001; Drauz 2002; see also Morgan ch. 7). These cases – together with the difficulties of handing bilateral dialogues when there are now ninety countries with an antitrust law – have shown the limits of bilateral agreements. As a consequence, antitrust authorities have started to grant more attention and resources to multilateral initiatives.

Multilateral frameworks: Initiatives and resistance

As indicated above, there were a few attempts after the end of the Second World War to push along a multilateral framework for antitrust. There have been many more since the 1990s that have followed different routes. Those different routes revealed conflicting perspectives and divergent opinions as to the purpose and desired scope of multilateral agreements.

The OECD route

The OECD revised its 1967 Recommendations in 1986 (OECD 1986) and then again in 1995. But those guidelines remained, throughout the revision process, fairly restricted in scope. They related only to practices that might have an impact on trade and dealt neither with other forms of international cartels nor with cross-border mergers. In parallel, the OECD was promoting international discussion of competition policy matters within its long-standing work group, the Competition Law and Policy Committee (CLP) and within a working group that brought together members of the CLP and of the OECD Trade Committee.

The CLP has worked particularly well as a forum for promoting soft convergence of competition policies among its members and for providing technical assistance to certain OECD observers and non-members. It has not, however, achieved much success in rule-making or dispute settlement. Convergence was more in terms of understandings and principles than in terms of rules, processes, and practices (cf. Marcussen ch. 9).

EU leadership in the WTO

In 1994, EU Commissioner Van Miert convened a group of "wise men" to think of the stakes and challenges for competition policy. Published in 1995, the Van Miert report called for the elaboration of a "plurilateral framework for competition ensuring the respect of certain basic competition principles" (Commission Européenne 1995). Karel van Miert was also instrumental in pushing along the constitution in 1996 of a Competition Working Group in the World Trade Organization (WTO). At the beginning, this group had a limited mandate but the EU was hoping to push it towards the negotiation of international rules (Van Miert 1997).

A few years later, the EU was again taking the lead, suggesting that competition should be tackled in the new round of negotiations. In April 1999, the former EU Competition Commissioner, Sir Leon Brittan, was proposing that "in negotiating a WTO agreement, we should aim for gradual convergence of approaches to anti-competitive practices that have a significant impact on international trade." Reactions to the EU position have been far from enthusiastic. Developing countries seemed overall fairly skeptical of the economic interest for them of adopting a multilateral framework. The US also insisted that any agreement should be based on a voluntary basis and that it would be difficult to frame competition in a way similar to trade (WTO 2000; Pons 2002). Given the failure of the Seattle and Doha trade summits to reach agreement on an agenda for a new round of multilateral negotiations, it is now unclear how or whether competition will be considered by the WTO in the future.

American initiatives

In parallel to these developments driven by the EU, the US launched its own initiative in 1997: the International Competition Policy Advisory Committee (ICPAC). Over the course of two years, the ICPAC held extensive public hearings in Washington with the participation of business executives, economists, lawyers and competition officials from around the world. In the end, the ICPAC recommended against the development at that time of binding competition rules subject to dispute settlement procedures within the WTO. Instead, it made a number of propositions based on non-binding agreements (ICPAC 2000). The idea was that binding agreements – as the EU was pushing for within the WTO – were not the only way to develop cooperation in the field of competition policy or to facilitate further convergence and harmonization. The ICPAC argued that countries might be prepared to cooperate in meaningful ways but may not be ready to be legally bound under international law. The ICPAC report therefore proposed a Global Competition Initiative to foster dialogue not only amongst antitrust officials but also between officials and broader communities with a view to bringing about common understandings and a common culture, greater convergence of laws and analyses.

International Competition Network – the global temptation

At the moment when the WTO round seemed stalled and the prospects for pushing along a binding multilateral agreement within the WTO framework were not good, the conclusions of the ICPAC report were opportune and came in handy. They paved the way to the setting up of the International Competition Network.

The genesis

In September 2000, Joel Klein (then heading the antitrust division of the US Department of Justice) was busy selling the Global Competition Initiative project. A conference coorganised in Brussels by the

International Bar Association and the European Commission, celebrating the tenth anniversary of the EC Merger Regulation, was in that
respect a defining moment. Klein then proposed to move along with the
ICPAC recommendations (Klein 2000). During his closing speech, EU
Commissioner Mario Monti expressed his support for the initiative in
warm and appreciative terms, as a constructive step in the right direction. Mario Monti's warm and rapid reaction was probably informed in
part by what was taking place in Europe at the time. In 2000, a European Competition Network had been created that brought together
European competition authorities, with a view to sharing knowledge
and experiences and to builing the foundations of a more solid and
systematic cooperation at the European level (ENA 2002).

The initiative for a global competition network was boosted by
another gathering in October 2000 at the Fordham Corporate Law
Institute in New York. Again under the auspices of the International
Bar Association, representatives from the main antitrust authorities
and the international legal community were brought together. Several
brainstorming meetings took place during that conference and in the
following months between senior competition officials from different
parts of the world. At the same time, the new Bush administration
seemed in principle to support the initiative.[5] The project was gaining
momentum.

Then came the GE/Honeywell case in 2001. At first sight, this could
have jeopardized any kind of cooperation initiative. What happened
in fact was the contrary – the case seemed to make such an initiative
all the more necessary and urgent (Akbar 2002). Hence, discussions
between interested parties continued, essentially along the lines of the
ICPAC report. At the yearly conference of the Fordham Corporate Law
Institute, on 25 October 2001, top officials from international antitrust
authorities representing thirteen countries plus the EU announced the
establishment of the International Competition Network (ICN). The
founding document indicated that "ICN will provide antitrust agencies from developed and developing countries a stronger and broader
network for addressing practical competition enforcement and policy
issues."[6]

The International Competition Network: A virtual forum

The ICN is defined by a number of original features – reflecting both
the necessity to bring together a multiplicity of actors in a flexible

manner and a willingness to differentiate it from existing fora such as the OECD or the WTO.

The first and probably the most striking of those features is its quasi-virtual nature. The ICN is a "project-oriented, consensus-based, informal network of antitrust agencies from developed and developing countries that will address antitrust enforcement and policy issues of common interest and formulate proposals for procedural and substantive convergence through a results-oriented agenda and structure" (ICN website). Membership is voluntary and open to any national or multinational competition authority. There were fourteen members at the creation, more than sixty members by the time of the first conference in Naples in September 2002 and close to eighty in 2004.

Running the ICN is a steering group that consists of representatives from antitrust agencies "that are committed to going forward with the mission of the ICN." Concretely, this has meant that the oldest and more established antitrust agencies have been dominant in the steering group. Each member serves a two-year term but the mandate can be renewed. The steering group is responsible for identifying projects and defining work plans that will then be approved by ICN members during the annual conference. The ICN does not have and does not plan to have a permanent secretariat, nor does it have a budget. Members pay for themselves and the agency holding the chair pays that year for secretarial costs.[7]

Not only is the ICN a virtual network. It is also an open one. This concretely means that while only antitrust agencies can be members, there is an attempt at stimulating interaction with a wider community (cf. Marcussen ch. 9). The targets are "non-governmental advisers," that is members of international organizations, representatives from consumer and industry associations, practitioners of antitrust law, economists and members of the academic community. The founding fathers often assert their willingness to stimulate the emergence of what they call a "community of interest." Annual conferences provide the opportunity for a physical rallying point where this "community" comes together. The private sector – and particularly US law firms – has been extremely involved, providing significant input and support to the network.

Finally, the ICN is a meta-organization (see Ahrne and Brunsson ch. 4): it is project-based and characterized by an ad hoc structure – where working groups are transient and transitory. Working groups can include non-governmental advisers but they will be led by representatives from antitrust agencies. At the moment of creation four working groups were set up, each dealing with projects that were singled out as particularly important and as being of priority. There are now six working groups: mergers, membership, funding, capacity building, antitrust enforcement in regulated sectors and operational framework. The ICN's work projects have brought substantial results notably in three areas: the control of multi-jurisdiction mergers, capacity building in developing and transition economies and competition advocacy (Roebling et al. 2003).

In short, the ICN has undeniably had a promising and rapid start, with concrete steps taken and already some positive outcomes. In particular, the promotion of global "best practices" around certain issues, like mergers, has been seen as a clear success, revealing the strength of a flexible network (Jalabert-Doury 2003; Roebling et al. 2003). However, some other commentators insist that the ICN, even though it represents an improvement on "anarchic" international ventures, is nevertheless inferior to WTO-type solutions both in terms of reduction of jurisdictional conflicts and of efficiency (Budzinski 2004). In addition, as European Commissioner Mario Monti commented in the fall of 2002, "it remains to be seen to what extent this ultra-light structure is able to support the increasing expectations heaved onto it" (Monti 2002).

Interesting in that respect is the persistence of divergence between competition authorities, despite membership to the network – as for example in the Microsoft case. Striking also is the resilient unwillingness on the part of some ICN members to enter into binding rules, even though those may stem from ICN working groups.[8] In parallel, it is worth mentioning that another venture was recently created that looks very much like the ICN, but targets civil society at large. Called the International Network of Civil Society Organizations on Competition (INSOC), it emulates the ICN structure and follows its missionary ambitions, aiming at promoting "a healthy competition culture by coalition building between civil society and other interested organizations" (Foer 2003; www.incsoc.net). The rapid success of the ICN has therefore already prompted followers to copy its template – a template that might be particularly well adapted to transnational governance (see Marcussen ch. 9; and McNichol ch. 17 for parallel developments).

Discussion and conclusions

The story we have told is that of the progressive emergence of a transnational governance forum. There have been, to date, three main stages in what has been a long process.

Internationalization of a national regulation

The first stage was one of rather direct but limited transfer of what was initially a national set of rules. In the years following the end of the Second World War, the peculiar American antitrust tradition was exported and imported in a small number of countries and in emerging transnational spaces such as the European Coal and Steel Community or the GATT. This first stage reflected the geopolitical dominance of the United States at the time and the radical questioning of a system – cartelized economies – that was associated with dark moments in European and world history. In that context, the United States projected its principles, practices and institutions well beyond national borders and did so in three ways. First, it imposed them in a direct and coercive manner in countries like Germany or Japan. Second, it pushed them through the emerging system of transnational organizations and institutions, which it was fostering at the time. Finally, it projected them in a more passive and indirect way by becoming a model for a number of countries but also for the budding Western European space. This process of transfer came with a fair amount of resistance locally and was associated with a degree of translation and local adaptation (Djelic 1998).

The second stage came much later and it was stimulated by three parallel developments – Europeanization, the end of Communism and globalization. Since the late 1980s, antitrust principles, institutions and practices have spread quickly from two main centers – the United States and the European Commission – to a large number of countries, close to 100 altogether. In this second stage, the process of transfer and adoption became ritualized, often reflecting a quest for institutional legitimacy (Meyer and Rowan 1977; DiMaggio and Powell 1983). It was mediated by antitrust experts from the American and European antitrust authorities, who spoke in the neutralized language of efficiencies and "best practices" often translated into scientific economics (see Drori and Meyer ch. 2). The process of transfer had apparently lost some of the political dimension it had had at the onset of the Cold War.

This second stage has been characterized by a two-pronged movement. First, there has been less translation and adaptation of the texts and principles than in the 1950s. In fact, in certain countries – particularly in EU candidate countries – the texts and principles were copied more or less word for word (ENA 2002). Secondly, though, by the early 2000s there is still a fair amount of decoupling between principles and local implementation (see Meyer et al. 1997a). National regimes still differ significantly from each other; interpretation and implementation are still very much shaped and influenced by local conditions, national legacies, pre-existing institutional constraints and available resources.

From parallel national jurisdictions to transnational governance

The third stage of the process started in the late 1990s and is still very much in the making. This third stage is the attempt to transform a landscape of multiple national antitrust jurisdictions into a unified sphere of transnational governance. This stage is now symbolized by the emergence of the ICN. But looking at the transnational history of antitrust, we see that the path to transnational governance set by the ICN is only one and for now the most successful of three paths that were successively identified and tested.

A first path to transnational governance in antitrust matters was illustrated above by the OECD route. A public transnational forum, the OECD, with the legitimacy of an expert body on general economic issues but with no direct power of constraint or coercion upon its members – and even less so on non-members – published recommendations and guidelines. The idea was that national agencies would spontaneously and voluntarily seize upon those guidelines and frames developed by an external, "neutral" and scientific public body to work towards a coordination of their practices in antitrust matters. The reach of the OECD route would initially have been limited to member countries.

A second path was barely threaded in the story recounted above; however a key actor – the European Commission – considered it very seriously. This was the project to use a pre-existing transnational space – the World Trade Organization – to develop a set of binding rules that would apply to all members of the WTO, altogether around 150 countries today. The reach in this case would undeniably have been global and rather efficient in terms of imposing a common framework.

The International Competition Network (ICN) was a third possible path – and for now this seems to be where transnational governance in antitrust matters is heading (for parallels with governance in financial and accounting matters see Marcussen ch. 9; Botzem and Quack ch. 13). The idea was to create a transnational space where all – or at least a majority of – national and regional actors of antitrust could come together to negotiate and agree upon homogenization if not full convergence of regimes and practices as well as enhanced coordination to deal with the peculiar challenges of the transnational arena. The reach is more or less global since around 100 countries today have antitrust regimes and those countries represent about 85 percent of world GNP. The idea, furthermore, was to open the ICN to all actors, from the public, semi-public or private sectors who had in one way or another an interest in antitrust.

Actors and scenarios of transnational governance

These three paths to transnational governance are characterized by quite distinct features. They point to different approaches to governance in the transnational space – and in fact to different ways of thinking about governance in general. The OECD route points to what we call here the "Experts" scenario. Initiatives within the WTO reveal the temptation of the "Statist" scenario. Finally, the ICN path belongs to what we call the "Community" scenario (see also Djelic and Quack 2003). The characteristics of those three scenarios are brought together in summary form in Table 14.2.

In the "Experts" scenario, the transnational rule-maker as an institution is clearly separate from purported rule-followers – even though some representatives from the latter may be involved in the process of rule-making. The legitimacy of rule-makers lies in their association with expertise – often in this century combined with "scientific" claims and credentials (Drori and Meyer ch. 2). The process of rule-making is entirely expert-driven and the products of rule-making are norms or standards, in any case of the soft law type (as described in Ahrne and Brunsson ch. 4; Jacobsson and Sahlin-Andersson ch. 12; Mörth ch. 6). The logic or mode in which transnational rule-makers may have an

Table 14.2. *Three possible scenarios for transnational governance*

	"Experts" (OECD)	"Statist" (WTO)	"Community" (ICN)
Rule makers vs rule followers	Separate	Separate	Combined
"Product" of governance process	Standards	Binding rules (close to laws)	Beliefs
Mode, logic of rule making	Expert driven	Political negotiation with expert input	Negotiation with expert input and with a view to create "communion"
Mode, logic of rule monitoring	"Expert awe"	Coercion, constraints	Socialization
Pluses and minuses	Will not work without a very strong legitimacy of the expert body – not really the case in our story	Efficient. Strong and hard rules will be likely to come though with exceptions and "decoupling."	Easy to start. Potentially leads to stronger and more stable homogenization. Not very constraining in the first place.

impact on purported rule-followers is what we call "Expert awe" – the belief in the superiority and legitimacy of expertise based on scientific claims. In the pure form of this scenario – and this was the case in the OECD story – there is no power of coercion or constraint linking rule-maker and purported rule-followers.

For want of a better word, we call the second scenario of transnational governance, the "Statist" scenario, in reference to the temptation to transfer the type of rule-making and rule-monitoring characteristic of Westphalian nation-states to the transnational arena. In that scenario, the transnational rule-maker is again clearly separate from purported rule-followers. This time, it has the features of a transnational institution or organization deriving its legitimacy from the mandates given to it by nation-states. The process of rule-making as a consequence is a political process – that takes the form of bargaining and negotiation between member countries with a greater or lesser degree of expert input. The products are binding rules, the transnational equivalent of hard laws. Quite often, those binding rules are associated with a set of exceptions and partial or temporary exemptions that reflect the political nature of the negotiation process (Zeiler 1999; see also WTO website). The transnational institution or organization has at its disposal the means and tools to make the rules "binding" – to impose their adoption, and sometimes to constrain or even coerce member units into implementing them.

The third scenario we call the "Community" scenario and it is different on a number of counts. First of all, there is no differentiation between rule-makers and purported rule-followers. The community of those – in the wide sense of the term – likely to be concerned by a particular set of rules of the game take it upon themselves to define and agree upon those rules (see Hedmo et al. ch. 15; McNichol ch. 17; Engels ch. 16). In the story we have told, the community brings together both organizational members (directly) and individual ones (indirectly). The ICN is a meta-organization at its core (Ahrne and Brunsson ch. 4) with a very open periphery. The logic or mode by which rules are made in this third scenario is one of negotiation but with the ultimate objective of reaching a situation of "communion." The process of negotiation comes to reflect, naturally, a potential imbalance in terms of resources, clout, power and influence. Undeniably, in the antitrust story we have been telling, negotiations are and will be biased in favor of developed countries and regions with an older tradition of antitrust (see also Marcussen ch. 9). The prominent position in the ICN of US antitrust authorities and of US law firms implies that the competition "gospel" is there unlikely to diverge too much from US antitrust dogma. At the same time, what communities of that sort are intent on producing, before anything else, are common beliefs. In the antitrust story, a key objective of the ICN is to foster a common conviction in the superiority of the market and competition and to bring about a deep common understanding of what those terms mean and imply (see Djelic ch. 3). Once such a common base of principles has been stabilized and crystallized – once, in other words, the stage of deep philosophical "communion" is reached – homogeneous standards, norms and practices should follow all the more naturally and easily. The link between rule-making and rule-following in this kind of scenario is the mechanism of socialization with associated processes in particular of "naming and shaming" (Boli ch. 5). The impact of this type of mechanism may be slow to come. But, in the long term, it may be better suited than external constraint or coercion for bringing about effective homogenization and coordination of standards and practices.

The story is still very much in the making but important steps have been taken on the "community" route. In the contemporary story of transnationalization of antitrust, the community scenario predominates even though it is partially hybridized with an "expert" and scientific logic (Drori and Meyer ch. 2). The path currently threaded privileges the development of normative institutions or rules of the game – common beliefs and cultural values – over the setting-up of structures, organizations and binding regulation (see Ahrne and Brunsson ch. 4). It appears to favor mechanisms of self-regulation, socialization and self-responsibilization over logics of coercion and external constraints. This does not mean, however, that power issues are evacuated from the process, quite on the contrary as we have seen. The concept of hegemony, however, appears more directly useful and applicable in this context (Foucault 1980). The ways in which the games of negotiation and collective decision-making will combine and interact with hegemonic processes in the coming years still remains to be seen. The ICN, however, appears to be an illustrative case of a type of "transnational social space" (Morgan 2001) that may in the future become increasingly widespread.

Notes

1. While we focus here on the United States, Canada also was a pioneer in antitrust legislation.
2. Within the UNCTAD framework, the EU is for instance helping the development of a regional competition policy within the Common Market for Eastern and Southern Africa (COMESA) with a budget of around 750,000 euros (Monti 2001).
3. Certain thresholds – the latter defining when firms ought to notify a concentration – are based on measures of assets or revenue (USA and EU for instance), while others are based on market share tests (Brazil, Slovenia and Turkey for instance).
4. In the US a filing fee of US$45,000 applies per acquiring person per transaction; in Croatia, leader in this league, the filing fee is US$140,000. Altogether, given multijurisdictional deals, a complex deal, even though not problematic in terms of anti-competitive concerns, may lead to a total cost in excess of US$1 million.

5. An indication of that can be found in the nomination of Bill Kolavsky, who had been directly involved in the ICPAC initiative, at the post of Assistant Attorney General of the Department of Justice. Bill Kolavsky was subsequently extremely influential in setting up the International Competition Network.
6. From here on, a lot of the information provided on ICN comes from the following website: http://www.internationalcompetitionnetwork.org/about.html. The thirteen countries at the foundation were: Australia, Canada, France, Germany, Israel, Italy, Japan, Korea, Mexico, South Africa, the United Kingdom, the United States, and Zambia, to which should be added the European Union.
7. A group in charge of collecting external funding was created recently to support, in particular, developing countries, which may lack the financial resources to participate actively.
8. This can be seen from the proceedings of the Seoul conference, for instance, in the case of recommended practices for merger control.

15 | *The emergence of a European regulatory field of management education**

TINA HEDMO, KERSTIN
SAHLIN-ANDERSSON AND
LINDA WEDLIN

Introduction

Management education has expanded dramatically around the world
over recent decades. The expansion has been particularly salient in
Europe, where existing business schools have flourished, and new ones
have proliferated. As business schools have grown, so has the number
of programs on offer, particularly Master of Business Administration
(MBA) programs. Linked to this expansion, professional associations,
the media, states, expert groups, international organizations, and many
other entities perform monitoring and assessment activities and circu-
late extensive information about management education. Accreditation
and ranking are two such activities, originating in the US but nowadays
also well established in Europe. Since the late 1990s, management education providers in Europe have been accredited after going through
quality assessment processes of, for instance, the European Quality
Improvement System (EQUIS), and the leading US accrediting organization, the Association to Advance Collegiate Schools of Business
(AACSB). Schools and programs have also been assessed in international rankings in major business newspapers and magazines. These
rankings were largely inspired by those conducted by US newspapers,
and were also influenced by European and US accreditation standards
and by the characteristics of the most prestigious management programs worldwide.

Accreditation and ranking are not only ways of monitoring, assessing, and spreading information about management education; we
argue that they have become new modes of regulation for management education. Their emergence affects other forms of regulation
and the development of management education in general. The examples provided here exemplify a re-regulation of management education
that challenges the traditional role of the state in regulating higher

educational systems in Europe. These new, soft modes of regulation have emerged transnationally, albeit in close interaction with governmental and intergovernmental regulatory systems.

The interplay between various assessment and regulatory activities shapes a regulatory field with a dynamic interconnection between those regulating and those being regulated. The concept of a regulatory field is elaborated in the following section. The empirical sections of this chapter describe the development of management education, and of rankings and accreditation activities in Europe. We then move on to analyze the interplay of those developments and thus the formation of a regulatory field. The chapter ends with some tentative conclusions about the impact of the developing regulations on the future of management education in Europe.

Regulatory impacts on field developments

Management education encompasses a diverse mix of schools and programs: independent business schools and university-based business programs; full-time, part-time, and distance-learning MBA programs; and executive management training programs – to name but a few. However, with the extended rankings, accreditation, and general media coverage, management education programs increasingly tend to be regarded as comparable and as all belonging to the same category, to an organizational field.

An organizational field consists, according to the now classic definition by DiMaggio and Powell (1983: 148) of "those organizations that, in the aggregate, constitute a recognized area of institutional life: key suppliers, resource and product consumers, regulatory agencies, and other organizations that produce similar services or products." DiMaggio and Powell and later others (e.g. DiMaggio 1987; Leblebici et al. 1991; Greenwood et al. 2002; Lawrence et al. 2002) have shown that once such a field is established, strong mechanisms drive organizations in the field to become increasingly similar. Hence, it is not surprising to find that management education worldwide is currently being re-structured along similar lines, and that management education seems to be becoming increasingly similar.

Together with a definition of organizational field, DiMaggio and Powell's (1983) article contributed the frequently cited typology of mechanisms explaining and bringing along increasing isomorphism:

coercive, mimetic, and normative mechanisms. A closer look at the interconnectedness of these mechanisms reveals the impact of regulation on field formation and development. DiMaggio (1983) showed that state expansion had a profound impact on the field of art. Through issuing rules for certain grants, the state exerted coercive pressure on organizations in the field. Through such regulatory measures, the state also exerted more indirect influence on the other two isomorphic processes.

The most enduring impact of federal support, DiMaggio argued, may not be direct effects on individual organizations, but rather indirect influences on the structure of organizational fields (DiMaggio 1983: 148). Those organizations that gained state support came to be perceived as more successful by their peer organizations and hence tended to be imitated (DiMaggio 1983). Organizations, in general, tend to imitate organizations perceived as more legitimate and successful (DiMaggio and Powell 1983: 152; Sahlin-Andersson and Sevón 2003). Mimetic mechanisms can thus follow on coercive ones. As to normative types of mechanisms, they are driven by professions. Professions are subject to the same coercive and mimetic pressures as are organizations, and are often closely linked to and supported by the state (DiMaggio and Powell 1983: 153); and so this pressure can be also more or less indirectly affected by state policies. Apparently, states can exert important influence on fields, even when they do not directly control or influence individual organizations.

The papers by DiMaggio (1983) and DiMaggio and Powell (1983) were written during a period of state expansion and increasingly complex and rationalized state intervention. The situation with regards to higher education (Hedmo 2004) and other social sectors started to change in the late 1980s together with a transformation of states (cf. Djelic ch. 3; Jacobsson ch. 10). These changes of states as regulators do not mean, however, less regulation; rather, new groups of regulators and regulations have emerged and grown in importance (Knill and Lemkuhl 2002). Many such regulatory organizations are of an international or transnational character (Boli and Thomas 1999). The community of regulators includes not only states, but also a complex pattern of various types of interconnected organizations (Rose and Miller 1992). As a consequence, the contemporary regulatory landscape is profoundly transformed.

Much regulation builds around soft rules, that is, non-hierarchical forms of regulation that are not legally binding (Mörth 2004 and ch. 6). Soft rules transcend the regulation–de-regulation divide. What is often termed "de-regulation" involves a new type of regulation, a line of thinking that has been pursued in the concept of "responsive regulation" (Ayres and Braithwaite 1992; see also Moran 2002). States, international organizations, professional associations, and non-governmental organizations may be included in the formation of regulatory networks and be subject to regulations formed in those networks.

This development calls for an understanding, not only of how regulation influences operations, but also how the regulators interact with each other and with other organizations in their field. Newly emergent regulators cannot be assumed a priori to play a prominent role, but their activities, struggles, and interrelationships with other organizations should be subject to the same field-analysis as other organizations.

Organizational fields, according to Scott et al. (2000), "incorporate both organization sets – individual organizations and their exchange partners and competitors – and organization populations – aggregates of organizations exhibiting similar forms and providing similar or related services." DiMaggio and Powell (1983: 148) made a similar point when noting that "the field idea comprehends the importance of both connectedness and structural equivalence." This twofold meaning of fields allows researchers to analyze the generative interplay and transformation of actors, meanings, and activities. The identities of actors guide action, but are at the same time shaped and re-shaped as activities and events unfold (March and Olsen 1998).

Field analysis points to the importance of considering the interlinked dynamics between individual organizations. It is important to look both at relationships among organizations in the same category in a given field (such as relationships among education providers or regulators) and at relationships between those regulating and those being regulated. Regulators form what we call a "regulatory field." With this concept we seek to show how a regulatory set-up of a sector emerges through interactions between regulators but also across regulators and those who are being regulated.

With the concept of regulatory field we acknowledge that not all activities mentioned above – such as rankings, and media coverage of MBA programs – were originally intended to serve a regulatory function. However, as the new monitoring and assessment efforts emerge, build on each other, and become intensely intertwined, they come to form a regulatory field that frames and influences individual actors – be they education providers, participants in educational programs, or rule-setters or monitors of programs. Our studies show that the intertwined educational providers, regulators, and monitoring bodies develop in relation to each other, so that the whole field ends up constituting a "regulatory knot."

The re-regulation described above has been observed in studies of various sectors and regions. However, both the expansion and re-regulation of management education appears especially salient in Europe and so it seems reasonable to focus our study on the emergence of a European regulatory field of management education. However, our analysis shows that developments in Europe are largely influenced by and intertwined with developments in other parts of the world – primarily the US. This suggests that the dynamics found in this particular case may not be unique either to management education or to Europe.

Methods and data

Our analysis is based on three sets of data. A first set captures the development of management education units and programs in Europe over the past forty years. The data was collected from secondary sources such as guidebooks and directories of business schools and MBA programs, and academic literature pertaining to the historic development of management education in Europe and elsewhere (Engwall 1992; Daniel 1998; Engwall and Zamagni 1998; Locke 1989; Moon 2002). The picture that emerges is one of dramatic expansion of management education.

This expansion has translated into a wide variety of programs and schools and intensified efforts to compare, judge, and spread information about these programs and schools. Such information circulates through expanded media coverage, including ranking lists. Our second set of data shows the development of this media coverage with a special focus on the development of European rankings of management education. The data builds upon material from newspapers and from the websites of major business newspapers and magazines, personal interviews with journalists from the *Financial Times*, and personal interviews with the deans and/or PR/media directors of six European business schools. This set of data also indicates strong expansion, and shows how this expansion has emerged in close interplay with the development and expansion of management education programs, and also with non-European rankings and other monitoring and regulating modes.

The third set of data concerns the emergence of a European system of accreditation, another development that has taken place in close interaction with the expansion of management education. This data draws on documentation and archival material from the European Foundation for Management Development (efmd). This organization initiated the European accreditation system for management educa-tion in the mid-1990s. The data also includes personal interviews with efmd members involved in the process of structuring this pan-European system.

All three data sets were compiled between 1998 and 2003. The data was analyzed first separately and thereafter together, so as to discern both distinct and common features and to capture the interrelated-ness of the processes. Each of these sets of data is contextualized so that it becomes clear how each development is both influenced by and influences other developments.

A regulatory space is formed

A small number of business schools were established in the early twen-tieth century in Europe but developments intensified from the 1950s onwards when many business schools and university-based programs in business studies were established (Engwall 1992). As these programs expanded, their offers became more complex and diversified – coming to include MBAs, executive education, and corporate university train-ing. Even though new programs adopted similar labels, proliferation also led to variation. This, in turn, increased the need for comparisons and standardization. This development becomes especially clear as we follow the proliferation of MBAs.

The first MBA programs were offered by US business schools in the early twentieth century (Daniel 1998; Crainer and Dearlove 1999). Since then, MBA programs have been established all over the US and later all over the world. The first European MBA program was estab-lished with the foundation of the Institut Européen d'Administration des Affaires (INSEAD) in 1958 followed by new programs around Europe in the 1960s and 1970s. The expansion increased dramatically in the 1980s and 1990s (Daniel 1998). Some programs arose from collaboration between European management education providers and their US partners; others were formed as the European management education providers imitated well-known programs or widespread models and guidelines.

These processes were similar in pattern to other Americanization (Djelic 1998) and imitation processes (cf. Westney 1987; Sahlin-Andersson 1996; Sevón 1996; Sahlin-Andersson and Sevón 2003), in that models were only partly imitated; as models were imitated they were subject to translation and edited to fit local expectations and circumstances. Thus European MBA programs came to display considerable variation, arising from national differences and the timing and procedures at program initiation (Mazza et al. 2005).

MBA and similar management education programs were formed outside or on the fringe of the state-regulated education system. In systems that were mainly state controlled, these programs provided an opportunity for educational organizations to expand operations in ways not prescribed by the state. This meant that "anyone" could offer such a program, and a number of MBA programs were established by less well-known schools and by organizations outside the national higher education systems. In addition, several European countries deregulated their higher education systems, which meant that management education more generally became less subject to coercive state control than had previously been the case (Hedmo 2004).

With their proliferation, MBA programs became an institutionalized part of European higher education. It became more or less taken for granted that at least the large universities and business schools should offer such programs. Because the label "MBA" was used for all such programs, despite great differences in format, they were all subject to comparison and to the widespread expectation that this label should correspond to a certain content. Providers of and participants in MBA programs also requested regulation so that they could determine what the term "MBA" stood for and ensure the quality of the programs on offer. The increased cost of management education coupled with enrolment growth and the increasing diversity of such education gradually eroded trust; this erosion of trust has been shown to drive the so-called "evaluation industry" with reference to higher education

(Trow 1998). Thus, in the absence of coercive regulation, a regulatory space (cf. Young 1994) was created for specifying what the label did and should stand for.

The expansion of rankings

In the late 1990s, ranking lists of MBA programs and business schools proliferated in international business newspapers and magazines. In January 1999, the London-based *Financial Times* published the first international ranking of European and American MBA programs (Financial Times 1999 (25 January)). This was the second attempt by the newspaper to launch a credible international ranking list; the first attempt, in 1998, met with heavy criticism before it was even published, and was withdrawn awaiting response from and consultation with business schools (Crainer and Dearlove 1999: 177). Another ranking was published in May 1999, this time pertaining to executive education. Both rankings were repeated in 2000, but were expanded and made more comprehensive. A ranking of international executive MBA programs was launched in 2001 (Financial Times 2001 (22 October)). In 2000, *Business Week* published its biennial ranking of "The Best Business Schools," featuring thirty US business schools. The same year, *Business Week* also included a separate ranking of seven European and Canadian business schools, thereby including non-US schools in their surveys for the first time (Business Week 2000 (2 October)). In 2001 *The Wall Street Journal* published its first ranking of international business schools, based on a survey of company recruiters (*The Wall Street Journal*, 30 April 2001), and in 2002 a comprehensive international MBA ranking was published in *The Economist*.

The "model" for the new rankings came largely from the US, where business school rankings have been published and produced since the 1970s (Elsbach and Kramer 1996; Daniel 1998; Crainer and Dearlove 1999; Segev et al. 1999; Wedlin 2006). The *US News and World Report* and *Business Week* started to produce their rankings in 1983 and 1988, respectively; both these journals ranked schools offering MBA programs (Graham and Morse 1999; Business Week 2000 (2 October)). The proliferation of rankings in the late 1990s shows that interest in international comparisons and global ranking lists had surged.

The decision by the *Financial Times* to produce rankings was part of an effort, started in 1995, to establish an authoritative business education section to attract young, business-school-trained managers to read the newspaper and to subscribe. As more newspapers increased their coverage of management education issues, competition between them led other media outlets to start publishing or to extend rankings of business schools and MBA programs. Ranking of business schools and management education became in a sense a "market."

The decision to produce rankings was also spurred by demand from leading European business schools for an international ranking list that would include European schools, to balance US rankings featuring US schools only (Interview, business education correspondent, *Financial Times*, 29 March 2001). A brief review of the ranking lists in 2000, reveals that the same schools dominate most of them. In the *Financial Times* Harvard, Wharton and Stanford held the top three positions, with the top-ranked European schools being placed lower – London Business School (LBS) eighth, INSEAD ninth, and the International Institute for Management Development (IMD) eleventh (Financial Times 2000 (24 January)). For the executive education list the ranking was similar: Harvard, Columbia, and Stanford were top of the list for open enrolments, followed by IMD fourth, LBS eleventh, and Instituto de Estudios Superiores de la Empresa (IESE) twelfth (Financial Times 2000 (23 May)). In the *Business Week* European list, INSEAD took the lead, coming before LBS, IESE, and IMD (Business Week 2000 (2 October)). Even though US business schools were prominent in the lists, European schools also held top positions, and thus they found the lists to be a way of establishing a reputation in the international field of management education (Wedlin 2006).

Rankings provide a means of distinguishing "serious" from "less serious," or "good" from "bad" business schools – something desired by business schools themselves. Such an argument for rankings was expressed by the director of Manchester Business School in a *Financial Times* interview: "It takes a lot of time and money and it is a pain at times, but it is a necessary condition for being in the MBA market. It does provide a minimum kitemark"; furthermore, "it puts us on an elite list and gets us into the game" (Financial Times 2000 (8 September)). Participation in international rankings is voluntary for schools, and they have to submit information to the ranking bodies. To date, most business schools participate in all major international rankings. This may be changing, as some leading American schools, including Harvard, have announced that they will pull out of some of the rankings; however, it is too soon to discern the implications of this.

This quest for order and distinction in the field emerged together with another development at the time, namely, the initiation of a European accreditation scheme. One business school director expressed the desire for discipline and order more clearly, and linked this to the development of accreditation:

I find that for [us] it is important that the European level of competence, and professionalism and standards is at the highest possible level . . . We actually paid, together with a few others, an initial sum of money to help efmd develop their approach, because, again, we feel it is important that the European playing field is somehow disciplined and you don't have all these fly-by-night schools, you know, fragmentation. So in that sense it is very important for us. But, for us as a school *per se*, I have to say that I don't think we got major insights out of the accreditation process. Nobody asks whether we are accredited or not; it's our reputation which is strong and drives it for us. (Interview, business school director, 2000 15 February)

The development of a European accreditation system

Like ranking, accreditation has its roots in the US. Since the early twentieth century it has been the main model to regulate the performance of American higher education providers and programs. Accreditation rests on quality standards that are predetermined by professionals in various academic disciplines, and the activity is run and administered by independent, non-governmental organizations (Kimmel et al. 1998; Eaton 2000). The primary American organization for accrediting business schools and programs is AACSB (Porter and McKibbin 1988).

In the 1990s, systems for accrediting management education were also started around Europe at the national level, these systems being mainly intended for programs at the master's and MBA levels. In 1997, accreditation was introduced at the European level by the efmd. The European Quality Improvement System (EQUIS) hosted by efmd was the first system based on pan-European standards; in addition, it covered schools that operated both within and outside European national higher education systems.

Efmd consisted of and represented the interests of leading European business schools, national and regional counterparts, and corporations (www.efmd.be). Over the past twenty years, efmd has claimed that one of its primary tasks was to "raise the quality of its members' management development activities" (efmd 1985). In the 1980s and 1990s when the number and diversity of business schools and management education programs were increasing dramatically in Europe, quality was more frequently discussed and quality innovations such as the Strategic Audit Program, used to monitor the quality of management education, were set up (efmd 1991). Efmd also initiated widespread cooperation with national accreditation associations within and outside Europe, both to share experience and compare evaluation procedures and quality standards.

In the early 1990s, the need for an efmd-based European accreditation scheme was frequently debated. The idea was at first met with a clear lack of enthusiasm from most efmd business school members, as accreditation was perceived as being too rigid and "uniform" for the diversified field of European management education. What finally persuaded efmd to continue with its plan was the discovery that the American AACSB was seriously planning to export its accreditation activity to Europe. It then became necessary to react and respond to the AACSB strategy, to defend and promote European "values" by constructing a European parallel to the AACSB system.

Other current developments also motivated the creation of an efmd-based accreditation scheme. One such driving force was the establishment of EU policies for creating the internal market, which also extended to higher education. In addition, efmd had more organization-related motives for launching the accreditation. Like many international organizations, efmd was struggling to maintain membership, attention, resources and meaningful tasks. Efmd found accreditation to be an important means of defending its position as an important European forum in management development. The development of regulatory activities and attempts to make these activities legitimate and significant were ways for the organization to attract members, interest, resources and legitimacy.

The idea of developing the accreditation scheme was initiated by efmd but the setting up of the EQUIS system was a collaborative effort. The project was prepared and formed inside an independent unit called the European Quality Link (EQUAL), which consisted of efmd and European accreditation organizations operating at the national level. Cooperation also meant dispute and disagreement among EQUAL members. One source of contention was the tendency of EQUAL members to defend their own systems and quality standards during meetings; another was the change in direction that happened in the European system. Initially, the intention was that EQUIS should be active only in those national contexts in which evaluation procedures such as accreditation were absent. Quite soon, however, it became clear that EQUIS was moving towards becoming a system operating solely at the European transnational level. It then became obvious to one EQUAL member, the British Association of MBAs (AMBA), that the future role of EQUIS could threaten the survival of its own accreditation system that was moving towards greater international acceptance. As a result, AMBA withdrew from EQUAL in 1997 to focus more on marketing its own system on the international market.

The standards and procedures of EQUIS were formed both in imitation of the competing AACSB accreditation system and in negotiation between the various schemes and standards of individual EQUAL members. In order to be Europe specific, the system incorporated a "European dimension," which represented the international dimension of schools and their connections with the larger business world (efmd 1997). To handle the diversity of European management education institutions and programs and to "guarantee" the system's success throughout Europe, EQUIS adopted a "flexible approach" which also allowed for continuous development and refinement of the accreditation scheme.

In 1997, nineteen member schools of efmd voluntarily agreed to undergo the EQUIS accreditation process (www.efmd.be). The purpose of this commitment was to legitimize EQUIS both internally and externally, and to finance implementation of the accreditation system. In exchange, the pioneering schools were promised the possibility of testing and refining the standards of the EQUIS system (efmd 1998a). By July 2005, eighty-seven education providers had received EQUIS accreditation. These institutions were not only situated in Europe, but also in North and South America, Africa, Australia, and Asia (www.efmd.be).

A regulatory field

The above account depicts how European management education largely grew at the margins of national higher education systems, and how partly new actors, such as professional organizations and the media, have become engaged in regulating management education activities. European MBA-type programs were initially set up in imitation of US models, but were translated to fit the diverse schools and systems of higher education. Even though programs looked different in different settings, they tended to use the same labels (e.g., "business school" and "MBA"). The European situation of widely dispersed and institutionalized, yet diverse management educational programs, gave rise to a demand for comparison, assessment, and regulation on the part of students, employers, and program organizers. This opened up a space for new regulatory actors and activities, such as accreditation and rankings, to emerge and spread.

Regulatory activities were partly driven by business schools' demands for distinction and "order" in the field. However, although educational institutions in Europe are now eager to become accredited and take considerable interest in published rankings, the demand for and interest in them largely arose after they were introduced. An expanding market for MBA programs and management education has driven the demand for rankings and accreditation, and the emerging regulatory activities have in turn contributed to forming a European field and market for management education (on marketization, see Djelic ch. 3; Engels ch. 16).

The rankings and accreditation systems, and the interplay between them, form new modes of regulation in Europe. Such regulation is not directly coupled to systems of sanctions or resource allocation. Moreover, such regulation is voluntary and includes large elements of self-regulation. Those regulated have been involved as members of the regulating organizations, and also as financial supporters and participants in getting the systems started; thus the regulator and those regulated are not hierarchically coupled to each other (cf. Brunsson and Jacobsson 2000; Jacobsson and Sahlin-Andersson ch. 12). In this sense, the new regulatory systems are very different from the system of national directives, formerly the main way of regulating higher education in Europe (Engwall and Zamagni 1998). The regulation does not arise from groups where representatives of various nations meet, but rather in groups that cut across and go beyond national boundaries; the new regulation could be characterized as transnational rather than national or international.

The European accreditation and rankings schemes developed in response to each other, in interaction with education providers and as responses to other accreditation and ranking. This suggests that we cannot understand the development and impact of one of these activities without taking the other into account and thus we need to analyze the interrelationships among regulators, or the development of the regulatory field, in order to explain the regulatory developments. In the next section we further analyze the interrelationships among the various regulators, and show how they have led to the formation of expansive regulatory activities.

Collaboration and competition among regulators

Competition between regulators and program providers, concerning what values should dominate European management education, was an important impetus for the issuance and expansion of new regulations. The development of regulations has arisen out of regulators' interest in controlling the criteria according to which programs and schools were being assessed, and in maintaining or acquiring dominance in the field of management education. The European efforts arose in imitation of US exemplars, but were at the same time driven by a desire to distinguish the European style of management education from the US one, and to retain a European identity.

These competitive struggles were combined with cooperation, primarily amongst the accreditation organizations. Several non-European schools have shown interest in undergoing the EQUIS accreditation system. In this expansion, efmd and the AACSB have started to cooperate. In 2001 the two organizations mutually accredited an Asian business school, but still on the basis of each organization's particular quality standards. This "strategic alliance" was perceived as a competitive advantage for both parties, as the accreditation model became more widely disseminated and taken for granted globally. The development in Europe has been driven by and is driving accreditation efforts beyond the borders of Europe; thus the European regulatory field is intertwined with global fields of management education and regulation.

The regulatory efforts developed in reaction to each other, but they also built on and benefited from each other. The development of accreditation featured in the media, and spurred discussions about quality among business schools and in the media. As the accreditation system developed, the media conducting the rankings also built it into their own evaluation systems. The *Financial Times* has an unwritten policy of only covering accredited MBA programs and schools in their weekly "business education section" (Interview, business education correspondent, *Financial Times*, 29 March 2001). The *Financial Times, The Wall Street Journal, US News and World Report*, and other rankers, use accreditation to select the business schools to include in the initial surveys for the rankings.

Rankings and the European accreditation scheme developed at approximately the same time, and were interlinked and mutually dependent. This partly follows from the fact that rankings and accreditation rest on different principles of discernment: while accreditation rests on inclusion, rankings rest on exclusion. A ranking puts in place a hierarchy between those included, and the inclusion of some means the exclusion of others. Rather than stressing conformity, the system enhances differentiation between actors along a standardized axis.

As the European accreditation system became established and widely known, an increasing number of schools applied to become accredited. Many of these did not conform very well to the criteria on which the system was originally based. For example, while the first group to be accredited consisted mainly of independent and well-known business schools, over time many less well-known schools applied, as did departments that were less autonomous parts of state-controlled universities. The criteria for accreditation were gradually adapted to encompass this broader group of management education providers. The expansion of accreditation led to an enhanced interest in rankings, because leading schools were seeking to differentiate themselves from other accredited schools.

Moreover, with the expansion, non-state, voluntary regulations came to overlap and be combined with state regulations; state representatives manifested interest in reforming their regulatory systems in response to the voluntary ones, and sought to imitate aspects of them. In this way a mechanism formed in which expanded regulation led to requests for new and further expanded – complementary and competing – regulation. In 1998 a demand was made within the EQUAL unit by recently appointed members from Eastern and Central Europe, for the development of specific guidelines for European MBA programs (Interview, project manager of EQUAL, 10 May 1999). Efmd developed such guidelines and claimed that these would assist schools, students, and employers in striving to achieve transparency and convergence, based on the best practice in the market. According to efmd, the guidelines serve another important purpose, namely, to contribute to the effort to establish national and governmental regulatory systems for MBA programs. A third purpose served by the guidelines is to contribute to the further development and expansion of EQUIS by incorporating MBA guidelines into that system (efmd 1998b).

The legitimacy of the regulators is not, however, a given. For regulators to appear legitimate and attractive, they incorporate input from "leading" business schools into their ranking and accreditation schemes. Thus, the design and impact of the regulations were as much dependent on those regulated, as those regulated were dependent on the regulations. In legitimizing the regulations, we also find interrelationships among the regulators that have resulted in extended regulations as well as in the issuance of standards, guidelines, and recommendations.

Criticism has been directed towards the media as a ranking body and towards the varying procedures they use in conducting rankings. Business schools and professional organizations have demanded new and extended quality standards and guidelines to "regulate" the practice of ranking (Dearlove and Jampol 1999; efmd 2000). And within efmd, business school members expressed a need for establishing an independent ranking list based on the EQUIS standards. The American body running the admissions test for business education, the General Management Admissions Council (GMAC), has taken another such initiative. This organization developed the "MBA Reporting Criteria" in 2000, with the intention of establishing norms for how ranking information was to be reported and to provide access to such information through the Council's website. All information submitted to GMAC for publication on the website is audited, securing the accuracy and consistency of the data. The council reported strong support for this initiative among business schools, and by June 2004, 148 schools throughout the world (primarily from the US and Europe) had declared their intention of adopting the criteria and submitting information to the database (www.gmac.com). The GMAC initiative was developed together with business schools, and supported by the accrediting organizations AACSB, AMBA, and efmd as "strategic partners" in GMAC. This initiative also found support from some ranking organizations that were aiming to establish their rankings as legitimate and controlled sources of information and assessment (Interview, business education correspondent, *Financial Times*, 29 March 2001).

The above account describes the emergence of an extended system of regulatory activities intertwined with the proliferation of management education throughout Europe. Regulatory systems have been formed through highly incremental processes, where the development of some regulations led to the further issuance of new regulations. We have shown the importance of collaboration, competition, and imitation not only among education providers, but also between regulators and providers of education, and among regulators. We conceptualize this as an emerging regulatory field, which has shaped the development of the European and global management education fields. We argue that the interplay among program organizers and regulatory actors has formed the backbone of the establishment of European management education as a recognized area of institutional life.

Regulatory field struggles

When analyzing sets of actors and activities and the interrelationships among them in terms of a regulatory field, we put the regulations, regulatory actors, regulatory activities, and the interrelationships among them to the fore in the analysis, and concentrate on how these are framed and formed through activities and relationships among those comprising the field. In this way, we point more clearly to the importance of the regulators than has generally been the case in research into organizational fields. Even if no single actor controls the regulations issued or even seeks to govern by issuing regulations, together these monitoring, rule-setting, and assessment activities form into a field that regulates. We have also focused on a new set of influential regulators: professional organizations and the media. The new forms of regulation arose outside state regulatory systems, but not entirely independent of states. The emergent accreditation system was partly supported by the European Union, and over time it has both been influenced by and has influenced the various national state regulatory systems throughout Europe.

Our analysis has shown how the regulatory field has become an arena for struggle between various interests as to the criteria for defining activities within the field, and as to who has the authority to decide and control the criteria for judging the activities and the members of the field. In addition, it is an arena where organizations struggle for resources and attention and for their own survival. Through these struggles, the field has expanded both geographically and in terms of the number of regulating activities, creating space for new and extended regulatory efforts. Although both those regulating and those being regulated "welcome" the extended regulation, and seek to control which regulations and criteria will come to dominate the field, our analysis suggests that the market for assessments and regulation is driven more by the supply of new forms of regulatory activities than by voiced demand for information. The paths of development of management education and the regulatory field analyzed here are clearly mutually dependent.

In our analysis of the emergent regulatory field we have identified the role of interaction among regulators and those being regulated, and have sought to show how new regulations as well as an emergent common categorization of management education has evolved through such reciprocal interaction. We have shown that this field has emerged, not only through interactions among those actors comprising the field, but also through the imitation of and in reaction to neighboring fields. European management education and its regulation have largely been formed as imitations and reactions to developments in the United States, and as the regulatory field has formed it has also increasingly overlapped and mixed with the US field, so that what seems to emerge is a more global regulatory field of management education mainly influenced by pioneer US efforts (for parallels see Botzem and Quack ch. 13; Djelic and Kleiner ch. 14).

Conclusions: The impact of emerging regulations on European management education

This chapter has examined the emergence of a European regulatory field of management education. This regulatory field is still developing and expanding, and it remains to be seen what impact it will have in practice. However, our analysis points to some tendencies that suggest the direction this development will take; we will conclude this chapter by briefly commenting on these tendencies.

One salient motive for developing European regulation has been to protect and emphasize the European dimension of management and management education (see Shenton 1996). The importance of competing with US schools, regulators, regulations, and the American model of management education was repeatedly expressed by the Europeans.

One may ask whether the European regulatory systems will serve to maintain or even strengthen the European dimension of management education. Even from the short history presented here we can draw some tentative conclusions. We have shown the considerable overlap and mentioned the intertwining collaboration and competition between US and European regulators and regulations: strong forces seem to be working for the globalization of regulations, regulators, and those regulated. Once schools have started to take an interest in being assessed and regulated, specific European regulations have proven insufficient, and schools have sought accreditation from bodies such as AACSB and have taken an interest in both US and European rankings. Likewise, accrediting organizations and rankers have turned more global too. For the regulators to legitimate and to be listened to, they need to have at least some of the most prestigious schools on their lists. In this intertwined game, played between schools and regulators and between the regional and global levels, it seems difficult to maintain regional distinctions.

Another background to the emerging regulatory systems was the diversity of management education that arose as programs proliferated. A common observation, developed in institutional theory, is that institutionalization, diffusion, and imitation lead to homogenization. As we have followed the proliferation of management education programs we have observed a more indirect relationship between diffusion, institutionalization, and homogenization than has usually been assumed in previous research. When MBA programs were started in Europe, this led both to similarities and variation. As the MBA spread and became a well-known and institutionalized form of management training, it was translated to suit different settings and thus a variety of MBA programs emerged. Concurrently, expectations arose that the well-known and widespread label should designate a certain content and qualification. Hence, the spread of the MBA has not led directly to homogenization; rather, a recognized category was formed, which in turn comprised the basis for the regulatory field of European management education. Whether these regulations will make management education programs become increasingly similar, or whether they will simply strengthen widely held expectations that management education programs should be similar – or at least comparable along some common dimensions – remains an open empirical question.

In tracing the spread of management education we have seen that a few schools and programs developed into prototypes to be imitated. Despite this, expansion has led to considerable variation. Hence, if we only look at interactions among schools, the dominance of the more prestigious programs is not so evident. When taking the development of the regulatory field into the picture, the circulation of ideas, ideals, and prestige displays a more complex pattern, but one in which the dominance of the leading schools appears more clearly than if we only look at the processes by which individual programs develop or at how schools imitate each other. Regulations have been formed on the basis of criteria that were largely adopted from the most prestigious schools. In addition, representatives of these schools appear as central actors in a number of regulating bodies and activities, and their participation was crucial for the initiation of the new regulatory systems in Europe. Hence, even though the European management education regulatory field may at first not appear to be hierarchical, but may rather give the impression of being quite dispersed, closer examination reveals a highly centralized and stratified pattern wherein a few schools appear not only to be regarded as models to be imitated, but also tend to become models used for shaping regulations.

At the beginning of this chapter, we indicated that modes of regulation similar to those analyzed here have recently emerged in several areas. Such regulation is at least formally voluntary, not being exerted by states, but rather by professional groups, international organizations, media, and other transnational units; it is built on expertise and is of a transnational character. Such regulations have been depicted as fragmented governance structures (Brunsson and Jacobsson 2000; Scott et al. 2000). A first glance at our material confirms this view. Seen from a traditional perspective, according to which states are assumed to be the dominant regulators, the lack of a state center seems to lead the observer to conclude that the governance system is fragmented or anarchic. Even though our analysis identifies a market governance system rather than a hierarchical one (cf Djelic ch. 3), because this governance develops as a regulatory field it does form quite a coherent and consistent pattern. It is, however, a system without a regulatory centre and with only very indirect or loose couplings between regulations and sanctions or resource allocations.

Note

* Authors are listed in alphabetical order. We thank Marie-Laure Djelic, John Meyer, Huggy Rao and the participants in seminars at Score and Uppsala University for comments on earlier versions of this paper. This research has been funded by the research program, "Transnational Regulations and the Transformation of States," headed by Bengt Jacobsson and Kerstin Sahlin-Andersson and financed by the Swedish Research Council, and by the CEMP Research Program, headed by Lars Engwall and financed by the European Union.

16 Market creation and transnational rule-making: The case of CO₂ emissions trading*

ANITA ENGELS

Introduction

Many have celebrated the creation of pollution markets as the triumph of markets over states. Along with a general move towards market-based approaches in environmental regulation and other fields of public policy (see Djelic ch. 3), successful examples of these new markets can be cited, including the creation of pollution rights, resource use quotas, and credits for reducing environmental impacts (Daily and Ellison 2002). The most prominent example is the so-called Acid Rain Program introduced by the United States in the 1990s to reduce the country's overall SO_2 (sulfur dioxide) emissions (Ellerman et al. 2000). These developments have been grist to the mill for advocates of the free market who criticize government intervention for its inefficiencies and the distortions it creates.

From the perspective of advocates of the free market, environmental pollution or overuse of natural resources occur when property rights over the environment or natural resources do not exist or are poorly enforced. Prices then do not adequately reflect the scarcity of a resource or the damage to an environmental good, and consequently produce market failures. Thus, to avoid pollution and overuse, property rights must (and can) be established and enforced, and the transfer of those rights should be allowed, thus creating a market in which undistorted price signals emerge. The market is thereby seen as the solution to environmental problems, whereas regulation would only create more distortions (Anderson and Leal 1991, 1997). However, many of these "free market environmentalists" fail to recognize the importance of the state in market creation and maintenance. This chapter will argue that government intervention is necessary at least to define and enforce the basic rules that underlie markets, and that states and markets are intimately linked in different phases of market development.

The goal of this chapter is to define market creation *as* rule-making and intervention by states and other actors. It looks specifically at the interactions between national and transnational spaces, and it does so by drawing upon two different bodies of literature. The first provides a sociological understanding of markets and of the processes through which markets are created and maintained. The second highlights the importance of transnational processes for state action and explores interactions between states and many other actors such as non-governmental organizations (NGOs) and transnational corporations (TNCs). The creation of a market for CO_2 emission rights is sub-divided into four phases, arranged here in chronological order but overlapping significantly. During those phases, actors were mainly concerned with rule-making for a market that was emerging but implications for future rule-monitoring are also discussed in the final section.

Understanding the role of rule-making for the creation of markets

Theories about markets and market creation have proliferated in the social sciences over the past decades, highlighting the embeddedness of markets in social, cultural, and political contexts and the constant interplay of economic and social processes. For the purposes of this paper, we will not review the multiplicity of debates across sociology and other social sciences (see for that Zelizer 1988; Swedberg 1994; Lie 1997; O'Riain 2000; Keister 2002 and Guillén et al. 2002). However, key insights are common to those perspectives and distinguish them from an understanding of markets in the neo-classical economics tradition. First, markets are seen as particular social arrangements that greatly vary in form. Second, markets are defined as having a specific history, involving creation, stabilization and maintenance over time, and eventual dissolution or transformation. Third, it is understood that markets must be organized; they do not spontaneously arise and develop into a self-sustaining order. Finally and therefore, markets depend on "market-making" and "market-sustaining" activities by various actors and institutions, most prominently among them states.

Markets are thus viewed as outcomes of other processes and rule-making is an essential dimension of market creation. Fligstein (2001) argues that states allow markets to stabilize over time by externally defining property rights, governance structures, and rules of exchange.

The historical analysis of nation-building reveals that market and state creation often go together. Emerging states and nations required the construction of stable markets just as much as they required the ability to wage wars against external enemies or the development of rudimentary welfare systems. Likewise, the survival and economic viability of firms depend on the stability of markets more than anything else; thus, markets equally require states (Fligstein 1996).

The role of the state in emissions trading is even more obvious. For environmental regulation, the definition of property rights is not only necessary to create a stable and predictable environment but in fact to create in the first place the very commodity subject to trading. The right to emit a ton of CO_2 is not a tangible good. Carruthers and Stinchcombe (1999) have shown the inherent difficulties of trading non-tangible goods. Knowledge is central to the process. It is used to create standards and homogenize the commodity, and "knowledge about an asset has to be socially established in such a way that many buyers and sellers in a market believe the same things about it" (Carruthers and Stinchcombe 1999: 357).

Carruthers and Stinchcombe (1999) make a general argument that can be applied to the case of emission rights. The process depends on successfully establishing the knowledge and the belief that the right to emit one ton of CO_2 equals any other right to emit one ton of CO_2 available on the market. This equality must hold regardless of how, by whom, and to whom it was originally issued. This is not obvious at all, and Levin and Espeland (2002) have demonstrated how different forms of commensuration had to be achieved before the US Acid Rain Program could turn a ton of SO_2 into a tradable commodity. They differentiate between technical, value, and cognitive commensuration. Technical commensuration comprises software, hardware, and bureaucratic solutions for problems related to defining, measuring, registering, and verifying pollution units. Value commensuration is achieved by defining the rules and procedures through which prices become attached to tradable units. It is crucial to ensure the credibility of prices by creating simultaneously conditions of scarcity and of liquidity. The process of cognitive commensuration creates new objects and new actors through classification; both SO_2 and individual polluters change their meanings and acquire new properties.

These commensuration aspects naturally also play a role in the creation of a market for CO_2. However, the case of CO_2 is more complex.

This is true for technical reasons; it is, for example, much more difficult to avoid CO_2 emissions if energy consumption remains constant or grows. It is also true because of the global nature of the CO_2 threat; in contrast the Acid Rain Program was designed for the United States as a national market. Global climate change has been monitored through international negotiations since the early 1990s.[1] Central to these negotiations is an acknowledgment of the fact that climate change cannot be prevented or mitigated by political action at the individual state level only (for parallels see Bensedrine and McNichol 2003). Rather, it needs to be addressed by the widest available negotiation framework: the United Nations with its more than 190 members. Ideally, a market for emission rights would have a global scope. Market creation and in particular the process of commensuration will be much more difficult if CO_2 emission rights are tradable across several jurisdictions that have divergent political and legal traditions.

Despite its intrinsic difficulties, the creation of a market for CO_2 is particularly interesting because it represents a new mode of rule-making that transcends both national environmental regulation and intergovernmental environmental negotiations. This chapter discusses the extent to which the market for CO_2 has been created through a process of transnational rule-making. Transnational rule-making involves new types of actors alongside governments and sometimes in competition with them. In the case of CO_2 emissions trading, these actors include transnational corporations, environmental NGOs, national and international industry and business associations, and expert groups ranging from scientific advisory bodies to private consulting firms.

The process also involves new modes of rule-making, beyond legislation and negotiation. First, a newly emerging global civil society (Anheier et al. 2001) has accompanied the climate negotiations (the so-called Rio process). Hence, various non-governmental actors have observed, commented, and evaluated the ongoing negotiations to such an extent that many of them have acquired an official observer status. Intergovernmental negotiations have been deeply embedded in this wider network of actors and activities. Even though their direct influence on negotiations is difficult to measure, they set the conditions under which a given decision becomes accepted as legitimate and appropriate. Second, private business initiatives, NGO-business partnerships, and various experts have been engaged in efforts to demonstrate the feasibility and the superior economic rationality of emissions trading. Much imitation and mutual learning has resulted from these experiments.

These examples support the hypothesis that "[t]he transnational level is a space in itself where interactions take place and behavioral patterns get structured." (Djelic and Quack 2003: 8). Both the United Nations and the European Union can be viewed as transnational spaces in the latter sense. The EU has taken the lead in developing an emissions trading scheme mandatory for member states. European governance can be described as a distinct mode of supranational governance that emerged through the interactions of different member states (Albert and Kopp-Malek 2004). This new governance space, in turn, shapes national governance processes (Eising and Kohler-Koch 1999; Kohler-Koch 1999; Djelic and Quack 2003). The interactions between national and transnational spaces are therefore a basic concern for anyone trying to understand the complexities of transnational rule-making. This chapter looks at interactions between national regulatory processes and transnational rule-making. Which type of actor becomes dominant at which stage of market creation? Which modes of rule-making emerge, and how are competing sets of rules treated by different actors? If national and transnational rule-making interact, can this be described in terms of top-down or bottom-up processes (Djelic and Quack 2003:302–33)? These questions are addressed in the following sections.

Creating a market for CO₂: Interactions between national and transnational rule-making

The creation of a market for CO₂ emissions trading dates back to 1996/97, and has gone through several phases. We summarize below how this process has evolved and propose what can be learned from it in terms of transnational rule-making. Empirical evidence is drawn from various sources, among them the author's own data collection through participant observation and expert interviews (BIAC/OECD/IEA 1999; DETR 2000; Feemster 2000; Gummer and Moreland 2000; Zapfel and Vainio 2002; Christiansen and Wettestad 2003; Engels 2003; Minnesma 2003).

First phase: the United States and the Kyoto Protocol

In the 1980s, scientists and civil society paid increasing attention to climate change linked to an exponential increase of greenhouse gas emissions. By 1990, the potential associated threats to human well-being prompted a call for an internationally negotiated treaty that would limit and eventually reduce CO_2 and other greenhouse gas emissions. Climate change was regarded as a global environmental problem, similar to stratospheric ozone depletion and species extinction. However, powerful industry resistance to any reduction of CO_2 emissions was difficult to overcome. Things evolved towards the late 1990s and some instruments to achieve emission reductions were perceived as more compatible with industry goals than others.

The most influential proposal in this respect was to introduce a market for tradable emission rights. The United States was the major proponent of this proposal. When international negotiations were advancing towards binding agreements on emission reductions in 1996, US negotiators were reluctant to take any measures that would force their domestic industries to curb CO_2 emission levels. The introduction of flexible mechanisms, among them emissions trading, would allow industry to postpone expensive on-site reductions and foster emission reductions in developing countries instead.

This was not a totally new approach in the US. In a country where state–industry relations in the field of environmental protection had historically been adversarial, the Environmental Protection Agency (EPA) experimented in the 1970s with market-based approaches that could be more readily accepted by industry than any form of command-and-control. These early experiences did not have the expected outcomes but they laid the groundwork for more far-reaching programs at a later stage. In the 1980s and early 1990s, when governments in most industrialized countries introduced regulations to reduce sulfur dioxide emissions, the EPA introduced the Acid Rain Program, the first large-scale emissions trading scheme in the world. The scheme became fully operational in 1995 and was soon perceived as an overall success (Schmalensee et al. 1998; Stavins 1998).

The EPA was therefore eager to repeat this political success by using the tool as an instrument to reduce global CO_2 emissions.[2] It was probably also the only way to reconcile the political split within the US on climate change. Skeptics who questioned the credibility of climate change research had a huge influence on public debates in the US (see parallels with McNichol ch. 17). Another important argument was that emission reductions would harm the US economy. The introduction of flexibility was thus an important precondition for any commitment to stabilize or reduce future CO_2 emissions. Support came mostly from US-based economists who argued that the greatest cost reductions could be achieved through a trading scheme that included developing countries and countries in transition. The rationale was that costs for reducing emissions would be high in wealthy OECD countries, but substantially lower in countries with less developed economies. This approach met fierce opposition in the EU and most developing countries. The latter insisted that they had been exempted from any binding reduction commitment in the Framework Convention on Climate Change in 1992, and that they had no intention of giving up their exemption. The former argued that flexible mechanisms would prevent industry from achieving true reductions, and that any form of emissions trading would mean that rich countries could buy themselves out of their obligation and would therefore endanger the integrity of the Convention and follow-up agreements.

The first phase of the negotiations can thus be described as the attempt by one party to shape transnational rules of the game according to its regulatory traditions and to the needs of its domestic economy. This attempt took place during the course of the UN climate negotiations leading up to the 1997 Kyoto Conference. Although the official format was "intergovernmental," negotiations came together with intense unofficial lobbying activity bilaterally and multilaterally. Furthermore, the negotiation process itself was critically observed by a growing community of environmental NGOs and other interest groups – business and professional associations, often organized as international NGOs (INGOs); consultants; and transnational organizations which are part of the UN system (see Boli ch. 5).[3]

During this phase, the US delegation was the dominant player and emissions trading would not have been part of the Kyoto Protocol without the US push. The combined opposition of developing countries and the EU was unsuccessful in keeping emissions trading out of the Protocol (IISD 1997). However, the US original scheme – namely, the broad inclusion of developing countries and countries in transition – was altered. The participation of developing countries was made voluntary and associated to other structuring rules having to do with environmental integrity and the right to unrestricted economic growth. These secondary rules limited the ability of First-World countries to shirk their own reduction obligations by buying emission rights from poorer countries.

The first phase of the creation of a market for CO_2 emissions trading was thus deeply embedded in political conflicts along the North–South divide, and in a perceived opposition between environmental integrity and economic rationality. The general mode of rule-making was a bottom-up move from one national base to the transnational space. Even though the formal framework was intergovernmental negotiation, the dependence on scientific input (see Drori and Meyer ch. 2) and the broad inclusion of NGOs, INGOs and other external observers point to a complex transnational rule-making process.

Second phase: United Nations, British Petroleum and transnational trading schemes

After Kyoto, the situation changed dramatically. In the United States, the Republican-dominated Congress blocked the development of a national CO_2 policy. Moreover, the fact that developing countries would not participate in future trading, made it much less attractive for the US to push further, through the United Nations, for an emissions trading scheme. Under the Clinton administration, the US slowly withdrew from the negotiation table and moved (as in many other arenas) to a more inward-oriented phase (Lutzenhiser 2001). This dynamic intensified under the administration of George W. Bush, culminating in the official withdrawal from the Kyoto Protocol and UN negotiations in March 2001.

However, once a paragraph allowing emissions trading was introduced into the Protocol, other actors took over and developed suggestions for market institutions and tools. Broker companies, financial service providers, and exchanges developed practical solutions for the technical problems associated with an international trading scheme. Organizations such as the United Nations Conference on Trade and Development (UNCTAD) and the International Energy Agency (IEA) carried out trade simulations and marketing activities to improve acceptance of emissions trading in the business community. More and more companies switched from direct opposition against any kind of CO_2 reduction to a position they called preparing for a "carbon-constrained future." For some of them this included a growing interest in the mechanisms of emissions trading. Moreover, some European countries realized that they were still far from reaching their own domestic emissions targets and hence sought alternatives or additions to their established policy programs. Slowly, the development of emissions trading gained momentum.

The rationale behind these efforts was to develop a unified trading scheme with general rules, applicable to all trades and by all participants (the "grand" model). The UN appeared as the only framework capable of developing such a scheme. The hope was that one unified approach towards emissions trading would have immediate top-down effects on national regulatory regimes (for a parallel see Djelic and Kleiner ch. 14). However, arriving at general agreements proved difficult within the UN framework because there were so many different actors involved and rule-making had to be based on the consensus principle. The process of value commensuration was particularly problematic, as emissions from wealthy OECD countries were valued differently from emissions in developing countries. Likewise, environmental protection groups questioned the equality of CO$_2$ units achieved by ex-ante emission reductions and by ex-post carbon sequestration (e.g. by storage of CO$_2$ in forest, soils, or the deep ocean). By the end of the 1990s, negotiation activity was particularly intense. The various attempts at developing registration, verification, and trading procedures can be looked at through the case of technical commensuration. There were parallel projects to define an overall technical and infrastructural framework for the international trading scheme, but reconciling those projects proved impossible.

In parallel, a large transnational corporation decided to step forward with a progressive stance towards greenhouse gas reductions. The oil company, British Petroleum (BP), with business units in about 150 countries, decided to adopt a 10 percent reduction target for its own operations voluntarily, allowing emission rights trading among its business units. Significant expertise and resources were invested into developing an internal trading scheme. Several authors have analyzed the background to this shift in business strategy (e.g. Levy and Newell 2000). This move provoked a split among the world's largest oil companies. Shell, and to some extent the Mexican oil company, Pemex, followed BP in its frontline efforts while Exxon-Mobil, Chevron-Texaco, and others remained opposed to limiting greenhouse gas emissions (Pulver 2004).

To the outside world this was a watershed. That one of the leading oil companies regarded climate change as a threat serious enough to develop precautionary action represented strong support for the negotiations. Several factors may have motivated BP: first, the introduction of internal emissions trading helped achieve efficiency gains in a company generally regarded as inefficient. Second, the shifts by BP and Shell can be explained by the "home-country effect" in which the economic, regulatory, and social environment of the home country provide a framework for negotiating what is in the company's economic interest (Levy and Kolk 2002; Pulver 2004). BP and Shell headquarters were in Europe, where governments saw future limitations to CO_2 emissions as a necessity, where influential groups had developed a critical view of oil companies and demanded environmentally friendly and socially responsible corporate behavior, and where climate change was widely perceived as a real threat.

There were fewer problems with commensuration in the BP frame than had been the case within the UN framework, as emission sources and reduction pathways were more homogenous. Moreover, the North–South divide that was so important in UN negotiations did not exist; business units in developing and developed countries both belonged to the same profit-seeking entity. To increase the credibility of its new approach to CO_2 emissions, the company formed a partnership (or strategic alliance) with the NGO Environmental Defense (for parallels see McNichol ch. 17). The NGO provided technical input, but mostly the association signaled that this was a serious effort and that no fraud was involved. This was the first truly global corporate emissions trading system for greenhouse gases anywhere in the world. It started with twelve BP business units in 1998 and operated across all units in 2000 and 2001. Once the decision was made at top management level, the scheme was relatively easy to implement, despite resistance. The CO_2 reduction goal of 10 percent was written into the contracts of business unit CEOs; success or failure had direct implications for their personal evaluation.

Emissions trading quickly became integrated into company practice. The community of traders (e.g. of oil and gas) working within BP were able to incorporate emissions into their trading routines.[4] The company saw the possibility to gain first-mover advantages if emissions trading were ever established in the framework of the Kyoto Protocol. In parallel to this trading activity, the company initiated a significant effort to propagate the instrument in other contexts, both nationally and internationally.

Both the UN and BP attempts to create inclusive trading schemes can be described as top-down movements. Both actors hoped to create enough momentum from the top to convince the bottom to join in the trading scheme. The objective was a unified trading scheme with common rules and a nearly comprehensive inclusion of market participants. Whereas top management at BP had control over business units and was able to achieve this aim, the UN system was more fragmented, and no single actor had enough clout to steer the process.

Third phase: multiple domestic activities

By the late 1990s, there was a growing awareness that any form of international trading scheme would be delayed for several years if it had to go through the UN system, and that rules would be set in that context by the lowest common denominator. Moreover, the player who introduced emissions trading in the first place (the US) dropped out entirely and refused to develop domestic policies at the federal level aimed at reducing emission levels. Still, initiatives emerged in the US, but at the state level and in the private sector (Dunn 2002). The state of New Jersey was the first to develop specific standards to reduce greenhouse gas emissions. Several senators from Midwestern states became interested in options to alter agricultural land management systems to increase the soil's capacity for carbon sequestration. States like Iowa and Wisconsin took the lead in connecting this kind of research with plans to develop rudimentary carbon trading systems.

Supported by NGOs like the Pew Charitable Trusts and the Joyce Foundation, other business-led activities experimented with trading credits, often in the form of futures (promises to reduce emissions in the years to come). Several large US-based companies like DuPont entered into networks and strategic alliances with other large companies to develop trading tools. Examples include the Partnership for Climate Action, brought together by the US advocacy group Environmental Defense, which aims at developing market mechanisms for greenhouse gas reductions; and the Business Environmental Leadership Council, brought together under the umbrella of the Pew Center on Global Climate Change. The most advanced trading scheme in the US is the newly founded Chicago Climate Exchange, where actors as diverse as the Iowa Farm Bureau, the City of Chicago, the World Resources Institute, IBM, Motorola, and Ford have come together to develop a marketplace for reducing and trading greenhouse gas emissions. However, these different initiatives coexisted without mutual interconnection or influence. Incompatibilities persist to this day, and without any federal backing, it is unclear who will monitor and enforce emission reduction agreements.[5]

Efforts were also fragmented in the EU. Without any larger scheme on the horizon, some member states decided to explore domestic trading schemes. Denmark introduced a CO_2 quota scheme in 1999 for its power sector. This was part of a general reform of the electricity sector with a move towards market mechanisms (Pedersen 2000). Norway also showed some interest. At the end of 1999, a Royal Commission proposed a comprehensive national quota system for greenhouse gases. Establishing a domestic trading scheme was seen as a way of preparing the country for future international trading (Schreiner 2000). The government of the Netherlands issued tenders for reductions in greenhouse gas emissions (carbon credits) achieved through private sector investments in renewable energy and energy efficiency measures in Central and Eastern Europe (Minnesma 2003).

The most elaborate scheme was developed in the UK. Shortly after Kyoto, a task force identified emissions trading as a potentially key element of the UK's long-term climate strategy (Rees and Evers 2000). Through close collaboration between industry and regulating agencies, the UK Emissions Trading Scheme (ETS) was created as the world's first national greenhouse gas emissions trading system. Trading began in April 2002. The UK climate change policy is based on a national emissions reduction target of 12.5 percent (from base 1990 levels) that was negotiated as part of EU burden-sharing under the Kyoto Protocol. Mostly due to a sweeping switch from coal to gas in the beginning of the 1990s, the UK is likely to achieve its national reduction target in the commitment period of 2008–12, and has announced a more challenging domestic goal of 20 percent reduction below 1990 levels by 2010 (Gummer and Moreland 2000). The government uses a combination of climate change levy for energy-intensive industries and CO_2 emissions trading scheme open to all UK-based companies. Nearly a thousand companies were engaged in trading during the first year, and the government announced its intention to establish the UK as the centre for greenhouse gas emissions trading in any future international trading scheme.[6]

This phase was marked by several parallel attempts to create domestic trading schemes and to develop coordinated national policies relying on market-based mechanisms. Although the proliferation of efforts allowed for the testing of different designs, it made more difficult the future task of harmonization. The UK trading scheme was most likely to become the model for international trading, and the early elaboration and implementation of the scheme represented a huge step forward by the UK government into the regulatory future. However, none of those initiatives became dominant and there was increasing concern, within the EU, about the fragmentation of initiatives. As a consequence, the European Commission came forward with a Green Paper in March 2000 outlining a proposal for a EU-wide trading scheme (European Commission 2000).

Fourth phase: EU mandatory trading scheme for all member states

The most important current rule-making effort is taking place within the EU. When it became obvious that progress on international emissions trading would be impossible in the UN framework, the European Commission took the lead with the ambitious aim of establishing an EU-wide mandatory trading scheme as early as 2005 (the EU Emission Allowance Trading Scheme (EATS)). This came as a surprise, since the EU position during negotiations of the Kyoto Protocol had been against emissions trading. A variety of factors accounted for this change in position (Christiansen and Wettestad 2003). The European Commission increasingly saw a need to develop effective instruments that would facilitate emission reductions in the EU. It had failed to generate sufficient support for a proposed EU carbon/energy tax in the early 1990s. More conventional policy approaches were seen as too expensive. Despite the lack of official support by the US government, numerous US experts who had gained experience with emissions trading gradually convinced key EU policy-makers of the virtues of emissions trading. Support both from the European Parliament and the Council encouraged the Commission to proceed with developing a Framework Directive for emissions trading. The emerging patchwork of different national schemes posed the threat of market fragmentation; for example, "[t]he Danish and UK systems trade different gases, encompass different sectors and use different blends of allowance- and credit-based trading" (Dunn 2002: 33). Although it is theoretically possible to trade between schemes, a single European market was clearly preferable. Finally, the fact that BP regarded its scheme as a success boosted support among industry sectors for the EU move towards a market-based policy approach.

Technical questions proved quite complex at the EU level, because each domestic climate policy now had to be integrated into a unifying scheme. Against partial resistance both from the UK (which wanted the EU scheme modeled after its own) and Germany (which was against the trading approach), the European Commission decided in December 2002 on the final modalities of the future trading scheme. At an unprecedented pace, the Directive came into force in July 2003. Partly in reaction to the developing EU EATS, BP suspended its internal trading scheme. Throughout the year 2000, BP employees working on its internal program were relentless in promoting it as a model for international trading in general. They also strongly influenced the form of the UK trading scheme. However, it became increasingly clear to BP that the EU plans differed in many important ways from the BP trading scheme, and that harmonizing these different approaches would be costly. In addition, BP had already achieved its 10 percent reduction target. As a consequence, the trading scheme was phased out quietly in early 2002.

The EU EATS quickly set new standards and rules, notwithstanding several schemes already in place. This is not to say that it unreasonably created new structures where old ones could have sufficed in a more bottom-up approach. The EU Directive is the outcome of a thorough negotiation process, accompanied by extensive expert advice and comments; the ultimate rationale was to create a huge market based on credible and enforceable reduction goals. After the Framework Directive was launched by the European Parliament, individual member states had no choice but to accept trading as a basic policy tool and to develop domestic institutional infrastructure allowing companies to trade. Some minor issues were left to the discretion of member states, but the cases of the UK and Germany make it clear that Europeanization of environmental policies has taken place, with wide-ranging implications for industrial and trade policies. Current

rule-making for the creation of a CO_2 market can best be characterized as a top-down process from the transnational European space to
member state legislatures. This is even more obvious with regard to
accession countries, as they must adopt these EU policies right from
the start (for parallels see Djelic and Kleiner ch. 14).

Because of its sheer size (it may in the future include as many as
twenty-eight countries), the EU trading scheme is expected to become
the role model for all subsequently developed international trading
schemes. "In terms of scale and structure, the EU EATS has the potential to be the world's 'prototype' for international emissions trading,
particularly if it delivers demonstrable cost-efficient emission reductions." (Hobley and Hawkes 2003: 20).[7] The EU Linking Directive
(April 2004) took a first step in this direction by defining the terms
under which emission reductions from outside the EU can enter the
European market.

Market creation and transnational rule-making: Conclusions and outlook

The multilayered history we have told here of successive and parallel
attempts at creating a market for CO_2 emissions trading clearly shows
that rule-making is at the core of market creation. The concept of
tradable emission rights is based on the idea that CO_2 emissions create
negative externalities, necessitating government intervention to reduce
global emissions to a socially optimal level. For any trading scheme to
work, emissions must be restricted to those who have acquired the right
to do so. An artificial scarcity is created that corresponds to a more
socially beneficial level of emissions, but the tradability of the right to
emit is guaranteed. As has been shown, this is a very complex regulatory
process, and many different actors at various levels of decision-making
have been involved.

The process of commensuration is complex, costly, and embedded
in political controversy. *Technical* commensuration involves the definition of baselines; reporting and monitoring techniques; and building up
software, hardware, and institutional solutions for issuing, buying, and
selling emission rights. The diversity of technical expertise within the
UN framework provided an abundance of technical solutions, but due
to a lack of leadership and difficult decision-making structures, no standardized solution emerged. *Value* commensuration proved especially

difficult in the UN framework because it was subject to manifold political controversies along two dimensions: first, the North–South divide and second, the environment–economy debate. Value commensuration was much easier to achieve in relatively homogeneous settings, such as within transnational corporations, individual states, or the EU. The EU trading scheme provided an important contribution towards *cognitive* commensuration as it simplified and homogenized the different categories relevant for emissions trading. Whereas the national schemes that preceded the EU EATS varied greatly (e.g. CO_2 quotas, carbon credits, emission allowances), the EU provided a coherent classification under which tradable units from member states and from sources outside the EU can be treated equally. Commensuration indeed is an important and complex process and many different actors are involved in ensuring that emission rights can be traded under a credible and efficient trading scheme. The creation of a CO_2 emissions market is thus an example of market creation *as* rule-making where states and many other actors interplay.

Rule-making in this example is inherently transnational. As no single state provides a large enough market in itself, any future CO_2 emissions trading scheme is bound to cross national boundaries. Three different transnational rule-making spaces were discussed: that of BP, the negotiation framework of the United Nations, and the policy process in the EU. In fact, these spaces are not mutually exclusive but form overlapping jurisdictions, and their contributions to the creation of a wider CO_2 emissions market have influenced one other. Partly, the overlap is created by individual actors; key individuals have moved from governments to intergovernmental bodies, from intergovernmental bodies to INGOs, from consulting firms to oil companies, and from research institutes to governments (for parallels on the role of individuals see Djelic ch. 3; Marcussen ch. 9; McNichol ch. 17). These individuals move freely between spaces and act as carriers of ideas and meanings.

However, if we look for specific modes of transnational rule-making, it is useful to separate those three spaces. In the initial phase of the process, the UN framework appeared as the most appropriate space to set up a new market. Still, the consensus principle, a heterogeneous constituency, and political conflicts made it impossible to reach an agreement at this level of decision-making. This phase established the market-based policy tool as an acceptable and feasible option, engendering, though, a wide variety of possible solutions. A smaller and more coherent political unit was needed to select from these different possibilities and to choose a coherent set of rules. Although many observers were surprised to see the EU EATS emerge "out of the blue," the EU was better poised than other regulatory actors to develop an integrated scheme. But it also built on previous efforts and would probably not have included emissions trading without the UN and BP initiatives.

Transnational rule-making is open to a much wider variety of actors than rule-making in domestic settings. This chapter has looked at the involvement of transnational corporations, business associations, technical and organizational consultants, environmental NGOs, state agencies and other regulatory bodies. The proliferation of actors in the context of transnational rule-making has several important implications: first, the process is less predictable. The dominant players in creating a market for CO_2 emissions have changed several times throughout the period. Likewise, the most dynamic level switched back and forth between national and transnational spaces, and also among different transnational spaces (UN, EU, and BP). In more than one example, established and institutionalized approaches were supplanted by new schemes. This leads to the second implication: investments in rule-making or market creation are risky; they may develop into dead ends and be overrun by newer approaches. The most visible example is the UK Emissions Trading Scheme, which was developed to realize first-mover advantages and to strengthen the UK position in any future trading scheme. Now that the European scheme has superseded the UK scheme, many fear that early UK leadership will turn into lost investments (Sorell 2003). Third, more rule-makers without democratic legitimacy play a role in the transnational space: e.g., experts, NGOs, and transnational corporations (see Mörth ch. 6). Martinelli points out the problematic implications for legitimacy if transnational corporations are accorded a role in the building of global governance, as most "enjoy power without responsibility, since most of their decisions are accountable only to shareholders and not to all the other many individual groups affected by them" (Martinelli 2003: 301). However, this problem also applies to NGOs and expert communities which usually are neither elected nor governed by anyone external, and therefore are only accountable to direct members or supporters. The wider implications of this for the legitimacy and acceptability of transnational regulation need to be addressed (see Jacobsson and Sahlin-Andersson ch. 12 for discussions on compliance and authorization).

We have seen that both bottom-up and top-down processes occur in transnational rule-making. It sometimes appears as if national and transnational spaces compete for leadership. However, rarely are wider schemes modeled after schemes at a "lower" level. In the case of CO_2 emissions trading, the rudimentary rules provided by the Kyoto Protocol were not exclusively guided by the US, who had the only functioning emissions trading scheme running at that time. Neither was the EU EATS modeled after the UK ETS. A possible explanation might be that transnational rule-making will be more acceptable if it is perceived as "neutral" rather than merely reflecting an existing national model. The example of CO_2 emissions trading also supports the hypothesis that, once an environmental problem has entered the transnational stage, the specific modes of transnational regulation have repercussions on national modes as well. The competitive regulatory process at the transnational level provides a broader variety of policy instruments than would emerge in national regulatory processes, which are usually confined by national regulatory styles, and established networks. However, once a broader variety of options exists, and the advantages and disadvantages of policy tools become more visible, established national regulatory regimes become more open to policy alternatives. Likewise, the new role of NGOs and pressure groups as important actors in the field does not halt at borders defined by national sovereignty (see also McNichol ch. 17).

Although this article has not focused on the question of rule-*monitoring*, some preliminary hypotheses can be suggested. Experiences with the US Acid Rain Program have shown that strict enforcement and high penalties for non-compliance are essential to the efficacy of an emissions trading scheme. Therefore, the process of rule-monitoring may be even more important than the process of rule-making for a future CO_2 emission market. In the EU EATS, the execution of control and enforcement duties remains the responsibility of member states (Peeters 2003). The specific mode of transnational rule-monitoring is simultaneously wider and narrower than national modes of rule-monitoring. It is wider in the following sense: multiple external observers (NGOs, associations, and other pressure groups) unofficially observe the process in parallel and in competition with official channels. This group of actors increasingly plays the role of watchdog. Moreover, many such actors have professionalized in past years to a degree which transforms them from simple pressure groups into quasi-scientific experts. Their monitoring activities often fall into the category of "naming and shaming," which is a very indirect form of sanctioning non-compliance. This phenomenon can be seen as part of the process of moral rationalization, by which certain forms of legitimation increasingly diffuse to all spheres of modern political and economic life (see Boli ch. 5). Transnational rule-monitoring is also narrower, however; national regulators are ultimately responsible for the implementation of a regulation, even if much of the rule-making process has taken place in the transnational field. The principle of national sovereignty limits the extent to which compliance can be officially monitored by transnational institutions.

Finally, this last point leads to the special case of the EU. It is unique in that its member states volunteer to transfer elements of their national sovereignty to a higher level. The EU as a space for transnational rule-making and rule-monitoring is influenced by an ensemble of changing member states, emerging European institutions (e.g., Commission, Parliament and Constitution), and a scientific expertise increasingly focused on European issues. Neil Fligstein's hypothesis about the close links between market creation and state formation assumes a new meaning in the context of emissions trading. Although the EU cannot be regarded as a new super-state, market creation might here serve as a means to further political and economic integration. It is undisputed that harmonizing environmental legislation stabilizes and enlarges the relevant market. But the process of enlarged market *creation* may perform the additional function of strengthening European governance structures. If this is true, creating a completely new market is even more promising than transforming existing markets in the cumbersome process of harmonization.

Notes

* The empirical work on which this chapter is based is a cross-national comparison of Germany, the Netherlands, the UK, and the USA on national pathways to emissions trading in the context of transnational processes. I would like to thank Oliver Kessler, Georg Krücken, Nikolas Wada, and the editors for thoughtful comments on an earlier draft.

1. For an overview of the negotiation process, see Mintzer and Leonard (1994), and the reporting service of the International Institute for Sustainable Development, available at http://www.iisd.org/climate/.

2. Interview Environmental Protection Agency, Washington DC, 30 May 2000.

3. Interviews International Energy Agency, Paris, 21 April 2000; Environmental Defense, New York, 23 May 2000; German Watch, Bonn, 7 March 2000; Emissions Trading Marketing Association, 28 August 2000; Hamburg Institute of International Economics, 30 November 2000; World Bank, Washington DC, 7 April 2000.

4. Interviews BP Geneva, 4 March 1999 and 19 April 2000; BP London, 6 September 2000; Environmental Defense, New York, 23 May 2000; Stanford University, 16 March 2004.

5. Interviews Chicago Climate Exchange, Chicago, 8 December 2000; Pew Center on Global Climate Change, Arlington, 29 May 2000; Environmental Protection Agency, Washington DC, 26 February 2004; World Resources Institute, Washington DC, 27 February 2004.

6. For updates see http://www.defra.gov.uk/environment/climatechange/trading/uk.

7. See also Atle Christiansen of the Oslo-based consultancy firm Point-Carbon in a press release (http://www.planetark.org/dailynewsstory.cfm/newsid/19024/story.htm).

17 | Transnational NGO certification programs as new regulatory forms: Lessons from the forestry sector

JASON MCNICHOL

Introduction – An emergent form of rule-making on the international stage

During the 1990s, attempts by non-governmental organizations (NGOs) to introduce new certification and labeling (C&L) programs stood at the center of broader efforts to use market instruments to improve environmental and social well-being in transnational commodity production (see also Engels ch. 16). Recognizing that consumers, activists and governments were suspicious of industry-sponsored codes of conduct that often smacked of "green-washing," leaders of high-profile firms became far more willing to consider independent certification as the decade progressed (Knight 1995; Wasik 1996; Nash and Ehrenfeld 1996; Murphy and Bendell 1997; Economist 1999). At the same time, a number of environmental and social justice NGOs, conceding that traditional corporate boycott campaigns were often ineffective and alienated potential allies, joined the certification bandwagon in earnest (e.g., Friends of the Earth 1996). By the mid-1990s, a variety of new initiatives emerged to reward companies whose practices accorded with NGO-defined environmental and social criteria. These certification programs appeared in a range of industries, including forest products, textiles, footwear, fisheries, rugs and children's toys (see e.g. Nash and Ehrenfeld 1996; Rothstein 1996; Kruijtbosch 1997; Lynch 1997; Coop America 1999; Bartley 2003).

Although these programs were diverse, they nonetheless shared three major characteristics. First and most obviously, voluntary certification and labeling program advocates championed their initiatives as market-based alternatives to traditional command-and-control regulation. In this regard, C&L programs were ideologically and

normatively consistent with the broader ascendance of market ideology in matters of oversight, both in advanced consumer countries
and across multilateral agencies seeking to influence state policies
in emerging economies (Adams 1990; Salzman 1991; OECD 1997;
Bartley 2003; see also Djelic ch. 3). Secondly, these initiatives sought,
albeit imperfectly and amid substantial conflicts, to formulate and
champion new shared beliefs about what scientifically reasonable standards governing "responsible" or "sustainable" production practices
should entail (cf. Drori and Meyer ch. 2). Finally, as nominally non-
governmental initiatives that sought to introduce these new "consensus" rules as voluntary standards, C&L advocates were effectively
supporting a new variety of "soft law" alongside a variety of other
regulatory innovations that were orchestrated outside traditional multilateral and state organs (cf. Jacobsson and Sahlin-Andersson ch. 12;
Mörth ch. 6).

Given these seemingly auspicious beginnings, the observer of newly
emerging C&L programs in the mid-1990s may have had reasons
to be optimistic regarding their future. But ten years later, the fate
of these initiatives remains uncertain and contested. As coalitions of
NGOs sought to assert new principles and criteria regarding social and
environmental performance in countries around the world, widespread
conflict emerged in their respective industries. The ensuing debates –
between retailers, producers, watchdog groups, and even governmental bodies – have been well publicized in the media of advanced
western countries. Some programs have emerged from such conflicts
to become powerful, influential actors in certain domestic markets,
whereas others have foundered. In a handful of industries, especially
timber and textiles, NGO-led certification and labeling programs have
appeared to influence the character of both national and multilateral
regulatory discussions. Intriguingly, they have done so in spite of their
limited uptake in the international trade of goods and services they
target.

The exercise that follows brings a sociological lens to bear on these
programs, arguing they are best understood as emergent multinational
coalitions seeking to introduce new norms and rules into the regulatory
fields of action surrounding commodity production. Adopting such a
framework, the chapter engages in a case study of non-governmental
oversight initiatives in one of the most active sectors – the wood products industry. After noting that these programs have been characterized
by a complex logic of interaction and contestation across different

constituencies and domestic regulatory arenas, I introduce in the next section a synthetic sociological model from which to describe and explain their evolution and significance. The model is then applied to assess the comparative evolution of the most longstanding of these programs in the wood products sector. The discussion concludes with observations for our current understanding of rule-making in the global economy.

International rule-making around social and environmental standards: Toward a synthetic sociological model

How should scholars of transnational regulation best assess the character and significance of third party certification and labeling programs in international commodity trade? Do they represent novel forms of rule-making and enforcement, or are they simply extensions of existing modes and logics of oversight within nations? Do voluntary, market-based oversight initiatives threaten or weaken existing state-based forms of oversight, as some critics allege, or do they complement them? Recent social scientific efforts to describe and analyze transnational regulatory politics provide a strong foundation on which to consider these questions.

Drawing on recent work in sociological institutionalism, comparative political economy, and other traditions, Figure 17.1 depicts a simplified representation of overlapping governance fields that might surround a hypothetical multinational commodity chain.[1] The sphere on the left side of the diagram represents the domestic governance field of a producer nation, whereas the sphere on the right side of the diagram represents that of a consumer nation. Governance fields are characterized by formal laws and regulations, "soft" laws such as voluntary standards and "best practice" guidelines, tacit norms and conventions, and cultural beliefs that, together, constitute the regulatory arena within which firms operate. The commodity chain, which links producers, intermediaries, and consumers along a series of exchange relations within and across states, is represented by the solid line linking both countries. The area where both fields overlap represents the transnational field of action that both countries are linked to through their participation in a multinational commodity market. The major actors that populate governance fields are noted in the top portions of the spheres. Shared constructions and emergent structures – ranging from shared meanings and norms at the more micro level to laws and power

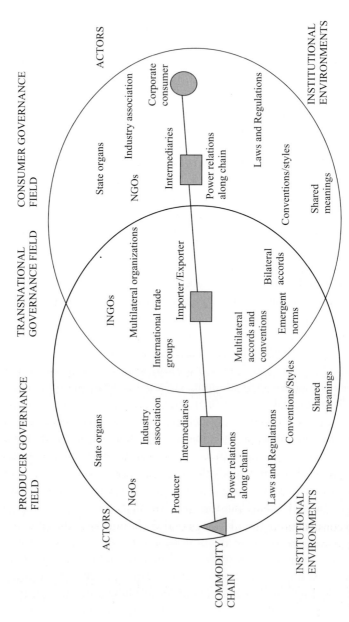

Figure 17.1 Simplified schematic of overlapping governance fields

relations at the macro level – are noted in the bottom portions as properties of domestic institutional environments.

Figure 17.1 is necessarily static in its representation – norms, rules, and relations of power along commodity chains are characterized at a given moment in time. But, of course, in reality the characteristics of governance fields can and do change; the social movement-like characteristics of C&L programs are a case in point. Recent work in sociological institutionalism analyzing "markets as politics" suggests that, during times of relative stability, dominant interests with the most power seek to maintain rules and means of enforcing them that privilege their interests and minimize destabilizing forces. However, during times of crisis when the existing "rules of the game" are called into question by other actors, "challengers" acting as institutional entrepreneurs can seek to change these rules by mobilizing a variety of resources and building alliances. In moments of opportunity, these entrepreneurs can use political skill to reframe understandings of self-interest and forge new coalitions to support new rules of governance (Fligstein 1997, 2001; McNichol 2002).

Thus, the model presented in Figure 17.1 suggests that transnational attempts to develop new forms of socio-environmental oversight are best understood as taking place within strategic action fields located primarily (but not exclusively) at the domestic level. From the perspective of this model, international certification programs emerge as new actors to mobilize, lobby, and wrestle with constraints and opportunities within a transnational field of governance, but they unfold over time as social forms within actually existing domestic markets. Over time, domestic characteristics (such as relations of power or regulatory regimes) can in turn be transformed by these transnational mobilizations.[2] As Figure 17.1 suggests, these characteristics can include pre-existing relations of power along the commodity chain, existing rules and norms that govern firm behavior, and the shared cultural constructions and meanings that shape understandings of self-interest among actors.

Case study: Well-managed forestry and the Forest Stewardship Council[3]

How might this sociological understanding of contestations over market governance help us better identify the nature and significance of international rule-making, particularly in non-governmental oversight regimes? Among widely traded international commodities, the timber products sector has seen some of the most organized and sustained non-governmental certification activity in recent years; the dominant organization coordinating these efforts – the Forest Stewardship Council (FSC) – has emerged to become one of the most well-known C&L programs in the world (McNichol 2002; Bartley 2003). The FSC, and the mobilizations to introduce new rules into global wood markets it coordinates, thus offer a case study ripe for analysis.

Founded in 1993 as a consensus-based, multi-stakeholder, international body with representatives from the North and South, the Forest Stewardship Council sought to formulate common principles and criteria that would define minimum environmental, social and economic standards to be met in the production setting (Forest Stewardship Council 1995a, 1995b, 1996). National and regional FSC "working groups" would consult with local stakeholders to adapt these principles and criteria to different socio-economic and biophysical environments. Firms that voluntarily underwent inspections by accredited third-party certifiers and met these regionally adapted criteria would be certified as "well-managed" by the FSC and could apply a label to their products. In defining its principles and criteria, the FSC was championing specific scientific and moral claims over what constituted "well-managed" forestry (see Boli ch. 5; Drori and Meyer ch. 2). Table 17.1 summarizes the ten common criteria that participating producers would need to meet to carry the organization's label in the marketplace.

In seeking to build such a program, the FSC faced formidable challenges: it sought to harness a possible "green premium" among consumers to generate incentives for firms to "do the right thing"; it struggled to articulate universal criteria while attempting to be responsive to local variation; it worked to balance often competing social and economic as well as environmental dimensions of "sustainability"; and it committed itself to consensus-based, cross-stakeholder cooperation among interests in the North and South. Given these seemingly utopian goals, some early critics unsurprisingly dismissed the effort as well-intentioned but misguided (for an especially critical assessment see Kiekens 1997; see also Varangis et al. 1995).

More than a decade later, though, the FSC had proven the critics wrong, at least partially. As of late 2005, the program counted over 645 members, organizations and individuals, from a broad spectrum of interests in the North and South (Forest Stewardship Council 2005a).

Table 17.1. *International principles and criteria established by the FSC (abridged) (source: FSC)*

Principle title	Principle description
#1: Compliance with laws and FSC Principles	Forest management shall respect all applicable laws of the country . . . and international treaties and agreements to which the country is a signatory, and comply with all FSC Principles and Criteria.
#2: Tenure and use rights and responsibilities	Long-term tenure and use rights to the land and forest resources shall be clearly defined, documented and legally established.
#3: Indigenous peoples' rights	The legal and customary rights of indigenous peoples to own, use and manage their lands, territories, and resources shall be recognized and respected.
#4: Community relations and workers' rights	Forest management operations shall maintain or enhance the long-term social and economic well-being of forest workers and local communities.
# 5: Benefits from the forest	Forest management operations shall encourage the efficient use of the forest's multiple products and services to ensure economic viability and a wide range of environmental and social benefits.
#6: Environmental impact	Forest management shall conserve biological diversity and its associated values, water resources, soils, and unique and fragile ecosystems and landscapes, and, by so doing, maintain the ecological functions and the integrity of the forest.
#7: Management plan	A management plan – appropriate to the scale and intensity of the operations – shall be written, implemented, and kept up to date. The long-term objectives of management, and the means of achieving them, shall be clearly stated.
#8: Monitoring and assessment	Monitoring shall be conducted – appropriate to the scale and intensity of forest management – to assess the condition of the forest, yields of forest products, chain of custody, management activities and their social and environmental impacts.
#9: Maintenance of high conservation value forests	Management activities in high conservation value forests shall maintain or enhance the attributes which define such forests. Decisions regarding high conservation value forests shall always be considered in the context of a precautionary approach.

(cont.)

Table 17.1. *(cont.)*

Principle title	Principle description
#10: Plantations	Plantations shall be planned and managed in accordance with Principles and Criteria 1 – 9, and Principle 10 and its Criteria. While plantations can provide an array of social and economic benefits, and can contribute to satisfying the world's needs for forest products, they should complement the management of, reduce pressures on, and promote the restoration and conservation of natural forests.

It had certified over 50 million hectares in more than 60 countries, including productive forests in Europe and North America, and, to a lesser extent, Africa, South America, and Asia (Forest Stewardship Council 2002; 2005b). Products bearing the FSC logo could be found in retail shops, furniture outlets, and in the catalogs of builders and architects in dozens of countries around the world. In the first years of the new century, governments, leading retailers, a broad spectrum of NGOs, and even some timber companies were celebrating the FSC as a leading exemplar of what new business–NGO partnerships could make possible in the transnational marketplace (e.g. Jenkins and Smith 1999; Friends of the Earth 2005; The Home Depot 2005; United Nations Department of Economic and Social Affairs 2005).

These successes, however, were accompanied by a number of contradictions and uncertainties. Most dramatically, the penetration of FSC protocols varied wildly across different domestic markets, as shown in Table 17.2 (tropical countries, not listed, had only 18 percent of FSC's total certified lands at that time). In some countries, such as Britain and Sweden, the FSC had high penetration, whereas in other major producer and consumer nations, such as the United States, Canada, Finland, and many tropical countries, market growth was minor or non-existent. Uneven success was accompanied by a series of troublesome developments: in most countries where the FSC sought to gain a foothold, controversies erupted and the organization found itself engulfed in widespread conflicts over its legitimacy and justifications of its standards. At the same time, state and industry groups launched rival schemes that sought to undermine the

Table 17.2. *Overview of market penetration and acceptance of FSC, 2001*

Country	% of FSC total worldwide	FSC hectares	Sites	Available hectares	FSC % total domestic productive lands
Canada	0.49	125,126	10	125,863,000	0.10
Finland	0.00	0	0	20,675,000	0
Netherlands	0.28	69,808	10	314,000	22.23
Poland	15.04	3,806,160	8	8,300,000	45.86
Sweden	39.98	10,117,431	21	21,236,000	47.64
United Kingdom	4.17	1,055,238	29	2,108,000	50.06
United States	11.97	3,030,014	89	198,123,000	1.53

Note. Data compiled from FAOSTAT (Food and Agriculture Organization of the United Nations) database for year 2001 and FSC sources.

credibility of the FSC, challenging its status as an exemplary program (McNichol 2002). The future of the FSC remains uncertain indeed.

The FSC as an articulated para-regulatory advocacy coalition

How best can we analyze the Forest Stewardship Council as a new form of rule-making in the transnational economy? We can begin by reconsidering the genesis and institutional development of the FSC through the sociological approach outlined above. Figure 17.2 points to those historical forces that fostered the emergence of the FSC. Three major shifts in dominant perceptions among forestry regulation stakeholders helped de-legitimate the status quo in the late 1980s and early 1990s, creating opportunities for entrepreneurship. First, activist environmental NGOs (ENGOs) in Europe and North America (such as Friends of the Earth) had engaged in sustained publicity campaigns linking image-conscious retailers with destructive forestry practices in tropical countries. For brand-name retailers such as B&Q in Britain and The Home Depot in the United States, activist ENGO pressure and perceptions that consumers were worrying more about tropical deforestation converged. Second, well-established ENGOs (including WWF-UK, WWF International, and the Rainforest Alliance), along with a growing cadre of "eco-entrepreneurs" from private firms and community forestry projects, had come to the conclusion that existing

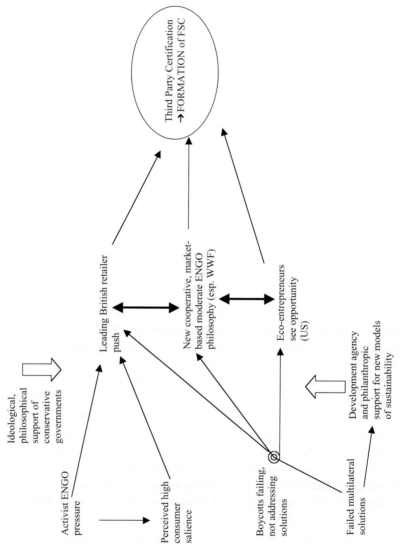

Figure 17.2 Overview of social formation of FSC, 1990–1993

multilateral efforts to stem Third-World forest degradation were not encouraging improvements in forestry practices. Third, these three constituencies – retailers, moderate NGOs, and eco-entrepreneurs – began to formulate alternative strategies in a general political environment that was becoming increasingly fond of market-based approaches (cf. Djelic ch. 3).

Thus, the FSC did not develop merely as a response to the growing preference of European and American shoppers for "guilt free" wood. On the contrary, its advocates took advantage of a widespread crisis of confidence in the tropical timber trade to manufacture a market for FSC protocols. They did so by strategically mobilizing selected retailers and suppliers, leveraging the shaming power of radical watchdog groups (cf. Boli ch. 5), drawing upon the material and institutional resources of sympathetic philanthropies and states, and engaging in a careful process of legitimation for "well-managed" wood.

At the center of this effort stood a coordinated network of entrepreneurial individuals[4] in Europe and North America who sought to use the purchasing power of high-visibility retailers and corporate consumers to pressure suppliers to seek FSC certification (for the role of networks of individuals see also Djelic ch. 3; Engels ch. 16; Marcussen ch. 9). By enlisting the support of powerful retailers (such as The Home Depot) and public consumers (such as local and state/provincial governments), advocates were able to create demand. At the same time, they sought to build supply by lobbying regional governments to support pilot projects on state lands, encouraging sympathetic landowners to become early adopters, and engaging in a "good cop, bad cop" relationship with more radical NGOs who continued to press forward with shaming campaigns and boycotts attesting to the poor production practices of uncertified companies (cf. Boli ch. 5). All the while, the coalition behind the FSC continued to marshal the symbolic and material resources of respected philanthropies, existing regulatory authorities, and intergovernmental agencies for support and legitimation of what they argued were scientifically and morally sound criteria for well-managed forestry operations.

In sum, the FSC operated as an articulated para-regulatory advocacy coalition (for parallels see Djelic and Kleiner ch. 14; Hedmo et al. ch. 15; Jacobsson and Sahlin-Andersson ch. 12; Marcussen ch. 9). The FSC was articulated as an organization linking regional and national initiatives within a transnational governance structure;[5] it functioned as a para-regulatory body attempting to define and enforce new governance rules outside traditional state regulatory structures; and it was constituted by a coalition of NGOs and firms that shared common normative convictions as advocates for a new form of governance.

This institutionalization project, however, proved extraordinarily difficult. First, the FSC grappled with a number of internal problems: tensions between local groups and the international secretariat; institutional paralysis when constituencies could not reach consensus on standards; disagreements over market strategy and alliances; funding deficits; and several other obstacles to the building of an institution. But internal struggles were only the beginning. Over time, the FSC drew the attention of producers, other industry groups, governments, NGOs, and multilateral organs. From a sociological institutional standpoint, we can locate these actors in the common social spaces – strategic action fields – within which the FSC was embedded, as is done in Figure 17.3.

As a multinational, non-governmental coalition, the FSC found itself sitting at the crossroads of two axes of action: national versus supranational and governmental versus non-governmental. At the supranational level, intergovernmental stakeholders included multilateral institutions and development agencies, such as the UN and World Bank, treaties and special trade bodies relating to forestry, and multilateral governance regimes such as the EU. Non-governmental actors included transnational NGOs, trade associations, competing industry-sponsored forestry working groups and schemes and multinational firms. At the national level, relevant state actors and institutions encompassed governments, regulatory agencies and state-mediated certification schemes. Non-state actors included most of the economic agents whose networks formed the commodity chains at issue – producers, mills and processors, traders, retailers and other aggregate consumers (such as cities and builders). Domestic non-state actors also encompassed non-governmental organizations operating at the national level, including both pro-and anti-certification coalitions, and ranging from small landowners to consumer organizations to conservationists.

Figure 17.3 helps illustrate how and why those various actors took note and responded to the FSC's actions. The FSC did not mobilize in a regulatory vacuum; other interested groups were already operating under shared understandings of governance that constituted the

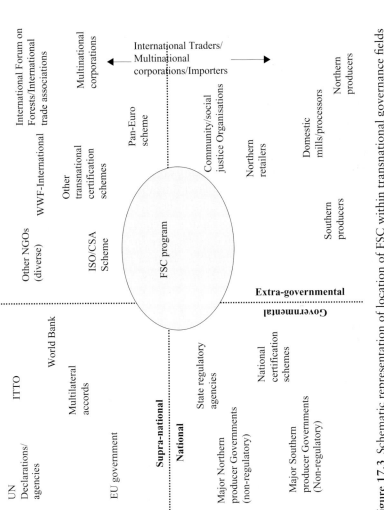

Figure 17.3 Schematic representation of location of FSC within transnational governance fields

regulatory arena in which they operated. As the FSC became an actor in
these overlapping fields of action, it sought to introduce new normative
claims regarding "good" forestry as well as control mechanisms that
could potentially alter the formal and informal "rules of the game." It
is no wonder, then, that the FSC witnessed widespread backlash and
counter-mobilizations in countries where it operated.

The counter-mobilizations the FSC witnessed – over its legitimacy,
cost-effectiveness, scientific merits, and legality – erupted both within
nations and multilaterally. That being said, while the FSC sat at the
cross-roads between state/non-state and national/transnational fields
of action, its history suggests that most of the FSC's work, and most
of the conflicts that such work triggered, was manifest first among
"extra-non-state" actors and institutions. And, although the transnational field later constituted a significant area of action conditioning the
FSC's efforts (e.g., through multilateral legitimation or transnational
coalition mobilization, as we shall see shortly), variation in the FSC's
experiences was first evident primarily at the national level. The primacy of domestic forces is well illustrated by the divergent experiences
of the two countries where the FSC received its strongest and most
ambitious start: Britain and the United States.

Explaining success and failure at the domestic level

Britain: An ideal-typical case of success and uncertainty

For most observers, the history of independent forest certification
in Britain was, until recently, celebrated as the ideal-typical success
story (see, for instance Murphy and Bendell 1997). There were indeed
impressive early successes in Britain; nevertheless, ongoing struggles
question the sustainability of the program's future there.

In the early 1990s, leading retailers joined with a dominant national
ENGO to build a "buyers group" committed to sourcing its wood
exclusively from third party certified "well managed" forestry operations by 2000.[6] Formalizing their commitment under the international Forest Stewardship Council umbrella, by 1996 the buyers group
had enlisted the participation of 47 companies, representing about 22
percent of domestic wood consumption (WWF-UK sources). Meanwhile, on the supply side a motivated FSC regional standards "working
group" began canvassing participation by private and state interests
to formulate regional FSC standards for British forestry operations.
However, as the FSC coalition garnered growing attention, a group

of domestic producer interests reacted in earnest, launching its own alternative labeling program and attacking the legitimacy of the FSC. A public relations battle for legitimacy and allegiances ensued between the two groups, and many observers reckoned that the FSC and the third party oversight principles it stood for were doomed.

Just when the battle was at its ugliest, the government forestry regulatory authority – the Forestry Commission – stepped in to broker a compromise. It proposed to develop a government-sponsored "Woodland Assurance Scheme" (UKWAS) that would be acceptable to both groups. After a series of meetings and rounds of drafts with the full gamut of unhappy interests, the Forestry Commission introduced a new state-sponsored scheme in 1999. While nominally not beholden to the FSC, this scheme pleased it sufficiently to allow the organization to recognize the UKWAS standards as equivalent. The compromise was seen as a resounding success for the FSC and the rules and norms for which it stood. Within two years, over 50 percent of productive British woodlands were FSC-certified (FSC sources). But the underlying struggle over the balance of power between ENGO and industrial interests was not over; by early 2000 a number of domestic producers had found renewed strength to oppose the FSC by allying themselves with a rival industry-controlled scheme operating in Continental Europe.

What explains the impressive (albeit imperfect) success of the FSC in Britain? The early, robust growth of the buyers group owed itself to five major factors:

(1) the relative power and leverage garnered by a closely coordinated network of leading retailers supported by a dominant ENGO;
(2) the success the buyers group had seen in encouraging major foreign suppliers to get certified, with the implication that smaller domestic landowners could be locked out of the market;
(3) the skilled ability of FSC supporters to build a broad coalition by reframing their cause to resonate with prevailing cultural beliefs and understandings;
(4) the passive, but significant, legitimation of FSC efforts by British and EU governments; and
(5) a carefully choreographed "good cop, bad cop" coordination strategy between the moderate FSC-WWF coalition and more radical NGOs (especially Friends of the Earth).

As this coalition began to succeed, however, a number of domestic woodland owners correctly surmised that it would shift the balance of power away from existing, less demanding state oversight, and reduce the amount of leverage they possessed through close relationships with the Forestry Commission. While the subsequent anti-FSC backlash had the sympathy of the state through 1997, two major factors led to a major shift in state strategy and the successful development of a compromise. First, as both primary owner of productive woodlands in the UK (through Forest Enterprise) and champion of British competitive interests and international reputation, the Forestry Commission was highly motivated to find a solution that enabled the domestic industry to strengthen its market share. Second, the new Forestry Commission representative, acting as a mediator, showed particular talent and skill in keeping opposing interests at the table to forge a compromise. Working closely with the FSC, he helped shepherd through a final draft of the government-sponsored UK WAS program that assured domestic landowners that they were not beholden to the FSC while, de facto, institutionalizing the FSC norms and rules. However, as a resilient industry-controlled rival grew in stature in Continental Europe the following year, landowners saw a new opportunity to wrest away the creeping control and legitimacy of the FSC. By 2001, they had begun to leverage their new alliances successfully with European allies to renew their struggle against the FSC, principally by questioning its legal authority at the EU-level.

The United States: Great potential, great conflict

Like Britain, the United States was the birthplace of much of the initial enthusiasm and entrepreneurship that led to the formation of the FSC. And, like its cousin across the Atlantic, the US effort boasted of many of the same promising pre-conditions – widespread public concerns over tropical forest degradation, boycott campaigns, and ideological support for market-based alternatives – that helped ensure a strong start for the FSC in Britain. Unlike in Britain, however, the ensuing effort to institutionalize the FSC's mandate was met with only modest successes and serious threats stemming from an industry-sponsored alternative.

In the United States, support for the FSC first emerged from a small group of woodworkers, community forestry activists who had worked abroad, and a few small manufacturers and landowners who shared convictions that developing a market mechanism to support sustainable forestry operations was the right thing to do. Joining forces with colleagues abroad to form the FSC in 1993, the American coalition took its cue from British counterparts and began forming domestic buyers groups. These groups were eventually amalgamated into a single organization, the Certified Forest Products Council, which counted among its members retail powerhouses such as The Home Depot and Nike.

While demand-side mobilization proceeded at a modest pace, supply-side efforts were meeting with far more resistance. The major domestic producer lobbying organization (the American Forest and Paper Association) took notice of those efforts early on, and in 1995 introduced its own, alternative labeling scheme. As in Britain, a public relations battle ensued, but at a much grander level. Meanwhile, several of the FSC's own working groups in the US became mired in conflicts between different stakeholders as they sought to develop regional standards.

As of late 2001, a draft of FSC national standards had been completed, but several US working groups were still hammering through debates over regional indicators. Concurrently, the major industry alternative program was set to launch aggressively its own "third party" certification option, replete with a label and claims of authenticity that would entirely bypass the structure of the FSC. All the while, the commitment of large retailers to preference FSC products remained tentative and tepid, and very few FSC-certified goods were making it to store shelves. As of early 2003, the fate of the FSC alongside the industry alternative – co-existence, harmonization of standards, or the eventual dissolution of the FSC and the NGO-based para-regulatory form it represented – remained unknown (Cashore et al. 2003).

Juxtaposed to the British case, many of the underlying mechanisms shaping the US experience are obvious. But others are subtler. An examination of power relations along the commodity chain for wood products in the US reveals a domestic producer industry that is far more powerful than in Britain. The United States is the single largest wood producer in the world. The powerful and centralized trade association (the American Forest and Paper Association) mounted, from the very beginning, a well-coordinated and aggressive campaign to weaken the FSC. Yet the relative power of domestic producers can only be part of the story; had major retailers worked aggressively in tandem with leading NGOs to pressure domestic suppliers in unison, supply-side responses might have been more sympathetic. Furthermore, the United

States did witness some early enthusiasm from private and state forestry operations (e.g., the State of Pennsylvania, and firms such as Collins Pine, and Seven Islands). But unlike in Britain, the take-up of supply appeared to stall.

Five factors help explain why a potentially promising beginning partially derailed in the United States. First, the coalition seeking to build domestic demand remained relatively loose. Powerhouses such as The Home Depot supported the FSC publicly but did not coordinate their efforts with other buyers. Domestic NGO support of the FSC was uneven and fractious. Some leading NGOs opposed the program because it might encourage wood consumption; sometimes, even regional offices of the same organization (such as the Sierra Club) differed in their opinions. Second, existing regulatory norms in the forestry sector in the United States – adversarial, lawsuit based, and divided between federal and state jurisdictions – militated against centralized and informal compromise and coordination between actors. Antitrust laws also prohibited the kind of competitive cooperation among retailers to pressure suppliers seen in Britain. Third, land tenure patterns and practices of forestry operations in the United States made the prospect of certification much less necessary and more cumbersome and expensive. Fourth, from the very beginning the FSC coalition faced a much more uphill battle in efforts to naturalize their cause alongside existing shared cultural symbols and beliefs regarding forestry practices and oversight. Finally, although the FSC actively sought state legitimation through pilot projects on public lands early on, few state bodies came forward to endorse the effort publicly.

The big picture: Emergent outcomes in the transnational arena of action

As those two cases illustrate, domestic political struggles over forest certification regimes certainly bore the stamp of their unique national institutional environments. Nonetheless, it remains true that most countries first found themselves party to political debates over the FSC because they were tied economically and politically to the preferences and social movement tactics of retailers and NGOs working multinationally. The FSC sought to introduce an international consensus framework on standards and procedures for certification under which national and regional initiatives would be coordinated. The social movements that gave birth to the FSC were indeed multinational, but they shared a common belief that an effective response to abuses in the transnational timber trade would require building credibility and consistency in the international marketplace through the adoption of one system and the use of a single, widely recognized label (cf. Djelic and Kleiner ch. 14; Engels ch. 16; Hedmo et al. ch. 15). As advocates built the FSC internationally based on this shared conviction, they sought to articulate their activities to further the work of allies working in countries around the world. And in so doing, they helped ratchet up the mobilization of struggles over the oversight of forestry practices to the transnational level.

Multinational commodity chains as conduits for transnational coordination

The FSC was founded to provide a single, credible system and corresponding label that could be used to certify well-managed wood products in markets all around the world. For major buyers and traders who were seeking a means to assure watchdog groups and other constituencies that wood products came from "sustainable" and legally felled sources, the availability of a single, international, widely recognized label was vital. The FSC's expressly international reach reflected, of course, the multinational character of the industry. As noted above, early support came from activists and retailers worried about tropical country imports to Europe and North America. However, trade flows within the northern hemisphere soon also came under the scrutiny of watchdog groups. Domestic boycotts and shame campaigns coordinated with European NGOs against major producers in British Columbia, for instance, helped compel several large Canadian companies exporting to Europe to consider FSC certification.

Thus, while the politics of certification unfolded largely among domestic actors, watchdog groups and retailers first mobilized across national borders. Multinational commodity chains were the first targets for certification supporters. European pressure groups sought to influence oversight of production practices in tropical countries by compelling major buyers in their home countries – namely retailers – to support certification (see North 1997). They adopted similar tactics to apply pressure on North American and European producers. The buyers groups that formed in Western Europe were the "engines" propelling pressures for certification along multinational commodity chains.

The transnationalization of conflict over control

The FSC was not the only actor in forest certification debates to work at the international level in the 1990s; producers, governments, and other interested groups also scaled up their international activities at the end of the decade. Because the FSC offered buyers an oversight system providing consistent credibility for products sourced from around the world, major industry groups had to coordinate their efforts to provide governments and corporate consumers with international alternatives if they wanted to retain control of the process.

As early as 1997, traders and producers across Europe were already discussing the possibility of launching an EU-wide industry alternative to the FSC. Recognizing that the FSC was, in fact, an effort to shift the balance of power over forest oversight away from states and towards environmental NGOs, outspoken industry leaders sought to mobilize their colleagues to mount a preemptive strike. By 2000, industry trade associations in Europe and North America had begun to develop their own international certification and labeling programs. In Europe, many smaller producers and some larger ones were advocating for the Pan European Forest Certification Scheme (PEFC), which sought to coordinate a number of national industry-sponsored initiatives. Oddly, the PEFC appeared to support many of the same values and procedural requirements – including "stakeholder consultation," a chain of custody system, and community input – as the rival it was trying to replace (for parallels see Botzem and Quack ch. 13; Hedmo et al. ch. 15). So why, then, did many producer organizations so vehemently support the PEFC as a weapon to unseat the FSC? The answer is control of the process. While some of the concerns of smaller landowners over the FSC – especially over time and expense incurred – were indeed better addressed by the PEFC framework, the PEFC was propelled mostly by a desire of producers to strengthen control over the certification process (Vallejo and Hauselmann 2001).

In North America, the major US trade group for wood producers, the American Forest and Paper Association (AF&PA), followed suit with its own "Sustainable Forestry Initiative" (SFI) program. In 2000, the

SFI went "international," offering a certification (and future labeling) option for non-American producers (Hansen et al. 2000). Within a few months of the announcement, a Canadian producer had been certified under the SFI's protocols. From the perspective of the AF&PA, providing foreign producers with the option of seeking certification under the SFI program was necessary to address the needs of customers and the public – the retailers and NGOs – who were still clamoring for a transparent, credible, and uniform system (Virga 2001).

Thus, from the perspective of FSC leaders and other observers, the underlying motivations for industry-sponsored attempts to provide alternative international schemes were very clear. Industry counter-mobilizations sought to keep control over the certification process away from ENGOs and firmly in the hands of industry-brokered alternatives backed by national and multilateral government bodies (Garforth 2001; Synnot 2002).

Conclusions: Implications for theories of transnational regulatory politics

Findings in this chapter suggest that non-governmental certification and labeling programs may be understood as efforts to "build in" procedural and normative innovations into existing governance fields – fields that are also populated by domestic actors that involve themselves in arbitrating and negotiating between those innovations and existing, state-based, governance structures. These efforts have helped deepen broader trends toward the rationalization of scientifically- and morally-justified norms regarding "responsible" production practices in an international regulatory arena operating according to market principles (e.g. Conroy 2001; see also Boli ch. 5; Djelic ch. 3; Drori and Meyer ch. 2).

"National" versus "global" influences on markets

The current study helps reaffirm and sharpen recent sociological attempts to overcome a tendency to privilege either national or transnational forces in thinking about the making of transnational markets. Commodity markets are indeed becoming more transnationalized – the wood trade is a case in point. Nonetheless, the governance fields that serve to define and constitute the nature of relationships in those markets are located primarily within national borders. Even in the highly internationalized wood trade, existing markets are populated by actors located in national institutional environments, and most struggles over governance occur within national borders – even when they are organized as international efforts by multinational coalitions.

While confirming that most action occurs at the national level, the findings also suggest that transnational influences can and do condition relations of power, conventions, and shared cultural constructions in the domestic sphere. In the present study, multinational institutional entrepreneurs, acting on behalf of the FSC, served as conduits for these influences, but so did international trade associations, multilateral organs, aid agencies, academics, MNCs, and even foreign states.

These findings are consistent with recent work that has sought to theorize on the politics of regulation in the transnational economy. Such efforts often map how state and non-state actors interact at both transnational and domestic levels to construct, challenge, and reproduce regulatory outcomes associated with environmental, health, and labor issues (e.g. Keck and Sikkink 1998; Evans 2000; Sears et al. 2001; Vogel and Kagan 2001; Djelic and Quack 2003). These scholars document how economic transactions join firms together in multinational commodity chains, but they also note how multilateral regimes, non-governmental organizations, and other interest groups increasingly coordinate activities across states. At the same time, however, globalization has not flattened the diverse topography of national institutional environments. Rather, differences in regulatory requirements, industrial structure, organizational culture, and other domestic-level characteristics among producer and consumer nations help explain the diversity of environmental and social outcomes associated with transnational commodity production, trade, and consumption. Furthermore, characteristics of national institutional environments and the strategies adopted by actors within them can "trickle up" to affect multilateral and transnational institutions and processes. Transnational influences can also "trickle down" to the domestic level, but national institutional environments are relatively "sticky" and change relatively slowly. Such an understanding of the nature of globalization is consistent with the argument made here that processes giving birth to new transnational forms of governance cannot be fully explained without examining how they play out in the domestic arenas where rules governing markets are actually constituted and enforced.

The role of the state in "non-state" governance struggles

It has become almost a truism in social theory circles to reaffirm that states "matter," but the current study suggests that state institutions may matter in "non-state" para-regulatory efforts in specific ways. Even in conflicts largely constituted by non-state actors, sovereign states accord legitimacy to NGOs and help enforce rules. When stakeholders disagree over the content or application of new non-state para-regulatory initiatives, they turn to public regulatory authorities as potential allies and arbiters. Over time, the participation of state regulatory entities becomes increasingly important to the success of C&L programs, through their roles as mediators, arbiters, and legitimacy providers. State agencies are often called in to codify, standardize, and legitimate standards and practices that define common rules for certification programs (Palmer 1996).

Based on the findings of this study, we can speculate that state engagement with "non-state" institution-building is concretely evident in many forms, including: participation or mediation in stakeholder meetings; commissioning "white papers" on the appropriateness or efficacy of an NGO effort; facilitating conflict resolution; and standardization of "national" program requirements. All the while, even in countries such as the US where state participation in programs such as the FSC has been minimal, public entities also serve as both producers and consumers of the very commodities at issue in non-governmental oversight programs. As such, public entities are often quite visible and capable of bestowing symbolic legitimacy on the particular non-state protocols they choose to support.

In acknowledging the powerful ways in which state agencies are involved in non-state para-regulatory efforts, this study nonetheless also shows that non-state actors have asserted new forms of autonomy in the regulatory sphere. As the case study of the FSC demonstrates, all action in governance fields is not state-mediated. The FSC and other NGO-controlled programs are typically governed entirely by non-state actors; state representatives can only serve as "observers" in its governing bodies and standards-setting groups. Paradoxically, the FSC relies on state bodies for necessary legitimation and mediation but remains a non-state actor all the while.

Conflict and consensus-building: Rationalizing new norms in global production practices

Even if third party C&L programs ultimately fail to penetrate large segments of international markets, the foregoing analysis of the wood products sectors suggests that such programs may contribute to other, potentially more profound transformations, in the regulatory arena. The Forest Stewardship Council has influenced formal and informal understandings among state and private actors regarding what should be regulated in international wood markets, who should be empowered to enforce such rules, and how enforcement should be undertaken. Such spillover has occurred principally through creeping isomorphism and the convergence of norms regarding scientific and moral attributes of "well-managed" forest products (see Boli ch. 5; Drori and Meyer ch. 2).

Competing alternative programs that originally appeared to thwart the FSC's efforts have slowly morphed, seemingly paradoxically, to embrace and embody (at least on paper) many of the same rules and norms within their operations (cf. Botzem and Quack ch. 13; Hedmo et al. ch. 15). In the case of the wood products sector, there is no doubt that industry and state alternatives have sought to remake themselves in order to weaken criticism from FSC-favoring opponents. In the two domestic case studies highlighted in this project, after bouts of pointed criticism in the media, competing initiatives re-invented themselves to claim, at least symbolically, support of many of the same principles originally advocated by the FSC. They did so by appealing to "best practices," buttressed by scientific studies and emerging international documents delineating what standards and criteria are desirable, good, or just (see, for example, Bass 1996; American Forest and Paper Association 2000; cf. Boli ch. 5; Drori and Meyer ch. 2).

Trends toward convergence are also evident within intergovernmental and aid bodies. For instance, since 1998, the World Bank has worked with WWF-International in a "partnership" to certify 200,000,000 hectares of "well-managed" forest area around the world under principles and criteria largely compatible with the FSC (WWF–World Bank Press Release 17 August 1998; Counsell 2003); the MacArthur Foundation has become a strong advocate of certification programs (Jenkins and Smith 1999); and a variety of UN and aid agencies, while not in agreement about the FSC's viability, nonetheless embrace its broader mandates for non-governmental participation and oversight in community forestry. Clearly, a number of these trends began concomitantly with the FSC and stemmed from broader new fascination with "market-based" instruments to promote sustainability; the FSC was certainly not the sole engine behind them (cf. Djelic ch. 3). Nonetheless, substantial evidence exists that the coalition driving the development of the FSC has worked directly and indirectly to win explicit and implicit support for its objectives from these organizations.

The observation that the Forest Stewardship Council has been perhaps most effective as a challenger seeking to influence the taken-for-granted rules and norms that define regulatory oversight suggests that NGO-coordinated C&L programs may lose individual battles but nonetheless help to deepen the rationalization of emerging norms and rules regarding what practices should be evaluated and which actors have the authority to do so.

Notes

1. Figure 17.1 is taken from McNichol (2002), on which the following analysis is partly based.
2. For a more detailed discussion of the conditions and characteristics of "trickle up" and "trickle down" effects between national institutional systems and transnational institution-building, see Djelic and Quack (2003).
3. The case study presented here is based on McNichol (2002).
4. The core group of advocates included representatives form WWF-UK and B&Q (a major retailer) in Britain, community forestry activists working in Asia and Latin America, regional members of the Rainforest Alliance, Sierra Club and other environmental organizations in Canada and the United States, independent eco-labeling authorities in Europe and North America and eclectic groups of woodworkers and "green" landowners (McNichol 2002).

5. The FSC governance structure requires that regional and national "working groups" formulate specific indicators that accord with international
   criteria but are also adapted to regional environmental, social and economic conditions.
6. This group had targeted 1995 in 1990 but it changed its target as 1995
   approached. In 2000, the group again shifted its objective to 75 percent
   certified sourcing by 2005 (Worldwide Fund for Nature 2000).

18 Institutional dynamics in a re-ordering world

MARIE-LAURE DJELIC AND KERSTIN
SAHLIN-ANDERSSON

Introduction

The chapters in this volume point to a profound re-definition of structuring frames for action and of normative and cognitive reference sets. In other words, all chapters, individually and as a whole, document significant institutional transformation. The transnationalization of our world, sometimes hastily labeled "globalization," is not only – indeed, far from it – about flows of goods, capital or people. Nor is transnationalization simply a discourse even though it does have important discursive dimensions. Our transnationalizing world is a re-ordering world, a world where institutional rules of the game are in serious transition. Furthermore, the chapters in this volume clearly suggest – and many mundane contemporary experiences confirm it – that the impact of re-ordering processes is significant and consequential for our everyday lives.

Rather than focusing on impact, though, this volume wanted to contribute to our understanding of transformation processes. How are new modes of governance – rules and regulations and the organizing and monitoring activities that sustain, reproduce and control them – shaped and how do they come about? A defining theme for this volume has been the genesis and stabilization of transnational governance. We have applied a revisited field perspective to approach this theme. We understand transnational fields to be complex combinations of institutional forces, spatial and relational topographies and propose that those three dimensions are constitutive of transnational governance.

As a consequence, we have considered transnational governance in the making from three complementary angles. First, we have looked in Part I at the institutional forces that are, in the end, the fundamental rules of the game of the rule-making process in our world – the meaning and cultural structure that defines and shapes positions, patterns of activities and interactions. Second, we have considered the spatial dimension of transnational governance. Part II gives a sense of the dynamic topography of actors. The chapters show a profoundly evolving landscape where old actors in the regulatory game – and its associated organizing and monitoring activities – are being thoroughly transformed and reinvented. At the same time, new types of actors are progressively getting involved. Third, and finally, we have looked into the relational dimension. Parts II and III display the dynamics of interaction associated with the re-ordering process. Contributions in Part III, in particular, are in-depth and generally longitudinal regulatory stories. They tell us about modes and logics of interaction and negotiation in complex constellations and reveal power plays and patterns of coalition-building. They also provide evidence of multidirectional and dense interactions across many different boundaries – public/private, state/non-state, and national/transnational.

In this concluding chapter we start with a synthetic overview of the contemporary regulatory explosion and its main features as they emerge from reading together the contributions to this volume. We follow, then, with an elaboration of the meaning, spatial and relational dimensions of regulatory dynamics. We end with a focus on notions of power and interest as we see them playing out in our re-ordering world.

A regulatory explosion

The contributions to this volume show that our re-ordering world is indeed marked by more – not less – rule-making activity. The intensity of the latter is such, in fact, that it would probably be more accurate to talk of regulatory "activism." Regulatory activism can take the form of a re-regulation of certain spheres that had already been regulated before but generally at the national level. This is the case, for example, with education, health, labor markets (Jacobsson 2004) or accounting and financial reporting. All those spheres are increasingly subject to transnational regulatory activities and initiatives.

Regulatory activism also takes the form of an expansion into virgin territories – towards spheres of social life that were not regulated before. This is the case, for example, with environmental and pollution issues (Frank et al. 2000; McNichol and Bensedrine 2003; Power 2003); ethical, social and environmental aspects of corporate activities; the life and rights of animals (Forbes and Jermier 2002);

administrative procedures (Brunsson and Jacobsson 2000; Beck and Walgenbach 2002) or with the structuring of love and intimate relationships (Franck and McEneaney 1999). The present world, indeed, is a "golden era of regulation" (Levi-Faur and Jordana 2005).

Soft regulation with potentially hard consequences

With the transnationalization of regulatory activities, the nature of rule-making has changed significantly. In the introduction to this volume we distinguished between four dimensions of regulatory developments: who is regulating, the mode of regulation, the nature of rules, and compliance mechanisms. We have found examples and illustrations, throughout this volume, of transformations along all four dimensions. Many new regulations are issued by states and by intergovernmental bodies but we have documented an expansion of regulating constellations that transcend the state/non-state divide. We have also seen how parts of states are engaging in regulatory games so that state regulation ends up having a kaleidoscopic character. The development, in other words, cannot be described as a simple move from state to non-state regulation – but it is a development where state regulators are increasingly embedded in and interplay with many other regulatory actors.

With this development come changes in modes of regulation and compliance mechanisms. Many new rules are voluntary. This means that those who are to comply should be attracted to following the rules rather than forced to do so. Some of the new regulatory regimes are constituted as "markets" where the incentives for following rules are essentially financial. The new market for CO_2 emissions rights is a good illustration. Other rule systems are also structured as markets but with reputation, trust and legitimacy as a combined set of incentives. This is the case with accreditation and rankings in management education, forestry certification schemes or the UN global compact for corporate social responsibility. Compliance can also be obtained as new rules are presented as progressive and contributing to prosperity, broadly understood, rather than as controlling tools. Rules in this case tend to be framed by science and expertise.

Regulation and rule-making, in their contemporary form, come together with intense organizing and monitoring activities that sustain and reproduce emerging rules as well as targeting adoption and implementation. In the background to the multiplication of soft rules, we find the potential threat that states would come to issue harder rules – both more restrictive and less open to interpretation and adjustment by those who are following rules. In fact soft rules can be either a way to buffer the field from harder forms of regulation or a first step towards harder forms of regulation. This suggests important dynamics where regulations develop and expand in response and reaction to each other. These dynamics clearly involve power relations and structures of authority, including when the latter are hidden under the apparent neutrality of references to science and expertise.

Even when they lean on the shoulders of potentially harder modes of controlling, soft rules are typically formed in general terms. They are open, as a consequence, to negotiations and translations by those who are regulated. In fact, this form of regulation requires the active participation of those being regulated both during the phase of interpretation and also at the moment of elaboration or during monitoring. Soft rules are generally associated with complex procedures of self-presentation, self-reporting and self-monitoring. This was shown to be the case, for example, in higher education, forestry certification or corporate governance.

A direct consequence of extended soft regulation is therefore a multiplication of resources put on formalized systems of self-presentation and monitoring in many organizations. This had been identified by Power (1997) in his studies of the audit society, and is confirmed by several chapters in this volume as well as in recent writings on the US Sarbanes-Oxley Act and its impact (e.g. Power 2004). So, what could appear to be at first sight a "softening" of the rule system in fact fosters, most of the time, extended re-regulation and increased organizing and formalization.

Governance with governments

There is often an assumption that transnationalization and the opening of the world mean drastic reduction of rules everywhere – competition favors the weakest governance orders. We do not find that. Instead, we provide the picture of a world where the intensity of rule-making activity is extremely high and if anything only increasing. Brought together, the contributions to this volume document an impressive overall progress of soft regulation, particularly with a transnational scope. They confirm that we have moved well beyond a Westphalian world, where sovereign isolates (nation-states) confront each other in an essentially anomic international arena. We also collectively show that states do not "withdraw" and remain very much involved in the regulatory game. But this regulatory game is changing profoundly and, in a process of close co-evolution, states are themselves going through significant re-invention. This book provides evidence of a transnational world characterized by increasing and intense "governance with government."

We also find that the actors who interact in the process – both those regulating and those regulated – tend to develop common identities. States have reformed to become more businesslike as they incorporate management tools and modes of organizing (e.g. Hood 1991). Nonprofit and non-governmental organizations are also restructuring to become more businesslike (e.g. Powell et al. 2006). Corporations on the other hand are expected to act as "citizens" of global society (e.g. Zadek 2001) and to claim and assume a degree of political power and responsibility. Distinctions between public and private sectors are getting blurred and a clear tendency is for all those various kinds of actors to be increasingly defined, controlled and governed as organizations (Brunsson and Sahlin-Andersson 2000).

With this degree of multi-polarity, expanded regulation reflects coordination and ordering ambitions. This is not a world where some units are assumed to have authority over others; instead relations among organizations are increasingly shaped in market terms. Monitoring tends to be done through mechanisms of socialization and on the basis of an increasingly rationalized global moral order. This soft path to regulation should, however and as noted above, not always be taken at face value. Control remains an objective but is increasingly hidden and neutralized behind references to science and expertise. There are clear power games and power stakes in transnational governance fields. A seemingly paradoxical example is that states may gain power and influence rather than "wither away" as assumed in a lot of the literature. As states form coalitions and constellations beyond their territories; as they increasingly rely on neutralized discursive references to expertise and science, they may gain in the process significant leverage both over local constituencies and in transnational arenas.

A governance spiral

Transnational governance expands in part through a self-reinforcing spiral. Regulation and the monitoring, evaluating and auditing activities that come together with it only seem to breed greater needs and calls for still further regulation and governance. Many chapters in this volume document an apparently unstoppable escalation of regulation and governance. They point to three main mechanisms that altogether feed the governance spiral. These mechanisms are moved respectively by distrust, the question of responsibility and the search for control.

In line with previous research (Power 1997; 2004) we have shown that the movement towards expanded regulation is driven in part by a lack of trust. A diffuse distrust generates the need for activities that reveal, make transparent and set rules, with a view to building more trust. Those activities, however, may in fact not only solve problems but also reveal and suggest new problems and new questions. In the process, rather than building trust, they could be undermining it further, leading to still more requests for auditing, monitoring and regulation. The chapters in this volume suggest that this could be particularly true in the case of transnational governance as it is characterized by three specific features. First, the absence of a formal and sovereign holder of legitimacy in the transnational arena entails the relative fragility of rules and monitoring activities. There is competition out there for claims to authority and the regulatory arena can be described as a regulatory market – where demand and offer stimulate and reinforce each other. Some of it may even have the feel of a market (regulatory) bubble. Second, in the absence of other legitimacy holders, science and expertise tend to impose themselves. There is quite an ambivalent relationship to science, however, in our societies. While science in general is legitimate and legitimating, individual experts and individual pieces of expertise are often contested. Third, this contestation is reinforced by the trend towards deliberative and participative democracy, so characteristic of our transnationalizing world. Deliberative democracy means expanded claims to be involved in and contribute to rule-making and rule-monitoring. Ultimately, this is bound to generate regulatory or governance "inflation" – where "your" regulation fosters "my" monitoring or counter-regulation, and so forth.

Hence, behind exploding regulatory and governance activities, one finds a distrust spiral that is fostered and reinforced by three defining and structuring forces of fields of transnational governance – scientization, marketization and deliberative democracy. We also find a "responsibility spiral" to be partially connected. Governance and regulation are in part about allocation of responsibility. When rules are precise and focused, responsibilities are relatively clear. With the multiplication of regulatory and governance activities, responsibilities get diffused and dispersed. Furthermore, the movement towards soft regulation has a tendency to re-route responsibility away from rule-setters and towards rule-followers. Voluntary rules that are open to translation mean that those who choose to follow the rules and to follow them in certain ways are held responsible. This double blurring of responsibilities may drive the need for regulation and governance still further and at the local level expanded soft regulation may foster a culture of defensiveness (see Power 2004). Organizational representatives then have to allocate extended resources not only to follow rules but also to explain why they choose to follow certain rules in particular ways or why they should not be held responsible.

A third mechanism feeding the spiral evolves around the search for control. We have pictured the transnational world as a world in motion, with unclear and shifting boundaries and organizations in flux. On the regulatory market, the way to reach control or to react to regulations that are not favorable to one's position and strategy is essentially to organize and drive a competing regulatory set-up. We saw examples of this in the field of management education. When European business schools realized that US accreditation and ranking systems increasingly shaped the norms for what counted as good management education, they reacted. Feeling marginalized within the existing governance frame, they structured and defined competing and complementary ranking and accreditation systems. Similar control spirals have emerged in many areas, particularly with the development of the European union and of a European identity. In a world where transnational regulation is expanding, the way to seek control is not by avoiding regulation. A more promising strategy is active involvement to issue and support a satisfactory regulatory scheme.

Consequential incrementalism

All empirical stories in this volume underscore the important role of time and the highly progressive and bumpy road to transnational

governance – with long moments of standstill, periods of backlash
and an undeniable role for historical opportunities and chance. Institutional rules of the game do not change according to a pattern of
punctuated equilibrium and radical ruptures. Instead, the chapters in
this volume show that institutional change is highly progressive and
step by step, often inscribed in long historical developments and generally associated with resistance, struggles, conflicts, negotiations or
cooperation. Institutional change is, in other words, an incremental
process. However incrementalism does not imply that the transformations generated would be only minor adaptations; many chapters
document the highly consequential and transformative impact of re-
ordering processes. Institutional change as it characterizes our contemporary transnationalizing world is both incremental and highly consequential, with a profound transformative impact (see also Djelic and
Quack 2003; Thelen and Streeck 2005).

We have pointed to a number of drivers for the explosion of regulatory and governance activities with a transnational scope. At a first
level of analysis, that of the detailed description of a particular regulatory process or history, complexity is striking All our empirical stories
tell of multiple actors involved, shifting coalitions and unstable interests, long and bumpy historical developments with a multiplicity of
stages, competing logics, conflicts and resistance, of bricolage and the
varying presence of national solutions or parts thereof. Each regulatory story therefore tends to picture a unique path, highly complex
if not merely chaotic. The multiplication of stories, though, and their
systematic confrontation and comparison, make it possible to identify
important regularities behind this apparently extreme complexity.

Institutional forces in fields of transnational governance – the meaning dimension

The regularities stem in great part from a set of institutional forces
that increasingly and progressively structure transnational governance.
Those institutional forces are powerful, and in a sense paradigmatic,
rules of the game for contemporary regulation and associated organizing and monitoring activities.

The first such institutional force is scientization – the "extraordinary and expansive authority of modern scientific rationalization" as
revealed in the overwhelming role and presence in our contemporary

world of scientific agencies, scientists, scientific products and argumentation. A sub-dimension of scientization is the strong drive towards measurement and quantification. Expertise and the legitimacy of science have a tendency to express themselves in figures, measurement and statistical relations. The ontology, methods and models characteristic of mathematics, physics and natural sciences have all but triumphed. They have a tendency to be purely and simply conflated with "science," marginalizing as it were alternative understandings of the scientific endeavor.

A second institutional force, increasingly shaping fields of transnational governance, is marketization. The powerful contemporary marketization drive reflects a belief that markets are superior arrangements for the allocation of goods and resources and this in every sphere of economic, social or even cultural and moral life. This "belief" in markets is itself institutionalizing fast and, as a consequence, markets are increasingly defined and perceived as the "natural" way to organize and structure human interactions.

Organizing is a third institutional force highly structuring of fields of governance. Organizing is a way to create order transnationally in the absence of a world state and of a world culture. In our transnational world, it often takes the particular form of "meta-organizing" – coordination and control being largely of the "soft" kind.

A fourth institutional force is what we have called in this volume moral rationalization. Rationalized and scientized assessment and celebration of virtue and virtuosity become increasingly prominent in the transnational public realm and act as a powerful sustaining and structuring force of transnational governance.

Deliberative democracy is a fifth institutional force shaping the context of transnational governance and, as it were, the rules of the game of transnational regulation and monitoring. The transnational world is increasingly permeated by a view of democracy that emphasizes dialogue and deliberation and the autonomy of participating actors. A sub-dimension associated with deliberative and participative democracy is the explosion and expansion of soft forms of governance.

Reinforcing interplays

Those five institutional forces and the two associated sub-dimensions are closely intertwined; in fact they nurture and foster each other.

Scientization, for example, is often an important background to the contemporary elaboration of soft regulation or the rationalized celebration of virtue and virtuosity. Meta-organizations rely on soft regulation – standardization in particular, often quite closely coupled with measurement and quantified objectives. Deliberative democracy and discussions around soft regulation generate "markets" for rules and therefore reinforce the marketization trend. The progress of marketization has, in turn, a tendency to rely on both formal organizing and scientized expertise as a two-dimensional backbone. The spread of markets and marketization in many different spheres of social life also suggests open participation and "free" or competitive involvement, pushing even further the trend towards deliberative democracy and soft regulation. The disclosure and transparency associated with deliberative democracy and soft regulation are often further rationalized and can even be articulated with formal celebrations of virtue and virtuosity. As to moral rationalization, it is generally revealed and expressed through sustained organizing efforts.

The close and mutually reinforcing interplay between those institutional forces generates, we propose, a highly structured and ordered world. Despite the absence of a world culture and political order, we find in fact a tight and constraining frame. Institutional forces should not be treated as external to the actors – as representing an environment to which actors are merely adapting. Rather, they are constitutive of the actors. Institutional forces frame and constitute organizations and individuals – their interests, values, structures, contents and meaning, activities and the nature and form of their interactions. There is another sense in which institutional forces are not external to actors and activities. If one adopts a long-term perspective, they reflect and express the aggregation of strategies, interests and activities. They have been historically and progressively constructed, even if they tend today to function as an external and progressively hardening "iron cage" (Weber 1978).

From battlefields to stabilization?

Ultimately, though, we are still talking about battlefields. The five institutional forces identified above and their two associated subdimensions are sometimes colliding and conflicting with other institutional sets – generally structured at a national level. Those national institutional systems are still powerful systems of constraints – localized ones for the most part but with a potential reach in other geographical spaces (Westney 1987; Djelic 1998). Building again on the physics metaphor, we view this as the confrontation of different fields of forces. In some cases, forces will work in parallel or similar directions. In other cases, they will counter each other and there will be powerful resistance. Contributions to this volume nevertheless seem to suggest three things. First, the progress of the institutional forces identified above is quite fast on the whole and probably only accelerating because of the mutually reinforcing dynamics described before. Second, this institutional frame is not potent and powerful only in fields of transnational governance – its impact is progressively being felt, in both direct and indirect ways, in governance processes that remain for various reasons still strongly national or local. Third, behind those institutional forces, their competition and their struggles, there are individuals, groups, organizations or networks; sets of colliding and conflicting interests; interactions and power plays.

When considered together and in their interaction, these institutional forces are increasingly turning into meta-rules of the game for governance and rule-making in our world. The structuring we are talking about is essentially of a normative and cognitive kind. This meta-institutional frame sets and defines a "meaning" or "cultural" system that constrains the way we think and talk about governance, the way we undertake, negotiate and structure it, the way we sustain and reproduce it – across, between but also, increasingly, within national boundaries. This institutional frame, this meaning or cultural system, and its components as we described them in this volume, follow the route of all institutional sets. They progressively become taken for granted and as it were fade into the background and become "invisible." This transnational culture increasingly sets and defines the "natural" way of doing, acting and being – and even resistance, reaction and protest activities tend to express and inscribe themselves within rather than outside the institutional frame.

It is interesting, in that respect, to consider the anti-globalization movements that define themselves as strong critiques of some of the logics of transnationalization described in this volume. Many features of anti-globalization movements in reality reinforce, rather than question, the advancing transnational meaning and cultural system presented here (see e.g. Keraghel and Sen 2004). Anti-globalization movements are highly organized, very much along meta-organization principles. Anti-globalization movements have appropriated, for themselves and their own functioning, claims to deliberative democracy and soft regulation and they even refer to expertise and science. Finally, they also make use of the tools associated with moral rationalization to build and diffuse their critique.

The dynamic topography of transnational governance – the spatial dimension

Fields of transnational governance are undeniably fields of forces and, as we showed in this volume, highly structured ones. Those fields, however, also have a spatial dimension.

The notion of space and its evolution

The notion of "governance space" could have two main dimensions. First, the term could refer to the space where governance is being constructed. Second, the term could refer to the space where governance applies. A clear analytical and empirical differentiation between those two dimensions would point towards a sharp separation between rule-makers and rule-followers. In a Westphalian world, this separation would tend to be particularly marked. In a Westphalian world, furthermore, the horizon would remain essentially national. The space where governance was constructed would broadly follow the contours of the nation-state and political administration. The space where governance applied would be tightly congruent with a particular national territory or sub-parts thereof.

In a transnationalizing world, the spatial dimension of governance appears to be much more complex, fluid and multi-dimensional. First, the notion of space is not always or systematically associated with a political and geographical territory. As the chapters in this volume document, there are governance spaces but those can range all the way from referring to a geographical and political territory, to an organizationally structured arena marked by a degree of physical reality (i.e. buildings) or, finally, to virtual spaces structured through a combination of technology and cognitive frames. Second, governance spaces are neither unitary nor centralized as would be the case in a Westphalian scenario where the nation-state would essentially represent the governance kernel. Rather governance spaces in a transnational world are de-centered and multi-centred, or even fragmented. A multiplicity of governance initiatives are often going on in parallel, in complex patterns of cooperation, competition or simple juxtaposition. Third, governance spaces have a horizon that is not, by a long way, simply national. Actually, the chapters in this volume document a blurring of boundaries. Governance spaces span multiple levels – the sub-national, the national, and the transnational – and a sharp differentiation between those levels becomes in fact increasingly less meaningful and useful. Fourth, and finally, the analytical separation between a space where governance is constructed and a space where governance applies becomes less relevant in a transnational world. There is here, also, a blurring of categories and boundaries. As the chapters in this volume illustrate, rules are increasingly being constructed, at least in part, by those who will then have to follow them.

At the same time, however, even if boundaries are blurring and easily crossed, those different levels remain a reality of a sort. They are always present, to be used and brought up when necessary in the interest of actors seeking influence, as tools to allocate blame and responsibility or as excuses to avoid difficulties and liabilities. In other words, sub-national, national and international levels largely become discursive categories at the disposal of actors, to be used as they take part in transnational, national or local governance games.

Who are the actors?

Transnational governance spaces are densely populated. There is a large and, in appearance, ever increasing number of actors involved in regulation and associated organizing and monitoring activities. Regulation and governance breed even more regulation and governance. This in itself in part explains the explosion in the sheer numbers of actors involved. We have seen, though, that the evolution of regulatory modes, leading to the widespread diffusion of softer types of rules, fosters regulatory competition, and as such is also a factor explaining the multiplicity of actors involved.

Out of this diversity and multiplicity, we can still differentiate between four broad categories. The first category contains those actors that are parts of or directly associated with nation-states and political administrations. States and political administrations are feeling the marketization impact. They are being re-defined as collections or networks of organizations that have to interact and compete on transnational regulatory markets. Hence, multiple agencies, administrative departments, public networks or groups are active quite independently in many different governance spaces. States and administrative units have undeniably lost their monopoly position over regulation. Nevertheless, they remain powerfully involved in regulatory and governance processes. We even find two particular and quite consequential roles for those types of actors. First, when we compare the empirical studies of governance presented in the chapters above, we find that an endorsement by states and/or administrative units gives in general much greater clout and strength to a set of rules, particularly when it comes to local and national adoption and implementation. Second, the threat of coercion undeniably remains a power resource in the hands of states even in times so clearly characterized by soft and interactive forms of regulation and governance.

In the second category of our four broad categories, we can put international organizations of a public nature and transnational political constructions: the IMF, the World Bank, the GATT and later the WTO, the OECD, or the various manifestations of the European Union amongst others. It is undeniable that the role, place and clout of this second category of actors have increased powerfully and significantly, particularly since the end of the Second World War. The progress of this category of actors on the world scene has been closely associated with the increasing density of transnational governance. And this has gone in two directions. Those international or transnational arenas and organizations have fostered and stimulated the generation of transnational governance. The explosion of transnational governance has in turn stabilized and reinforced those actors, their power and reach.

A third category brings together what we call here "reinvented old actors." A general trend is for former "rule-takers" and "rule-followers" to increasingly be involved in governance processes. A consequence is that many economic and societal actors have to reinvent themselves as active participants in transnational governance. Universities, corporations, the media or professions are striking exemplars of those actors who reinvent themselves. This reinvention is sometimes so profound as to give rise to new types of actors altogether. The horizon is changing radically and requires adaptation to new meta-rules of governance. From having been rule-takers and rule-followers, who sometimes tried to bypass externally imposed regulation and constraints, those actors have to turn into governance co-constructors in spaces that span multiple levels. This, of course, has profound implications for the features and competences that those actors need to develop.

The fourth category contains what we broadly call "new" actors. By "new" we essentially mean two things. Those actors – organizations, networks or entities – can be "new" in terms of their structures, features and qualities. They can also be "new" in the sense of having stood until then quite far away from regulatory and governance activities. They could, obviously, also be "new" on both counts. Non-governmental organizations, whether national or international, enter into this category. They are becoming increasingly important and powerful actors of transnational governance (Boli and Thomas 1999; Cutler et al. 1999; Mörth 2004). Standards or experts organizations, here again with a national and/or a transnational dimension, have also multiplied (Brunsson and Jacobsson 2000), following upon and reinforcing at the same time the scientization trend identified above.

In Parts II and III of this volume, we also point to another type of "new" actor that we propose to call the "transnational community of interest." The transnational network of central bankers, the International Competition Network, the International Accounting Standards Committee, the AACSB, the efmd or the Forest Stewardship Council are all illustrations, we suggest, of "transnational communities of interest." This type of entity is somewhere in between an epistemic and expert community, a profession and a meta-organization and a combination of all those. It has a transnational nature and dimension by construction and it spans and bridges national boundaries. Just like the banyan tree, it has at the same time an overarching identity and multiple deep and solid local roots. The overarching identity tends to be more cognitive, normative and cultural than physical and structural. In fact some of those transnational communities of interest can be close to virtual networks and organizations.

We propose that this type of actor is increasingly present and involved in processes of transnational governance. It has a tendency to bring its members together around a project, often a regulatory one. This type of entity or actor can bring together only public or state-related members – as in the case of the transnational network of central bankers. It can also bridge the boundaries between public and private spheres and actors – as the cases of the International Competition Network, the International Accounting Standards Committee and the efmd all illustrate. Finally, it can also bring together many different non-state members. Those transnational communities of interest can be more or less open or closed. They tend, though, to be expansive and missionary in the sense that their *raison d'être* is to rally around a project not only their members but also entities potentially well beyond that membership. Interestingly, the expansive and sometimes highly inclusive nature of those "actors" means that they can turn from regulatory actors into regulatory spaces.

Institutional dynamics of transnational governance – the relational dimension

Transnational governance is highly structured by powerful institutional forces while at the very same time it is a richly populated spatial topography. This combination generates a partly paradoxical situation where activities, interplays and interactions are extremely intense in what is ultimately a fairly constrained and rigid landscape.

Paradoxical dynamics . . .

Governance is characterized in our transnational world by intense activity and activism, by dense and multidirectional interplays and interactions. We have seen above some of the main mechanisms behind that level of activity. At the very same time, though, it appears that the more intense and dense activities and interplays become, the more they are working towards the strengthening and stabilization of those structuring institutional forces identified above.

There is, in fact, a paradoxical loop here. Meta-rules of the game, as they progressively stabilize, foster the development of regulatory activities and the intensification of interplays. This happens through the diffusion of marketization, organizing, and deliberative democracy principles that justify and call for multiple and multidirectional involvements and initiatives. The movements thus generated can appear at first relatively chaotic. Steps are taken in many different directions and the rhythm seems to be constantly accelerating. However, the combination in this volume of different "stories" of transnational governance points to an emergent and stabilizing order. The intensity of activities and the density of interplays reinforce, in the end, the meta-rules of the game and the institutional "cage" in which transnational governance appears to be set. This means that a lot of what, at first sight, seems to be regulatory competition should ultimately be re-interpreted as many steps pushing in a parallel direction. In other words, competition in the short term contributes to the emergence of collective stabilization in the longer term.

We therefore propose a reading of transnational arenas of governance as highly constrained and constraining fields – if not monolithic ones – with an intense surface activity that tends to generate and reproduce order behind an appearance of complexity and competition. The longitudinal study of the re-ordering of the accounting standards field provides a great illustration. At a first level, Botzem and Quack (ch. 13) document a multiplicity of initiatives, competing actors and efforts, a lot of movement back and forth, resistance, conflicts, give and take. At the same time, they also point to standardization in the long term – accounting rules and standards progressively become more homogeneous, more similar and compatible across and between national boundaries. This process of standardization both emerges through and reinforces further the dense activity trend. Looking at the evolution of market and competition regulation, Djelic and Kleiner (ch. 14) find more or less the same kind of progressive standardization under the guise of intense activity – partly competitive and even conflictual. McNichol's account of the emergence of certification programs in the forestry sector (ch. 17) and Engels' analysis of the creation of a market for CO^2 emissions rights (ch. 16) can also be read through such a lens.

. . . *Often unrecognized*

A further finding is that this collective stabilizing tends not to be noticed by the actors involved while competitive pressures are being acutely perceived. In fact, we would propose that intense competition at an apparent and superficial level tends to blind both actors themselves and most observers to the profound ordering and stabilization associated with meta-rules of the game. There are many illustrations of that throughout Parts II and III of this volume. Disagreements, conflicts and competition between the representatives of two standardization systems in higher education – EQUIS and AACSB – tend to overemphasize differences and competition when both standardization frames in fact proceed from parallel logics and push the field, overall, in the same direction. If we look at it this way, then differences become only minor variations around a common theme. The same could be said about conflict and competition between standards in many other fields – the cases of accounting rules and competition regulation presented in this volume are two more illustrations.

The literature on "globalization" has a tendency to picture our world as being highly complex and unpredictable, if not on the verge of "chaos." The emphasis on complexity and unpredictability appear in fact both in proselytising accounts and in more critical analyses of "globalization." What we find is different. We propose that complexity, chaos and instability are there but only at a surface level. We document and provide evidence in this volume that our world is much more simple and orderly than it superficially appears. This order and simplicity emerge from and reflect meta-rules of the game, a set of powerfully structuring institutional forces.

The same applies, we propose, to the notion of diversity. At a first level the topography of transnational governance suggests a rich pool of actors concerned with and to a greater or lesser degree involved in governance. Behind multiplicity, however, we also provide evidence of significant progressive convergence. A central bank is much more like another central bank today than it would have been twenty years ago. NGOs increasingly look alike, even when some work for and others against the same project. Hence, multiplicity is not necessarily synonymous with diversity and we argue that our transnationalizing world is characterized by a double and partly contradictory trend. The number of actors involved in and concerned by regulation and governance has increased. However, each "species" or category of actors has had a tendency to become increasingly homogeneous, leaving less and less space for variation inside a given category. Even more homogenization also happens across categories. Actors all tend to be rationalized organizations with a will and an identity of their own (Brunsson and Sahlin-Andersson 2000; Meyer and Jepperson 2000).

The expansive network

Those paradoxical dynamics reveal and express themselves increasingly in what we see as a cornerstone of contemporary governance, namely the "expansive" network. There is a parallel and reinforcing influence between the formalization of a governance issue and the structuration of an associated governance "network." The process goes in fact both ways as most contributions in this volume show. The existence of a governance issue fosters the emergence and development of a governance network. But the structuration of a network can also transform a particular, often limited, project into a transnational governance issue.

We have seen above that the "communities of interest" structured around a particular governance theme hover somewhere in between governance actors and governance spaces. The tendency is for those communities of interest to be expansive networks with a view to diffusing the regulatory project and question at least as much as proposed standards and regulatory solutions. The expansion can take different forms. The network can remain closed but highly active in diffusion dynamics – through direct and mediated contacts, targeting various kinds of relays, investing socialization fora (e.g. training institutions or media outlets). This type of strategy is exemplified in this volume by the transnational network of central bankers.

The network can also choose the "variable geometry" strategy. A core group of members retains the high hand on governance dynamics while regularly opening itself, in the context of particular events, to concerned parties. This strategy is illustrated by the International Competition Network and to some extent also in the case of accounting standards. This type of partial and ad hoc opening is a way to co-opt concerned parties and related opinion makers progressively. An associated strategy can be to foster the emergence and development of parallel and relay networks. This is nicely illustrated in the case of the International Competition Network by the recent emergence of INSOC (the International Network of Civil Society Organizations on Competition) – a civil society network that follows and appropriates the missionary aims and ambitions of the ICN.

Finally, expansion can merely refer to the progressive opening up of the governance network to the point where, ultimately, all actors in a field could be integrated. The fields of higher management education and the processes of standard elaboration in the forestry sector seem to develop in this direction. This is also, one could argue, the apparent logic in the governance field that is structuring itself transnationally around the issue of corporate social responsibility.

The expansive nature of the network can go all the way towards including resistance and opposition groups. In this way, the expansive network combines perfectly with the paradoxical dynamics underscored above. Conflicts, competition and discussions are given significant space while all actors become progressively set and inscribed within the same structuring meta-rules without always realizing it. The increasing multiplicity of actors involved can therefore come together with a progressive and rapid convergence and standardization, and hence in fact with less diversity. Meanwhile, the very structure of networks can evolve and they can develop their own organizing dynamics. While some networks will retain a fluid structure, others can transform over time and develop to become formal organizations.

A representation of institutional dynamics

To get at a real understanding of transnational governance, an undeniable challenge is to grasp how surface dynamics generate background stability and how the progress of background stability fosters surface dynamics, in a self-reinforcing loop. This finding is represented visually in figure 18.1, where we get a three strata cut on transnational governance fields. Those fields have a "dark side" – the set of increasingly powerful institutional forces. Those forces are active and generate dense activity at the surface of the field but with ultimately a stabilizing and reinforcing impact for themselves. The "dark side" is thus labeled because it has a tendency to be invisible, undetected, and taken for granted.

Transnational governance has a highly dynamic "bright side," bright in the sense here of visible, that can be mapped and described. This bright side is made up of dynamic topographies of actors that negotiate, enact, transform, resist, translate or embrace evolving rules of the game. The activity at that surface level is dense but increasingly powerfully set and embedded in, constrained and directed by, homogenizing meta-rules of the game. Institutional forces shape, constrain and embed both dynamic topographies of actors and surface regulation. In their rule-setting and governance activities, dynamic topographies of actors express and enact, spread, stabilize and reproduce but also try to resist and potentially bend the institutional "cage" in which they are more or less comfortably set and inscribed.

The struggle is increasingly unfair, though, we argue. On the bright side of the field, a lot of energy is spent on what are, ultimately,

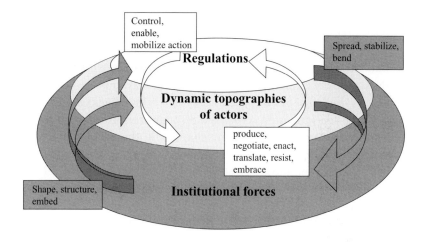

Bright side of the field

Dark side of the field

Figure 18.1 Institutional dynamics of regulations

battles around minor variations. On the whole, the impact of activities that follow the structuring logic of meta-institutional forces can be quite real. Headlong battles against the progressively stabilized meta-institutional forces are getting increasingly difficult, on the other hand, if not doomed from the start.

Power, influence and hegemony in transnational governance

As a last word, it seems important to go back and draw attention to issues of power, interests and influence. Fields of transnational governance tend to wrap themselves in discursive references to efficiency and best practices – legitimized by science and measurement or market mechanisms and validated through rational benchmarks and scales. The discourse and self-presentation of actors involved in transnational governance processes is often neutralized, that is, void of references to issues of power and interests.

All chapters in this volume show that the institutional dynamics of regulation include in fact contestation, struggle, and power plays. The elaboration and development of new kinds of regulations are in great part interest-driven and reflect logics of power and control. Actors use the neutral language of science and expertise; they invoke co-ordination and a common good. When we consider governance processes in more detail, however, and take in the longitudinal dimension in particular, we find that those processes evolve with struggles and conflicts between self-interested actors and through the formation of coalitions and counter-movements. Many chapters in this volume also provide evidence that interests are not stable but that they are shaped and re-shaped over time and across situations. The institutional embeddedness of actors – or the softness of actors – does not mean in other words that interests are absent. Rather, what this suggests is that the shaping of interests and their evolution through time should also be subject to analysis.

Many chapters in this volume illustrate vividly the importance of interest- and power-driven logics including in highly institutionalized settings. It is quite clear from our empirical evidence that the complexity of the transnational world does not always block individual interests and activities, indeed far from it. We often find the opposite – organizations or networks and even individual persons can become extremely powerful and influential as they navigate through the densely organized transnational world and gain significant leverage in the process. A number of features, in this respect, appear to be particularly significant, amongst which size, centrality and resources are all unmistakable. We will only focus, though, as a concluding theme, on another dimension that appears to be key – what we call here the "first mover advantage."

This first mover advantage can be reflected at many levels. Those who set and define the rules early on – or who at least are involved at an early stage – are more likely to be able to influence the emergent regulation to their advantage, to fit and serve their own interests and to increase their position of power and capacity to control. There is another way in which the first mover advantage plays itself out. Those participating in defining the rules of the game are more likely to understand the rules better and to be able to maneuver within and around them. Knowledge means control and power and understanding of the rules of the game gives a headstart to those actors that were involved early on in rule-setting.

At the macro and meta-level this takes on a particular dimension. Brought together, the contributions to this volume clearly show that there is a kind of meta-first mover advantage in favor of the United States and of American actors. The detailed regulatory studies in Parts II and III document a unique and often powerful role and place of American actors and blueprints in regulatory processes, both at the origins and at critical and key moments. The transnational regulatory explosion is, already at this level, an "Americanization." There is another sense, even more significant, in which the contemporary regulatory and governance explosion is a form of "Americanization." The institutional forces, the fundamental rules of the game of the rule-making process in our world, as defined and described in Part I, also reflect undeniably the power and influence of American actors, groups, networks, organizations and cultural and cognitive blueprints. This power and influence is particularly linked historically to the post Second World War period and is associated in part with the threading of an international organizational net – key nodes being the World Bank, the IMF, the OECD, the United Nations and its satellites, the GATT and the WTO.

The important consequence, naturally, is that American actors, organizations and networks often have a headstart in transnational governance fields that are shaped according to institutional principles with which they are in a sense "genetically" familiar. The concept of hegemony (Gramsci 1971) is applicable here or as Foucault would put it "power is everywhere; not because it embraces everything, but because it comes from everywhere" (Foucault 1990[1978]: 93). This book, however, should encourage us to go beyond simple conceptions of power and/or hegemony. We should be looking further into the complex interplay of hegemonic logics and more classical and "visible" resource-based and interest-based power games. There lies, we suggest, an important dimension of the institutional dynamics of contemporary regulation and governance.

References

Abbott, K. and Snidal, D. 2001. "International 'Standards' and International Governance", *Journal of European Public Policy* 8(3): 345–70

Abdelgawad, W. 2001. "Jalons de L' Internationalisation du Droit de la Concurrence", *Revue Internationale de Droit Économique* 15(2): 161–96

Adams, R. 1990. "The Greening of Consumerism", *Accountancy* 105: 80–3

Afonso, A., Schuknecht, L. and Tanzi, V. 2003. "Public Sector Efficiency: An International Comparison", *ECB Working Paper*, No. 242, July

Ahrne, G. 1998. "Stater och andra Organisationer", in Ahrne (ed.) *Stater som Organisationer*. Stockholm: Nerenius & Santérus

Ahrne, G. and Brunsson, N. (eds.) 2004a. *Regelexplosionen*: Stockholm EFI, Stockholm School of Economics

Ahrne, G. and Brunsson, N. 2004b. "Soft Regulation from an Organizational Perspective", in Mörth (ed) *Soft Law in Governance and Regulation*. Cheltenham: Edward Elgar, pp. 171–90

Ahrne, G. and Brunsson, N. 2005. "Organizations and Meta-organizations", *Scandinavian Journal of Management* 21: 429–49

Ahrne, G., Brunsson, N. and Garsten, C. 2000. "Standardizing through Organization", in Brunsson and Jacobsson (eds.) *A World of Standards*. Oxford: Oxford University Press, pp. 50–68

Akbar, Y. 2002. "Grabbing Victory from the Jaws of Defeat – Can the GE/Honeywell Merger Facilitate International Antitrust Policy Co-operation?", *World Competition Law and Economics Review* 25(4): 403–22

Albert, M. and Kopp-Malek, T. 2004. "The Pragmatism of Global and European Governance: Emerging Forms of the Political 'beyond Westphalia'", *Millenium: Journal of International Studies* 31(3): 453–71

Alchian, A. A. and Demsetz, H. 1972. "Production, Information Costs and Economic Organization", *American Economic Review* 62 (December): 777–95

Aldestam, M. 2004. "Soft Law in the State Aid Policy Area", in Mörth (ed.) *Soft Law in Governance and Regulation*. Cheltenham: Edward Elgar, pp. 11–36

Allen, T. J. and Cohen, S. I. 1969. "Information Flow in Research and Development Laboratories", *Administrative Science Quarterly* 14: 12–19

Altbach, P. 1999. "The Logic of Mass Higher Education", in Fagerlind, Holmestand, and Stromqvist (eds.) *Higher Education at the Crossroads.* Stockholm: Institute of International Education, pp. 97–112

Alvesson, M. and Berg, P-O. 1992. *Corporate Culture and Organizational Symbolism.* Berlin: de Gruyter

Amdam, R-P., Kvålshaugen, R. and Larsen, E. (eds.) 2003. *Inside the Business School.* Copenhagen: Copenhagen Business School Press

American Forest and Paper Association. 2000. *2001 Edition: Sustainable Forestry Initiative Standard.* Washington, DC: American Forest and Paper Association

Anderson, B. 1983. *Imagined Communities.* London: Verso

Anderson, T. and Leal, D. 1991. *Free Market Environmentalism.* Boulder, CO: Westview

Anderson, T. and Leal, D. 1997. *Enviro-capitalists.* Lanham MD: Rowman & Littlefield

Anheier, H., Glasius, M. and Kaldor, M. (eds.) 2001. *Global Civil Society 2001.* Yearbook. Oxford: Oxford University Press

Appadurai, A. 1996. *Modernity at Large.* Minneapolis, MN: University of Minnesota Press

Archer, M. 1988. *Culture and Agency.* Cambridge: Cambridge University Press

Aries, P. 1962. *Centuries of Childhood.* New York: Alfred A. Knopf

Aristotle, 1984. *The Nichomachean Ethics.* Oxford: Oxford University Press

Aronowitz, S. 1988. *Science as Power.* Minneapolis: University of Minnesota Press

Ashford, M. 1998. *Con Tricks.* New York: Simon & Schuster

Auboin, R. 1955. *The Bank for International Settlements, 1930–1955.* Princeton University: International Finance Section

Ayres, I. and Braithwaite, J. 1992. *Responsive Regulation.* Oxford: Oxford University Press

Babb, S. 2001. "The Rise of the New Money Doctors in Mexico", paper presented at the Political Economy Research Institute, University of Massachusetts, Amherst, 7–8 December

Baert, P. and Shipman, A. 2005. "University Under Siege? Trust and Accountability in the Contemporary Academy", *European Societies* 7: 157–86

Baldwin, D. (ed.) 1993. *Neorealism and Neoliberalism.* New York: Columbia University Press

Baldwin, R., Scott, C. and Hood, C. (eds.) 1998. *A Reader on Regulation.* Oxford: Oxford University Press

Ballwieser, W. (ed.) 1998. *US-amerikanische Rechnungslegung*. Stuttgart: Schäffer-Poeschel Verlag

Barca, F. and Becht, M. 2001. *The Control of Corporate Europe*. Oxford: Oxford University Press

Bardach, E. 1977. *The Implementation Game*. Cambridge, MA: MIT Press

Barnard, C. 1968. *The Functions of the Executive*. Cambridge, MA: Harvard University Press

Barnes, B. 1985. *About Science*. Oxford: Basil Blackwell

Barnett, A. 1996. "The Creation of Democracy?", in Hirst, P. and Khilnani, S. (eds.), *Reinventing Democracy*. London: Blackwell Publishers, pp. 157–75

Bartlett, C. A. and Ghoshal, S. 1989. *Managing Across Borders*. London: Hutchinson Business Books

Bartley, T. 2003. "Certifying Forests and Factories: States, Social Movements, and the Rise of Private Regulation in the Apparel and Forest Products Fields", *Politics and Society* 31(3): 433–64

Bass, S. 1996. "Principles of Certification of Forest Management Systems and Labelling of Forest Products", paper presented at International Conference on Certification and Labelling of Products from Sustainable Managed Forests, Australia, 26–31 May

Bassiouni, M. C. 2003. *Introduction to International Criminal Law*. Ardsley, NY: Transnational Publishers

Beck, N. and Walgenbach, P. 2002. "The Institutionalization of the Quality Management Approach in Germany", in Sahlin-Andersson and Engwall (eds), *The Expansion of Management Knowledge*. Stanford: Stanford University Press, pp. 145–74.

Beck, U. 1992. *Risk Society*. London: Sage

Becker, G. 1958. "Competition and Democracy", *Journal of Law and Economics*, 1: 105–09

Becker, G. 1971. *The Economics of Discrimination*. Chicago: Chicago University Press

Becker, G. 1991. *A Treatise on the Family*. Cambridge, MA: Harvard University Press

Bellah, R. (ed.) 1993. *Émile Durkheim on Morality and Society*. Chicago: University of Chicago Press

Bellah, R., Madsen, R., Sullivan, W., Swidler, A. and Topton, S. 1985. *Habits of the Heart*. Berkeley: University of California Press

Bello, W. F. and Mittal, A. 2001. *The Future in the Balance*. Oakland, CA: Food First Books

Ben-David, J. 1990. *Scientific Growth*. Berkeley: University of California Press

Ben-David, J. and Zloczower, A. 1962. "Universities and Academic Systems in Modern Societies", *European Journal of Sociology* 3: 45–85.

Berger, P. 1967. *The Sacred Canopy*. Garden City, NY: Doubleday

Berghahn, V. 1986. *The Americanization of West German Industry*. Cambridge: Cambridge University Press

Berman, H. and Kaufman, C. 1978. "The Law of International Commercial Transactions (Lex Mercatoria)", *Harvard International Law Journal* 19(1): 221–77

BIAC/OECD/IEA 1999. *Workshop on Climate Change: Industry view on the Climate Change Challenge with Special Emphasis on the Kyoto Mechanisms*. Paris, 8 March

Birkinshaw, J. and Hood, N. (eds.) 1998. *Multinational Corporate Evolution and Subsidiary Development*. London: Macmillan

Black, J. 2002. "Critical Reflections on Regulation", discussion paper No. 4. London: Centre for Analysis of Risk and Regulation, London School of Economics

Blair, M. M. 1995. *Ownership and Control*. Washington: Brookings Institution

Blau, P. 1963. *The Dynamics of Bureaucracy*. Chicago: University of Chicago Press

Blinder, A., Goodhart, C., Hildebrand, P., Lipton, D. and Wyplosz, C. 2001. "How do Central Banks Talk?", *Geneva Reports on the World Economy*, No. 3. Geneva: International Center for Monetary and Banking Studies

Bloom, A. 1987. *The Closing of the American Mind*. New York: Simon and Schuster

Bohlen, J. 2001. *Making Waves*. Montreal: Black Rose

Boli, J. 1999. "World Authority Structures and Legitimations", in Boli and Thomas (eds.) *Constructing World Culture*. Stanford: Stanford University Press, pp. 267–300

Boli, J. 2005. "Trends in world culture", *International Journal of Comparative Sociology* 46(5/6)

Boli, J. and Thomas, G. M. 1997. "World Culture in the World Polity: A Century of International Non-governmental Organization", *American Sociological Review* 62: 171–90

Boli, J. and Thomas, G. M. (eds.) 1999. *Constructing World Culture*. Stanford: Stanford University Press

Boli, J., Elliott, M. A. and Bieri, F. 2004. "Globalization", in George Ritzer (ed.) *Handbook of Social Problems*. Newbury Park: Sage, pp. 389–415

Bond, M. 2000. "The Backlash against NGOs", *Prospect Magazine*, April. Available at http://www.globalpolicy.org/ngos/backlash.htm

Borgatti, S., Everett, M. and Freeman, L. 1999. *UCINET 6.0 Version 1.00*. Natick: Analytic Technologies

Bornemann, A. 1940. *J. Laurence Laughlin*. Washington: American Council on Public Affairs

Borrás, S. and Jacobsson, K. 2004. "The Open Method of Co-ordination and New Governance Patterns in the EU", *Journal of European Public Policy*, 11(2): 185–208

Boström, M. 2003. "How State-Dependent is a Non-State-Driven Rule-Making Project? The Case of Forest Certification in Sweden", *Journal of Environmental Policy and Planning* 5(2): 165–80

Bourdieu, P. 1977. *Outline of a Theory of Practice*. Cambridge: Cambridge University Press

Bourdieu, P. 1984. *Distinction*. Cambridge, MA: Harvard University Press

Bourdieu, P. 1989. "Social Space and Symbolic Power", *Sociological Theory* 7(1): 14–25

Bowker, G. C. and Star, S. L. 1999. *Sorting Things Out*. Cambridge, MA: MIT Press

Bowles, P. and White, G. 1994. "Central Bank Independence: A Political Economy Approach", *The Journal for Development Studies* 31: 235–64

Bradley, K. and Ramirez, F. O. 1996. "World Polity and Gender Parity: Women's Share of Higher Education, 1965–1985", *Research in Sociology of Education and Socialization* 11: 63–91

Braithwaite, J. and Drahos, P. 2000. *Global Business Regulation*. Cambridge: Cambridge University Press

Brännström, L. 2004. "Reglering i en Metaorganisation – Fallet ILO", in Ahrne and Brunsson (eds.) *Regelexplosionen*. EFI. Stockholm School of Economics, pp. 127–53

Bratton, W. et al. 1996. "Introduction: Regulatory Competition and Institutional Evolution", in Bratton et al. (eds.) *International Regulatory Competition and Coordination*. Oxford: Clarendon Press, pp. 1–58

Braunthal, G. 1965. *The Federation of German Industry in Politics*. Ithaca: Cornell University Press

Bronfenbrenner, M. 1962. "Observations on the Chicago Schools", *Journal of Political Economy* 70 (February): 72–5

Broz, J. L. 1997. *The International Origins of the Federal Reserve System*. Ithaca: Cornell University Press

Brunsson, N. 1999. "Standardization as Organization", in Egeberg and Lægreid (eds.) *Organizing Political Institutions*. Oslo: Scandinavian University Press

Brunsson, N. and Jacobsson, B. (eds.) 2000. *A World of Standards*. Oxford: Oxford University Press

Brunsson, N. and Sahlin-Andersson, K. 2000. "Constructing Organizations: The Example of Public Sector Reform", *Organization Studies* 21(4): 721–46

Budzinski, O. 2004. "The International Competition Network, Prospects and Limits on the Road towards International Competition Governance", *Competition & Change* 8(3): 223–42

Bundgard-Pedersen, T. 1997. "The Europeanization of Standardisation". Doctoral dissertation, Copenhagen University

Business Week, 2000. "The Best B-Schools", 2 October: 75–97

Cairns, D. 1996. "The Role of International Accounting Standards in Improving and Harmonising Financial Reporting", *Corporate Governance* 4(2): 48–59

Callaghan, J. 1987. *Time and Chance*. London: Collins

Calori, R., Atamer, T. and Nunes, P. 2000. *The Dynamics of International Competition*. Thousand Oaks, CA: Sage

Caparoso, J. A. and Stone Sweet, A. 2002. "Conclusion: Institutional Logics of European Integration", in Stone Sweet, Sandholtz and Fligstein (eds.) *The Institutionalization of Europe*. Oxford: Oxford University Press, pp. 221–36

Capie, F., Goodhart, C., Fisher, S. and Schnadt, N. 1994. *The Future of Central Banking*. Cambridge: Cambridge University Press

Carlson, S. 1991/1951. *Executive Behaviour*, Acta Universitatis Upsaliensis, Studia Oeconomiae Negotiorum 32. Stockholm: Almqvist & Wiksell International

Carlsson, B. and Nachemson-Ekwall, S. 2003. *Livsfarlig Ledning*. Stockholm: Ekerlids

Carlsson, R. H. 2001. *Ownership and Value Creation*. Chichester: Wiley

Carpenter, J. N. and Yermach, D. L. (eds.) 1999. *Executive Compensation and Shareholder Value*. Boston, MA: Kluwer Academic

Carruthers, B. and Stinchcombe, A. 1999. "The Social Structure of Liquidity: Flexibility, Markets, and States", *Theory and Society* 28: 353–82

Cashore, B., Auld G. and Newsom, D. 2003. "The United States' Race to Certify Sustainable Forestry: Non-State Environmental Governance and the Competition for Policy-Making Authority", *Business and Politics* 5(3): 219–57

Castells, M. 1996. *The Rise of the Network Society*. Oxford: Blackwell Publishers

Chabbott, C. and Ramirez, F. O. 2000. "Development and Education", in Hallinan (ed.) *Handbook of the Sociology of Education*. New York: Klewer/Plenum, pp. 163–87

Chernow, R. 1998. *Titan*. New York: Random House

Christensen, T. and Lægreid, P. (eds.) 2001. *New Public Management*. Aldershot: Ashgate

Christiansen, A. and Wettestad, J. 2003. "The EU as a Frontrunner on Greenhouse Gas Emissions Trading: How Did it Happen and will the EU Succeed?", *Climate Policy* 3: 3–18

Cini, M. 2001. "The Soft Law Approach: Commission Rule-making in the EU's State Aid Regime", *Journal of European Public Policy* 8(2): 192–207

Clark, A. M. 2001. *Diplomacy of Conscience*. Princeton, NJ: Princeton University Press

Clark, B. 1972. "The Organizational Saga in Higher Education", *Administrative Science Quarterly* 17(2): 178–83

Clark, B. 1993. *Creating Entrepreneurial Universities*. Surrey: Pergamon Press

Clarke, S. 1967. *Central Bank Cooperation 1924–31*. New York: Federal Reserve Bank of New York

Coats, A. W. 1963. "The Origins of the 'Chicago School(s)'?", *Journal of Political Economy* 71 (October): 487–93

Cole, S. 1992. *Making Science*. Cambridge: Harvard University Press

Coleman, J. 1982. *The Asymmetric Society*. Syracuse: Syracuse University Press

Collectif Dalloz 2004. *Le Nouveau Process Pénal après la Loi Perben*. Paris: Dalloz

Collins, R. 1980. "Weber's last Theory of Capitalism: A Systematisation", *American Sociological Review* 45: 925–42

Collins, R. 1982. *Sociological Insight*. New York: Oxford University Press

Commission Européenne 1995. "La Politique de Concurrence dans le Nouvel Ordre Commercial", *Rapport du Groupe des Experts*. Brussels: DG IV

Commission of the European Community 1995. *Accounting Harmonisation*. COM 95 (508) EN

Conroy, M. E. 2001. "Can Advocacy-Led Certification Systems Transform Global Corporate Practices? Evidence and Some Theory", Working Paper Series No. 21. Amherst: University of Massachusetts Political Economy Research Institute

Coop-America. 1999. *National Green Pages: A Directory of Products and Services for People and the Planet*. Washington, DC: Coop America

Corwin, R. 1970. *Militant Professionalism*. New York: Appleton-Century-Crofts

Counsell, S. 2003. *Briefing the World Bank Forest Strategy/Policy And Forest Certification*. London: Rainforest Foundation UK. Available at: http://www.rainforestfoundationuk.org

Crainer, S. and Dearlove, D. 1999. *Gravy Training*. San Francisco: Jossey-Bass

Crouch, C. 1986. "Sharing Public Spaces: States and Organised Interests in Western Europe", in: Hall (ed.) *States in History*. Oxford: Basil Blackwell, pp. 177–210

Crozier, M. 1964. *The Bureaucratic Phenomenon*, Chicago: University of Chicago Press

Cubeddu, R. 1993. *The Philosophy of the Austrian School*. London/New York: Routledge

Cukierman, A., Webb, S. and Neyapti, B. 1992. "Measuring the Independence of Central Banks and Its Effects on Policy Outcome", *The World Bank Economic Review* 6: 353–98

Cunningham, F. 2002. *Theories of Democracy*. London: Routledge

Cupitt, R., Whitlock, R. and Whitlock, L. W. 1996. "The (Im)mortality of International Governmental Organizations", *International Interactions* 21. Reprinted in Diehl, P. 2001. *The Politics of Global Governance*. London: Lynne Rienner Publishers, pp. 44–61

Cutler, A. C. 2002. "Private International Regimes and Interfirm Cooperation", in Hall and Biersteker (eds.) *The Emergence of Private Authority in Global Governance*. Cambridge: Cambridge University Press, pp. 23–42.

Cutler, A. C., Haufler, V. and Porters, T. (eds.) 1999. *Private Authority and International Affairs*. New York: State University of New York Press

Cyert, R. and March, J. 1963. *A Behavioral Theory of the Firm*. Englewood Cliffs, NJ: Prentice Hall

Czarniawska, B. and Joerges, B. 1996. "Travels of Ideas", in Czarniawska and Sevón (eds.) *Translating Organizational Change*. Berlin: de Gruyter, pp. 13–48

Czarniawska, B. and Sevón, G. 1996. (eds.) *Translating Organizational Change*. Berlin: de Gruyter

Dahl, M. 2004. "Organizing Scrutiny. International Organizations Making States 'Auditable'", paper presented at the EIASM Workshop in Lofoten, June 7–8

Dahl, R. 1999. "Kan Internationella Organisation vara Demokratis ka?", in *Bör demokratin avnationaliseras?*. Sweden: *Statens Offentliga Utredningar* 11: 55–78

Dahlkvist, M. and Strandberg, U. 1999. "Kommunal Självstyrelse som Maktspridningsprojekt?", in Amnå (ed.) *Maktdelning*. Sweden: *Statens Offentliga Utredningar* 76.

Daily, G. and Ellison, K. 2002. "How to Make Carbon Charismatic", in Daily and Ellison (eds.) *The new economy of nature*. Washington DC: Island Press, pp. 35–60

Daley, L. and Mueller, G. 1982. "Accounting in the Arena of World Politics. Crosscurrents of International Standard-setting Activities", *Journal of Accountancy* (February): 40–50

Damm, W. 1958. "National and International Factors Influencing Cartel Legislation in Germany", PhD Dissertation. Chicago: University of Chicago

Daniel, C. A. 1998. *MBA: the First Century*. London: Associated University Press

David, P. and Greenstein, S. 1990. "The Economics of Compatibility Standards: An introduction to recent research", *Economics of Innovation and New Technologies* 1: 3–41

Davis, P. E. and Steil, B. 2001. *Institutional Investors*, Cambridge, MA: MIT

Deacon, B. 2005. "From 'Safety Nets' Back to 'Universal Social Provision'", in *Global Social Policy* 5(1): 19–28

Dean, M. and Pringle, R. 1994. *The Central Banks*. New York: Penguin Books

Dearlove, D. and Jampol, J. 1999. "Ranking the Rankings", in *The Directory of MBAs* (3rd edn) Herts, UK: Edition XII Limited and EFMD, pp. 38–44

De la Porte, C. and Nanz, P. (2004) "The OMC – a Deliberative Democratic Mode of Governance? The Cases of Employment and Pensions", *Journal of European Public Policy* 11(2): 267–88

DeloitteToucheTohmatsu 2003. *IAS Plus*. Available from http://www.iasplus.com/restruct/chrono.htm (Accessed 4 July 2003.)

DETR 2000. *A Greenhouse Gas Emissions Trading Scheme for the United Kingdom*. Available from http://www.detr.govuk/environment/consult/ggetrade/index.htm

Devuyst, Y. 2001. "Transatlantic Competition Relations", in Pollack and Shaffer (eds.) *Transatlantic Governance in the Global Economy*. Lanham, MA: Rowman and Littlefield Publishers, pp. 127–52

Dezalay, Y. 1993. "Professional Competition and the Social Construction of Transnational Regulatory Expertise", in McCahery, Picciotto and Scott (eds.) *Corporate Control and Accountability*, Oxford: Clarendon Press, pp. 203–15

Dezalay, Y. and Garth, B. 1996. *Dealing in Virtue*. Chicago: The University of Chicago Press

Dezalay, Y. and Garth, B. 2002a. *The Internationalization of Palace Wars*. Chicago: University of Chicago Press

Dezalay, Y. and Garth, B. (eds.) 2002b. *Global Prescriptions*. Ann Arbor: University of Michigan Press

Dezalay, Y. and Sugarman, D. 1995. *Professional Competition and Professional Power*. London, New York: Routledge

DiMaggio, P. 1983. "State Expansion and Organizational Fields", in Hall and Quinn (eds.) *Organizational Theory and Public Policy*. Beverly Hills, CA: Sage, pp. 142–72

DiMaggio, P. 1987. "Classification in Art", *American Sociological Review,* 52(4): 440–55

DiMaggio, P. and Powell, W.W. 1983. "The Iron Cage Revisited: Institutional Isomorphism and Collective Rationality in Organizational Fields", *American Sociological Review* 48: 147–60

D'Iribarne, P. 1989. *La Logique de l'Honneur.* Paris: Editions du Seuil.

Djelic, M-L. 1998. *Exporting the American Model.* Oxford: Oxford University Press

Djelic, M-L. 2002. "Does Europe Mean Americanization? The Case of Competition", *Competition and Change* 6(3): 233–50

Djelic, M-L. 2004. "Social Networks and Country-to-Country Transfer: Dense and Weak Ties in the Diffusion of Knowledge", *Socio-Economic Review,* 2(3): 341–70.

Djelic, M-L. and Quack, S. (eds.) 2003. *Globalization and Institutions.* Cheltenham, UK: Edward Elgar

Djelic, M-L. and Quack, S. 2005 "Rethinking Path Dependency: The Crooked Path of Institutional Change in Post-War Germany", in Morgan, Whitley and Moen (eds.) *Changing Capitalisms?* Oxford: Oxford University Press, pp. 137–66

Dobbin, F. 1994. *Forging Industrial Policy.* Cambridge: Cambridge University Press

Dore, R. 1976. *The Diploma Disease.* Berkeley: University of California Press

Doremus, P. N., Keller, W., Pauley, L. and Reich, S. 1998. *The Myth of the Global Corporation.* Princeton, NJ: Princeton University Press

Dostaler, G. and Ethier, D. 1989. *Friedrich Hayek.* Paris: Economica

Douglas, M. 1966. *Purity and Danger.* London: Routledge & Kegan Paul

Douglas, M. 1986. *How Institutions Think.* Syracuse University Press.

Drake, P. W. 1989. *The Money Doctor in the Andes.* Durham: Duke University Press

Drauz, G. 2002. "Unbundling GE/Honeywell: The Assessment of Conglomerate Mergers under EC Competition Law", *Fordham International Law Journal* 25(4): 885–908

Drori, G., Meyer, J., Ramirez, F. and Schofer, E. 2003. *Science in the Modern World Polity.* Stanford: Stanford University Press

Drori, G. and Moon, H. 2006. "The Changing Nature of Tertiary Education: Neo-Institutional Perspective onto Cross-National Trends in Disciplinary Enrollment, 1965–1995" in Baker and Wiseman (eds.), *The Impact of Comparative Education Research on Institutional Theory.* Elsevier Science

Dryzek, J. S. 1999. "Transnational Democracy", *The Journal of Political Philosophy* 7(1): 30–51

Dryzek, J. S. 2000. *Deliberative Democracy and Beyond.* Oxford: Oxford University Press

Dumont, L. 1986. *Essays on Individualism.* Chicago: University of Chicago Press

Dunn, S. 2002. "Down to Business on Climate Change. An Overview of Corporate Strategies", *Greener Management International* 39: 27–41

Dunning, J. (ed.) 2000. *Regions, Globalization and the Knowledge-Based Economy.* Oxford: Oxford University Press

Durkheim, E. 1961. *The Elementary Forms of Religious Life.* New York: Collier-Macmillan

Dussauze, E. 1938. *L'Etat et les Ententes Industrielles.* Paris: Librairie Technique et Economique

Dyson, K., Featherstone, K. and Michalopoulos, G. 1995. "Strapped to the Mast: EC Central Bankers Between Global Financial Markets and Regional Integration", *Journal of European Public Policy* 2: 465–87

Eaton, J. S. 2000. "Accreditation", in Forrest and Kinser (eds.), *Higher Education in United States.* Santa Barbara, CA: ABC-CLIO

Economist. 1999. "Sweatshop Wars", 27 February

Economist. 2003. "Central Bank Transparency – As Clear as Mud", 7 August

Edenhammar, H., Jakobson, T., Wachtmeister C. J. and associates, 2001. *Investor Relations i Praktiken.* Stockholm: Ekerlid

Efmd 1985. *Report on 1984–85. Programme of Activities 1985–86. Objectives, activities and services*

Efmd 1991. *Annual Report 1991*

Efmd 1997. "Green Light for the European Quality Improvement System" (press release)

Efmd 1998a. "Improving the Quality of Management Education", *Forum* 3: 4–7

Efmd 1998b. "EQUAL European Guidelines", *efmd Bulletin* 11: 11

Efmd 2000. "Strategic Points for efmd's Future", *efmd Bulletin* 3: 1

Eichengreen, B. 1992. *Golden Fetters.* New York: Oxford University Press

Eifinger, S., de Haan, J. and Koedijk, K. 2002. "Small is Beautiful: Measuring the Research Input and Output of European Central Banks", *European Journal of Political Economy* 18: 365–74

Eising, R. 2002. "Policy Learning in Embedded Negotiations: Explaining EU Electricity Liberalization", *International Organization* 56: 85–120

Eising, R. and Kohler-Koch, B. 1999. "Governance in the European Union. A Comparative Assessment", in Kohler-Koch and Eising (eds.) *The Transformation of Governance in the European Union.* London: Routledge, pp. 267–85

Ekelund, R., Hebert, R., Tollison, R., Anderson, G. and Davidson, A. 1996. *Sacred Trust*. New York: Oxford University Press

Ellerman, A. D., Joskow, P., Schmalensee, R., Montero, J. and Bailey, E. 2000. *Markets for Clean Air*. Cambridge: Cambridge University Press

Eliot, T. S. 1968 (1949) "Notes Toward the Definition of Culture", in *Christianity and Culture*. New York: Harcourt Brace Jovanovich

Ellul, J. 1973. *Les Nouveaux Possédés*. Paris: Fayard

Ellul, J. 1977. *Le Système Technician*. Paris: Calmann-Levy

Ellul, J. 1978. *The betrayal of the West*. New York: Seabury

Elsbach, K. and Kramer, R. 1996. "Member Responses to Organizational Identity Threats Encountering and Countering the Business Week Rankings", *Administrative Science Quarterly* 41(3): 442–76

Emery, F. and Trist, E. 1965. "The Causal Texture of Organizational Environments", *Human Relations* 18(1): 21–32

ENA Association 2002. "Dossier Spécial – La Concurrence", *ENA hors les murs*, 318 (February)

Engels, A. 2003. "Welthandel mit CO_2-Emissionszertifikaten? Globalisierung von Risikomanagement im internationalen Vergleich", in Kegler and Kerner (eds.) *Technik Welt Kultur*. Cologne: Böhlau Verlag, pp. 255–70

Engwall, L. 1978. *Newspapers as Organizations*, Farnborough: Saxon House

Engwall, L. 1992. *Mercury Meets Minerva*. Oxford: Pergamon Press

Engwall, L. 1994. "Bridge, Poker and Banking", in Fair and Raymond (eds.), *The Competitiveness of Financial Institutions and Centres in Europe*. Amsterdam: Kluwer, pp. 227–39

Engwall, L. 1997. "The Swedish Banking Crisis: The Invisible Hand Shaking the Visible Hand", in Morgan and Knights (eds.), *Regulation and Deregulation in European Financial Services*. London: Macmillan, pp. 178–200

Engwall, L. and Zamagni, V. (eds.) 1998. *Management Education in Historical Perspective*. Manchester: Manchester University Press

Engwall, L., Alvarez, J. L., Amdam, R. P. and Kipping, M. 2004. *The Creation of European Management Practice*. Final Report, Brussels: European Commission

Eriksen, E. O. and Fossum, J. E. (eds.) 2000. *Democracy in the European Union*. London: Routledge

Eriksen, E. O. and Fossum, J. E. 2002. "Europe in Search of its Legitimacy", paper presented to the NOPSA Triennal Conference, Aalborg, 15–17 August

Etzioni, A. 1961. *A Comparative Analysis of Complex Organizations*. New York: Free Press

European Commission 2000. *Green Paper on Greenhouse Gas Emissions within the European Union.* Brussels

Evans, L. and Nobes, C. 1996. "Some Mysteries Relating to the Prudence Principle in the Fourth Directive and in German and British Law", *The European Accounting Review* 5(2): 361–73

Evans, P. 2000. "Fighting Marginalization with Transnational Networks: Counter-Hegemonic Globalization", *Contemporary Sociology*, 20(1): 230–41

Evenett, S. J., Lehmann, A. and Steil, B. (eds.) 2000. *Antitrust Goes Global.* Washington DC: Brookings Institution Press

Falk, R. 1999. *Predatory globalization.* Malden, MA: Polity Press

Fama, E. 1980. "Agency Problems and the Theory of the Firm", *Journal of Political Economy*, 88 (April): 288–307

Federal Reserve Bank of Boston 1984. *The International Monetary System.* Conference Series No. 28, Boston, May

Federal Reserve Bank of Boston 1999. *Rethinking the International Monetary System.* Conference Series No. 43, Boston, June

FEE 1992. *Analysis of European Accounting and Disclosure Practices.* London: Routledge

Feemster, R. 2000. "Emissions Trading: Is the Netherlands Jumping the Gun?", in *Earth Times News Service.* Available at http://www.earthtimes. org/nov/climatechangeemissionsnov15_00.htm

Financial Times. 1999. "Ranking Can Both Help and Rankle", 25 January

Financial Times. 2000. "A High Degree of Diversity at the Top Schools": I–IV, 24 January

Financial Times. 2000. "Sea Change in the Market is Gathering Pace": I–IV, 23 May

Financial Times. 2000. "Consensus the Ideal", 8 September

Financial Times. 2001. "Concerns are Raised by Global Thrust", 22 October

Finnemore, M. 1993. "International Organization as Teachers of Norms: The United Nations Educational, Scientific, and Cultural Organization and Science Policy", *International Organization* 47: 567–97

Finnemore, M. 1996a. *National Interests in International Society.* Ithaca, NY: Cornell University Press

Finnemore, M. 1996b. "Norms, Culture, and World Politics: Insights From Sociology's Institutionalism", *International Organization* 50: 325–47

Finnemore, M. and Sikkink, K. 1998. "International Norm Dynamics and Political Change", *International Organization* 52(4): 887–917

Flexner, A. 1930. *Universities: American, English, German.* New York: Oxford University Press

Fligstein, N. 1990. *The Transformation of Corporate Control.* Cambridge: Harvard University Press

Fligstein, N. 1996. "Markets as Politics: A Political-cultural Approach to Market Institutions", *American Sociological Review* 61: 656–73

Fligstein, N. 1997. "Fields, Power, and Social Skill: A Critical Analysis of the New Institutionalisms", unpublished manuscript: University of California at Berkeley

Fligstein, N. 2001. *The Architecture of Markets*. Princeton, NJ: Princeton University Press

Flower, J. 1997. "The Future Shape of Harmonization: The EU Versus the IASC Versus the SEC", *The European Accounting Review* 6(2): 281–303

Foer, A. A. 2003. "On launching an International Network of Public Interest Organizations for Competition Policy. The American Antitrust Institute Column, March 3, 2003". Available at www.antitrustinstitute.org/recent2/237.cfm

Forbes, L. and Jermier, J. 2002. "The Institutionalization of Bird Protection: Mabel Osgood Wright and the Early Audobon Movement", *Organization & Environment* 15: 458–74

Forest Stewardship Council – FSC. 1995a. FSC Process Guidelines for Developing Regional Certification Standards. Oaxaca: Forest Stewardship Council

Forest Stewardship Council – FSC. 1995b. *FSC Protocol for Endorsing National Initiatives*. Oaxaca: Forest Stewardship Council

Forest Stewardship Council – FSC. 1996. *Forest Stewardship Council Principles and Criteria for Natural Forest Management*. Oaxaca: Forest Stewardship Council

Forest Stewardship Council. 2002. *Coverage Data*. Available at http://www.fsc-oax.org

Forest Stewardship Council. 2005a. *List of Members* (1 December 2005). Available at: http://www.fsc.org/keepout/en/content_areas/77/82/files/List_of_FSC_members_200_5_12_01.pdf

Forest Stewardship Council. 2005b. *About FSC*. Available at: http://www.fsc.org/en/about/what_is

Forsgren, M. and Björkman, I. (eds.) 1997. *The Nature of the International Firm*. Copenhagen: Handelshojskolens forlag

Foucault, M. 1980. *Power/Knowledge*. New York: Pantheon Books

Foucault, M. 1990/1978. *The History of Sexuality: An Introduction*, Vol. I. (R. Hurley trans.). New York: Vintage Books

Fourcade-Gourinchas, M. 2001. "Politics, Institutional Structures and the Rise of Economics: A Comparative Study", *Theory and Society*, 30(3): 397–447

Fourcade-Gourinchas, M. and Babb, S. 2002. "The Rebirth of the Liberal Creed: Path to Neoliberalism in Four Countries", *American Journal of Sociology* 108(3): 533–79

Foxley, A. 1983. *Latin American Experiments in Neoconservative Economics*. Berkeley and Los Angeles: University of California Press

Frame, J. D., Narin, F. and Carpenter, M. 1977. "The Distribution of World Science", *Social Studies of Science* 7: 501–16

Frank, D. and Gabler, J. 2001. "The Composition of Knowledge: Change in Faculty Makeup Over Time", unpublished manuscript: Department of Sociology, Harvard University

Frank, D. and Gabler, J. 2006. *Reconstructing the University: Worldwide Changes in Academic Emphases over the 20th Century*. Stanford CA: Stanford University Press

Frank, D., Hironaka, A. and Schofer, E. 2000. "The Nation-State and the Natural Environment Over the Twentieth Century", *American Sociological Review*, 65: 96–116

Frank, D. and McEneaney, E. 1999. "The Individualization of Society and the Liberalization of State Policies on Same-Sex Sexual Relations, 1984–1995", *Social Forces* 77 (March): 911–44

Frank, D., Meyer, J. and Miyahara, D. 1995. "The Individualist Polity and the Prevalence of Professionalized Psychology: A Cross-national Study", *American Sociological Review* 60: 360–77

Freedom House 2000. "Democracy's Century. A Survey of Global Political Change in the 20th Century", Washington DC: Freedom House. Available at www.freedomhouse.org/research/demcent.htm

Freeman, R. B. 1976. *The Over-Educated American*. New York: Academic Press

Friedman, M. 1962. *Capitalism and Freedom*. Chicago: Chicago University Press

Friedman, M. 1968. "The Role of Monetary Policy", *American Economic Review*, 58(1): 1–17

Friedman, M and Friedman, R. 1979. *Free to Choose*. New York: Avon Books

Friedman, T. 2000. *The Lexus and the Olive Tree*. New York: Anchor Books

Friends of the Earth 1996. *The Good Wood Guide*. London: Friends of the Earth

Friends of the Earth. 2005. *The Good Wood Guide*. Available at: http://www.foe.co.uk/campaigns/biodiversity/resource/good_wood_guide/

From, J. 2002. "Decision-Making in a Complex Environment: A Sociological Institutionalist Analysis of Competition Policy Decision-Making in the European Commission", *Journal of European Public Policy* 9(2): 219–37

Frykman, H. and Mörth, U. 2004. "Soft Law and Three Notions of Democracy: The Case of the EU", in Mörth (ed.) *Soft Law in Governance and Regulation*. Chellenham: Edward Elgar, pp. 155–70

Gale Research 2000. *Awards, Honors and Prizes* (17th edn.) Two volumes, Valerie J Webster(ed.). Detroit: Gale Research

Gallarotti, G. 1995. *The Anatomy of An International Monetary Regime.* New York: Oxford University Press

Garforth, M. 2001. Personal communication on 17 January in Edinburgh, Scotland

Garton Ash, T. 2004. *Free World.* London: Allen Lane Penguin

Geertz, C. 1980. *Negara.* Princeton: Princeton University Press

Gerber, D.J. 1998. *Law and Competition in Twentieth Century Europe.* Oxford: Oxford University Press

Gibney, M. E. 2003. *Globalizing Rights,* Oxford: Oxford University Press

Gilardi, F. 2005. "The Institutional Foundations of Regulatory Capitalism: The Diffusion of Independent Regulatory Agencies in Western Europe", in Levi-Faur and Jordana (eds.), *The Rise of Regulatory Capitalism.* The Annals of APSA, Vol. 598. London: Sage, pp. 84–101

Gill, S. 2003. *Power and Resistance in the New World Order.* New York: Palgrave/Macmillan

Gill, S. and Law, D. 1993. "Global Hegemony and the Structural Power of Capital", in Gill, S. (ed.) *Gramsci, Historical Materialism and International Relations.* Cambridge: Cambridge University Press, pp. 93–124

Ginzel, L. E. Kramer, R. M. and Sutton, R. I. 1993. "Organizational Impression Management as a Reciprocal Influence Process: The Neglected Role of the Organizational Audience", *Research in Organizational Behavior,* 25: 227–66

Glaum, M. 2000. "Bridging the GAAP: the Changing Attitude of German Managers towards Anglo-American Accounting and Accounting Harmonization", *Journal of International Financial Management and Accounting* 11(1): 23–47

Goffman, E. 1956. "The Nature of Deference and Demeanor", *American Anthropologist* 58 (June): 473–502

Goffman, E. 1959. *The Presentation of Self in Everyday Life.* New York: Doubleday Anchor Books

Goodin, R. E. 2003. *Reflective Democracy.* Cambridge: Cambridge University Press

Gouldner, A. 1964. *Patterns of Industrial Bureaucracy.* New York: Free Press

Grafström, M. 2002. "Power of the Pink Press. Business News in Sweden, 1976–2000", Master's thesis, Department of Business Studies, Uppsala University

Graham, A. E. and Morse, R. J. 1999. "How We Rank Graduate Schools", www.usnews.com/usnews/edu/beyond/gradrank/gbrank.htm

Gramsci, A. 1971. *Selections from the Prison Notebook* (Q. Hoare and G. Smith, eds. and trans.). London: Lawrence and Wishart

Green, E. 2003. "What Tasks Should Central Banks Be Asked to Perform?", paper presented at Sveriges Riksbank's conference on "Central Bank Efficiency", Stockholm, 23–24 May

Green Cowles, M. 1995. "Setting the Agenda for a New Europe: The ERT and EC 1992", *Journal of Common Market Studies*, 33 (December): 501–26

Green Cowles, M. 2001. "The TABD and Domestic Business–Government Relations", in Green Cowles, Caporaso and Risse (eds.) *Transforming Europe*. Ithaca, CT: Cornell University Press

Greenwood, J. 1997. *Representing Interests in the European Union*. London: Macmillan

Greenwood, J. and Aspinwall, M. (eds.), 1998. *Collective Action in the European Union*. London: Routledge

Greenwood, R., Suddaby, R. and Hinings, C. R. 2002. "The Orizing Change: The Role of Professional Associations in the Transformation of Institutionalized Fields", Academy of Management Journal 45(1): 58–80

Greider, W. 1987. *Secrets of the Temple*. New York: Simon & Schuster

Guillén, M. 2001. "Is Globalization Civilizing, Destructive or Feeble? A Critique of Five Key Debates in the Social Science Literature", *Annual Review of Sociology* 27: 235–60

Guillén, M., Collins, R., England, P. and Meyer, M. (eds.) 2002. *The New Economic Sociology*. New York: Russell Sage Foundation Publications

Guler, I., Guillén, M. and Macpherson, J. 2002. "Global Competition, Institutions and the Diffusion of Organizational Practices: The International Spread of ISO 9000 Quality Certificates", *Administrative Science Quarterly* 47: 207–32

Gummer, J. and Moreland, R. 2000. *The European Union and Global Climate Change*. Prepared for the Pew Center on Global Climate Change, Arlington VA

Gumport, P. 2000. "Academic Restructuring Organizational Change and Institutional Imperatives", *Higher Education* 39: 67–91

Haas, E. B. 1990. *When Knowledge is Power*. Berkeley: University of California Press

Haas, P. 1989. "Do Regimes Matter? Epistemic Communities and Mediterranean Pollution Control", *International Organization* 43(3): 377–403

Haas, P. 1992. "Introduction: Epistemic Communities and International Policy Coordination", *International Organization* 46(1): 1–35

Habermas, J. 1993. *Justification and Application*. Cambridge: MIT Press

Hadenius, S. and Söderhjelm, T. 1994. *Bankerna i pressen 1984–1990*. Stockholm: Fritzes

Håkansson, H. and Johanson, J. 1998. "The Network as a Governance Structure: Interfirm Cooperation Beyond Markets and Hierarchies", in Brunsson and Olsen (eds.) *Organizing Organizations*. Bergen: Fagbokforlaget, pp. 47–63

Haley, J. 2001. *Antitrust in Germany and Japan*. Seattle: University of Washington Press

Hall, P. and Soskice, D. 2001. *Varieties of Capitalism*. Oxford: Oxford University Press

Hall, R. D. and Biersteker, T. J. (eds.) 2002. *The Emergence of Private Authority in Global Governance*. Cambridge: Cambridge University Press

Haller, A. 1992. "The Relationship of Financial and Tax Accounting in Germany: A Major Reason for Accounting Disharmony in Europe", *The International Journal of Accounting* 27: 310–23

Haller, A. 2002. "Financial Accounting Developments in the European Union: Past Events and Future Prospects", *The European Accounting Review* 11(1): 153–90

Haller, A., Raffournier, B. and Walton, P. (eds.) 2000. *Unternehmenspublizität im internationalen Wettbewerb*. Stuttgart: Schäffer-Poeschel Verlag

Hancher, L. and Moran, M. (eds.) 1989. *Capitalism, Culture, and Economic Regulation*. Oxford: Clarendon Press

Hannerz, U. 1996. *Transnational Connections*. London: Routledge

Hansen, E., Forsyth, K. and Juslin, H. 2000. Forest Certification Update for the ECE Region, Summer 2000. New York and Geneva: United Nations

Haraway, D. 1996. *Modest-witness@Second-Millenium: FemaleMan-Meets-OncoMouse: Feminism and technoscience*. New York: Routledge

Heckscher, E. 1962. *Mercantilism* (2nd edn). London and New York: George Allen and Unwin/Macmillan

Hedmo, T. 2004. "Rule-making in the Transnational Space: The Development of European Accreditation of Management Education", unpublished doctoral thesis No. 109. Dept. of Business Studies, Uppsala University

Heintz, B., Müller, D. and Roggenthin, H. 2001. "Gleichberechtigung zwischen globalen Normen und lokalen Kontexten. Deutschland, Schweiz, Marokko und Syrien im Vergleich", *Kölner Zeitschrift für Soziologie und Sozialpsychologie* 53: 398–430

Held, D. 1995. *Democracy and the Global Order*. Cambridge: Cambridge: Polity Press

Held, D., McGrew, A., Goldblatt, D. and Perraton, J. 1999. *Global Transformations*. Stanford: Stanford University Press

Hellman, N. 2000. *Investor Behaviour*. Stockholm: Economic Research Institute

Henisz, W., Zelner, B. and Guillén, M. 2004. "International Coercion, Emulation and Policy Diffusion: Market-Oriented Infrastructure Reforms, 1977–1999", University of Michigan: William Davidson Institute Working Paper 713

Henning, R. 2000. "Selling standards", in Brunsson and Jacobsson (eds.) *A World of Standards*. Oxford: Oxford University Press, pp. 114–24

Higgott, R., Underhill, G. R. D. and Bieler, A. 2000. *Non-State Actors and Authority in the Global System*. London: Routledge

Hinings, C. R. and Greenwood, R. 2002. "Disconnects and Consequences in Organization Theory?", *Administrative Science Quarterly* 47(3): 411–28

Hirst, P. 1994. *Associative Democracy*. London: Polity Press

Hirst, P. 1997. *From Statism to Pluralism*. London: UCL Press

Hirst, P. Q. and Thompson, G. 2000. *Globalization in Question* (2nd edn.). Cambridge: Polity Press

Hobley, A. and Hawkes, P. 2003. "The EU Emission Allowance Trading Scheme: A Prototype for Global GHG Emissions Allowance Trading?", *Environmental Finance*, May: 17–20

Hodgson, G. 2001. *How Economics Forgot History*. London: Routledge

Hoffman, A. and Ventresca, M. 2002. "Introduction", in Hoffman and Ventresca (eds.) *Organizations, policy, and the natural environment*. Stanford: Stanford University Press, pp. 1–38

Hoffman, P. 1951. *Peace can be Won*. New York: Doubleday

Hofstede, G. 1980. *Culture's Consequences*. Beverly Hills: Sage

Hogwood, B. W. and Gunn, L. A. 1984. *Policy Analysis for the Real World*. Oxford: Oxford University Press

Home Depot, Inc. 2005. *Certification*. Available at: http://www.homedepot.com/HDUS/EN_US/corporate/corp_respon/certification.shtml

Hood, C. 1991. "A Public Management for All Seasons?", *Public Administration*, 69: 3–19

Hood, C. 1995. "The New Public Management in the 1980s: Variations on a Theme", *Accounting, Organization and Society*, 20(2–3): 93–109

Hood, C., Scott, C., James, O., Jones, G. and Travers, T. 1999. *Regulation Inside Government*. Oxford: Oxford University Press

Hopwood, A. 1994. "Some Reflections on the Harmonization of Accounting in the EU", *European Accounting Review* 3(2): 241–53

Hu, Y. S. 1992. "Global or Stateless Firms are National Corporations with International Operations", *California Management Review* 34: 107–26

Hwang, H. 2003. "Planning Development", unpublished PhD dissertation, Stanford University

ICPAC 2000. *ICPAC Final Report*. Available at www.usdoj.gov/atr/icpac/finalreport.htm

Iggers, G. 1968. *The German Conception of History*. Middletown: Wesleyan University Press

IISD (International Institute for Sustainable Development) 1997. "Report of the Third Conference of the Parties to the United Nations Framework Convention on Climate Change: 1–11 December 1997", *Earth Negotiations Bulletin* 12: 76. Available at http://www.iisd.ca/download/pdf/enb1276e.pdf

Ikenberry, J. 1990. "The International Spread of Privatization Policies: Inducements, Learning and Policy Bandwagoning", in Suleiman and Waterbury (eds), *The Political Economy of Public Sector Reform and Privatization*. London: Westview Press, pp. 88–110

IMF 2001. *IMF Survey*, Vol xxx, No. 7, April

Inhaber, H. 1977. "Scientists and Economic Growth", *Social Studies of Science* 7: 517–24

Inkeles, A., and Smith, D. 1974. *Becoming Modern*. Cambridge: Harvard University Press

J. P. Morgan 2001. *Who's Who in Central Banking 2002*. London: Central Banking Publications Ltd

Jacobsson, B. 1987. *Kraftsamlingen. Politik och Företagande i Parallella Processer*. Lund: Doxa/Studentlitteratur

Jacobsson, B. 2000. "Standardization and Expert Knowledge", in Brunsson and Jacobsson (eds.) *A World of Standards*. Oxford: Oxford University Press, pp. 40–49

Jacobsson, B., Lægrid, P. and Pedersen, O. K. 2003. *Europeanization and Transnational States. Comparing Four Nordic States*. London: Routledge

Jacobsson, B., Lægreid, P. and Pedersen, O. K. 2004. "The Transnationalisation of Nordic Central Administrations" in *Zeitschrift für Staats- und Europawissenschaften*, Heft1. Berlin: De Gruyter Recht

Jacobsson, K. 2001. Innovations in EU Governance: The Case of Employment Policy Co-ordination, Stockholm University, Score working paper series 2001–12

Jacobsson, K. 2004. "Between Deliberation and Discipline: Soft Governance in EU Employment Policy", in Mörth (ed.) *Soft Law in Governance and Regulation*. Cheltenham: Edward Elgar, pp. 81–102

Jacobsson, K., Mörth, U. and Sahlin-Andersson, K. 2002. "Den frivilliga regleringens attraktionskraft", in Boström, Forssell, Jacobsson and Tamm-Hallström (eds.), *Den organiserade frivilligheten*. Lund: Liber, pp. 163–89

Jácome, H. and Luis, I. 2001. "Legal Central Bank Independence and Inflation in Latin America During the 1990s", IMF Working Paper WP/01/212. Washington: IMF

Jalabert-Doury, N. 2003. "The International Competition Network, Convergence in Merger Control?" *International Business Law Journal* 6: 697–710

James, C. 2001. "Reconciling Divergent Enforcement Policies: Where do We Go from Here?", address by the Assistant Attorney General, Antitrust Division US Department of Justice, 28th Annual Conference on International Law and Policy, Fordham Corporate Law Institute. New York, 25 October. Available at http://www.usdoj.gov/atr/public/speeches/9395.htm

Jang, Y. S. 2000a. "The Worldwide Founding of Ministries of Science and Technology, 1950–1990", *Sociological Perspectives* 43: 247–70

Jang, Y. S. 2000b. "The Expansion of Modern Accounting as a Global and Institutional Practice", unpublished PhD dissertation, Stanford University

Jasanoff, S. 1990. *The Fifth Branch*. Cambridge: Harvard University Press

Jenkins, M. and Smith, E. (eds.) 1999. *The Business of Sustainable Forestry*. Washington DC: Island Press

Jensen, M. C. and Meckling, W. H. 1976. "Theory of the Firm: Managerial Behavior, Agency Costs and Ownership Structure", *Journal of Financial Economics* 3 (October): 305–60

Jepperson, R. 1991. "Institutions, Institutional Effects, and Institutionalism", in Powell and DiMaggio (eds.), *The New Institutionalism in Organizational Analysis*. Chicago: University of Chicago Press

Jepperson, R. 2002. "Political Modernities: Disentangling the Two Underlying Dimensions of Institutional Differentiation", *Sociological Theory* 20(1): 61–85

Johnson, D. and Turner, C. 2000. *European Business*. London: Routledge

Johnson, J. 2002. "Financial Globalization and National Sovereignty: Neoliberal Transformation in Post-Communist Central Banks", paper prepared for delivery at the annual meeting of the American Political Science Association, 29 August–1 September

Johnston, A. I. 2001. "Treating International Institutions as Social Environments", *International Studies Quarterly* 45: 487–515

Jönsson, C. 1990. "Den Transnationella Maktens Metaforer: Biljard, Schack, Teater Eller Spindelnät?", in Hansson and Stenelo (eds.) *Makt och Internationalisering*. Stockholm: Carlssons

Jordan, G. 2001. *Shell, Greenpeace and the Brent Spar*. Basingstoke: Palgrave

Jordana, J. and Levi-Faur, D. (eds.) 2004. *The Politics of Regulation*. Cheltenham, UK: Edward Elgar, pp. 145–74

Jutterström, M. 2004. "Att påverka beslut", doctoral dissertation, Stockholm: EFI

Kagan, R. 2000. "How Much Do National Styles of Law Matter?", in Kagan and Axelrad (eds.) *Regulatory Encounters*. Berkeley, Los Angeles: University of California Press, pp. 1–32

Katzenstein, P., Keohane, R. and Krasner, S. 1998. "International Organization at Fifty: Exploration. and Contestation in the Study of World Politics", *International Organization*, 52: 4

Keane, J. 2003. *Global Civil Society*. Cambridge: Cambridge University Press

Keasey, K., Thompson, S. and Wright, M. 1997. "Introduction: The Corporate Governance Problem – Competing Diagnoses and Solutions", in: Keasey, Thompson and Wright (eds.) *Corporate Governance*. Oxford: Oxford University Press, pp. 1–17

Keck, M. and Sikkink, K. 1998. *Activists Beyond Borders*. Cornell, NY: Cornell University Press

Keegan, W. 1984. *Mrs Thatcher's Economic Experiment*. London: Penguin

Keister, L. 2002. "Financial Markets, Money, and Banking", *Annual Review of Sociology* 28: 39–61

Keohane, R. 1982. "The Demand for International Regimes", *International Organization* 36(2): 325–55

Keraghel, C. and Sen, J. 2004. "Explorations in Open Space. The World Social Forum and Cultures of Politics", *International Social Science Journal* 56(182): 483–93

Khagram, S. and Levitt, P. 2004. "Towards a Sociology of Transnationalism and a Transnational Sociology", Working Paper 24, Hauser Center: Kennedy School of Government, Harvard University

Khoury, S. 1990. *The Deregulation of the World Financial Markets*. London: Pinter

Kiekens, J.-P. 1997. *Certification: international trends and forestry and trade implications*. IFF

Kimmel, S. L., Marquette, R. P. and Olsen, D. H. 1998. "Outcomes Assessment Programmes; Historical Perspective and State of the Art", *Accounting Education* 13(4): 851–69

Kingdon, J.W. 1984. *Agendas, Alternatives and Public Policies*. Boston: Little Brown & Co

Kipping, M. 2002. "Development and Dynamics of Business–Government Relations", in Amatori and Jones (eds.), *Business History around the World*. New York: Cambridge

Kipping, M. and Engwall, L. (eds.) 2002. *Management Consulting*. Oxford: Oxford University Press

Kirp, D. 2003. *Shakespeare, Einstein, and The Bottom Line*. Cambridge: Harvard University Press

Kirton, J. J. and Trebilcock, M. J. 2004. *Hard Choices, Soft Law*. Aldershot: Ashgate

Kivinen, O. and Ahola, S. 1999. "Higher Education as a Human Risk Capital", *Higher Education* 38(2): 191–208

Kleekämper, H. 1995. "Aktuelle Entwicklungen beim IASC", *Betriebswirtschaftliche Forschung und Praxis* (BFuP) 4/95: 414–31

Kleekämper, H. 1998. "IASC – Das Trojanische Pferd der SEC?", in Ballwieser (ed.) *US-amerikanische Rechnungslegvng*. Stuttgart: Schäffer-Poeschel Verlag, pp. 351–67

Klein, J. 2000. "Time for a Global Initiative?", speech by the Assistant Attorney General, Antitrust Division US Department of Justice at the EC Merger Control 10th Anniversary Conference. Brussels, 14 September. Available at http://www.usdoj.gov/atr/public/speeches/6486.htm

Klein, N. 2002. *No Logo*. New York: Picador USA

Kleiner, T. 2003a. "Building up an Asset Management Industry: Forays of an Anglo-saxon Logic into the French Business System", in Djelic and Quack (eds.) *Globalization and Institutions*. Cheltenham, UK: Edward Elgar, pp. 57–82

Kleiner, T. 2003b. "Antitrust Legislation", in Northrup, C. (ed.) *US Economic History Encyclopedia*. Santa Barbara: ABC-CLIO, pp. 435–7

Knight, A. P. 1995. *How Green is my Front Door?* Hampshire, UK: B&Q plc

Knill, C. and Lehmkuhl, D. 2002. "Private Actors and the State: Internationalization and Changing Patterns of Governance", *Governance* 15(1): 41–63

Knorr Cetina, K. and Bruegger, U. 2002. "Global Microstructures: The Virtual Societies of Financial Markets", *American Journal of Sociology*, 107(4): 905–50

Kobrin, S. J. 2002. "Economic Governance in an Electronically Networked Global Economy", in Hall and Biersteker (eds.) *The Emergence of Private Authority in Global Governance*. Cambridge: Cambridge University Press, pp. 43–75

Koch-Weser Ammassari, E. 2004. "Constructing the European Higher Education Area: Institutional Policy and Student Experiences Across Countries", paper presented at the 36th World Congress of the International Institute of Sociology in Beijing

Kogut, B. and Macpherson, M. 2004. "The Decision to Privatize as an Economic Policy Idea: Epistemic Communities, Palace Wars and Diffusion", INSEAD Working Paper

Kohler-Koch, B. 1996. "The Strength of Weakness: The Transformation of Governance in the EU", in Gustavsson and Lewin. (eds.) *The Future of the Nation-State*. London: Routledge

Kohler-Koch, B. 1999. "The Evolution and Transformation of European Governance", in Kohler-Koch and Eising (eds.) *The Transformation of Governance in the European Union*. London: Routledge, pp. 14–35

Kohler-Koch, B. and Eising, R. (eds.) 1999. *The Transformation of Governance in the European Union*. London: Routledge

Koot, G. 1987. *English Historical Economics, 1870–1926*. Cambridge: Cambridge University Press

Kotter, J. D. 1982. *The General Managers*, New York: Free Press

Krasner, S. 1983. *International Regimes*. Ithaca, NY: Cornell University Press

Krastev, I. 2000. "Post-communist Think Tanks: Making and Faking Influence", in Stone (ed.) *Banking on Knowledge*. London: Routledge, pp. 142–61

Kristensen, P. H. and Zeitlin, J. 2005. *Local Players in Global Games*. Oxford: Oxford University Press

Krucken, G. 2003. "Learning The 'New, New Thing': On the Role of Path Dependency in University Structures", *Higher Education* 46: 315–39

Kruijtbosch, M. 1997. *Rugmark: a Brief Resume of Concept to Reality for Visual Guarantee of Carpets Made Without Child Labour*. India Committee of the Netherlands

Kudo, A. and Hara, T. 1992. *International Cartels in Business History*. Tokyo: University of Tokyo Press

Küng, H. 1998. *A Global Ethic for Global Politics and Economics*. Oxford: Oxford University Press

Lal, D. 2000. "The Challenge of Globalization: There is no Third Way", in Vasquez (ed.) *Global Fortune*. Washington: Cato Institute, pp. 29–41

Larson, R. 1997. "Corporate Lobbying of the International Accounting Standards Committee", *Journal of International Financial Management and Accounting* 8(3): 175–203

Lawrence, T., Hardy, C. and Phillips, N. 2002. "Institutional Effects of Interorganizational Collaboration: The Emergence of Proto-Institutions", *Academy of Management Journal* 45(1): 281–91

Lawrence, T., Winn, M. and Jennings, P. D. 2001. "The Temporal Dynamics of Institutionalism", *Academy of Management Journal* 26(4): 624–44

Leblebici, H., Salancik, G. R., Copay, A. and King, T. 1991. "Institutional Change and the Transformation of Interorganizational Fields: An Organizational History of the US Radio Broadcasting Industry", *Administrative Science Quarterly* 36 (September): 333–63

Leeson, R. 1998. "Patinkin, Johnson and the 'Shadow of Friedman'", Working Paper 167 (March), Economics Department Murdoch University, Australia

Lehmkuhl, D. 2003. "Structuring Dispute Resolution in Transnational Trade: Competition and Coevolution of Public and Private Institutions", in Djelic and Quack (eds.) *Globalization and Institutions*. Cheltenham UK: Edward Elgar, pp. 278–301

Lenhardt, G. and Stock, M. 2000. "Hochschulentwicklung und Bürgerrechte in der BRD und der DDR", *Kölner Zeitschrift für Soziologie und Sozialpsychologie* 52(3): 520–40

Levi-Faur, D. 2005. "The Global Diffusion of Regulatory Capitalism", in Levi-Faur and Jordana (eds.) *The Rise of Regulatory Capitalism*. The Annals of APSA, Vol. 598. London: Sage, pp. 12–32

Levi-Faur, D. and Jordana, J. (eds.) 2005. *The Rise of Regulatory Capitalism*. The Annals of APSA, Vol. 598. London: Sage

Levin, P. and Espeland, W. 2002. "Pollution Futures: Commensuration, Commodification, and the Market for Air", in Hoffman and Ventresca (eds.) *Organizations, Policy, and the Natural Environment*. Stanford: Stanford University Press, pp. 119–47

Levine, D. (ed.) 1985. *Georg Simmel on Individuality and Social Forms*. Chicago: University of Chicago Press

Levy, D. and Kolk, A. 2002. "Strategic Responses to Global Climate Change: Conflicting Pressures on Multinationals in the Oil Industry", *Business and Politics* 5: 131–51

Levy, D. and Newell, P. 2000. "Oceans Apart? Business Responses to Global Environmental Issues in Europe and the United States", *Environment* 42(9): 8–20

Lewin, K. 1936. *Principles of Topological Psychology*. New York: McGraw Hill

Lewin, K. 1947. "Channels of Group Life", *Human Relations* 1: 143–53

Lewin, K. 1951. *Field Theory in Social Science: Selected Theoretical Papers* (D. Cartwright (ed.)). New York: Harper & Row

Lexis, 1975, Paris: Larousse

Lie, J. 1997. "Sociology of Markets", *Annual Review of Sociology* 23: 341–60

Liljeros, F. 1996. "Elitinnebandy: Skapandet av en Elitidrott", Working Paper, Stockholm University: Department of Sociology

Lindblom, C. E. 1977. *Politics and Markets*. New York: Basic Books

Little, D., Kelsay, J. and Sachedina, A. A. 1988. *Human Rights and the Conflict of Cultures*. Columbia, SC: University of South Carolina Press

Ljunggren, S-B. 1997. *Att Rida Tigern*. Stockholm: Timbro

Locke, J. 1997. *Political Essays*. Cambridge: Cambridge University Press

Locke, R. 1989. *Management and Higher Education since 1940*. Cambridge: Cambridge University Press

Loft, A., Mouritsen, J. and Rohde, C. 2004. "Making Accounting the Danish Way", Working Paper, Copenhagen Business School

Lowen, R. S. 1997. *Creating The Cold War University*. University of California Press

Loya, T. and Boli, J. 1999. "Standardization in the World Polity. Technical Rationality over Power", in Boli and Thomas (eds.) *Constructing World Culture*. Stanford: Stanford University Press, pp. 169–97

Luhmann, N. 2000. *Organisation und Entscheidung*. Opladen: Westdeutscher Verlag

Luo, X. R. 2002. "From Technical Skills to Personal Development: Employee Training in US Organizations in the 20th Century", in Sahlin-Andersson and Engwall (eds.) *The Expansion of Management Knowledge*. Stanford: Stanford University Press, pp. 195–211

Lütz, S. 1998. "The Revival of the Nation-State? Stock Exchange Regulation in an Era of Globalized Financial Markets", *Journal of European Public Policy* 5(1): 153–68

Lutzenhiser, L. 2001. "The Contours of US Climate Non-policy", *Society and Natural Resources* 14: 511–23

Lynch, J. W. 1997. "Environmental Labels: A New Policy Strategy", *Forum for Applied Research and Public Policy* 12(1): 121–3

Lynn, E. L., Heinrich, C. J., Hill, C. J. 2001. *Improving Governance*. Washington, DC: Georgetown University Press

Maddox, R. F. 2001. *The War within World War II*. Westport: Praeger

Magnusson, L. 1994. *Mercantilism*. London: Routledge

Magretta, J. 1999. *Managing the New Economy*, Boston, MA: Harvard Business School

Mahdudi, A. 1980. *Human Rights in Islam*. Leicester: Islamic Foundation

Majone, G. (ed.) 1996. *Regulating Europe*. London: Routledge

Maliszewski, W. 2000. "Central Bank Independence in Transition Economies", Centre for Social and Economic Research (CASE), London School of Economics and Political Science, September

Manent, P. 1986. *Les Libéraux*, Vols. I and II. Paris: Hachette Littérature

March, J. G. 1981. "Decisions in Organizations and Theories of Choice", in Van de Ven and Joyce (eds.) *Perspectives of Organizational Design and Behavior*. New York: Wiley, pp. 205–44

March, J. G. 1994. *A Primer on Decision Making*. New York: Free Press

March, J. G. 1999. "A Learning Perspective on the Network Dynamics of Institutional Integration", in Egeberg, M. and Laegreid, P. (eds.) *Organizing Political Institutions*. Oslo: Scandinavian University Press, pp. 129–55

March, J. and Olsen, J. P. 1989. *Rediscovering Institutions*. New York: The Free Press

March, J. and Olsen, J. P. 1998. "The Institutional Dynamics of International Political Orders", *International Organization* 52(4): 943–69

March, J. and Simon, H. 1958. *Organizations*. New York: John Wiley and Sons

March, J., Schulz, M. and Zhou, X. 2000. *The Dynamics of Rules*. Stanford: Stanford University Press

Marcussen, M. 2000. *Ideas and Elites*. Aalborg: Aalborg University Press

Marcussen, M. 2004. "OECD Governance Through Soft Law", in Mörth (ed.) *Soft Law in Governance and Regulation*. Cheltenham: Edward Elgar, pp. 103–28

Marcussen, M. 2005. "Central Banks on the Move", *Journal of European Public Policy* 12(5): 903–23

Margolis, J. and Walsh, J. 2003. "Misery Loves Companies: Rethinking Social Initiatives by Business", *Administrative Science Quarterly* 48: 268–305

Martin, J. 1950. *All Honorable Men*. Boston: Little Brown

Martin, J. 2002. *Organizational Culture*. Thousand Oaks: Sage

Martin, J. L. 2003. "What is Field Theory?", *American Journal of Sociology* 109(1): 1–49

Martin, L. (ed.) 2005. *International Institutions in the New Global Economy*. Cheltenham: Edward Elgar

Martinelli, A. 2003. "Markets, Governments, Communities and Global Governance", *International Sociology* 18(2): 291–323

Mattli, W. 2003. "Public and Private Governance in Setting International Standards", in Kahler and Lake (eds.) *Governance in a Global Economy*. Princeton: Princeton University Press, pp. 199–225

Mattli, W. and Büthe, T. 2003. "Setting International Standards: Technological Rationality or Primacy of Power?", *World Politics* 56(1): 1–42

Maurice, M. and Sorge, A. (eds.) 2000. *Embedding Organizations*. Amsterdam : John Benjamins

Maxfield, S. 1997. *Gatekeepers of Growth*. Princeton: Princeton University Press

Mayer, D. 1994. *The Constitutional Thought of Thomas Jefferson*. Charlottesville: University Press of Virginia

Mazey, S. and Richardson, J. (eds.) 1993. *Lobbying in the European Community*, Oxford: Oxford University Press

Mazon, P. 2003. *Gender and the Modern Research University*. Stanford: Stanford University Press

Mazuri, A. 1975. "The African University as a Multinational Corporation: Problems of Penetration and Dependency", *Harvard Educational Review* 45: 191–210

Mazza, C., Sahlin-Andersson, K. and Strandgaard Pederson, J. 2005. "European Constructions of an American Model: Developments of Four MBA Programs", *Management Learning* 36(4): 471–91

McAdam, D., Tarrow, S. G. and Tilly, C. 2001. *Dynamics of Contention*. New York: Cambridge University Press

McEneaney, E. 2003. "Elements of a Contemporary Primary School Science", in Drori et al. *Science in the Modern World Polity*. Stanford: Stanford University Press, pp. 136–54

McKenzie, R. 2000. *Trust on Trial*. Cambridge, MA: Perseus Publishing

McLean, B. and Elkind, P. 2003. *The Smartest Guys in the Room*. New York: Portfolio

McNamara, K. 2002. "Rational Fictions: Central Bank Independence and the Social Logic of Delegation", *West European Politics* 25: 47–76

McNeely, C. 1995. *Constructing the Nation-State*. London: Greenwood Press

McNichol, J. 2002. "Contesting Governance in the Global Marketplace: A Sociological Assessment of NGO–Business Partnerships to Build Markets for Certified Wood Products", PhD Dissertation, Department of Sociology: University of California at Berkeley

McNichol, J. and Bensedrine, J. 2003. "Multilateral Rulemaking: Transatlantic Struggles around Genetically Modified Food", in Djelic and Quack (eds.) *Globalization and Institutions*. Cheltenham UK: Edward Elgar, pp. 220–244

Melamed, D. 2000. "Promoting Sound Antitrust Enforcement in the Global Economy", speech by the Acting Assistant Attorney General, Antitrust Division, US Department of Justice, before the Fordham Corporate Law Institute 27th Annual Conference on International Antitrust Law and Policy, New York, 19 October. Available at http://www.usdoj.gov/atr/public/speeches/6785.htm

Mendel, P. 2001. "Global Models of Organization", unpublished PhD dissertation, Stanford University

Mendes, P. 2003. "Austrian Neoliberal Think Tanks and the Backlash against the Welfare State", *Journal of Australian Political Economy* 51: 29–56

Merton, R. 1957. "Bureaucratic Structure and Personality", in *Social Theory and Social Structure*, Glencoe, IL: Free Press, pp. 195–206

Merton, R. 1970/1938. *Science, Technology and Society in Seventeenth Century England*. New York: Ferting Howard

Merton, R. 1973/1942. *The Sociology of Science*. Chicago: University of Chicago Press

Meyer, J. 1970. "The Charter; Conditions of Diffuse Socialization in Schools", in Scott (ed) *Social Processes and Social Structures*. New York: Holt, Rinehart and Winston. pp. 564–78

Meyer, J. 1986. "Myths of Socialization and of Personality", in Heller, Sosna and Wellbery (eds.) *Reconstructing Individualism*. Stanford: Stanford University Press

Meyer, J. 1994. "Rationalized Environments", in Scott and Meyer (eds.) *Institutional Environments and Organizations*. Thousand Oaks, CA: Sage, pp. 28–54

Meyer, J. 1996. "Otherhood: The Promulgation and Transmission of Ideas in the Modern Organizational Environment", in Czarniawska and Sevón (eds.) *Translating Organizational Change*. Berlin: de Gruyter, pp. 241–52

Meyer, J. 2000. "Globalization – Sources and Effects on National States and Societies", *International Sociology* 15: 233–48

Meyer, J. 2002. "Globalization and the Expansion and Standardization of Management", in Sahlin-Andersson and Engwall (eds.) *The Expansion of Management Knowledge*. Stanford: Stanford University Press, pp. 33–44

Meyer, J. and Jepperson, R. 2000. "The Actors of Modern Society: The Cultural Construction of Social Agency", *Sociological Theory* 18(1): 100–20

Meyer, J. and Rowan, B. 1977. "Institutionalized Organizations: Formal Structure as Myth and Ceremony", *American Journal of Sociology* 83: 340–63

Meyer, J. and Scott, W. R. 1983. *Organizational Environments*. Beverly Hills, CA: Sage

Meyer, J., Boli, J. and Thomas, G. M. 1987. "Ontology and Rationalization in the World Cultural Account", in Thomas et al. (eds) *Institutional Structure*. Newbury Park, CA: Sage, chapter 1

Meyer, J., Boli, J., Thomas, G. and Ramirez, R. 1997a. "World Society and the Nation-State", *American Journal of Sociology* 103(1): 144–81

Meyer, J., Frank, D., Hironaka, A., Schofer, E. and Tuma, N. 1997b. "The Structuring of a World Environmental Regime, 1870–1990", *International Organization* 51(4): 623–51

Meyer, L. 2004. *A Term at the FED*. New York: HarperCollins Publishers Inc

Michels, R. 1928. *Cartels, Combines and Trusts in Postwar Germany*. New York: Columbia University Press

Micklethwait, J. and Wooldridge, A. 1996. *The Witch Doctors*, Heinemann: London

Micklethwait, J. and Wooldridge, A. 2000. *A Future Perfect*. New York: Crown Business

Milgrom, P., North, D. and Weingast, B. 1990. "The Role of Institutions in the Revival of Trade: The Law Merchant, Private Judges and the Champagne Fairs", *Economics and Politics* 2(1): 1–23

Miller, H. 1962. "On the 'Chicago School' of Economics", *Journal of Political Economy* 70(1): 64–9

Minnesma, M. 2003. "Dutch Climate Policy. A Victim of Economic Growth?", *Climate Policy* 3: 45–56

Mintzberg, H. 1973. *The Nature of Managerial Work,* New York: Harper & Row

Mintzer, I. and Leonard, J. (eds.) 1994. *Negotiating Climate Change: The Inside Story of the Rio Convention.* Cambridge: Cambridge University Press

Mises, von, L. 1935/1920. "Economic Calculations in the Socialist Commonwealth", in Hayek (ed.) *Collectivist Economic Planning.* London: Routledge and Sons

Mohr, J. 2005. "Implicit Terrains: Meaning, Measurement, and Spatial Metaphors in Organizational Theory", in Ventresca and Porac (eds.) *Constructing Industries and Markets.* New York: Elsevier

Monks, R. A. and Minow, N. 1995. *Corporate Governance.* Cambridge MA: Blackwell Business

Monnet, J. 1976. *Mémoires.* Paris: Fayard

Monti, M. 2001. "International Co-operation and Technical Assistance: A View from the EU", speech by the European Commissioner for Competition, UNCTAD 3rd IGE Session, Geneva, 4 July. Available at http://europa.eu.int/comm/competition/speeches/index_speeches_ by_the_ commissioner.html

Monti, M. 2002. "A Global Competition Policy?", speech by the European Commissioner for Competition at the European Competition Day, Copenhagen, 17 September. Available at http://europa.eu.int/comm/competition/speeches/index_speeches_by_the_commissioner.html

Moon, H. 2002. "The Globalization of Professional Management Education, 1881–2000", unpublished PhD dissertation, Stanford University

Moran, M. 2002. "Understanding the Regulatory State", *British Journal of Political Science* 32: 391–413

Moravcsik, A. 1993. "Preferences and Power in the European Community: A Liberal Intergovernmental Approach", *Journal of Common Market Studies* 31: 473–524

Morgan, G. 2001a. "Transnational Communities and Business Systems", *Global Networks* 1(2): 113–30

Morgan, G. 2001b. "The Development of Transnational Standards and Regulations and their Impacts on Firms", in Morgan, Kristensen and Whitley (eds.) *The Multinational Firm.* Oxford: Oxford University Press, pp. 225–52

Morgan, G. 2005. "Understanding Multinational Corporations", in Ackroyd, Batt, Thompson and Tolbert (eds.) *The Oxford Handbook of Work and Organization.* Oxford: Oxford University Press, pp. 554–76

Morgan, G. and Quack, S. 2000. "Confidence and Confidentiality: The Social Construction of Performance Standards in German and British Banking", in Quack, Morgan and Whitley (eds.) *National Capitalisms, Global Competition, and Economic Performance*. Amsterdam, Philadelphia: Benjamins, pp. 131–57

Morgan, G. and Quack, S. 2005a. "Institutional Legacies and Firm Dynamics: The Internationalization of British and German Law Firms", working paper, University of Warwick

Morgan, G. and Quack, S. 2005b. "Internationalization and Capability Development in Professional Services Firms", in Morgan, Whitley and Moen (eds.), *Changing Capitalism?* Oxford: Oxford University Press, pp. 277–311

Morgan, G., Kristensen, P. H. and Whitley, R. (eds.) 2001. *The Multinational Firm*. Oxford: Oxford University Press

Morgan, G., Whitley, R. and Moen, E. (eds). 2005. *Changing Capitalism?* Oxford: Oxford University Press

MorganStanley 2004. *Central Bank Directory 2004*. London: Central Banking Publications Ltd

Mörth, U. 1996. "Vardagsintegration i Europa", doctoral dissertation, Statsvetenskapliga Institutionen, Stockholms Universitet

Mörth, U. (ed.) 2004. *Soft Law in Governance and Regulation*. Cheltenham: Edward Elgar

Mulkay, M. 1983. *Science Observed*. London: Sage

Muris, T. 2002. "Competition Agencies in a Market Based Global Economy", speech of the Chairman of the Federal Trade Commission at the Annual Lecture of the European Foreign Affairs Review, Brussels, 23 July. Available at http://www.ftc.gov/speeches/muris/020723 brussels.htm

Murphy, D. and Bendell, J. 1997. *In the Company of Partners*. Bristol (England): Policy Press

Nadler, D. A., Spencer, J. L. and associates. 1998. *Executive Teams,* San Francisco, CA: Jossey-Bass

Nash, J. and Ehrenfeld, J. 1996. "Code Green: Business Adopts Voluntary Environmental Standards", *Environment* 38: 16–44

Nelson, R. 2001. *Economics as Religion*. University Park, Pennsylvania: Pennsylvania State University Press

Nicholls, A. 1984. "The Other Germany, the Neo-liberals", in Bullen, Von Strandmann and Polonsky (eds.) *Ideas into Politics*, London: Croom Helm, pp. 164–77

Niebuhr, R. 1960. *Moral Man and Immoral Society.* New York: Scribner

Nisbet, R. 1971. *The Degradation of the American Dogma*. London: John Dewey Society Lectures Series

Nisbet, R. 1980. *History of the Idea of Progress*. New York: Basic Books

Noaksson, N. and Jacobsson, K. (2003). *The Production of Ideas and Expert Knowledge in OECD*. Stockholm: Score reports 2003: 7

Nobes, C. 1985. "Harmonisation of Financial Reporting", in Nobes and Parker (eds.) *Comparative International Accounting*. Essex: Pearson Education, pp. 331–52

Nobes, C. and Parker, R. (eds.) 1985. *Comparative International Accounting*. New York: St. Martin's Press

Nobes, C. and Parker, R. (eds.) 2004. *Comparative International Accounting*. Essex: Pearson Education

Noble, D. 1982. "The Selling of the University: MIT–Whitehead Merger", *Nation* 234(5): 129

North, D. C. 1990. *Institutions, Institutional Change, and Economic Performance*. Cambridge: Cambridge University Press

North, R. 1997. "Out of the Woods", *The Times* (London), 31 May

Notes from Nowhere. 2003. *We Are Everywhere*. London: Verso

Nouveau Petit Robert. 1994. Paris: Dictionnaires Le Robert

O'Brien, R., Goetz, A. M., Scholte, J. A. and Williams, M. 2000. *Contesting Global Governance*. Cambridge: Cambridge University Press

OECD 1986. "Recommandation Révisée de l'OCDE de 1986 sur la Coopération entre Pays Membres dans le Domaine des Pratiques Commerciales Restrictives Affectant les Échanges Internationaux". C(86)44, 21 May

OECD 1997. *Eco-labelling: Actual Effects of Selected Programs*. Paris: Organization for Economic Cooperation and Development.

Ohmae, K. 1995. *The Pluralist State*. London: Macmillan

Olsen, J. P. 2003. "What is Legitimate Role for Euro-citizens?", *Comparative European Politics* 1(1): 91–110

Olson, O., Guthrie, J. and Humphrey, C. (eds.) 1998. *Global Warning*. Oslo: Cappelen Akademisk Forlag

One World Trust 2003. *The Global Accountability Report*, No. 1. London: Houses of Parliament. Available at http://www.oneworldtrust.org

O'Riain, S. 2000. "States and Markets in an Era of Globalization", *Annual Review of Sociology* 26: 187–213

O'Riain, S. 2001. "Flexible States in the Network Polity: The Case of Industrial Policy in the Republic of Ireland", Working Paper Department of Sociology, University of California (Davis)

O'Shea, J. and Madigan, C. 1997. *Dangerous Company*. New York: Times Books

Österdahl, I. 2004. "The ECJ and Soft Law: Who's Afraid of the EU Fundamental Rights Charter?", in Mörth (ed.) *Soft Law in Governance and Regulation*. Cheltenham: Edward Elgar, pp. 37–60

Pallas, J. 2004. "Talking Organizations", paper presented at a workshop on the Nordic Business Press in Copenhagen, 17–19 September

Palmer, J. 1996. "Monitoring Forest Practices", paper presented at the Economic, Social, and Political Issues in Certification of Forest Management, Kuala Lumpur, Malaysia, 12–16 May

Parsons, T. 1954. *Essays in Sociological Theory*. Glencoe: The Free Press

Peacock, A. and Willgerodt, H. (eds.) 1989. *Germany's Social Market Economy*. New York: Saint Martin's Press

Pedersen, S. 2000. "The Danish CO_2 Emissions Trading Scheme", *Review of European Community and International Environmental Law* 9(3): 223–31

Peeters, M. 2003. "Emissions Trading as a New Dimension to European Environmental Law: The Political Agreement of the European Council on Greenhouse Gas Allowance Trading", *European Environmental Law Review* March: 82–92

Peritz, R. 1996. *Competition Policy in America*. New York: Oxford University Press

Perrow, C. 1979. *Complex Organizations*, 2d edn. Glenview: Scott, Foresman

Peters, T. and Waterman, R. 1982. *In Search of Excellence*. New York: Harper and Row

Pettigrew, A. 1973. *The Politics of Organizational Decision-Making*. London: Tavistock

Pierre, J. 2000. *Debating Governance*. Oxford: Oxford University Press

Pire, B. (ed.) 2000. *Dictionnaire de la Physique*. Paris : Encyclopaedia Universalis/Albin Michel

Pittman, R. 1998. "Competition Law and Policy in the United States", Working Paper US Department of Justice, Washington, DC

Polanyi, K. 1944. *The Great Transformation*. New York: Rinehard & Co

Polanyi, K. 1968. *Primitive, Archaic and Modern Economics*. (G. Dalton, ed.). Boston: Beacon Press

Pons, J.-F. 2002. "Is it Time for an International Agreement on Antitrust?", Speech at Frauenchiemsee, 3–5 June

Porter, L. W. and McKibbin, L. E. 1988. *Management Education and Development, Drift or Thrust into the 21st Century?* NY: McGraw-Hill

Posner, R. 1972. *Economic Analysis of Law*. Boston: Little Brown

Powell, W. and DiMaggio, P. 1991. *The New Institutionalism in Organizational Analysis*. Chicago: University of Chicago Press

Powell, W. and Owen-Smith, J. 1998. "Universities and the Market for Intellectual Property", *Journal of Policy Analysis and Management* 17(2): 253–77

Powell, W., Gammal, D. L. and Simmard, C. 2006. "Close Encounters: The Circulation and Reception of Managerial Practices in the San Francisco Bay Area Nonprofit Community", in Czarniawska and Sevón (eds.) *Global Ideas*. Lund, Sweden: Liber. pp. 233–58

Power, J. 2001. *Like Water on Stone*. London: Allen Lane

Power, M. 1997. *The Audit Society*. Oxford: Oxford University Press

Power, M. 2003. "Evaluating the Audit Explosion", *Law & Policy* 25(3): 115–202

Power, M. 2004. *The Risk Management of Everything*. London: Demos

Premfors, R. and Roth, K. 2004. "En Demokratisyn och ett Forskningsfält", in Premfors and Roth (eds.) *Deliberativ Demokrati*. Lund: Studentlitteratur

Presidency Conclusions. 2001. European Council Meeting in Laeken, 14 and 15 December. Available at http://ue.eu.int/ueDocs/cms_Data/docs/ pressData/ en/ec/68827.pdf

Pressman, J. L. and Wildavsky, A. 1973. *Implementation*. Berkeley: University of California Press

Pulver, S. 2004. "Carbon Chronicles: An Environmental Contestation Model of the Climate Policies of ExxonMobil, BP, and Shell", paper presented at the Scancor workshop on Corporate Social Responsibility in the Era of the Transforming Welfare State, Florence, 6–8 May

Putnam, R. 2000. *Bowling Alone*. New York: Simon & Schuster

Quack, S. and Djelic, M.-L. 2005. "Adaptation, Recombination, and Reinforcement: The Story of Antitrust and Competition Law in Germany and Europe", in Streeck and Thelen (eds.) *Beyond Continuity*. Oxford: Oxford University Press

Quack, S., Morgan, G. and Whitley, R. (eds.) 2000. *National Capitalisms, Global Competition, and Economic Performance*. Amsterdam, Philadelphia: Benjamins

Ramirez, F. O. 2002. "Eyes Wide Shut: University, State, and Society", *European Educational Research Journal* 1(3): 255–71

Ramirez, F. O. 2005. "Growing Commonalities and Persistent Differences in Higher Education: Universities Between Globalization and National Tradition", in Meyer and Rowan (eds.) *The New Institutionalism in Education*. NY: SUNY University Press

Ramirez, F. O., Meyer, J., Wotipka, C. and Drori, G. 2002. *Expansion and Impact of the World Human Rights Regime*. Stanford: Stanford Institute for International Studies

Ramirez, F. O. and Wotipka, C. M. 2001. "Slowly But Surely? The Global Expansion of Women's Share of Science and Engineering Fields of Study", *Sociology of Education* 74: 231–51

Readings, B. 1996. *The University in Ruins*. Cambridge, MA: Harvard University Press

Reder, M. 1982. "Chicago Economics: Permanence and Change", *Journal of Economic Literature* 20: 1–38

Rees, M. and Evers, R. 2000. "Proposals for Emissions Trading in the United Kingdom", *Review of European Community & International Environmental Law* 9(3): 232–8

Rheinstein, M. 1974. *Einführung in die Rechtsvergleichung*. München: C. H. Beck'sche Verlagsbuchhandlung

Riddle, P. 1989. "University and State", doctoral dissertation, Department of Sociology, Stanford University

Rifkin, J. 2004. *The European Dream*. Cambridge: Polity Press

Ringer, F. K. 1969. *The Decline of the German Mandarins*. Cambridge, MA: Harvard University Press

Risse-Kappen, T. (ed.) 1995. *Bringing Transnational Relations Back In*. Cambridge: Cambridge University Press

Robertson, R. 1992. *Globalization*. London: Sage

Rockoff, J. 1999. "The UK Case", in Alvarez, Mazza, and Mur (eds.), *The Management Publishing Industry in Europe*. CEMP Report No. 5, pp. 182–217

Roe, M. J. 1994. *Strong Managers, Weak Owners*. Princeton, NJ: Princeton University Press

Roebling, G., Ryan, S. A. and Sjöblom, D. 2003. "The International Competition Network (ICN) Two Years on: Concrete Results of a Virtual Network", *Competition Policy Newsletter* 3 (autumn): 37–40

Rogers, E. 1983. *Diffusion of Innovations*, 3rd edn. New York: Free Press

Rose, N. and Miller, P. 1992. "Political Power Beyond the State: Problematics of Government", *British Journal of Sociology* 43(2): 173–205

Rosenau, J. and Czempiel, E.-O. (eds.) 1992. *Governance without Government*. Cambridge: Cambridge University Press

Rothstein, R. 1996. "The Starbucks Solution: Can Voluntary Codes Raise Global Living Standards?", *The American Prospect* July–August: 36–42

Rouam, C., Thinam J. and Lisbe, S. 1994. "La Politique de Concurrence de la Communauté à L'Échelle Mondiale : L'Exportation des Règles de Concurrence Communautaires", *EC Competition Policy Newsletter* 1(1): 7–11

Røvik, K. A. 2002. "The Secrets of the Winners: Management Ideas that Flow", in Sahlin-Andersson and Engwall (eds.) *The Expansion of Management Knowledge*. Stanford: Stanford University Press, pp. 113–144

Rowley, W., Wakil, O. and Campbell, N. 2000. "Streamlining International Merger Control", in *EC Merger Control Ten Years On*. London: International Bar Association/European Commission (ed.), 15–37

Roy, W. 1997. *Socializing Capital*. Princeton: Princeton University Press

Royal Swedish Academy of Sciences 1999. "The 1999 Nobel Prize in Chemistry", Press release, 12 October. Available at http://www.nobel.se/chemistry/laureates/1999/press.html

Ruggie, J. G. 1983. "Continuity and Transformation in World Politics: Towards a Neorealist Synthesis", *World Politics* 35(2): 261–85

Ruggie, J. G. 1993. "Territoriality and Beyond: Problematizing Modernity in International Relations", *International Organizations* 47(1): 139–74

Ruggie, J. G. 2002. "The Theory and Practice of Learning Networks. Global Social Responsibility and the Global Compact", *Journal of Corporate Citizenship* 5: 27–36

Ruggie, J. G. 2004. "Reconstituting the Global Public Domain: Issues, Actors and Practices", *European Journal of International Relations* 10(4): 499–532

Rupp, V. 1997. *Oude En Nieuwe Univeriteiten*. Den Haag: Sdu Uitgevers

Sahlin-Andersson, K. 1996. "Imitating by Editing Success: The Construction of Organizational Fields", in Czarniawska and Sevón (eds.) *Translating Organizational Change*. Berlin: de Gruyter, pp. 69–92

Sahlin-Andersson, K. 2000. "Arenas as Standardizers", in Brunsson and Jacobsson (eds.) *A World of Standards*. Oxford: Oxford University Press, pp. 101–14

Sahlin-Andersson, K. 2003. "The Impact of Privatisation: Management, Organisation, Regulation and Monitoring in Transition", proceedings from the International Conference on Public Health, Bergen, Norway, 15–17 June

Sahlin-Andersson, K. 2004. "Emergent Cross-Sectional Soft Regulations: Dynamics at Play in the Global Compact Initiative", in Mörth (ed.) *Soft Law in Governance and Regulation*. Cheltenham: Edward Elgar, pp. 129–54

Sahlin-Andersson, K. and Engwall, L. (eds.) 2002. *The Expansion of Management Knowledge*. Stanford: Stanford University Press

Sahlin-Andersson, K. and Sevón, G. 2003. "Imitation and Identification as Performatives", in Czarniawska and Sevón (eds.) *The Northern Lights*. Malmö: Liber, pp. 249–65

Salzman, J. 1991. *Environmental Labelling in OECD Countries*. OECD: Paris

Samuels, J. M. and Piper, A. G. 1985. *International Accounting*. London: Croom Helm

Schaub, A. 2000. "Assessing International Mergers: The Commission's Approach", speech of the Director General for Competition, European Commission, at the EC Merger Control 10th Anniversary Conference, Brussels, 14–15 September. Available at http://europa.eu.int/comm/competition/speeches/text/sp2000_015_en.html

Schloss, H. 1958. *The Bank for International Settlements*. Amsterdam: North-Holland Publishing Company

Schmalensee, R., Joskow, P., Ellerman, A. D., Montero, J. and Bailey, E. 1998. "An Interim Evaluation of Sulfur Dioxide Emissions Trading", *Journal of Economic Perspectives* 12(3): 53–68

Schmidt, P. 2004. "Law in the Age of Governance: Regulation, Networks and Lawyers", in Jordana and Levi-Faur (eds.) *The Politics of Regulation*. Cheltenham, UK: Edward Elgar, pp. 273–95

Schmidt, S. and Werle, R. 1998. *Coordinating Technology*. Cambridge MA: MIT Press

Schmitter, P. and Lehmbruch, G. 1979. *Trend Towards Corporatist Intermediation*. London: Sage

Schofer, E. 1999. "The Rationalization of Science and the Scientization of Society: International Science Organizations, 1870–1995", in Boli and Thomas (eds.) *Constructing World Culture*. Stanford: Stanford University Press, pp. 249–66

Schofer, E. and Meyer, J. W. 2004. "The Worldwide Expansion of Higher Education in the Twentieth Century", unpublished paper, Department of Sociology, University of Minnesota

Schofer, E., Meyer, J. and Ramirez, F. 2000. "The Effects of Science on National Economic Development, 1970–1990", *American Sociological Review* 65: 877–98

Scholte, J. A. 2000. *Globalization*. New York: Palgrave

Schreiner, P. 2000. "The Norwegian Approach to Greenhouse Gas Emissions Trading", *Review of European Community and International Environmental Law* 9(3): 239–51

Schumpeter, J. 1983. *Histoire de L'Analyse Économique*, 3 Vols. Paris: NRF-Gallimard

Scott, C. 2004. "Regulation in the Age of Governance: The Rise of the Post-Regulatory State", in Jordana and Levi-Faur (eds.) *The Politics of Regulation*. Cheltenham, UK: Edward Elgar, pp. 145–174

Scott, J. 2000. *Social Network Analysis*. London: Sage

Scott, W. R. 1998. *Organizations*, 4th edn. New Jersey: Prentice-Hall

Scott, W. R. 1995. *Institutions and Organizations*. London: Sage Publications

Scott, W. R. 2003. "Institutional Carriers: Reviewing Modes of Transporting Ideas over Time and Space and Considering their Consequences", *Industrial and Corporate Change* 12(4): 879–94

Scott, W. R. and Meyer, J. 1983. "The Organization of Societal Sectors", in Meyer and Scott (eds.) *Organizational Environments*. Beverly Hills CA: Sage, pp. 129–54

Scott, W. R., Ruef, M., Mendel, P. and Caronna, C. 2000. *Institutional Change and Healthcare Organizations*. Chicago: University of Chicago Press

Sears, R., Davalos, L. and Ferraz, G. 2001. "Missing the Forest for the Profits: The Role of Multinational Corporations in the International Forest Regime", *Journal of Environment and Development* 10(4): 345–64

Segev, E., Raveh, A. and Farjoun, M. 1999. "Conceptual Maps of the Leading MBA Programs in the United States: Core Courses, Concentration Areas, and the Ranking of the School", *Strategic Management Journal* 20: 549–65

Sevón, G. 1996. "Organizational Imitation in Identity Transformations", in Czarniawska and Sevón (eds.) *Translating Organizational Change*. Berlin: de Gruyter, pp. 49–67

Shanks, C., Jacobson, H. and Kaplan, J. 1996. "Inertia and Change in the Constellation of International Governmental Organizations, 1981–1992", *International Organization* 50: 593–627

Shenton, G. 1996. "Management Education Models in Europe: Diversity and Integration", in Lee, Letiche, Crawshaw and Thomas (eds.) *Management Education in the New Europe*. London: International Thomson Business Press, pp. 32–47

Shills, E. 1971. "No Salvation Outside Higher Education", *Minerva* 6: 313–21

Shionoya, Y. (ed.) 2001. *The German Historical School*. London: Routledge

Shore, C. and Wright, S. 2000. "Coercive Accountability. The Rise of Audit Culture in Higher Education", in Strathern, M. (ed.) *Audit Cultures*. London: Routledge

Siebert, F. S., Peterson, T. and Schramm, W. 1956. *Four Theories of the Press*, Urbana, IL: University of Illinois

Simmons, B. 2001. "The International Politics of Harmonization: The Case of Capital Market Regulation", *International Organization* 55(3): 589–620

Simmons, B., Dobbin, F. and Garrett, G. 2003. "The International Diffusion of Democracy and Markets", paper presented at the American Political Science Association Meetings, Philadephia, August

Skinner, A. 1999. "Analytical Introduction", in Smith (ed.) *The Wealth of Nations*, Books I–III. London and New York: Penguin Books, pp. 15–43

Sklar, M. 1988. *Corporate Reconstruction of American Capitalism, 1890–1916*. Cambridge: Cambridge University Press

Slaughter, A.-M. 2004. *A New World Order*. Princeton: Princeton University Press

Slaughter, S. and Leslie, L. 1997. *Academic Capitalism*. Baltimore: Johns Hopkins Press

Smith, A. [1776] 1999. *The Wealth of Nations*. Books I–III (A. Skinner, ed.). London and New York: Penguin Books

Smith, A. [1776] 2000. *The Wealth of Nations*. Books IV and V (A. Skinner, ed.). London and New York: Penguin Books

Smith, A. D. 1990. "Towards a Global Culture?", in Featherstone (ed.) *Global Culture*. London: Sage, pp. 171–91

Smith, J. and Johnston, H. (eds.) 2002. *Transnational Dimensions of Social Movements*. Lanham, MD: Rowman & Littlefield

Snyder, F. 1993. "Soft Law and Institutional Practice in the European Community", in Martin (ed) *The Construction of Europe*. Dordrecht/ London: Kluwer Academic Publishers, pp. 197–225

Soares, J. 1999. *The Decline of Privilege*. Stanford: Stanford University Press

Sorell, S. 2003. *Back to the Drawing Board? Implications of the EU Emissions Trading Directive for UK Climate Policy*. Sussex: SPRU

Spiliopoulou Åkermark, S. 2004. "Soft Law and International Financial Institutions – Issues of Hard and Soft Law from a Lawyer's Perspective", in Mörth (ed) *Soft Law in Governance and Regulation*. Cheltenham: Edward Elgar, pp. 61–80

Squires, S. E. 2003. *Inside Arthur Andersen*. Upper Saddle River, NJ: FT Prentice Hall

Starr, A. 2000. *Naming the Enemy*. New York: Zed

Stavins, R. 1998. "What Can We Learn from the Grand Policy Experiment? Lessons from SO_2 Allowance Trading", *Journal of Economic Perspectives* 12(3): 69–88

Stefancic, J. and Delgado, R. 1998. *No Mercy*. Temple University Press

Stewart, R. 1967. *Managers and their Jobs*, Maidenhead: McGraw-Hill

Stigler, G. J. 1976. "The Successes and Failures of Professor Smith", *Journal of Political Economy*, December: 1199–1213

Stiglitz, J. 2002. *Globalization and its Discontents*. New York: Norton

Stinchcombe, A. 1965. "Social Structure and Organizations", in March (ed.) *Handbook of Organizations*. Chicago: Rand McNally & Co, pp. 142–93

Strang, D. and Meyer, J. 1993. "Institutional Conditions for Diffusion", *Theory and Society* 22: 487–511

Strange, S. 1996. *The Retreat of the State*. Cambridge: Cambridge University Press

Strathern, M. 2000. "The Tyranny of Transparency", *British Educational Research Journal* 26(3): 309–21

Streeck, W. 1997. "German Capitalism: Does It Exist? Can It Survive?", in Crouch and Streeck (eds.) *Political Economy of Modern Capitalism*. London: Sage, pp. 33–54

Streeck, W. and Thelen, K. (eds) 2005. *Beyond Continuity*. Oxford: Oxford University Press

Suddaby, R. and Greenwood, R. 2002. "Colonizing Knowledge: Commodification as a Dynamic of Jurisdictional Expansion in Professional Service Firms", *Human Relations* 54(7): 933–53

Surowiecki, J. 2004. *The Wisdom of Crowds*. Doubleday

Suzuki, T. 2003. "The Epistemology of Macroeconomic Reality: The Keynesian Revolution from an Accounting Point of View", *Accounting, Organizations and Society* 28: 471–517

Svensson, J. 2003. "Twinning – Modernization Through Imitation", paper presented at the EGOS Colloquium in Ljubljana, July

Swedberg, R. 1994. "Markets as Social Structures", in Smelser and Swedberg (eds.) *The Handbook of Economic Sociology*. Princeton: Princeton University Press, pp. 255–82

Synnott, T. 2002. Personal communication. Oaxaca, Mexico

Tainio, R., Huolman, M., Pulkkinen, M., Ali-Yrkkö, J. and Ylä-Anttila, P. 2003. "Global Investors Meet Local Managers: Shareholder Value in the Finnish Context", in Djelic and Quack (eds.) *Globalization and Institutions*. Cheltenham, UK: Edward Elgar, pp. 37–56

Tamm Hallström, K. 2004. *Organizing International Standardization*. Cheltenham: Edward Elgar

Tapper, E. and Salter, B. 1992. *Oxford, Cambridge, and The Changing Idea of the University*. Buckingham: Open University Press

Tarrow, S. G. 1994. *Power in Movement*. Cambridge: Cambridge University Press

Teichova, A., Lévy-Leboyer, M. and Nussbaum, H. 1986. *Multinational Enterprise in Historical Perspective*. Cambridge: Cambridge University Press

Tengblad, S. 2002. "Time and Space in Managerial Work", *Scandinavian Journal of Management* 18(4): 543–65

Thomas, G., Meyer, J. W., Ramirez, F. and Boli, J. 1987. *Institutional Structure*. Newbury Park, CA: Sage

Thomas, R. D. 1970. "The Accountants International Study Group – The First Three Years", *International Journal of Accounting* Fall: 59–65

Thompson, J. 1967. *Organizations in Action*, New York: McGraw-Hill

Thorell, P. and Whittington, G. 1994. "The Harmonization of Accounting within the EU. Problems, Perspectives and Strategies", *The European Accounting Review* 3(2): 215–39

Thornton, P. 2004. *Markets from Culture*. Stanford: Stanford University Press

Tolbert, P. and Zucker, L. 1983. "Institutional Sources of Change in the Formal Structure of Organizations: The Diffusion of Civil Service Reform, 1880–1935", *Administrative Science Quarterly* 28: 22–39

Tolbert, P. and Zucker, L. 1996. "The Institutionalization of Institutional Theory", in Clegg, Hardy and Nord (eds.) *Handbook of Organization Studies*. London: Sage, pp. 175–90

Tomusk, V. 2004. "Three Bolognas and a Pizza Pie: Notes on Institutionalization of the European Higher Education System", *International Studies in Sociology of Education* 14: 75–95

Toulmin, S. 1990. *Cosmopolis*, New York: Free Press

Trow, M. 1998. "On the Accountability of Higher Education in the United States", in Bowen and Shapiro (eds.) *Universities and Their Leadership*. New Jersey: Princeton University Press, pp. 15–61

Tyack, D. and Hansot, E. 1982. *Managers of Virtue*. New York: Basic Books

UNCTAD. 2000. *World Investment Report 2000. Cross-border Mergers and Acquisitions and Development*. New York and Geneva: United Nations

Union of International Associations 2002/2003. *Yearbook of International Organizations*, 39th edn. München: K. G. Saur Verlag, cd-rom version

United Nations 1968. "Proclamation of Teheran, Final Act of the International Conference on Human Rights, Teheran, 22 April to 13 May 1968". UN Doc. A/CONF. 32/41 at 3

United Nations Department of Social and Economic Affairs. 2005. *Success Stories-2000 (Integrated Planning and Management of Land Resources, Agriculture and Forests)*. Available at: http://www.un.org/esa/sustdev/mgroups/success/SARD-2.htm

United Nations General Assembly 1948. "Universal Declaration of Human Rights". GA res 217A (III), UN Doc A/810 at 71

Unocal Corporation 2004. "Statement of Principles". Available at http://www.unocal.com/responsibility/princip.htm

Useem, M. 1984. *The Inner Circle*. Oxford: Oxford University Press

Valdès, J. G. 1995. *Pinochet's Economists*. Cambridge: Cambridge University Press

Vallejo, N. and Hauselmann, P. 2001. *PEFC: An Analysis*. Switzerland, Zurich: WWF

Van der Pijl, K. 1984. *The Making of an Atlantic Ruling Class*. London: Verso

Van der Pijl, K. 1998. *Transnational Classes and International Relations*. London: Routledge

Van Miert, K. 1997. "International Cooperation in the Field of Competition; A View from the EC", speech by the European Commissioner before the Fordham Corporate Law Institute 24th Annual Conference, New York, 16 October. Available at http://europa.eu.int/comm/competition/speeches/text/sp1997_073_en.html

Van Miert, K. 1998. "European Competition Policy", speech at the Management Policy Council, Brussels-De Warande, 6 May. Available at http://europa.eu.int/comm/competition/speeches/text/sp1998_053_en.html

Van Waarden, F. 1992. "Emergence and Development of Business Interest Associations. An Example from the Netherlands", *Organization Studies*, 13: 521–62

Van Waarden, F. and Drahos, M. 2002. "Courts and (Epistemic) Communities in the Convergence of Competition Policies", *Journal of European Public Policy* 9(6): 913–34

Van Zandt, D. 1991. "The Regulatory and Institutional Conditions for an International Securities Market", *Virginia Journal of International Law* 47: 32–47

Varangis, P., Crossley, R. et al. 1995. *Is there a Case for Tropical Timber Certification?*. Washington DC: World Bank

Vaughn, K. 1994. *Austrian Economics in America*. Cambridge: Cambridge University Press

Venit, J. S. and Kolasky, W. J. 2000. "Substantive Convergence and Procedural Dissonance in Merger Review", in Evenett, Lehmann and Steil (eds.) *Antitrust Goes Global*. Washington DC: Brookings Institution Press, pp. 79–97

Ventresca, M. and Kratz, M. 2004. "How Market Logics Enter the University: Evidence and Arguments from the Spread of 'Enrollment Management' in US Universities, 1975–2002", paper presented at the Stanford Institute of Higher Education, Stanford University

Ventresca, M., Szyliowicz, D. and Dacin, T. 2003. "Innovations in Governance: Global Structuring and the Field of Public Exchange-Traded Markets", in Djelic and Quack (eds.) *Globalization and Institutions*. Cheltenham, UK: Edward Elgar, pp. 245–77

Vernon, R. 1977. *Storm over the Multinationals*. Cambridge, MA: Harvard University Press

Vickers, J. and Yarrow, G. 1988. *Privatization*. Cambridge: MIT Press

Vifell, Å. 2002. Enklaver i Staten. Internationaliseringen av den Svenska Statsförvaltningen, Stockholm University, Score working paper series 2002–2

Viner, J. 1960. "The Intellectual History of Laissez-Faire", *Journal of Law and Economics* 3: 45–69

Virga, M. 2001. Personal communication on 29 March in Washington, DC

Vogel, D. and Kagan, R. A. 2001. National Regulations in a Global Economy, working paper, University of California at Berkeley

Vogel, S. K. 1996. *Freer Markets, More Rules*. Ithaca: Cornell University Press

Vorwold, G. 2000. "Das Modell 'FASB' in den USA – Ein Fehlschlag", *Internationales Steuerrecht* 19: 599–607

Wallerstedt, E. 2002. "From Accounting to Professional Services: The Emergence of a Swedish Auditing Field", in Sahlin-Andersson and Engwall (eds.) *The Expansion of Management Knowledge*. Stanford: Stanford University Press, pp. 246–74

Warkentin, C. 2001. *Reshaping World Politics*. Lanham, MD: Rowman & Littlefield

Wälti, S., Kübler, S. and Papadopoulos, Y. 2004. "How Democratic is Governance?", *Governance* 17(1): 83–113

Warren, R. L. 1967. "The Interorganizational Field as a Focus for Investigation", *Administrative Science Quarterly* 12: 396–419

Warren, R. L. 1972. *The Community in America*. Chicago: Rand McNally

Wasik, J. 1996. *Green Marketing and Management*. Cambridge and Oxford: Blackwell Business

Weber, M. 1949. *The Methodology of the Social Sciences*. New York: Free Press

Weber, M. 1958. *The Protestant Ethic and the Spirit of Capitalism*. New York: Scribner

Weber, M. 1959. *Le Savant et le Politique*. Paris: Plon

Weber, M. 1964. *The Theory of Social and Economic Organization*. New York: Oxford University Press

Weber, M. 1978. *Economy and Society*, 2 Vols. (G. Roth and C. Wittich, eds.). Berkeley: University of California Press

Wedlin, L. 2004. "Playing the Ranking Game: Field Formation and Boundary-work in European Management Education", unpublished doctoral thesis No. 108, Department of Business Studies, Uppsala University

Wedlin, L. 2006. *Ranking Business Schools. Forming Fields, Identities and Boundaries in International Management Education*. Cheltenham, UK: Edward Elgar

Westney, D. E. 1987. *Imitation and Innovation*. Cambridge, MA: Harvard University Press

Westphal, J. D., Gulati, R. and Shortell, S. M. 1997. "Customization or Conformity: An Institutional and Network Perspective on the Content and Consequences of TQM Adoption", *Administrative Science Quarterly* 42: 366–94

Weyland, K. 2003. "Theories of Policy Diffusion: An Assessment", paper presented at the American Political Science Association, Philadelphia, PA, 28–31 August

Whitley, R. 1999. *Divergent Capitalisms*. Oxford: Oxford University Press

Whitley, R. 2003. "Changing Transnational Institutions and the Management of International Business Transactions", in Djelic and Quack (eds.) *Globalization and Institutions*. Cheltenham, UK: Edward Elgar, pp. 108–33

Whitley, R. 2005a. "How National are Business Systems? The Role of States and Complementary Institutions in Standardizing Systems of Economic Coordination and Control at the National Level", in Morgan, Whitley and Moen (eds.) *Changing Capitalism?* Oxford: Oxford University Press, pp. 190–231

Whitley, R. 2005b. "Developing Transnational Organizational Capabilities in Multinational Companies: Institutional constraints on authority sharing and careers in six types of MNC" in Morgan, Whitley and Moen (eds.) *Changing Capitalism?* Oxford: Oxford University Press, pp. 235–76

Willets, P. 1996. *The Conscience of the World*. Washington, DC: Brookings Institution Press

Williams, R. 1981. *Culture*. London: Fontana Press

Williamson, J. 2000. "What Should the World Bank Think About the Washington Consensus?", *The World Bank Research Observer* 15: 251–64

Woodward, B. 2000. *Maestro*. New York: Simon & Schuster (large print edition)

World Federation of International Music Competitions. 2004. "About the Federation". Available at http://www.wfimc.org/public/index_fr.html

Worldwide Fund for Nature – United Kingdom. 2000. FSC News. WWF 95+ Group Newsletter: 8

Wotipka, C. M. and Ramirez, F. O. 2004. "A Cross-National Analysis of the Emergence and Institutionalization of Women's Studies Curricula", paper presented at the annual meeting of the American Sociological Association

WTO. 2000. Report (2000) of the Working Group on the Interaction between Trade and Competition Policy to the General Council. Available at http://docsonline.wto.org/imrd/

Wuthnow, R. 1987. *Meaning and Moral Order*. Berkeley: University of California Press

Wuthnow, R. 1989. *Communities of Discourse*. Cambridge, MA: Harvard University Press

Wuthnow, R. (ed.) 1991. *Between States and Markets*. Princeton: Princeton University Press

Yearbook of International Organizations 2001/2002, *2003/2004*. Union of International Associations, ed. Munchen: K. G. Saur

Yergin, D. and Stanislaw, J. 1998. *The Commanding Heights*. New York: Simon and Schuster

Yonay, Y. 1998. *The Struggle over the Soul of Economics*. Princeton: Princeton University Press

Young, J. 1994. "Outlining Regulatory Space: Agenda Issues and the FASB", *Accounting, Organizations and Society* 19(1): 83–109

Young, O. R. 1989. *International Cooperation*. Ithaca: Cornell University Press

Zadek, S. 2001. *The Civil Corporation*. London: Earthscan Publications

Zapfel, P. and Vainio, M. 2002. *Pathways to European Greenhouse Gas Emissions Trading*, Working Paper Fondazione Eni Enrico Mattei. Available at http://www.feem.it/web/activ/activ.html

Zeiler, T. 1999. *Free Trade, Free World*. Chapel Hill: University of North Carolina Press

Zeitlin, J. and Herrigel, G. (eds.) 2000. *Americanization and its Limits*. Oxford: Oxford University Press

Zelizer, V. 1988. "Beyond the Polemics on the Market: Establishing a Theoretical and Empirical Agenda", *Sociologica Forum* 3(4): 614–34

Zuckerman, H. 1989. "The Sociology of Science", in Smelser (ed.) *Handbook of Sociology*. Newbury Park: Sage, pp. 511–74

Zürn, M. 1998. *Regieren jenseits des Nationalstaats*. Frankfurt am Main: Suhrkamp

Zürn, M. 2000. "Democratic Governance Beyond the Nation-State – The EU and Other International Institutions", *European Journal of International Relations* 6(2): 183–222

Zürn, M. and Joerges, C. (eds.) 2005. *Law and Governance in Postnational Europe*. Cambridge: Cambridge University Press

Index